WORLD WAR ZOOS

WORLD WAR ZOOS

Humans and Other Animals
in the Deadliest Conflict of the Modern Age

John M. Kinder

The University of Chicago Press
Chicago

The University of Chicago Press, Chicago 60637
© 2025 by John M. Kinder
All rights reserved. No part of this book may be used or reproduced in
any manner whatsoever without written permission, except in the case of
brief quotations in critical articles and reviews. For more information,
contact the University of Chicago Press, 1427 E. 60th St., Chicago, IL 60637.
Published 2025
Printed in the United States of America

34 33 32 31 30 29 28 27 26 25   1 2 3 4 5

ISBN-13: 978-0-226-82766-7 (cloth)
ISBN-13: 978-0-226-82767-4 (e-book)
DOI: https://doi.org/10.7208/chicago/9780226827674.001.0001

Library of Congress Cataloging-in-Publication Data

Names: Kinder, John M. (John Matthew), 1975– author.
Title: World War zoos : humans and other animals in the deadliest conflict of the
    modern age / John M. Kinder.
Description: Chicago : The University of Chicago Press, 2025. |
    Includes bibliographical references and index.
Identifiers: LCCN 2024035547 | ISBN 9780226827667 (cloth) |
    ISBN 9780226827674 (ebook)
Subjects: LCSH: World War, 1939–1945. | Zoos—History—20th century.
Classification: LCC D810.A65 K54 2025 | DDC 940.53—dc23/eng/20240823
LC record available at https://lccn.loc.gov/2024035547

♾ This paper meets the requirements of ANSI/NISO Z39.48-1992
(Permanence of Paper).

Contents

Prologue: The Pandas at Pearl Harbor   vii

Introduction: Two World Wars   1

PART I. THE THIRTIES EXPERIENCE

1   The Monkey's Lament   15

2   Hitler's Zoos   31

3   The Bear at Buchenwald   44

4   Zoos in an Age of International Cooperation   56

5   A Dress Rehearsal in España   64

PART II. OPENING DAY ACTIVITIES

6   Zero Hour   77

7   The Freeze and the Thaw   91

8   The Rape of the Zoo   103

9   American Zoos (Finally) Go to War   115

10   Helpless Gazelles and Beasts on the Hunt   127

PART III. COMMISSARY AND ADMINISTRATION (STAFF ONLY)

11 Domestic Worries *141*

12 Zoos without Keepers *154*

13 Doing Their Bit *168*

PART IV. CARNIVORE ENCOUNTERS

14 Sacrificial Lambs *185*

15 Bombing the Zoo *199*

16 The Mask of the Chimpanzee *211*

17 Beastly Liberations *226*

18 KZ Zoo *239*

PART V. FUTURE EXHIBITS

19 Brave Zoo World *255*

Epilogue: Baboon or Bear? 277

Acknowledgments of a Recovering Zoo-Lover *289*
Notes *293*
Index *339*

Prologue:
The Pandas at Pearl Harbor

December 19, 1941. Twelve days since the Japanese attack on Pearl Harbor. The massive turbines of the SS *President Coolidge* churned the oil-slicked waters of Honolulu Bay. As the crew readied for launch, more than nine hundred passengers milled about in the mid-morning heat, anxious to leave the beaches of Waikiki far behind. Most were civilians: children separated from parents; missionaries returning from the Philippines; evacuees, tourists, prostitutes—even twenty-seven members of the Willamette University football team, which had arrived in Oahu four days before the US war began. Players bunked in steerage, a warren of cramped cabins and converted cargo holds below the waterline, where a small attachment of nurses manned a makeshift hospital for wounded sailors. One hundred twenty-five in all: some were riddled with bomb fragments, others "burned from head to foot."[1]

Near dusk, the ship motored out of port and joined the first convoy to leave Hawaii since the United States entered World War II. While those in the upper decks rolled bandages and tried to ignore the persistent rumors of submarines, Ruth Erikson, an officer in the navy nursing corps, and two others kept a twenty-four-hour watch on the men in their care. Decades later, Erikson recalled one patient in particular—an "older man, perhaps a chief"—his body so badly scorched he lost "intravenous fluids faster than they could be replaced." He held on for five days but eventually died and was buried at sea. The next day, shortly before dawn of Christmas morning, the *Coolidge* trudged beneath the Golden Gate Bridge and into San Francisco Bay. As visitors crowded

viii   Prologue

the docks, jostling to catch sight of loved ones, Allyn Jennings, general director of the New York Zoological Society, waited to greet the ship's most unusual refugees: a pair of giant pandas.

◉ ◉

The story behind the pandas at Pearl Harbor began months earlier when Pandora, the Bronx Zoo's sole remaining panda, unexpectedly took ill. At first Pandora refused to eat, playing with her pablum mush like a distracted child. Then came the convulsions, eyes lifeless, limbs shuddering. No doubt she heard the blaring of the sirens, felt the jolting of the zoo station wagon, as it crossed the bridge into Manhattan. Doctors at Columbia-Presbyterian Medical Center administered a sedative and ran a barrage of tests—X-rays, a spinal tap, an EEG—searching for the cause of the panda's rapid decline. But it was too late. At exactly 2:05 on the afternoon of May 13, after weeks of diminishing health, Pandora died of mysterious causes. She was three years old. And, war or no war, the Bronx Zoo was determined to replace her.[2]

As New Yorkers mourned the news, the zoo's director cabled its most prominent patrons, publishing magnate Henry Luce and his magnetic wife, the writer and future diplomat Clare Boothe Luce, to see about filling the panda-sized hole. At the time, the political power couple happened to be in China stumping on behalf of the humanitarian organization United China Relief. Agreeing to help, the Luces reached out to their friend Soong Mei-ling, wife of the Chinese nationalist leader Chiang Kai-shek, who immediately granted the zoo's request for assistance. With Japanese forces pushing ever closer to the wartime capital, "Madame Chiang" (as she was often known in the West) was eager to cement friendly relations with the United States. In her mind, a panda was a small price to pay for American goodwill.

To lead the search, China's photogenic first lady enlisted the help of David Crockett Graham, a missionary and naturalist who taught at the West China Union University in the ancient cultural capital of Chengdu, the largest city on the fringe of panda country.* Hunters

---

* The giant panda (*Ailuropoda melanoleuca*) is endemic to the dense and remote forested foothills of the Himalayas in Sichuan. The species was unknown in the West until 1869, when a local hunter showed a panda skin to Jesuit missionary and naturalist Father Armand

The Pandas at Pearl Harbor   ix

eventually captured a forty-two-pound infant panda and returned to Chengdu on September 30. Once there, Graham discovered that another party had bagged a second panda—"male . . . probably 10 or 11 months old . . . weighing about 60" pounds—a few days earlier, an unexpected bonus sure to please Madame Chiang's benefactors.

Half a world away, John Tee-Van left New York on a 34,868-mile journey to ferry the animals to the South Bronx. No one was better suited for the task. Tee-Van had spent two years in charge of the panda exhibit at the recently shuttered New York World's Fair. Slim, clean-shaven, with a crop of perpetually wind-blown hair, the forty-four-year-old also looked the part of a proper "zoo man"—just the sort of figure needed to conduct a mission of such public interest. Over the following months, Tee-Van traversed what would soon become a familiar wartime geography: New Zealand, Australia, the Netherlands East Indies, Singapore, Bangkok, Rangoon, the Burma Road, and finally the airfield at Chengdu, where bamboo decoy planes lined the runway.

Arriving at Graham's home at the end of October, Tee-Van was thrilled to discover the smaller of the two pandas sitting on the front porch, her "paw-supported chin resting on the arm of a wooden swing." In appearance and behavior, each animal was markedly different—a distinction the American attributed to their sexes. The female, Tee-Van recorded, was "coy and cuddly with a child-like desire to be as companionable as possible, while the male, more cleanly cut in color, slightly larger and more compactly formed, gave forth a very evident atmosphere of self-sufficiency—an 'I'm a he-man and quite able to take care of myself' attitude."[3] (Both, it turns out, were female.)

A few days later, the pandas were crated up and flown to the mid-river airport of Chongqing, China's wartime capital, where they were put up at the house of a Methodist missionary. As Tee-Van finalized his travel plans, thousands of residents passed by for a rare glimpse of the white-and-black *hsiung maou* (cat bear). Finally, on November 8,

---

David. In 1929, Kermit and Theodore Roosevelt III, sons of the former president, earned the dubious honor of being the first Westerners to shoot a panda. Seven years later, Ruth Harkness, a noted socialite and wife of a recently deceased animal collector, captured a live panda cub and brought it to San Francisco. She sold it (Su Lin) to the Brookfield Zoo, where it died in April 1938. Six others soon reached American shores: two to Chicago (Mei-Mei and Mei-Lan), two to St. Louis (Happy and Pao Pei), and two to the Bronx (Pan and Pandora).

Figure P.1. After the radio address, the smaller of the two pandas was guest of honor at a lunch held at the home of Chiang Kai-shek and Soong Mei-ling, where she proceeded to roll around and munch bamboo, to the great amusement of the Chinese generalissimo. Here, John Tee-Van rubs the panda's furry belly while Soong Mei-ling (*crouching*) and Soong Ai-ling (*standing*) look on approvingly. © Wildlife Conservation Society. Reproduced by permission of the WCS Archives.

Madame Chiang and her older sister Soong Ai-ling, wife of nationalist politician Dr. H. H. Kung, woke before dawn and rode through pouring rain to the city's radio station, recently bombed, where they met William J. Dunn, the Far East correspondent for the Columbia Broadcast System.

After a brief introduction, Madame Kung spoke first: "Hello friends in America: Amiable as these Pandas are, Mme. Chiang and I hope that they will represent more to you than the gift of two small animals. We intend this gift to be a token of our friendship for you and our appreciation of the sincere efforts made on China's behalf by the United China Relief campaign." In Madame Kung's mind, the pandas were ideal symbols of Chinese wartime gratitude. They were "peculiarly Chinese" (found in no other place on earth), rare (only seven had ever left China alive), and "cheerful" in appearance (a source of happiness in a world increasingly marked by sorrow). Most important of all, she presented the pandas as both icons of heroic resistance and tragic reminders of war's human toll. Before the war, the panda's home range was largely unknown, even to the Chinese. After four years of war, however, forty million Chinese people had been pushed from the coasts to the edge of panda country.

When it was her turn, Soong Mei-ling flattered her American listeners by regaling them with evidence of their generosity. Recounting a recent visit to a war orphanage, she intoned: "Whenever America was mentioned the eyes of the little children would immediately brighten, their breaths quicken and their ears perk up. They all knew that American children had saved nickels from ice cream and pennies from all day suckers in order to send vitamins to China's war orphans." At a time when three-quarters of Americans remained ambivalent about entering World War II, Madame Chiang Kai-shek praised the United States as a spiritual ally of war-torn China: "Unlike the fascist nations which consider it fair game to victimize the weak and the unfortunate, America is now supporting justice and humanity as earnestly as China who has fought and bled for these principles during the past four and a half years." China's gift of a "pair of chubby, comical, black and white furry Pandas," she concluded, was just a "very small way of saying 'Thank You.'"

It's unclear how many Americans heard their address. Although transmitted simultaneously on multiple channels, the broadcast failed to reach US airwaves. Nevertheless, Tee-Van was confident that the political significance of the pandas would be clear—if, that is, he managed to get them back to the States.

The following weeks were a blur of activity: trucks, boats, planes, passports, meetings with agents and local bureaucrats, and a never-ending search for edible bamboo. Late in the afternoon on November 14, Tee-Van loaded the pandas into the cramped cabin of a small twin-engine plane. The pandas rode in wooden crates, stacked on top of each other near the tail. As the Douglas DC-2 glided toward the southeast, the "male" panda thrashed wildly—scratching, barking, and "hurling the loose end of a chain that was attached to his harness"

Figure P.2. John Tee-Van and one of the pandas preparing to board a China National Aviation Corporation (CNAC) plane for a leg of the journey to the United States. © Wildlife Conservation Society. Reproduced by permission of the WCS Archives.

against the side of the cage. When night fell, the plane flew on in darkness, guided only by the light of the moon. Below was occupied territory. Finally, after five and a half hours, the pilot switched on the navigation lights and landed in Hong Kong.

The next morning, Tee-Van bundled the pandas onto a ship to the Philippines, where, after spending several days at a mountain villa outside Manila, the party boarded the SS *President Coolidge* for what Tee-Van hoped was the final oceanic leg of their journey. Once at sea, the pandas spent much of their day lazing about the ship's upper deck, where the ocean breezes cut the stifling tropical heat. (Chains stopped them from wandering too close to the sides.) All the while, a steady stream of passengers dropped by to take in the rare animals' antics—made all the more amusing by their seeming indifference to the geopolitical implications of their journey.

The *Coolidge* was somewhere east of the Solomon Islands when, shortly before 8:00 a.m. Hawaii time, a wave of planes from the Japanese Imperial Army swept down from the Oahu highlands toward Pearl Harbor. Within minutes, smoke from the burning ships blackened the sky. The damage was staggering: eight battleships sunk or damaged, hundreds of planes destroyed before they could even get off the ground, more than 3,500 Americans killed or wounded. When the crew of the *Coolidge* heard the news, they darkened the ship's portholes and painted the top deck a dull gray. According to Tee-Van, one officer even "threatened to camouflage the pandas, for he asserted their black and white coloration was entirely too conspicuous." Joking aside, and despite the protection of a navy cruiser, which had joined them shortly after leaving the Philippines, the *Coolidge* was deep in hostile waters, thousands of miles from the nearest US base. Only the sheer scale of the Pacific made it possible for the ship to reach Honolulu undetected by the Japanese.

◉ ◉

After the drama of their oceanic passage, the final leg of the pandas' journey proved comparatively uneventful. Not long after the *Coolidge* docked in San Francisco, the pandas were loaded into a rail car for a four-day trek to Manhattan's Grand Central Terminal. From there, it was just a short jaunt across the city to their new home in the Bronx Zoo. On December 31, a crowd of children, zoo officials, and Chinese politicians gathered in front of an artificial Tibetan monastery to witness the formal unveiling of New York's latest animal celebrities.[4] For the pandas, it was the end of a months-long ordeal, their lives endangered every step of the way—from the moment they were snatched up by hunters to their perilous voyage across the Pacific and beyond.

In retrospect, we might easily dismiss the entire drama as an illustration of the self-absorption for which prewar America was so rightly famous. Why, when Warsaw burned and Manchuria starved, were people willing to go to such lengths to ensure that New Yorkers could see a panda?

Yet for John Tee-Van and the rest of the Bronx Zoo staff, for the Soong sisters and the embattled armies of China, and for the millions of zoo visitors, Pan-Dee and Pan-Dah[†] were more than exhibited animals. They were symbols of national resilience, happy reminders of better days, and totems of everything that World War II threatened to destroy.

[†] In early 1942, the CBS radio program *Let's Pretend* sponsored a nationwide contest to name the Bronx Zoo pandas. Much to the consternation of zoo officials, the winner, eleven-year-old Nancy Lostutter of Columbus, Indiana, christened the larger "male" Pan-Dee and the smaller female Pan-Dah (though, over time, New Yorkers came to prefer "Susie").

INTRODUCTION

Two World Wars

I didn't grow up thinking about zoos in wartime. I was lucky in that respect. While zoos were part of the backdrop of my everyday life, war was always far away—abstract, obscure, more an idea than a lived reality. I saw war at the movies, of course, and sometime in high school I became acutely afraid of being drafted to help kick Saddam Hussein out of Kuwait. (I did not know that the US military draft had been suspended nearly two decades earlier.) Yet I can honestly say I spent my youth blissfully ignorant about what happens to zoos—and zoo animals—when countries go to war.

That changed during a short visit to Berlin in the late 1990s. After several days of playing tourist, my buddy and I decided to skip the museums and spend a quiet afternoon in the world-famous Tiergarten (literally, the "garden of beasts"), the 520-acre park/zoological garden/urban hangout in the center of the city. There, just outside the elephant enclosure, we stumbled upon a small memorial to the zoo's animal casualties in World War II. It featured a photograph of the zoo's famed pachyderm house—a concrete and iron structure made up to resemble some kind of Eastern temple—in the immediate aftermath of an Allied bombing raid. Where the structure once stood was a pile of rubble; the only evidence of the former residents' fate was a bloodied leg protruding from the wreckage. Even at the time, I struggled to contemplate what had happened: The screaming momentum of the falling bombs. The darkness lit by flashes of ignition. The stench of the elephants' bodies, smoldering and covered in effluence. The terror they must have felt just before the world crashed in.

But what bothered me then and what angers me still was the memorial makers' obvious reluctance to place the elephants' deaths into any sort of context. How did the animals get to Berlin in the first place? And how did they wind up in Allied bombsights? Was it a tragic accident, what now we might call "collateral damage"? Or were Germany's enemies trying to send a message? Also missing, I realized later, was any hint of the zoo's complicity in the war and, by extension, the pain and suffering experienced by so many Berlin Zoo residents. Instead, the memorial seemed content to portray the dead elephants in symbolic terms, innocent victims of a war in which zookeepers played no part.

In the years since, I've spent hundreds of hours thinking about what happens to zoos in wartime. This book is the result. It chronicles zoos' experiences in the deadliest decades of global history, beginning in the depths of the Great Depression, through the terrors of World War II, and finally to the conflict's aftermath in the atomic age. More than anything before or since, World War II represented an existential threat to the globe's zoological institutions. Some zoos were bombed into near oblivion. Others bore the indignities of foreign occupation, their precious collections looted or butchered by enemy troops. Even zoos spared the worst of the fighting had to wrestle with questions rarely asked in public: What should they do when supplies ran low? Which animals should be killed to protect the lives of others? And how could zoos justify keeping dangerous creatures that could so easily escape during an aerial attack?

Above all else, the war forced zoo leaders to reckon with humans' capacity to destroy life on a hitherto unimaginable scale. During the nineteenth century, the eradication of species like the great auk and passenger pigeon set off alarms about the fate of wild animals in a rapidly industrialized world. But World War II represented a threat of an entirely different magnitude, one that imperiled the future of civilization itself. In 1944, Henry Fairfield Osborn Jr., the president of the New York Zoological Society, declared, "We need to face the unpleasant fact that there are two world wars going on—one, man's destruction of man; the other, his destruction of the 'living resources' of nature, upon which his own existence depends."[1] Eight decades later, the latter conflict continues to rage with no end in sight.

I conceived this book with three goals in mind.

The *first*, and perhaps most obvious, is to catalog the impact of World War II on the world's zoos and the animals they held. In the immediate term, wartime shortages forced staff to seek novel means of locating food, securing workers, and attracting visitors. Yet the conflict's effects lingered far beyond 1945. Solly Zuckerman, the Jewish public servant who started at the London Zoological Society and later served as scientific advisor to Britain's strategic bombing campaign, described World War II as the "opening of the present phase in the evolution of zoos."[2] Before the conflict, the center of the zoo world was Western Europe, and Germany in particular. At war's end, the globe's largest animal collections were in the United States, a transformation that paralleled the rise of the nation as a cultural, economic, and military superpower. The war also permanently affected zoos' ability to acquire animals in the wild. As late as the 1930s, many zoos relied upon overseas animal dealers—or, better yet, safari-style expeditions—when seeking fresh specimens. Within half a decade of the war's end, however, a rising tide of anticolonial movements across Africa and Southeast Asia threatened to dissolve the centuries-old network of imperial exploitation and exchange that had long served as the zoo industry's invisible backbone. Today, it's illegal in most nations to take animals out of the wild for display in zoos. Although by no means the only factor involved, World War II spurred zoos to embrace strategies of on-site breeding and international exchange to fill their cages.

The book's *second* goal is to show how wartime zoos mirrored a hierarchical vision of the natural world, marking out inequalities between humans and animals, different species of animals, and different segments of humanity. In the guise of wholesome entertainment, wartime zoos sent stark messages about whose lives mattered most—and whose mattered not at all. Students of World War II often associate this kind of thinking with Nazi Germany, where Hitler's government not only turned antisemitism into a state religion but also carried out the deadliest genocide in modern history. But ideas about what Keith Thomas famously called "human ascendency"—the anthropocentric worldview that humans are preordained to rule the natural world—are hard-wired into the modern zoo, as much as advocates prefer to deny them.[3] Indeed, World War II–era zoos served as staging grounds for some of the most loathsome practices of the era: captivity, selective execution, forced removal, racial and ethnic discrimination, and more.

The book's *final* and, in my mind, most significant goal is to highlight humans' conflicted attitudes toward animals in periods of social trauma. At the outbreak of war, ordinary people will often go to extraordinary lengths on behalf of local pets, farmed animals, wildlife, and zoo animals. Following Vladmir Putin's invasion of Ukraine in 2022, for example, social media exploded with clips of brave men and women shuttling zoo animals to safety. One viral video captured workers trying to evacuate a van-full of kangaroos and wallabies from Feldman Ecopark near Kharkiv, just across the border with Russia.[4] Farther south, volunteers drove a lion and wolf on a four-day, 620-mile journey from Zaporizhzhia to a zoo in the Romanian city of Rădăuți—all without the benefit of tranquilizers. Sebastian Taralunga, a spokesman for one of the zoo extraction groups, testified to the spirit of collaboration the war had engendered: "Everybody agreed that in extreme times we have to have extreme measures and we decided to do whatever possible to bring these animals out of war."[5]

I'm certainly not the first to claim we can learn a lot about a society by looking at how it treats its most vulnerable inhabitants.[6] At the same time, it's important to ask tough questions about how that vulnerability is manufactured in the first place. Most zoos endure a precarious existence in the best of times.[7] A spate of disease, a well-publicized escape—perhaps even a change in local government—is all that it takes to send a seemingly healthy zoo spiraling toward collapse. These kinds of threats are compounded during wartime, when communities frequently shift their resource priorities toward the military and national defense. The chief victims, of course, are the animals themselves—the monkeys and hippos, rattlesnakes and alligators, rockhopper penguins and great spotted kiwi that rely upon their keepers to keep them alive. Trapped behind iron bars or gaping moats, nature's most ingenious predators can quickly succumb to accidents, starvation, or violent death.

In this sense at least, the fate of World War II–era zoo animals was neither aberration nor tragic accident. Long before the first shots were fired, zoo animals from Belgium to Burma were quite literally prisoners of forces beyond their control.

⊙ ⊙

But why should we care about zoos during World War II? It's a fair question. Zoos are strange places, after all. Just think about it. You take a bunch of animals, move them halfway around the globe, place them in cages (excuse me: "artificial environments"), feed them diets they'd never eat in the wild, and then charge the public for the privilege of looking at them. At their very best, zoos represent an important, albeit highly flawed, weapon in the ongoing battle against animal extinction. At their very worst, they are little more than family-friendly prisons where, in the words of philosopher Brian Massumi, animal incarceration is "converted into fun."[8] Either way, most of us aren't used to taking zoos and their history all that seriously.

If body counts are a measure of historical significance, zoos wouldn't rate highly, either. By any metric, zoo casualties represented the *least* of World War II's animal victims. Millions of horses died in the conflict, numbers that far exceeded those of elephants, tigers, and monkeys. In the opening weeks of the war, Britain alone slaughtered hundreds of thousands of domestic pets; countless more died elsewhere in the conflict—killed for food, burned alive by incendiaries, crushed by debris. Warring armies destroyed wildlife, contaminated ecosystems, disrupted animal migrations, and polluted watersheds, the effects of which would be felt for decades. By my rough math, no more than 25,000 zoo animals died because of World War II, a minuscule fraction of the hundreds of millions of cows, poultry, and pigs butchered to feed warring armies.[9] (Most of these would have been birthed, raised, killed, and cooked anyway, but you get my drift.)

I've also come to believe that many people don't want to take a hard look at zoos—especially not in wartime. Once, I was in the middle of a lovely conversation with a German archivist only to realize that something was lost in translation. When I finally rectified the problem ("No, not Jews . . . ZOOS"), I was met with a look of confusion and vague disappointment. Others have reacted with outright hostility, as if this subject were not only a waste of time but an insult to World War II's *real* victims. Writing in September 1938, at the height of the Spanish Civil War, Elisabeth Leigh dismissed public concern over wartime zoos as little more than barely disguised narcissism. "If we think at all about the fate of zoos in wartime," she declared acidly, it's only because we're worried about our own safety.[10] Even groups otherwise sympathetic to the topic of animal welfare frequently bristle at any attempt to suggest parallels between the lives of animals and their human counterparts. The Anti-Defamation League (ADL), for example, famously condemned the People for the Ethical Treatment of Animals' (PETA) "Holocaust on your Plate" campaign, which used images from concentration camps to draw attention to the horrors of factory farming.[11]

It would be foolish to ignore such misgivings. World War II is to date the most destructive event in human history since the Black Death. More than seventy-five million people died in the conflict, most of them civilians. The war unleashed the horrors of the Holocaust, pushed both sides to adopt campaigns of terror bombing, and sent the world order spiraling toward the prospect of nuclear annihilation. Why, against all of this, should we give a second thought to wartime zoos and the animals they kept?

Let's start with the fact that zoos were popular—and that can tell us a good deal about the societies that constructed and maintained them.[12] During the 1930s, zoos ranked among the best-attended forms of live entertainment on the planet, especially in the parts of Western and Central Europe where so much of World War II would be waged. Stories of zoo births and deaths regularly attracted front-page attention, and some of the most influential figures of the World War II era— Churchill, Mussolini, and Göring, among others—were avid zoo-goers. For most visitors, zoos represented a kind of fantasy, an escape from the dreariness or banality of everyday life. But they also carried a cultural weight that's difficult to appreciate today. In the decade prior to World War II, the governments of Italy, France, and the United States sank millions of dollars into zoo-building projects. Imperial Japan built zoos in occupied Manchuria and opened the first modern animal park on the Korean peninsula. Zoos were especially beloved in Adolf Hitler's Germany, where Nazi ideologues seized on metaphors from the natural world to fuel their paranoid visions of national supremacy.

Beyond their popularity, zoos served as anchors of normalcy for those who visited them. Walter van den bergh, director of the Antwerp Zoo during World War II, explained this point not long after the conflict's end:

Figure I.1. Prior to the German occupation of Holland in 1940, Amsterdam's Artis Zoo held a special place in the hearts of the city's Jewish population. Located in Amsterdam's Jewish quarter, a few blocks away from where a young Anne Frank would spend years in hiding, Artis was especially popular with Jewish children who lived nearby. This photograph shows siblings Leo and Bertie Serphos and their friend Rene Schap standing in front of Artis's penguin house in 1936. Both Bertie and Rene would be murdered during the Holocaust less than a decade later. United States Holocaust Memorial Museum, courtesy of Rita Serphos.

The Antwerp Zoo has a peculiar place in the affections of our citizens. For more than a hundred years it has been here in the heart of the city. Most citizens of Antwerp came here as children with their grandparents; they played here in their school days; they came here to concerts and exhibitions; many of them met their future fiancés here, and almost all of them did some of their courting here. Now they bring their children, and in years to come will bring their grandchildren.[13]

Not everyone shared the Belgian zoo director's obvious nostalgia. Throughout the war years, critics charged that zoo animals were simply too expensive to justify their maintenance. Far better, they argued, to butcher some, destroy others, and let the rest go free. Still, the war did little to sway the minds of the most enthusiastic patrons, who were often willing to excuse animal suffering as an unfortunate "accident" of history. Even in the conflict's darkest hours, zoo attendance often remained remarkably high—a tribute to people's enduring desire to see exotic animals and the familiar places that housed them.

At the same time, World War II zoos were microcosms of the cities (and nations) in which they existed. Many big-city zoos resembled miniature citadels complete with air raid wardens, enclosures stacked with sandbags, underground bomb shelters, and posters of happy animals doing their bit to defeat the enemy (whoever the enemy happened to be). Eager to contribute to the war effort, zoos hosted patriotic rallies, staged educational exhibits, carried out military-related research, and trumpeted the ideological goals of the Allies and the Axis. At the Berlin Zoo, director Lutz Heck, a close friend of Hermann Göring and an ardent Nazi in his own right, not only oversaw the Nazification of Germany's largest zoo but also used his close connections with the Wehrmacht to raid occupied zoos in the recently expanded Reich. Staff at Amsterdam's Artis Zoo hid Jewish refugees and resistance fighters from Nazi police. Meanwhile, across the Atlantic, the United States' most prominent zoo leader, William Mann, embarked on a secret mission to study the dietary habits of American GIs. Cooperating with the military allowed zoo professionals to stake a claim in the wartime state, one that would be cemented even further when the Cold War prompted a heightened interest in zoological matters among military and defense professionals.

Above all else, this story matters because, to borrow Claude Levi-Strauss's well-worn maxim, zoos are "good to think with."[14] During the war years, zoos offered people metaphors to help them understand experiences of imprisonment, powerlessness, and degradation. Propagandists used zoos to teach lessons about the virtues of sacrifice, while journalists deployed zoo stories to raise the spirits of war-weary readers. When viewed today, the experiences of wartime zoos provide a lens through which to explore the rise of Nazism, the moral dramas of collaboration and resistance, and the urge to rebuild in the wake of apocalyptic destruction. At the same time, the story of zoos in World War II can be read as an allegory of twenty-first-century crises, when collapsing ecosystems, rapid human population growth, and rising temperatures threaten wildlife across the planet.

Put simply, the story of zoos during World War II reminds us that war's traumas and upheavals weren't confined to the battlefield. Bombed, looted, starved, occupied: not even the city zoo could escape the conflict unscathed.

◉ ◉

Whenever I visit a zoo, the first thing I like to do is scope the official map. Although some zoos seem to encourage exploration, many are designed to funnel visitors down a specific trajectory—across artificial savannahs, through misty indoor jungles, past bathrooms and snack carts and children's playgrounds—until you wind up right where they want you: the gift shop. Books work the same way. You mark out a path, introduce your best material along the way, and hope readers take away something at the end.

This book follows a broadly chronological route, beginning in the Great Depression, which offered a preview of the crises to come, and ending around the dawn of the Cold War. I've adopted a bird's-eye view of zoos in this period, one that surveys the breadth of the global zoo industry—swooping in here, wheeling back there—as it migrates across the war's landscape. It's not a complete survey. I'll be the first to admit a not-so-subtle American bias in terms of both content and, more important, context. (The United States doesn't come off scot-free, but if you're a Nazi—or even Nazi-adjacent—I've got a feeling you won't find much to like in the pages that follow.) When the war began, there were hundreds of zoos around the globe, from internationally recognized institutions like the Berlin Zoological Garden, the world's largest with more than 3,000 individual animals, to countless roadside animal attractions. Certain institutions—the London Zoo in Regent's Park and Tokyo's Ueno Zoo, for example—appear with some regularity, if only because they are representative of larger trends. Even so, our path will take us to some unexpected places as well, including a petting zoo constructed by Japanese Americans in a government-run incarceration camp.

Two words of warning.

First, you can expect us to circle back to certain questions and moral quandaries more than once. To some degree, this is inevitable. As any frequent zoo visitor will tell you, most zoos are pretty much the same. They sound the same, they smell the same—they even tend to display the same species of animals. (This is part of the reason why many people find them insufferably dull.) Sure, we can draw up lists of the world's "best" and "worst" zoos; we can heap praise on immersive bioparks and point a self-righteous finger at places like Three Bears General Store (self-described as the "The Ultimate Shopping Destination in Pigeon Forge, Tennessee"), which uses displays of live Asiatic bears to sell candy, religious knickknacks, and cheap souvenirs. In the end, though, all zoos face a similar set of dilemmas: they need to keep their animals alive (or alive-*ish*); they have to make peace, even if haltingly, with the logic of captivity (the belief that humans have the right—the obligation—to keep animals under lock and key); and, with the exception of private menageries, they need to sustain public interest to stay afloat. In other words, if something happens at one zoo, you can bet it will happen at others.

All that said, the subtle differences between how zoos deal with seemingly inevitable problems can be quite telling. Take the issue of food. From a dietary perspective, an elephant is little more than a walking stomach, a bottomless void to be filled with literal tons of fresh vegetables, roughage, and grain (never mind water) over the course of a year. During World War II, zoos came up with all sorts of ways to stretch their meager food supplies, from repurposing unused land to grow crops to begging the public for table scraps. All the while, zoos were forced to make life-and-death decisions about whose hunger mattered most—and why. Should zoos prioritize quantity over quality? Or should they privilege the lives and appetites of the least-resource-hungry animals, even if they weren't likely to attract visitors?

World War II–era zoos also wrestled with the dilemma of whether—and when—to destroy the animals in their care. To be fair, zoos grapple with this question every day and always have. Although we'd like to think that the bulk of zoo animals die a "natural" death, all zoos engage in routine calculations about which specimens (because of age, sickness, and lack of public interest) are no longer worth keeping. Visitors are rarely privy to such matters, if only because they'd puncture the myth that zoos are animal-first institutions, more concerned with their caged inhabitants than those who come to view them. During World War II, however, the combined threats of resource deprivation, aerial bombardment, and fearmongering led zoos to shoot, strangle, poison, intentionally starve, and beat to death hundreds, possibly thousands, of animals in their care. Few zoo men believed such measures were strictly necessary. But the fact that many zoos did so nonetheless says a lot about their willingness to do anything and everything to survive the conflict.

Which brings me to my second warning: some of what follows will make for tough reading. Again, this is somewhat inevitable. Few people take pleasure in hearing stories about animal suffering—at least, few who would bother to read a book like this one. And zoo animals did indeed suffer in World War II: from disease, neglect, and starvation; from mental anxiety and the predation of foreign armies; and from the traumatic effects of bullets, falling incendiaries, and explosive armaments. Most disturbing of all is the fact that animal suffering is baked into the zoo even in the best of times. Put another way: World War II might have been a nightmare, but for the world's zoo animals, peacetime was often little better.

◉ ◉

A final note. Since the birth of the modern zoo in the late eighteenth century, numerous commentators have gravitated toward a single metaphor to describe the zoo and its mission: the ark.

For those who skipped Sunday school, a quick refresher: in the Hebrew book of Genesis, God commands Noah to build a giant wooden boat, three decks tall and stacked to the gills with mating pairs of every animal species. Once everyone is inside, He unleashes a torrential rainstorm as a punishment for mankind's stupidity and wickedness. As the rest of God's creatures drown, Noah's floating menagerie rides out the storm in relative comfort. True, Genesis doesn't tell us much about how Noah and his family manage the ordeal: the feeding; the washing; the inevitable sickness, pestilence, and disease. (One finds a similar reticence in many zoos.)

All the same, the story remains a favorite among those advocating on zoos' behalf. During World War II, the ark metaphor cast zoos as sites of refuge, spaces of life in a world consumed by death. To this day, zoo champions often use references to Noah's ark when arguing for zoos' role in helping stave off animal extinctions caused by human-induced climate change.[15]

Nevertheless, the story of zoos during World War II should make us wary about pushing this metaphor too far. I cannot find the passage (biblical scholars, please correct me) where Noah kills the parents of gorillas and other large animals to secure ark-worthy specimens, a practice common within the zoo industry well into the twentieth century. The biblical Noah does not have to decide which animals live and which ones die when food supplies begin to run out. (The prototypical prepper, he no doubt planned for forty days and then doubled it, just in case.) What's more, the twentieth-century "Noahs" featured in this book weren't content to hunker down and wait for the floodwaters to drop. A number, as we shall see, hoped to use the conflict to their own advantage, either by raiding the collections of others or by boosting their reputations as agents of the wartime state. In short, there's something decidedly self-serving about the zoo's reputation as an "ark in the park," a coinage that says less about what zoos do and more about what we want them to be.

More than that, though, the ark metaphor suggests a *post-flood* moment—a time when, the danger having passed, zoos could get back to some semblance of normalcy. But World War II did not represent a state of exception in which the normal rules of zoo life were put on hold. Quite the opposite. The war forced zoo folk and zoo-goers alike to confront what often lay just below the surface: the hierarchies that valued some creatures more than others; the difficult ethical questions about who lives and who dies; the intrusion of politics into the worlds of science and entertainment; the tension between internationalist ideals and nationalist jingoism; and the reliance of zoos on the fruits of empire (sometimes literally) to function.

What follows is the story of how the world's zoos survived the most destructive war in history—and what they sacrificed in the process.

PART I

The Thirties Experience

1

The Monkey's Lament

In July 1932, in a small railway city in the northwest of England, a resident at the Chester Zoo did the unthinkable. As happy zoo-goers looked on, a rhesus monkey chewed off a length of rope that hung in its open-air exhibit. It tied one end to a tree branch, fashioned a crude slipknot with the other, and passed its head through the noose. Then the monkey climbed to the top of the tree, let out a final scream, and leapt into space. "Death," the zoo's owner, George Mottershead, told the press, "was instantaneous."[1]

While the zoo convened a jury to sort out the matter, news of the monkey's apparent suicide quickly spread across the English-speaking world. Most scientists remained dubious. E. W. MacBride, a celebrated biologist from Imperial College, London, insisted that there had never been a "proved case of suicide in all nature."[2] Mottershead himself viewed the hanging as little more than a freak accident.[3]

Skeptics notwithstanding, tales of "zooicide" would have struck a special chord with readers in the decade prior to World War II. Laurel Braitman, a historian of animal psychology, argues that people's fascination with self-destructive animals stems from an all-too-human longing to contemplate our own demise,[4] a sentiment that would have resonated with millions of people living through the Great Depression.* Throughout the 1930s, the press abounded with macabre

---

* At the time of the monkey's fatal leap, the world was in the middle of the greatest epidemic of suicide of the century. Across the globe, untold numbers of people came to see themselves as "superfluous," better off dead than living. Although national averages varied,

16   Chapter 1

headlines about caged animals desperate to end their lives: "Sulking Tigress Goes on a Hunger Strike," "Rochester Zoo Has a Suicide Run," "Monkey Looks Once, Then Takes Fatal Jump."[5] In 1933, the Sydney *World News* reported how a crocodile at the Johannesburg Zoo "committed suicide" by spending the night in its "ice-cold swimming pool."[6] That same year, a paper in New Zealand recounted the sad tale of the Wellington Zoo sea lions. One after another, these "melancholy and expensive prisoners" had "taken matters into their own flippers," the story's writer insisted. "The popular belief is that they committed suicide on realizing that they were Wellington's guests for life."[7] The Perth *Mirror* in Western Australia even encouraged readers to send in their own stories of animal suicide; the author of the best letter would receive a prize of ten shillings.[8] To countless Depression-era animal lovers, suicidal monkeys and mournful sea lions would have appeared less like freaks of nature and more like fellow victims of a world from which they badly wanted to escape.

We can hardly blame them (the animals, I mean) for seeking a way out. The Depression years brought zoos a mountain of new problems, many of which would be aggravated even further in wartime. Between 1929 and 1933, American zoos' operating budgets plummeted by 30 percent. Faced with mass unemployment and burdened resources, many cities reduced zoo funding to a pittance. Public turnout nosedived as well. In Philadelphia, home of the oldest zoo in the nation, attendance plunged from 400,000 visitors in 1929 to 150,000 in 1932.[9] The situation was much the same at zoos around the world. In New Zealand, attendance at the Auckland Zoo declined from 155,292 in 1929 to 63,327 in 1932.[10] In 1930, the Melbourne Zoological Gardens slashed salaries and wages by 15 percent because of declining revenue.[11] With little money coming in, zoos struggled to pay workers, feed their animals, and fill cages. Times were so tough that the South Perth Zoo in

industrialized countries with high rates of urban unemployment tended to suffer the most. Predictably, totalitarian governments were loath to publicize their citizens' willingness to take their own lives. In Stalinist Russia, the Soviet press banned all references to homegrown suicides. Benito Mussolini's media machine did the same, while Adolf Hitler's newly installed government instructed newspapers to convey the "illusion that suicide was a problem of the past." See Christian Goeschel, *Suicide in Nazi Germany* (Oxford: Oxford University Press, 2009), 67.

Western Australia had to turn down offers of animals from other zoos. The reason? It could not afford to pay for the shipping.[12]

Faced with dropping revenues, zoos were forced to cut costs, especially on their greatest expense: food. In Tulsa, Oklahoma, zoo staff "scroung[ed] spoiled vegetables, pick[ed] up road-kill, and harvest[ed] park grass . . . to feed their 35 animals."[13] Other zoos grew crops, slaughtered draft horses, or fed their animals "Depression Diets" made up of less expensive substitutes of their normal fare.[14] In Providence, Rhode Island, the Roger Williams Park Zoo not only planted a large vegetable garden but claimed to teach its population of tropical birds to drink (and enjoy) cow's milk instead of their normal diet of fresh fruit.[15] The Moscow Zoo meanwhile announced a large-scale program to breed ostriches for their meat.[16]

In their hunger to entice visitors, Depression-era zoos borrowed heavily from their circus cousins, showcasing their flesh-and-blood residents as objects of cartoonish spectacle.[17] At the Antwerp Zoo, where the "official menu [was] about 50 per cent below par," staff trained elephants to beg visitors for pennies to buy food.[18] In Berlin, an orchestra of four elephants—two on drums, one turning the crank of a music box, one playing a triangle with its trunk—pantomimed playing music, while a fifth conducted from atop a small barrel.[19] Elsewhere, zoos force-fed snakes, dressed monkeys in costume, held animal "weddings," and trotted out all kinds of dog-and-pony shows to earn the pennies of cash-strapped zoo-goers.

None of this was unique to the Depression years.[20] Even in flush times, zoos are rarely the bastions of public learning they claim to be. It's no surprise, then, that zoo leaders in the 1930s often adopted a "whatever it takes" attitude when it came to grabbing headlines and drumming up business.[21] In 1937, for example, the London Zoo held its annual charity ball complete with a live orchestra, a simian host, and face-to-fur exposure to the zoo's most sparkling personalities. As the human guests swayed to the music, a trio of seated chimpanzees emptied their glasses, metal chains wrapped around their throats to make sure they did not try to dart for freedom. Even the elephants took a swing on the dance floor, lumbering among the backless dresses and black dinner jackets well into the night.[22]

Inevitably, zoos had little choice but to slim their collections, though this often proved easier said than done. While most zoos made a habit of selling older or excess animals, the economic crisis drove the market for unwanted zoo animals to a new low.[23] In June 1932, the *New York Times* reported that "depression made its way into the animal kingdom at the Central Park zoo" after an auction of "surplus animals" failed to attract a single buyer.[24] The zoo in Waco, Texas, had better luck and managed to sell its entire stock. Officials at the shuttered zoo cast the decision in altruistic terms, telling reporters it was "more important to feed hungry humans than hungry animals."[25] (One of its bears became the living mascot of Baylor University.) Many zoos resorted to more extreme methods, destroying animals whose maintenance costs outweighed their utility, a practice that would become increasingly common a decade later. Citing a need for economy, the Beaumaris Zoo in Hobart, Tasmania, slaughtered a leopard and a lion in May 1932. The zoo's curator, A. R. Reid, defended the decision on pragmatic grounds, claiming the move would save approximately thirty-five shillings a week in food bills.[26]

While zoos had always had their naysayers, the Depression spurred a fresh wave of criticism. One Australian "taxpayer" carped that maintaining the local zoo was "a cruel waste when so many human beings are on the hunger list."[27] In Michigan, a member of an anti-tax organization wondered why "idle animals are kept in luxury while Detroit people starve."[28] Critics also rejected the "silly platitude" that zoos fostered education, calling them "a survival of medievalism, cruel, unnecessary, and degrading to the community."[29] What was to be gained by condemning animals to lives of "terror or anger," particularly when long-range photography, motion pictures—even natural history museums—offered a more "correct vision" of zoo animals' wild selves? asked one angry Pittsburgh resident in 1931. "Better by far the spectacle of a dead polar bear surrounded by cakes of asbestos ice, or a stuffed eagle perched on the ledge of a plaster of Paris foundation, than the gruesome sight of a panting polar bear steaming under an equatorial sun, or the 'Glorious American Eagle,' tearing like a buzzard at the vermin in what plumage they have left him."[30]

At the same time, the hardships of the Depression sparked a renewed sense of empathy on behalf of zoos' captive inhabitants—and a heightened awareness of ordinary people's animal instincts. When gazing at the "panting, miserable lions" at New York's Central Park and Prospect Park zoos in October 1930, one Brooklynite wished he "had a rifle to put them out of their abysmal misery." If the current economic hardships continued, he warned darkly: "One Winter's day the stuffy, smiling lion house in Central Park may be more crowded than usual with hungry unemployed feeling the cold; an alarming tumult may arise and, upon armed keepers rushing to the scene, it will be found that instead of a lion having eaten a human, humans have eaten the lions! It will be a merciful release."[31] In an especially philosophical letter to the editor of the *Evening Post* in June 1932, a resident of New Zealand urged readers to imagine how they would feel if sentenced to a lifetime of captivity in a zoo cage. "The misery of confinement does not, in the case of the animals, carry with it the alternative of suicide, as might be the case were a human being deprived of liberty.[†] No human, having that option, would accept the lot we impose on animals."[32]

Even Solly Zuckerman, one of the best-known zoo men of his generation, characterized the interwar years as a "period of decay" after decades of zoo progress.[33] Born in Cape Town in 1904, he completed his medical studies at University College Hospital (London) before taking up a position at the London Zoo, where he carried out extensive research on the sexual behavior of apes. During World War II, Zuckerman set aside his zoological work to develop an anti-concussive helmet for civil defense workers and, starting in 1945, to serve as a scientific advisor of the British Bombing Unit Survey, which was responsible for assembling a postmortem study of the bombing campaign against Germany.[34] For all his diverse interests, however, Zuckerman remained intimately connected to the zoo throughout his life. In one of a series of influential books on zoological history, he criticized Depression-era zoos as "mere animal show-grounds." Few zoos, he argued, had "any meaningful scientific connections," and those that did were mired in backwardness. Whereas the field of zoology had shifted toward cutting-edge experimentation, zoos were "stuck in an earlier mould," more concerned with classifying the new species than pushing the

---

[†] The following month, the events at Chester Zoo would prove the letter writer wrong. For some zoo animals, suicide *was* an option, but I doubt that news of the monkey's death provided much comfort.

limits of veterinary science. Ultimately, Solly Zuckerman summed up the decade before World War II as a reactionary time—"not just in the world of politics, but also in that of zoos."[35]

Zoo-lovers were quick to jump to their defense. Admission was cheap (in some cities, it was free or only a few pennies), and unlike elite institutions, such as opera theaters or art museums, zoos had wide appeal across the social classes. Zoos also served an important economic interest, their advocates claimed, promoting tourism and funneling much-needed money into municipal coffers. (This, at a time when many zoos were going belly-up, was a bit of a stretch.) Further, zoos were said to serve as a mechanism of social discipline. Noting the rise of "enforced leisure" (unemployment) in the 1930s, some worried observers argued that institutions like zoos functioned as "crucial 'safety valve[s]' to occupy people's time." Funding zoos might be expensive in the short term, their champions pointed out, but it was a small price to pay to help keep the unemployed preoccupied and protect the people's "moral health."[36]

Ultimately, though, zoos often relied upon their oldest—and, in many respects, shakiest—justification: education. For centuries, circuses and traveling menageries had touted the high-minded appeal of their collections. In the early 1800s, the London Exeter Exchange, the largest menagerie in the city, stuffed "two tigers, a lion, a hyena, a leopard, a panther, two sloths, a camel, many monkeys, and a tapir" into a pair of rooms on the second floor of a commercial building—all with the aim of edifying their fee-paying customers.[37] Such claims were nonsense, of course, a fig leaf to those who saw live animal displays as an easy way to rake in cash. For all that, zoos' defenders would continue to tout the life-altering appeal of live animal interactions. Only in the zoo, opined one writer in 1937, can the visitor attain a "glimpse of the jungle . . . some realization of the world's past, some contact with nature; some humility that he seems to need and cling to in his present-day mechanized life."[38]

Dr. Huxley's Kiddie Zoo

Among the zoo's most fervent backers during the Depression years was the biologist Julian Sorell Huxley. It was a role he was born to play. His grandfather, Thomas H. Huxley, was a titan of Victorian science and a die-hard advocate of evolutionary theory (he was known as "Darwin's Bulldog"). His brother, Aldous, was the author of the science fiction novel *Brave New World*, and Julian himself was renowned for his ability to translate scientific ideas for a popular audience.[39] Huxley spent much of his career without a formal university affiliation, which allowed him to follow his intellect wherever it led: from biology and evolutionary theory to eugenics, political philosophy, even transhumanism, a term he coined. A fervent believer in "expanding the role of scientific and technical expertise in political-economic life,"[40] he collaborated with H. G. Wells on the massive three-volume biology textbook *The Science of Life*, and during World War II, Huxley was a regular on the BBC's *The Brains Trust*, a radio panel discussion show.[41] Huxley was no cinema icon: gangly, with a skinny neck, round spectacles, and a mop of uncombed hair, he looked more like a caricature of a village high school principal than a world-renowned public intellectual. But for over half a century, he was the public face of British science to millions of readers and listeners around the world.

In November 1935, Peter Chalmers Mitchell approached Huxley about taking over the role of secretary of the Zoological Society of London (ZSL), a position Mitchell had held since 1903. Unlike the zoo superintendent, who was largely in charge of feeding and maintaining the animals, the secretary dealt with "matters of general policy" and advised the zoo Fellows, mostly aristocratic types with a personal or family interest in the animal world. Huxley was intrigued, though he had some reservations. Unlike other zoo men of his era, Huxley did not believe that humans had a God-given right to "deprive animals of their liberty and make a spectacle of them" for amusement. As he recalled in his memoirs, "I see nothing wrong in confining invertebrates, fish, amphibians, and reptiles, even huge creatures like crocodiles, pythons and giant tortoises. Nor do I find it wicked to confine birds and mammals, but with the important proviso that they have enough space for exercise and opportunities to enjoy themselves." Unfortunately, many zoos (including Huxley's own) failed to live up to their side of the bargain, sentencing their largest—and, in some cases, most intelligent— animals to lives of mental anguish. "It is tragic to see the splendid giant gorilla moping and solitary in his little cage," he wrote, "and the lions and tigers reduced to endless and aimless pacing up and down."[42]

Regardless, Huxley believed that properly maintained zoos—organized along scientific principles and competently focused on animals' physical and mental health—served a vital civic purpose.[43] In an August 1936 lecture, Huxley emphasized the zoo's value in educating the public and awakening their interests in the wonders of the natural world. More than exhibiting the curious and the bizarre, the zoo functioned as a hub of scientific activity: it hosted lectures for teachers, promoted humane pet-keeping, answered letters from pet owners, and conducted original research in the fields of "parasitology, animal behaviourism, diet, and animal breeding." In Huxley's view, the zoo was a "practical course in biology," a chance for Londoners of all social strata to see evolutionary theory in action. Above all else, Huxley believed the zoo could, one newspaper reported, "counteract the gloomy view of life" implied by modern physics and chemistry.[44] As embodied by the zoo, biology was a fundamentally optimistic discipline—a science of beauty, variety, and improvement.

In his tenure as zoo secretary (1935–1942), Huxley worked to put a modern stamp on the collection. He changed the exhibit labels to provide more information about the animals' habitats and behaviors. He opened an art studio on the zoo grounds, established a magazine to promote the zoo's scientific agenda, and hired exiles from Nazi Germany, including several Bauhaus architects.[45] His greatest achievement was the construction of London's first petting zoo for children. In August 1935, not long before assuming the role of ZSL secretary, Huxley opened Pets Corner on a small, fenced-off section of the Fellows' Lawn. "This new enclosure here is, I think, a sign that we are continuing our policy of developing the part which the zoo plays in the life of London and indeed of Britain as a whole," he explained to the assembled press. For a fee of one shilling, children could ride a Galapagos tortoise, hand-feed a penguin, wrestle (and be photographed with) a chained chimpanzee, and pet a baby wolf.[46]

Although an instant success, the addition irked some of the zoo's stodgiest visitors.[47] One especially aggrieved "Lady" complained in the *Times* that the "children's playground" introduced the "first elements of unrest" into the zoo grounds. Yet Huxley tuned out his critics, knowing that the zoo needed to democratize its exhibits. No longer the privileged realm of London's elite, the zoo was increasingly part of a mass

Figure 1.1. Six-year-old Teddy Kennedy (*center*) and twelve-year-old Robert Kennedy (*left*) with Julian Huxley at the opening of the Children's Zoo in Regent's Park in June 1938. Trinity Mirror / Mirrorpix / Alamy.

amusement landscape.[48] On June 9, 1938, the renovated and relocated Royal Children's Zoo was unveiled to the public. With his older siblings Robert and Kathleen looking on, six-year-old Teddy Kennedy, future senator and son of the US ambassador to Great Britain, cut the ribbon.

The Colonial Exposition and Mussolini's Zoo

Regent's Park was not the only Depression-era zoo to undergo expansion. Throughout the 1930s, governments and wealthy patrons invested in zoo construction projects around the globe, the results of which are visible to this day. For nations suffocating under the weight of mass unemployment, zoos often appeared an ideal outlet for public investment: they required a large labor force, served a vital need for inexpensive recreation, targeted a wide swath of the citizenry, and ostensibly promoted an interest in science and natural history. Beyond

24   Chapter 1

all that, building zoos usually made for good politics, especially when the finished products aligned with uplifting narratives of national greatness.

One of Europe's most celebrated zoo-building projects began life in the early 1930s, when France hosted the *Exposition Colonial International de Paris*, a massive six-month showcase of the accomplishments of French colonialism. Spread out across the Bois de Vincennes, a nearly 2,500-acre park in the eastern suburbs of Paris, the Exposition featured scaled reproductions of Syrian mosques, pavilions from Somaliland, even sections of Angkor-Vat temple, alongside ethnological displays of indigenous peoples[‡] from throughout the empire.[49] The Exposition's chief organizer, Maréchal Lyautey, a French Army general best known for conquering Morocco, believed that France had an uplifting effect on colonies and peoples under its control. According to historian Patricia A. Morton, Lyautey saw the event as a "didactic demonstration of the colonial world order, based on cooperation among the colonizing powers and the West's responsibility to continue colonization and its good works."[50]

The most popular exhibit, the "Zoo de la Colonial," was located at the far end of the Exposition grounds near the Palestine Pavilion, a stone domelike structure made to resemble Rachel's Tomb. Forgoing the iron cages and box-like concrete exhibits of nineteenth-century zoos, the Colonial Zoo was modeled on the so-called "barless" designs found at Carl Hagenbeck's Tierpark in Stellingen, outside of Hamburg, which used hidden moats and tricks of perspective to create the illusion of freedom and open space. Zoo historians Eric Baratay and Elisabeth Hardouin-Fugier write that Hagenbeck's firm was a virtual partner in the Colonial Zoo: "The animals came from Stellingen, as did their keepers, their trainer, the writer Eiper and the design of the fake rocks, constructed of 250 tonnes of cement poured over wooden frames."[51] Lyautey hoped to use the zoo to showcase the "splendours" of the empire's wildlife in an exotic setting.[52] It worked. Between May 6 and November 15, 1931, some five million visitors flocked to the

---

[‡] These weren't the "human zoos" that were so popular in Europe and North America throughout the nineteenth century (and, shamefully, far into the twentieth). But they were close enough.

Colonial Zoo, which included animals from French colonies in North Africa, Indochina, Madagascar, Guyana, and elsewhere.

After the Exposition closed, the Colonial Zoo collection became the basis for the Paris Zoological Park (better known as the Vincennes Zoo), which opened in another part of the park three years later. Paris already had a zoo, the *Ménagerie du Jardin des Plantes*, which had been founded during the French Revolution. By the 1930s, however, not only had it fallen into disrepair, but it was desperately behind the times. Lions, tigers, and bears were held like "prisoners of the state," crammed into "microscopic vaults" devoid of fresh air and light. The new zoo, by contrast, was meant to bring Paris roaring into the twentieth century. According to one contemporary account, Vincennes's 2,500 pensioners (a term often used to describe France's zoo animals) lived in "quasi-freedom" amid a landscape of plaster terraces, concrete pools, and carefully manicured panoramas—all of it dominated by a sixty-five-meter-high mountain (known as the "Grand Rocher" or "Big Rock"), which also doubled as a water tower. No longer would zoo animals be allowed to spend their days in shameful lethargy, the zoo's director assured the press. Vincennes's animal population "worked" (doing what, it was never clear) and engaged in regular bouts of "physical culture," which along with vitamin-infused diets were considered essential for their long-term health.[53] In retrospect, we now know that Vincennes turned out to be just another zoo with all the same problems (lack of species-appropriate food, space, animal enrichment, and upkeep) as zoos the world over. Nevertheless, the zoo's promises of camouflaged captivity and physically cultured animals proved to be an instant success with the public. The day after the Vincennes Zoo was inaugurated on June 2, 1934, fifty thousand Parisians passed through its gates.

The zoo's driving force in its early years was its first director, Achille Joseph Urbain, who was already a superstar in the fields of immunology and microbiology. After graduating with a veterinary degree in 1906, he joined the French cavalry in World War I, where he won the *croix de guerre* for treating severely wounded soldiers. At war's end, he spent more than a decade training at the Pasteur Institute in Paris before joining the staff of the National Museum of Natural History in 1931. Bald, with a domed head and an elegantly groomed mustache, Urbain shared Huxley's view on the importance of good publicity.

Indeed, he was a virtual celebrity in mid-1930s Paris. On May 17, 1933, a year before the Vincennes Zoo was set to open, he delivered an address from a transmitter atop the Eiffel Tower. In January 1935, he left on an expedition to Chad and Cameroon accompanied by a journalist from *Le Journal*, which published sensationalistic biweekly accounts of the scientist's exploits. Three years later, a thinly fictionalized account of the trip appeared in Paris bookstores, further cementing Urbain's public image as the nation's preeminent zoo man.[54]

If the Vincennes Zoo had its roots in French imperialism, the renovation of the Rome Zoo bore the architectural hallmarks of Italian fascism. Opened in 1911, the Giardino Zoologico di Roma had also been built on a Hagenbeckian model of open-air enclosures, rocky landscapes, and theatrical use of water and perspective.[55] During the 1920s, Italy's fascist dictator, Benito Mussolini, loved to drop by the lion cages, whose inhabitants he equated with strength, brutality, and viciousness. Once, not long after coming to power, he announced, "I am possessed by a frenzied ambition which torments and devours me from within like a physical illness. It is, through my own will-power, to carve a mark on the age—like a lion with his claws, like this," slashing at the air with his fingers extended.[56] According to historian Giulia Guazzaloca, Il Duce "wanted to make respect for animals an ornament of fascist 'modernism.'" An avowed hunter (and never one to be tripped up by contradictions), Mussolini was eager to modernize Italy's image as a nation awash in animal abuse. In his mind, the "new Italian" had a patriotic duty to treat animals kindly, if only to quiet the complaints of foreign visitors to the country. "Anyone who abuses animals is no Italian," he bellowed, a message he hoped to instill in future fascists from infancy.[57]

In 1933, the zoo undertook a two-year overhaul of many major exhibits, which had been mutilated after two decades of haphazard change.[58] Architect Raffaele De Vico, best known as a designer of parks and scenic gardens, supervised the expansion, including the construction of a sea lion pool and a massive concrete reptile house, complete with an indoor crocodile pond. The new designs blended modern building techniques, references to Rome's imperial past, and the fascist celebration of monumentality. Once reopened, visitors entered the zoo by scaling three sets of steps before passing beneath a high archway. Looming above it all was the zoo's new aviary, a colossal

Figure 1.2. Like other strongmen of his era, Benito Mussolini was obsessed with the ferocity and power of lions. Tellingly, however, Il Duce satisfied his cult of machismo by playing with cubs rather than with dangerous adults. This 1924 photo shows him riding around in an open-top car with his pet lion cub, Ras. D and S Photography Archives / Alamy.

dome of intersecting steel rods like something from a Futurist art exhibit.[59] While the zoo would never attain the status of other European zoos, especially those of Germany, it nonetheless served as a monument to the power and modernity of the fascist state. This link was made especially clear when, in December 1935, hundreds of Romans turned out to gaze at the zoo's newest residents: a pair of lions recently looted in Italy's murderous campaign against Ethiopia.[60]

America's Zoo Deal

On the afternoon of November 26, 1931, fifteen unemployed men carried out a chemical weapon attack in midtown Manhattan. They had been enlisted in the city's "great war" against the rats of the Central Park Zoo. Each man carried a bucket of toast cubes dipped in a solution of digitalis and other plant toxins. The campaign was led by a pair of self-described "rodent control specialists," Irving and Hugo Billig, who had concocted seventy-five gallons of the deadly solution in the basement of the nearby Arsenal building. Over the next few hours, as groups of children followed along, the small army scattered 5,000 pieces of the lethal toast.[61] As the sun set, a lone photographer waited by his tripod to snap a picture of the first casualty.[62]

When the party returned early the next morning, corpses littered the zoo grounds. Park officials discovered twenty-seven lifeless bodies beneath the floor of the tiger cage; reports of dozens more came in over the next few hours. In his Fifth Avenue office, Irving Billig, a statistician by trade, estimated that as many as 4,500 rats had died after the first dosing, though the vast majority would never be found. Mother rats likely took much of the food back to their underground lairs to share with their young, he ecstatically explained to the *New York Times*. One piece of toast could easily poison an entire family.[63]

No nation invested more resources in constructing, maintaining, and, yes, disinfesting zoos during the Depression years than the United States. Under the auspices of Franklin Roosevelt's New Deal legislation, the federal government sank millions of dollars into zoo construction and renovation across the country. At the National Zoo in Washington, DC, federally funded workers built "three stone houses for hardy ruminants, a swan pond, a mile of cement footpaths and a rocky mount for high-climbing goats." St. Louis invested heavily in "barless caging," as did Detroit, which used $438,000 in federal funds to complete an "African Swamp," an exhibit for Siberian tigers, and a "South American pampas," based on a Hagenbeck design.[64] In New Orleans, workers from the Civil Works Administration dug a 1,200-foot-long lagoon, "forming what are now the water bodies of the Audubon Zoo's Louisiana Swamp, Jaguar Jungle and South American Pampas exhibits."[65] While at the Como Park Zoo in St. Paul, Minnesota, workers from the Works Progress Association (WPA) constructed a new monkey island, bear island, and main zoo building.[66]

Some zoo watchers would look back at the mid-1930s as a "golden age for American zoos."[67] In February 1935, Earl Chapin May reported that twenty million people had visited North American zoos in the previous year—an "all-time high" and a remarkable turnaround since the start of the decade.[68] American "zoo consciousness" was especially pronounced in New York City. With its three zoos—in the Bronx,

Central Park, and Prospect Park in Brooklyn—New York attracted millions of zoo visitors a year. The Bronx Zoo alone was the second-largest zoo in the world (only Berlin's animal collection was larger), and New York's three zoos collectively housed more "wild animals, birds and reptiles" than anywhere else.[69]

New York's zoos even had their own advocate in the form of Alfred (Al) Smith, the former governor who lost the presidential race to Herbert Hoover in 1928. While living at the governor's mansion in Albany, Smith had built an "executive zoo" housing various animals he acquired.[70] In December 1934, Smith was named "honorary night superintendent" at the newly renovated Central Park Zoo. Several nights a week he could be seen walking from his apartment at 820 Fifth Avenue to the zoo, where—decked out in his black evening coat and brown derby—he would spend half an hour feeding various animals by hand.[71] The next year, Smith was given the task of helping fill the empty cages of the Prospect Park Zoo, which was set to open on the Fourth of July despite the fact that it contained fewer than twenty animals.[72] As Prospect Park's "renting agent," Smith called in favors, delivered speeches, and gave interviews from his office on the thirty-second floor of the Empire State Building. In a particular moment of bravado, he penned a letter to Ethiopian emperor Haile Selassie accepting his offer to export a leopard and four lions to Brooklyn. Smith revealed the missive at a public gathering of the Citizens Committee for the Prospect Park Zoo in November 1935: "Dear Haile: Send 'em along, Yours, AL."[73]

They never arrived. Mussolini's armies got there first.

The Coming Storm

By the mid-1930s, even the most optimistic observers of global affairs were forced to recognize ominous signs on the horizon. The international order was swiftly unraveling, and the zoo might not be able to remain neutral for long. The fascist invasion of Ethiopia, a campaign that left some 250,000 Africans dead, threatened to wreak havoc on zoos' traditional hunting grounds. In October 1935, the United Press service reported that the war had "shut off one of the world's most abundant sources of wild animals," and professional animal dealers vowed to avoid the region until the violence abated.[74] In October 1937, Joseph Stalin's brutal purge of intellectuals and "anti-Soviet elements" reached the iron gates of the Moscow Zoo, when the director and several animal keepers were arrested on a litany of trumped-up charges, including scaring the bears with loudspeakers, feeding strychnine-laden sausages to the badgers, and staging ballet dances in the park.[75] Later that year, Western newspapers pointed to a change in the diet of Tokyo's zoo animals as a sign of a looming war economy. Noting the zoo curtailing its lions' meat rations and feeding its wolves sardines and vegetables, one newspaper noted: "A similar compulsory shift of eating and drinking and sartorial habits is foreshadowed for [Tokyo's] human inhabitants."[76]

And then there was the "pudgy little vegetarian with the Charlie Chaplin mustache"—Adolf Hitler.[77] To zoo-goers the world over, Hitler's Nazi Party was an enigma. How could a group of murderous fanatics come from a nation of purported animal lovers?

Not everyone lived to find out. On the afternoon of August 4, 1939, Adele Langer (age forty-three) and her two sons—Tommy (age six) and Jan Misha (age four and a half)—checked into the stylish Congress Hotel in downtown Chicago. The family had escaped, along with Adele's husband Karel, from Nazi-occupied Czechoslovakia, and the family's six-month visitor's visa was set to expire soon. After paying $8, she took a room on the hotel's thirteenth floor, and—sometime around 11 p.m. that evening—she heaved the two boys out the window of their room and then jumped. All three bodies smashed onto the sidewalk of Michigan Avenue more than a hundred feet below. Had she waited at home, only a few hours later Adele would have learned that the Canadian government had granted the family permanent asylum. Instead, Adele had left the house early so she could take her boys for a final visit to the zoo.

2

Hitler's Zoos

One sunny day in June 1935, Hermann Göring, the recently appointed commander of the resurgent German *Luftwaffe*, settled into a lawn chair at his summer home in the alpine retreat of Obersalzberg, near the Austrian border. At forty-two, he cut a strangely adolescent figure. Göring wore lederhosen (the short leather breeches traditionally favored by Bavarian woodsmen) and white stockings pulled up to his knees. His body was bloated after years of morphine addiction and heavy eating, and for all Göring's usual tidiness (he often changed shirts multiple times a day because of incessant sweating), a lock of unruly hair flopped back and forth across his wide brow. Cradled in his arms was a wriggling lion cub, one of several he and his new wife, the actress Emmy Sonnemann, would raise over the coming years. The scene resembled something from a satirical cartoon: Nazi versus kitten. The will to power against the power of will. The tighter Göring held on, the more the cub struggled to break free, pausing occasionally to gnaw on Göring's forearm or stare at tufts of grass only a few feet away. In the end, the future Reichsmarschall would not be deterred. As a photographer snapped pictures, Göring aped for the camera, squeezing the helpless lion to his face like a toddler with a stuffed toy.[1]

In later years, critics came to see Göring's pet lions as manifestations of a compulsive personality: an insatiable desire for all things grand and exotic. By all accounts, der dicke Hermann ("Fat Hermann") was a man of enormous appetites—a dandy for whom no excess was too excessive. He loved food, wine, uniforms (the more ornate, the better). He owned a private menagerie, a $265,000 toy train set, yachts, rare jewels, and enough antiques to furnish a small palace. When he wasn't amassing new titles, Göring collected art with the urgency of an addict, plastering the walls of his various homes with hundreds of paintings looted from countries under Nazi rule. (He had a special fondness for female nudes.) Viewed in this light, Göring's lion cubs seem like little more than stage dressing: props with which he might play out daily fantasies of life without limits.[2]

To his admirers, however, Göring's lions had the opposite effect. Compared to most Nazi leaders, who projected an image of humorless self-importance, Göring appeared softhearted, almost childlike. As early as July 1933, the *New York Times* described him as a "great lover of animals," a reputation that he would cultivate over the next decade.[3] The press circulated photos of Göring bottle-feeding the cubs by hand. In state-funded documentaries and kitschy postcards, he was shown fretting over his animal brood like an anxious father.[4] It was shameless propaganda, all of it. Still, how bad could these Nazis be if one of Hitler's chief lieutenants owned a baby lion named Mucki?

It would be a mistake to credit Germany's zoo-mania in the 1930s to figures like Hermann Göring and his *Führer*. The German public had long expressed a fascination with exotic animals, particularly if they happened to be confined to a nature reserve or an urban menagerie. During the 1800s, the rise in global trade, coupled with growing numbers of expeditions to Africa and Asia, fueled public curiosity about the natural world. When they weren't tramping through the countryside, German wildlife lovers collected insects, attended lectures on jungle exploration, and sought out novel ways to come face to face with the world's strange and exotic creatures.[5] Nineteenth-century Germans were especially fond of zoos, which promised to satisfy their hunger to experience the world's living bounty firsthand. By 1900, Germany boasted more zoos than any other country in Europe: an archipelago of iron cages and concrete islands that stretched from Breslau to Cologne.[6]

Nevertheless, the rise of National Socialism sparked even greater interest in animals and their welfare. Shortly after coming to power in January 1933, the Nazi Party enacted dozens of laws regulating the treatment of animals. In the first few months, they banned vivisection (live animal experimentation) and enacted new guidelines for animal slaughter. That August, Göring threatened to send people who "treat animals as inanimate property" to a concentration camp.[7] On November 24, 1933, the Nazi government passed the most comprehensive animal protection law of its time. Among other things, the *Reichstierschutzgesetz* (Reich Animal Protection Act) made it illegal to import horses with docked tails, force-feed domestic fowl, or "test the power of dogs on cats, foxes, and other animals." Much of the law was aimed at minimizing the pain animals routinely suffered at human hands. Harming a pet was punishable by up to two years in prison—an astounding sentence at a time when, in most countries, animals had no legal status whatsoever.[8]

That was just the beginning. Over the next decade, Nazi legislators continued to enact measures on the treatment of domestic animals and native wildlife. No issue was too large—or too small—to escape their interest. Lawmakers outlawed the slaughter of fish without anesthesia, established stricter hunting regulations, and set new standards for the most humane way to cook a lobster.* In the eyes of Nazi ideologues, animals were more than extensions of human property; they were part of a shared moral universe, deserving of protection for their own sake. Just as important, Nazi officials saw animal protection as a means of reinvigorating a nation still reeling from economic depression and spiritual collapse. The goal of the 1933 Animal Protection Law, it declared, was to "awaken and strengthen compassion as one of the highest moral values of the German people."[9]

When it came to animal protection, the Reich's most vocal spokesman was Adolf Hitler himself, whose reputation as a vegetarian and an animal lover spread across the Atlantic.[10] One pro-Nazi magazine described Hitler as an "exemplary friend of animals" who opposed vivisection and refused to eat meat "because of his general attitude toward life."[11] He was said to shield his eyes during scenes of animal violence on film, and fellow Nazis recalled Hitler weeping openly when he encountered injured animals on the street.[12] Hitler had a special hatred for hunting, which he considered both wasteful and needlessly

---

* How to kill lobsters the Nazi way: Step one, heat the water to a rapid boil; step two, toss the lobsters in one at a time, so that they die as quickly as possible. Any other technique was considered tantamount to torture.

Figure 2.1. Drawn by German American artist Arthur Johnson, this 1933 cartoon from the Berlin humor magazine *Kladderadatsch* shows rabbits, dogs, birds, and other animals heiling a uniformed Hermann Göring after the passage of antivivisection laws in Germany. Courtesy of Universitätsbibliothek Heidelberg.

Hitler's Zoos   35

cruel. "Killing animals, if it must be done, is the butcher's business," he once raged. "If only there were still some danger connected with hunting, as in the days when men used spears for killing game. But today . . . anybody with a fat belly can safely shoot the animal down from a distance. . . . Hunting and horse racing are the last remnants of a dead feudal world."[13]

Great Danes and Lion Cubs

While *some* individuals' feelings about *certain* animals were no doubt sincere, Nazis' collective practices toward animals were riddled with inconsistencies and contradictions. This is, of course, to be expected. Hitler and company were not exactly known for their intellectual coherence, and they were not afraid to lie, obfuscate—even deny reality itself—when it suited their purpose. (These were, after all, the very same folks who salivated over statuesque blond "super-men," despite the fact that many top Nazis—including Joseph Goebbels and Heinrich Himmler, Hitler's rat-faced secretary—bore little resemblance to the so-called master race.) More to the point, Nazism itself was, as historian Frank Uekoetter points out, an "amorphous conglomerate of concepts, notions, and resentments where even key concepts like *Volk* and race, community and *Führer* were open to divergent readings."[14] At times, ideas about protecting and conserving wildlife closely aligned with the goals of the Nazi state; at others, however, top Nazis were all too willing to discard their high-minded ideals in pursuit of individual pleasure and political power.

The Reich's most visible "animal lovers" were no exception. In his position as *Reichsforstminister* (Minister of the German Forests) and *Reichsjägermeister* (Master of the German Hunt), Hermann Göring established nature reserves, outlawed steel traps, and introduced harsher penalties for poaching native wildlife.[15] For all of that, he remained a lifelong hunter, often importing deer, mountain goats, and other large game to his various estates for the sole pleasure of shooting them dead.

Hitler's professed affection for animals proved to be more hypocritical still. He could be vicious to his pet German shepherd Blondi, and he frequently used animal epithets—swine, dogs, "little worms"—to denigrate his political opponents, both real and imagined.[16] After they refused to adopt Nazi racial policies in 1933, Hitler banned German vegetarian societies and jailed the movement's leaders.[17] As for his own famously ascetic diet, Hitler was not nearly as strict as his toadies led the public to believe. Throughout the 1930s, the *Führer* continued to indulge his appetite for Bavarian sausages and other meat dishes.[18] The architect Albert Speer, a regular guest at Hitler's vacation home in the Bavarian Alps, recalled watching the Reich Chancellor eat "caviar by the spoonful" until he discovered the fish eggs' cost. (The "idea of a caviar-eating Leader was incompatible with Hitler's conception of himself," Speer noted in his diary.)[19] One biographer, Robert Payne, postulates that Hitler's strict vegetarianism was, in large part, a "fiction invented by [Propaganda Minister Joseph] Goebbels to emphasize his total dedication, his self-control, the distance that separated him from other men."[20] This might be going a *bit* too far (after 1942, Hitler seems to have given up meat for good). What's indisputable is that Nazi propagandists used Hitler's diet as part of a broader campaign to cast National Socialism as a force of progress: pro-Germany, pro-animal, pro-nature, pro-life.

In fact, from today's perspective, Nazi animal protection laws look like little more than a thinly veiled attempt to harass German Jews. Early on, the antisemitic undertones of Nazi animal protection were somewhat subtle—at least when compared to what was to come. The April 1933 slaughter laws, for example, expressly prohibited the killing of livestock without anesthesia, a requirement that effectively outlawed kosher butchering. Antisemitism was also a driving force for attacks on vivisection, which antisemites like the composer Richard Wagner had long denounced as "Jewish science."[21] By the late 1930s, the Nazis abandoned all pretense of neutrality when it came to both animals and people. During the *Anschluss* of Austria in March 1938, German troops terrorized Jews by shooting all their dogs. On February 15, 1942, only a few weeks after deciding the "Final Solution to the Jewish Question," Hitler's government officially banned Jews from owning pets. For countless pet owners, the decree meant an unbearable choice: they could euthanize their beloved dogs, cats, and birds themselves, or they could hand them over to the German Animal Protection Association for immediate destruction.[22]

A few years after fleeing Nazi Germany, the Jewish philosophers Max Horkheimer and Theodor Adorno penned a short note on the

Nazis' purported affection for animals. It was damning, to say the least. "When captains of industry and fascist leaders have animals around them, they are not domestic poodles but Great Danes and lion cubs," Horkheimer and Adorno wrote. "They are there to add spice to power through the terror they inspire." The exiled philosophers rejected the notion that the Nazis valued animals for their intrinsic worth. Instead, they charged that "the Fascist's passionate interest in animals, nature, and children is rooted in the lust to persecute. . . . A creature is merely material for the master's bloody purpose."[23]

More than half a century later, Horkheimer and Adorno's critique remains compelling—and not simply because it resonates so perfectly with our view of Nazis as amoral killers. Well before the start of their genocidal campaigns, National Socialist thinkers embraced racist theories of evolution and biology to lend scientific credibility to their fantasies of mass slaughter. According to Arnold Arluke and Boria Sax, authors of a series of groundbreaking studies on animals in the Third Reich, the Nazis "saw human life as part of a larger biological order that they sought to create."[24] In the Nazi worldview, nature was a hierarchy: with racially pure Aryans at the top, animals and non-Aryans in the middle, and contaminated *Untermenschen* (subhumans) at the very bottom. Echoing the teachings of the antisemitic philosopher Ernst Haeckel, who believed that non-Europeans were closer to animals than to humans, Hitler proclaimed in 1927: "Take away the Nordic Germans and nothing remains but the dance of apes."[25] Today, the Nazis' frequent references to rats, lions, and other creatures might seem like metaphors; at the time, however, many National Socialists viewed politics in explicitly biological terms. Kill or be killed. Survival of the fittest.

The Nazification of German Zookeeping

Within this context, psychologist Colin Goldner argues, German zoos served as key "sites of 'representative biology' in which central ideological themes of the Nazi state, such as the theory of the heredity or race, could be made clear."[26] More than assemblies of wild beasts, zoos were living, breathing, roaring manifestations of the Nazi worldview: open-air prisons where the strong ruled the weak, "undesirables" were purged, and men in uniforms called the shots. Nazi propagandist Joseph Goebbels believed that zoo animals illustrated "eternal laws" about the virtues of aggression and the inevitability of conflict. An avid zoo-goer, he despised monkeys, which he described as the "embodiment of lechery." The lion, by contrast, he felt was a "picture of shackled force. Full of contemptuous arrogance. We humans are small and cowardly to this prince." A visit to a zoo in July 1924 inspired the Nazi propagandist to write a full-throated defense of political violence: "Is not nature also terrible? Is the struggle for existence—between man and man, state and state, race and race, continent and continent—not the cruelest process known to the world? The right of the stronger—we must again see this natural law clearer, then all fantasies of pacifism and eternal peace will fly away. . . . Go and speak of pacifism among the lions and tigers!"[27]

Although not all of Goebbels's cohort shared his zeal for caged animals, the Nazi regime was all too willing to throw its weight behind the nation's zoos. Nazi functionaries lent financial and political support to new zoos in Bochum, Duisburg, Heidelberg, Straubing, Hamm, Krefeld, and other cities.[28] They subsidized expansion projects and helped zoos negotiate bureaucratic red tape. Individual Nazi leaders also contributed animals to the nation's most prestigious collections. The recently opened Hellabrunn Zoo in Munich, a Nazi stronghold since the 1920s, was a particular favorite of the party's inner circle. Deputy *Führer* Rudolf Hess donated a young lioness; Göring passed along four pure-blooded wisents (European bison). In 1935, Hitler gave the zoo fifty-five mandarin ducks for a new free-range exhibit; two years later, he donated a pair of giraffes he received as a birthday gift from admirers in German East Africa.[29]

The Nazification of German zoos extended well beyond funding and donations. By their very nature, zoos in the 1930s were tailor-made for political exploitation. Zoos encouraged visitors to slow down, contemplate their place within the natural world, and—above all—*read the signs*, which the Nazis were all too happy to adapt to fit their worldview. Often located in urban parks with easy access to public transportation, zoos were able to accommodate large groups of people for hours on end—all of which made them ideal venues for staging political rallies. By the mid-1930s, the Nazi influence of German zoos would have been difficult to miss. Across the country, zoo visitors encountered buildings festooned with swastikas and draped in black, white, and red. As early as 1934, the Dresden Zoo offered reduced admission for officers in uniform, and German zoos collaborated with the Nazi leisure organization *Kraft durch Freude* (Strength through Joy) to promote tourism and interest in animals.[30] In the Tiergarten, a wooded 500-acre park in the center of the Reich capital, the Berlin Zoological Garden was a centerpiece of Nazi activity. It hosted gala dinners for military organizations, press balls for higher-ups in the propaganda ministry, and concerts for top Nazis and their families. On February 6, 1938, members of the paramilitary *Schutzstaffel* (SS) used the zoo to stage a donation campaign for *Winterhilfswerk des Deutschen Volkes* (Winter Relief of the German People), an annual charity drive. In a few years, Nazi storm troopers would engage in one of the bloodiest killing sprees in world history. But on that day, at least, they were tasked with a different mission: to lead German children on pony rides.

Like other professionals, German zoo leaders would have felt considerable pressure to go along with the Nazi agenda, whatever their personal inclinations. Well before Hitler's rise, German zoos tended to be overtly hierarchical institutions; upon reaching the top, a zoo director might stay in the position for years (even decades), ingratiating himself with the local political establishment. Zoo directors that bucked Hitler's plans could expect to lose their jobs at the very least—not that German zoo men were innocent victims of Nazi menace. Nearly all prominent zoo directors and natural scientists—including such future luminaries as the Nobel Prize–winning ornithologist Konrad Lorenz and Bernhard Grzimek, who won an Academy Award for his documentary *Serengeti Shall Not Die* (1959)—officially joined the Nazi Party. ("As a natural scientist, I have, of course, always been a National Socialist," Lorenz acknowledged later.)[31] Others cozied up to Nazi leaders or sought to leverage Hitler's purported interest in animals for their own benefit.

Among the ranks of the true believers, Otto Antonius, director of Vienna's world-famous Schönbrunn Zoo, deserves special mention. He was the dictionary definition of a modern zoo man: one part scientist, one part ringmaster. A tireless researcher, he authored nearly two hundred scientific publications on such varied topics as enclosure design, livestock breeding, and animal psychology.[32] He enjoyed tending the animals by hand and often could be seen walking amid the cages in a rumpled overcoat and felt fedora. He was also, in the words of his wartime superiors, an "ideal national socialist." Antonius joined the National Socialist Party (member #1307171) in 1932. When the Austrian government banned the party the following year, he kept up his membership in secret. He was eventually discovered and, in 1934, the Austrian Federal Chancellery removed him from his position. Stung, Antonius spent the next few years consumed by writing and research. In February 1936, he traveled to Poland, where he worked with the agriculturalist Tadeusz Vetulani on a scheme to "re-breed" forest tarpans, an extinct subspecies of wild horse. All the while, he continued to fight his suspension. On January 2, 1937, he was finally allowed to resume his position as zoo director, and, little more than a year later, the Nazi annexation of Austria meant that he no longer needed to disguise his political sympathies.[33]

The First Family of Nazi Zoo Men

No one embodied the tangled relationship between Nazism and German zoos more fully than Lutz Heck. He belonged to the first family of German zoo directors. His father, Ludwig, was the director of the Berlin Zoo from 1888 to 1931. His younger brother, Heinz, ran Munich's Hellabrunn Zoo, which reopened in 1928. Decades before Hitler's rise, the elder Heck was a kind of ur-Nazi: an archconservative and ardent eugenicist who schooled his boys in the importance of blood and race. In 1938, "Papa Heck" wrote: "My sons have often said to me of late: You were a National Socialist, you preached to us national socialist worldviews, long before the word was in use."[34]

From an early age, Lutz was poised to follow in his father's footsteps. Already a fervent nationalist, he spent four years in the German military during World War I. After the war, while studying zoology at the University of Berlin, Lutz joined fellow vets in a weeklong street battle against marching workers. He earned his doctorate in 1922 and began a stint at a small zoo in Halle. He returned to the Berlin Zoo two years later and, after rising to assistant director in 1927, became director in 1932. At forty, with a pockmarked face and thinning parted hair, Heck looked more like a suburban bank manager than the most famous zoo man in the Third Reich. But he had a special talent for

Figure 2.2. A hunting companion of Hermann Göring, Lutz Heck was director of the Berlin Zoo throughout the Nazi era. In this photo he is seen stroking the noses of some zebras in May 1940. Sueddeutsche Zeitung Photo / Alamy.

winning influential friends and soon proved himself a die-hard supporter of the Nazi cause. An avid hunter and outdoorsman, he was especially close to Hermann Göring. Among other favors, Heck personally supplied Göring with lion cubs and picked them up when they grew too large. A Nazi in all but name, Heck eventually made it official, joining the National Socialist Party (member #3934018) on May 1, 1937.[35]

Throughout this period, Lutz and his brother Heinz had a side project: resurrecting extinct animals through selective "back-breeding."[36] The brothers had been fascinated with the "game of past ages" since childhood, when they first encountered the stories of Siegfried's hunts in the medieval epic poem the *Nibelungenlied*.[37] They were especially interested in aurochs, a breed of wild oxen that once roamed the forests of central Europe. The last aurochs died in the Jaktorów forest, south of Warsaw, in 1627. But the Hecks believed that no animal was truly extinct as long as it had living descendants. The aurochs' genetic structure lived on; all they had to do, Lutz wrote, was "assemble the right material to start from and then know how to mix it."[38] The process was more art than science. The Hecks scoured Europe to locate animals that, in their eyes, exhibited the aurochs' wild temperament and primitive characteristics. Then, after returning to Germany, they spent years mixing and matching the various breeds—highlighting some traits, minimizing others—until both had managed to create a beast that resembled the semi-mythical creature of their childhood imaginations. In the autumn of 1938, a caravan of trucks carried seven of Lutz's aurochs to Göring's nature preserve in East Prussia, where they were left to wander in a 120-acre fenced pen.[39]

Today, zoologists tend to treat the Hecks' "near-aurochs" as little more than historical curiosities on par with "ligers" and other animal hybrids. In 1930s Germany, however, the Hecks' quest to restore this icon of German natural history paralleled Hitler's ultimate promise: to turn back the clock of modernity and restore the German Reich to its past glories. In the eyes of National Socialists, twentieth-century society was contaminated, weak, impure. Under Hitler, the Nazis would undo the centuries of civilization and unshackle the animal instincts that lived within all Germans. "I want violent, imperious, fearless, cruel young people," said Hitler. "The free, magnificent beast of prey must once again flash in their eyes. . . . In this way, I shall blot out thousands of years of human domestication. I shall have the pure, noble stuff of nature."[40]

In a world of cattle, Germany would be a nation of aurochs.

Potemkin Villages

On July 24, 1936, one week before the start of the Olympic Games,[†] the Berlin Zoo celebrated the grand opening of a new lion exhibit, an artificial rock mountain made from some 2.6 million pounds of sandstone.[41] Six days later, over a thousand international journalists attended a gala in the zoo ballroom hosted by Joseph Goebbels. As Nazi paramilitary bands played, guests ate dinner beneath the banners of

---

[†] In addition to the hundreds of buildings, the artificial lake, the hairdressing salons, and the thirty-eight dining halls, the official Olympic Village also included a "mini-zoo" featuring a small selection of storks, deer, and other "German" animals.

the fifty-three participating nations. Eventually, Goebbels welcomed the press in the "name of the Fuhrer," assuring the crowd that the Nazis had no intention of using the Olympics as state propaganda. "We want you to see Germany as it is," Goebbels insisted, "but we have no intention of showing you Potemkin villages."[42]

I can't help but wonder if anyone in the assembled audience remarked about the irony of Goebbels's statement, particularly given its setting. What, after all, is a zoo if not a kind of Potemkin village of the natural world? What other place does more to disguise nature's violence—and human violence toward it?

Goebbels's pronouncement was doubly ironic considering Lutz Heck's latest addition, a so-called Deutsche Zoo exhibiting the Reich's indigenous wildlife. Funded by concessions from the Prussian state ministry, it contained a bear exhibit, a small aviary, and enclosures for foxes, wildcats, and wolves—all of it set in an idealized "German landscape" of artificial rocks and carefully arranged flora. The Deutsche Zoo did little to hide its Nazi roots (signs were marked with swastikas), but that was the point.[43] The primary goal of the addition was to strengthen German zoo-goers' connection to the landscape, to its wildlife, and—in time—to Hitler's genocidal vision of purifying the Reich of its non-native inhabitants.

In the end, though, perhaps the most telling expression of Nazi zoo-mania was not found in Berlin or even Nuremberg, where Hitler's government financed the construction of a new zoo following the expansion of the Nazi Party grounds. It was hidden away in a beech forest outside the Thuringian city of Weimar. For decades, the region had been a site of pilgrimage for fans of the nineteenth-century poet Johann von Goethe, whose writings transformed the Ettersburg—the wooded limestone ridge that dominated the landscape—into a symbol of romantic freedom. During the late 1930s, however, the forest came to be home to another citadel of German national culture now infamous the world over.

Initially, it was to be called "Ettersberg Concentration Camp." Today, most of us know it by a different name: Buchenwald. And it had a zoo.

3

The Bear at Buchenwald

The unlikely story of the Buchenwald Zoological Garden began in July 1937, when the first advanced squad of imprisoned laborers arrived in the area.[1] By the following spring, Hitler's newest penal colony held some 2,500 inmates, who spent their days clearing forest, building roads, and constructing what would soon become Germany's largest *Konzentrationslager* (KZ) or concentration camp.[2] To outsiders, Nazi leaders maintained (falsely) that the camps were geared toward reeducating social deviants and providing "preventive custody" to political prisoners. In truth, the KZ system metastasized into a state within a state—a zone of absolute power where millions were starved, tortured, worked as slaves, and eventually transformed into corpses.[3] "It was a city of its own, built solely by the labour of the inmates," testified one longtime prisoner. "There were production workshops, a sawmill, pig-breeding facilities, a vegetable garden, a brickyard, quarries, a riding school . . . an infirmary, a general records department, a depot and a wood yard, hairdressers, guard and command towers, music bands, a sculptors' workshop and a woodcarving shop."[4] Separated from the SS residential areas, the inmates' camp consisted of a grid of squat buildings (barracks, assorted workshops, a crematorium) surrounding an open muster yard—all of it wrapped in a three-meter fence of electrified barbed wire.[5]

Everything about Buchenwald was designed to strip prisoners of their humanity. Driven like cattle through the front gates, the stunned inmates were promptly stripped, their heads shaven raw by camp barbers. Guards confiscated their possessions, including artificial limbs, and staff inspected the inmates' bodies for evidence of disease. (The camp pathological department would also take a special interest in body art, amassing a sizable collection of human leather with "colorful or otherwise interesting tattoos.") Once dressed, prisoners were forced to wear colored triangles on their clothing to identify their purported "crimes" (pink for homosexuals, purple for conscientious objectors, red for communists, yellow for Jews).[6] With tens of thousands of warm bodies at their disposal, camp doctors injected prisoners with typhus, subjected prisoners to hypothermia (in the name of "science"), and attempted to "cure" homosexuality using "gland implants and synthetic hormones."[7] Absolute despotism ruled, and camp guards delighted in terrorizing the prisoners. Eventually, many inmates became, according to one survivor, "mummified by exhaustion, starvation, and beatings."[8] The SS men gave the area a telling nickname—"The Singing Forest"—because of the sounds of the prisoners moaning when they were tied to the trees.[9]

Overseeing it all was Karl-Otto Koch, who commanded the camp from 1937 to 1941. It would be hard to conceive of a man more suited to life as a Nazi bureaucrat. The son of a minor government official, Koch fought on the front lines of World War I, where he spent much of the conflict as a POW. Spineless, utterly conventional in his habits, and with a penchant for cruelty, he joined the Nazi Party in 1931 and quickly rose through the party hierarchy. In 1934, Koch was assigned command of a concentration camp at Sachsenburg and then at Sachsenhausen, advancing to the rank of SS colonel. By the time he and his second wife, Ilse, arrived at Buchenwald, he was "reputed to be the most brutal camp commander" in the entire Reich, no small feat for a man who, only a few years earlier, was struggling to make ends meet as an insurance agent.[10]

The SS Colonel's Zoo

One of Koch's first pet projects after arriving at Buchenwald was overseeing the construction of a camp zoo. It was located just outside the prisoners' yard—close enough that the prisoners could peer through the barbed wire of their own enclosure to glimpse the confined animals. As with everything else at Buchenwald, prisoners provided the

Figure 3.1. Postcard published by the Waffen-SS in 1939 of two bears wrestling at the Buchenwald Zoo. The entire bear pit was designed, built, paid for, and maintained by prisoners. Archive of the Buchenwald Memorial.

lion's share of the labor, scrounging rocks and other materials from worksites to craft the animals' pens. The zoo's most iconic structure was a stone *Bärenzwinger* (bear enclosure). It resembled a miniature mountain and had been designed by the imprisoned Bauhaus architect Franz Ehrlich. (Before he was transferred to Berlin, Erhlich also decorated Koch's house and designed the typography for Buchenwald's ironic motto—*Jedem das Seine* [To Each His Own]—which greeted arriving prisoners above the camp's main gates.)[11] Tiny by the standards of a city zoo, the Buchenwald Zoological Garden came to house a mix of native and foreign creatures, including deer, monkeys, bears, and several species of birds.

These weren't the only animals kept at Buchenwald. Under Koch's direction, inmates and staff raised pigs, ducks, chickens, cows, and horses, along with thousands of Angora rabbits, guinea pigs, and mice for use in medical experiments. Prisoners were also forced to construct a *falkenhof* (falcon house) as a tribute to Hermann Göring. Prisoners labored at breakneck speed to complete the structure, often working from sunup to sundown with only scraps to fill their empty stomachs.[12]

When it was finally completed (at an estimated cost of 135,000 marks), the building featured a German-style aviary, a trophy room, a gazebo, and room for numerous animals. Besides birds of prey, the *falkenhof* contained deer, wild boars, foxes, marten, peacocks, and a mouflon (a subspecies of wild sheep native to Anatolia and Iraq).[13] Overseers lived in a "House of the Falconer" nearby, which in later years would be converted into living quarters for high-profile prisoners (former French prime ministers Léon Blum and Édouard Deladier would be interned there).

Koch had both personal and professional reasons for supporting the zoo project. A purported animal lover (weren't they all?), Koch claimed to enjoy little more than strolling among the animals' pens with his young son, Artwin. He also saw the zoo as an opportunity to provide the camp's officers and staff with much-needed recreation and entertainment. Deprived of the amusements of city life, SS men and their relatives would nonetheless get to observe the "beauty and

Figure 3.2. Taken from the family photo album, this image shows camp commander Karl-Otto Koch in the deer enclosure with his son, Artwin. The original caption states: "With Papi at Buchenwald Zoo, Oct. 1939." Archive of the Buchenwald Memorial.

48   Chapter 3

peculiarity" of animals they might never see in the wild, Koch declared in September 1938.[14]

Koch further hoped to use the animal displays to instill in his men (some barely out of their teens) a strict sense of behavior and personal decorum. Like other petty tyrants, Koch held a tight grip on the lives of his underlings, and he expected his SS men to live up to Nazi standards, which included what he saw as a healthy appreciation of the natural world.[15] Killing young deer in the nearby forest was strictly forbidden, as was damaging the animal enclosures.[16] In 1938, upon learning that SS guards had tortured some of the zoo's deer (feeding them tinfoil and tying their antlers to a fence), Koch threatened to report the "perpetrators of such loutish acts" to the SS commander in chief.[17] The following year, he raged that many of the zoo animals, "especially the monkeys," endured routine doses of harassment from camp staff and civilian workers.[18] In Koch's mind, it was fine to harass Buchenwald's human prisoners, but harming helpless animals was off-limits.

"To the Buchenwald Zoological Park"

If the Buchenwald Zoo was meant to amuse the SS guards, it was designed to torment the incarcerated, reminding them that they ranked no higher than caged beasts. Upon arrival, prisoners were marched past a hand-carved signpost directing them to the Buchenwald Zoological Park, leaving no doubt about their new status. Within the Nazi worldview, Buchenwald's thousands of slave laborers did not deserve the dignity or ethical considerations afforded to the zoo denizens. As far as Koch was concerned, the camp's human captives were expendable (to be shot, tortured, starved, experimented upon, and worked to death as the guards saw fit). Arbitrary punishment was encouraged, if only to send a message. Adding insult to injury, the SS forced the inmates to foot the bill for the zoo's expenses, squeezing "voluntary levies" from the prisoners to pay for everything from the animals' enclosures to their upkeep. Gustav Herzog, an inmate from Vienna, recalled a telling incident from 1939. In a rare moment of levity, a group of Jewish inmates allegedly struck a wolf during a snowball fight, causing the animal to rub open a "wound from a chain around its neck." When it had to be put down, the SS ordered the prisoners to pay 5,000

Figure 3.3. Hand-carved by inmates, the wooden signpost of the Buchenwald Zoo featured several bears, a tusked hog, and other animals perched atop a pile of stones. It reads: "To the Buchenwald Zoological Park." Courtesy of the Stadtmuseum Weimar.

reichsmarks to purchase a replacement.[19] The message was clear: prisoners ranked at the very bottom of the camp pecking order—below Koch and his family, below the SS officers and guards, and below the bears, deer, monkeys, eagles, dogs, pigs, and other animals held in the Nazi prison-state.

This was especially evident when it came to food. Throughout the zoo's short history, the animals at Buchenwald tended to enjoy far better diets than human prisoners. Even as thousands of inmates died of starvation, the monkeys consumed a regular diet of oatmeal, mashed potatoes with milk, and zwieback. As late as 1944, the bears "received meat every day," usually taken from the inmates' meager rations. A postwar report affirms that, despite regular food shortages, "the falconry was maintained to its fullest extent," while prisoners were forced to survive on slivers of bread and "cooked rutabagas." If inmates were allowed meat, recalled one former prisoner, it typically was "in such a state of decomposition" that it could not be fed to the zoo animals. The dynamic was the same when it came to the canines at the camp. While the human inmates starved, the roughly 120 SS dogs at Buchenwald dined on fresh eggs, meat, potatoes, and oats, supplemented by dog biscuits and an occasional dram of wine.[20]

It's no surprise, then, that some prisoners sought to spend as much time working at the zoo as possible. Peter Zenkel, the deputy prime minister of Czechoslovakia, who was imprisoned at Buchenwald from 1939 to the war's end, testified: "The prisoners always liked to work in the zoo because they could scrounge the food intended for the monkeys, pigs, dogs and other animals."[21] In October 1939, Hans Bergmann, a political prisoner and Jew from Vienna, sent a handwritten note to SS *Obersturmführer* Arthur Rödl, deputy commander at Buchenwald, "obediently" requesting to be reinstated as a bear keeper. The bears were becoming restless, and he was convinced that their current caretaker could not handle them on his own. Bergmann was especially concerned about the female Betti, who faced months of dangerous pregnancy. Despite his lingering war injuries ("heart shot, lung shot"), the Jewish prisoner was adamant that he could make a difference.[22]

It's a mistake, of course, to presume that prisoners felt anything particular for the caged animals under their care. For those looking to survive Buchenwald, feigning affection for the monkeys, deer, and bears could, quite literally, mean the difference between life and death. We can never really know whether Bergmann and others sought zoo work to outwit their SS overseers, scavenge food scraps, or escape even more deadly forms of slave labor. Still, it's not hard to imagine why some Buchenwald prisoners might become genuinely fond of their animal wards. They, too, knew what it was like to be confined, powerless, held against their will. Beyond that, though, the prisoners at Buchenwald were still human, as much as their guards treated them otherwise. And, for many humans at least, caring for animals is one of life's great pleasures.

Undoubtedly the most poignant window into inmates' complex feelings toward the zoo is *A Bear Hunt at KZ Buchenwald*, an illustrated satirical poem composed by camp survivor Kurt Dittmar in 1946. Handwritten and drawn in the months following the camp's liberation, the thirty-eight-page document tracks the history of Betti's short life at Buchenwald, from her arrival as a cub to her eventual death at the hands of a camp commander. From the beginning, it's obvious that the prisoners would rather eat Betti than raise her, a sentiment that never fully disappears. Hungry and subject to relentless beatings, Buchenwald's human inmates envy Betti's diet of sugar and fat and her relative freedom inside her newly constructed cage. Eventually, the SS introduce other animals to "ogle at"—deer, monkeys, foxes, wolves, eagles, and buzzards—crowding Betti's "*Lebensraum*" (living space) and filling the air with their screeches and yowls.[23]

At the climax of the poem, Betti, fed up with her new zoo mates and longing for freedom, bursts through the camp's electric fence and escapes into the nearby forest. Inmates try to lasso the she-bear and snare her in a wooden trap baited with honey, but nothing works. Finally, Buchenwald's deputy commander shoots Betti while riding on his motorcycle, taking her corpse back in his sidecar. Dittmar's illustration of the scene shows three prisoners distraught with grief at the sight of Betti's dead body. They too know what it's like to be "*jagdwild*" (game): tracked, trapped, hunted, and ensnared. As the guards drunkenly celebrate, the prisoners are forced to build a spit, where Betti's skinned body is rotisseried over an open flame, her charred flesh turning brown and crispy. Sadly, the prisoners don't get a single bite, not even a bone or the flesh off her skull. But they can dream—dream of a day when they can stuff themselves with bear ham and jacket potatoes and all the vegetables they desire, and dream of a day when their captors will be held accountable for their crimes.[24]

Although based on real events, Kurt Dittmar's *A Bear Hunt at KZ Buchenwald* does not purport to be history. There are too many creative flourishes, too many witty asides, to view it as a wholly objective accounting of Betti's failed escape from Buchenwald concentration camp. What we get instead is something more interesting: a meditation on the power and limits of empathy. In Dittmar's telling, Buchenwald's human inmates recognize that Betti's life always hangs by a thread, that she is valuable right up to the point when the SS decides otherwise. She too is a prisoner, even though she has better meals and a nicer cage. But that doesn't mean they won't try to steal her food or gnaw on her fleshless bones. In Dittmar's Buchenwald, prisoners can both weep over Betti's killing and hungrily drool over her sizzling corpse.

Figures 3.4–3.6. Illustrations from Kurt Dittmar's 1946 satirical poem, *A Bear Hunt at KZ Buchenwald*. *Top left*, cover; *bottom left*, image of the Jewish keeper feeding the bear cubs while other prisoners look on hungrily; *above*, the prisoners turn Betti's headless torso on the fiery spit, while the SS officers get drunk and celebrate. In real life, after picking Betti clean, Koch's men extorted 8,000 reichsmarks from camp prisoners to purchase a replacement. "Eine Bären-Jagd im KZ Buchenwald" by Kurt Dittmar, Gotha 1946, Archive of the Buchenwald Memorial, BwA- K-96-2.

Satanic Pastimes

As it turns out, Buchenwald was not the only concentration camp to have a "zoo." In the spring of 1939, French journalist Jean Fontenoy described something similar during a guided tour of the Sachsenhausen concentration camp, a large rural prison complex about twenty miles from Berlin.[25] Although the communist-turned-fascist did not wholly disguise the brutality of camp life—the shaved heads, the hard labor, the iron discipline of the guards—he nonetheless went out of his way to tamp down the concerns of French readers. The highlight of his visit was Sachsenhausen's animal collection, which included beavers, flamingos, a grieving marmoset named Mimile (a recent widower), and various birds of prey. The zoo's star attraction was a large ape that could perform a backward somersault on command. Before he was arrested, the beast's trainer had been a communist deputy in the Reichstag. Now, the camp commander explained, the young prisoner had discovered his true passion. As for getting out: that would have to wait. Like the backflipping ape, his handler was destined to remain at Sachsenhausen indefinitely.

Read today, accounts of concentration camp zoos are almost too preposterous to be believed. And yet they can teach us a great deal about the concentration camp system and, more to our purposes, the world of zoos beyond Buchenwald's gates.

For starters, the story of the Buchenwald Zoological Garden serves as another reminder of the paradoxical attitudes of Nazi leaders when it came to animals. Koch had no problem overseeing unthinkable violence against inmates (Eugen Kogon, author of *The Theory and Practice of Hell*, proclaimed that one of the "satanic pastimes" of the Koch regime was to "throw prisoners into the bears' cage to be torn limb from limb"), but he was outraged by any hint of cruelty to animals.[26]

At the same time, one cannot help but draw parallels between Buchenwald's zoo animals and the hundreds of thousands of inmates who passed through the camp's gates. The Nazis' carceral regime demanded docile bodies—both animal and human—and absolute control over life and death. In fact, camp guards often went out of their way to transform the techniques of the zoo—encagement, exposure to the elements, forced visibility—into means of torture. A 1945 report recounted a particularly sadistic episode when Koch decided to punish a "gypsy" who tried to escape. The man was forced into a wooden crate so small he had to sit hunched over. One side was covered in wire netting, and the wood was "held together with long nails driven from the outside," so that "with his slightest movement" the tips pierced his skin. He was put on display for "two days and three nights," until his screams "no longer sounded human." In the end, the prisoner, nearly mad from suffering, was "put out of his misery with a lethal injection."[27]

Yet it was the zoo's very ordinariness, its ties to everyday life, that ultimately made it such a powerful accessory to mass murder. Like so much else in the KZ system, it belonged to what writer (and Buchenwald survivor) David Rousset famously dubbed *l'univers concentrationnaire*, a "perverted version of the normal world, where word and acts came to have an infernal, reverse meaning, where life—food, music, zoo, medical care—served death."[28] Within this "weird kingdom," both the zoo and the falcon house functioned as psychological buffers and mechanisms of disavowal.[29] They allowed non-prisoners to take their minds off the relentless killing and maintain the fiction that the camp was civilized, modern, and humane. Indeed, for a short while, the falcon house became something of a tourist attraction among Weimar families. Buses ran to and from the city every Sunday, and visitors paid modest sums to admire the caged eagles, hawks, and other birds. The SS even sold picture postcards and illustrated "folding books" as precious keepsakes.

Far more important, however, was what the visitors didn't see: the inmates' yard, the crematorium, the rows of haggard faces.[30] In this sense, at least, the falcon house had much in common with zoos outside concentration camps—it offered a benign vision of captivity while shielding the public from the violence that made it possible.

4

Zoos in an Age of International Cooperation

Even as the rise of Hitler dragged German zoos further into the grip of militant nationalism, many zoo leaders publicly espoused a countervailing sentiment. While it's tempting to view the 1930s as a period of escalating hostility, every year pushing the world closer to war, the decade also marked what's been called a "golden age" of international cooperation.[1] All around the world, politicians, activists, and ordinary people called on leaders to ditch their homegrown prejudices and unite around ideals of solidarity, humanity, and mutual aid. The reasons why aren't difficult to understand. First, there was the global economic crisis, a catastrophe that enveloped the entire world in hunger and despair.[2] A close second was the specter of another world war, a threat so ominous that millions rallied to the cause of peace. For many, twentieth-century problems were simply too large and complex for any single nation to solve. Only by coming together—by marshaling their collective resources in a spirit of openness and shared values— could the global community hope to see a better day.

As the decade progressed, the "vogue for internationality" touched all walks of life, from foreign policy and economics to religion and popular culture.[3] Reformers led efforts to abolish war, conserve the natural environment, and, in the case of the International Olympic Committee, inspire "peaceful cosmopolitanism" through athletic competition.[4] Among the most vocal evangelists for international cooperation were members of the global eugenics movement, a loose coalition of biologists, corporate leaders, and racist ideologues that sought to "improve" humans' genetic destiny through controlled breeding.

Largely disavowed today, eugenics flourished throughout interwar North America and Western Europe—in no small part thanks to the close relationship forged by advocates in the United States and Germany.[5] In 1934, Henry Fairfield Osborn Jr., the former head of the New York Zoological Society and one of the nation's leading eugenicists, earned the dubious accolade of becoming the first American to be awarded an honorary doctorate in Hitler's Germany. Other US academics toured "racial hygiene institutes," attended Nazi heredity health courts, and defended the Reich's sterilization policies—all under the seemingly benign banner of international science.[6]

Zoos were ideally suited to exploit the internationalist fervor. From their birth in the late eighteenth century, modern zoos not only functioned as showcases of imperial power but were considered markers of a "modern, advanced culture."[7] As European imperialism spread across the globe, zoos publicized themselves as venues for foreign travel, places where city dwellers could explore the far corners of the earth. Instead of challenging visitors with "scathing critiques of capitalism, imperialism, and colonial exploitation," observes historian Nigel Rothfels, zoos presented an "idealized world where Europeans could walk among the exhibited animals . . . and feel comfortable, secure, and, of course, enlightened."[8] By the 1930s, many of the world's zoos had abandoned the worst of their colonial trappings, including the practice of exhibiting so-called "primitive" peoples.[9] Nevertheless, they continued to rely on a heady cocktail of exoticism and international adventure to attract visitors.

Zoos' embrace of internationalism was no less evident in the realm of design. Throughout the 1930s, zoo planners experimented with several new exhibit schemes, from Heinz Heck's "geo-zoo" in Munich to London's double helix-shaped penguin pool, which was built by the radical architect Berthold Lubetkin's Tecton Group in 1934. However, when it came to their animal stock, the world's zoos tended to draw upon only a handful of architectural models. Outside of iron cages, a zoo staple long after World War II, no exhibit design was more frequently emulated than the open-air *Freianlagen* (or "free enclosures") revolutionized by Carl Hagenbeck at his family's animal park near Hamburg. Zoo directors in such varied locales as Antwerp, Milan, Budapest, and San Francisco scrambled to create *Freianlagen* of their

58 Chapter 4

own. Carl Hagenbeck, as we have seen, designed the original Rome Zoo and inspired the Vincennes Zoo; his nephew John founded a zoo in Ceylon in 1928, while his sons Heinrich and Lorenz were hired to construct artificial landscapes in interwar Seattle, Detroit, and Chicago.

The best evidence of zoo directors' commitment to internationalism can be seen in their professional relationships. Zoos relied upon vast networks of acquisition and exchange—the kinds of contacts that could track down a Siberian tiger, negotiate kangaroo exports, and ease the shipment of poisonous snakes from the Amazon basin. Although zoo directors still made headlines for their "Bring 'em back alive"-style expeditions, they spent much of their working day on desk duty, securing international cargo insurance and plying their overseas counterparts with offers to buy, sell, or trade. Foreign zoo men weren't just competitors—they were colleagues and, in some cases, decades-long friends. As such, zoo professionals sought every opportunity to inspect each other's facilities. While planning the Vincennes Zoo, Achille Urbain and Édouard Sicaire Bourdelle embarked on what amounted to a grand tour of the continent's animal parks, soaking up advice in Munich, Budapest, Berlin, Rome, and Hamburg.[10] In 1936, Julian Huxley, recently installed as secretary of the London Zoological Society, made a similar trip, setting aside his political misgivings to visit zoos throughout the Third Reich.[11]

Zoo Directors Unite

The earliest organization of zoo professionals dates back to the late nineteenth century, when German-speaking zoo directors began to hold informal meetings during the spring animal auctions in Antwerp, Belgium. Founded in 1887, the *Zoodirektorenkonferenz* (Conference of Zoo Directors) usually met twice a year—in Antwerp and in Germany—where zoo men would share stories, detail the latest techniques in exhibit design, and do their best to put a scientific sheen on displays not so different than those found in traveling carnivals. After World War I, which had brought Antwerp's animal auctions to a sudden halt, German zoo directors began to look beyond the nation's borders to recruit new members. By the early 1930s, the newly renamed *Mitteleuropäische Zoodirecktorenkonferenz* (Central European Conference of Zoo Directors) included zoo men from Switzerland, Austria, Poland, Denmark, the Netherlands, Hungary, Sweden, and Bulgaria. Then, at the 1935 meeting in Basel, Switzerland, attendees adopted their most ambitious name yet: the *Internationalen Verbandes der Direktoren Zoologischer Gärten* (International Union of Directors of Zoological Gardens, or IUDZG).[12] For the group's first president, the Frankfurt a. Main Zoo's Kurt Priemel, the change represented the realization of a principle he'd articulated a decade earlier: "All work for the great and splendid idea of nature conservation must remain fragmented if it does not flourish in the soil of internationality."[13]

IUDZG members were not an especially diverse group. Although zookeeping was often a family affair (with wives and children expected to pitch in whenever possible), early IUDZG cohorts were composed entirely of men—most in their forties or fifties. Despite the group's democratic pretenses, strict membership requirements made it virtually impossible for anyone outside the upper echelons of the zoo world to join. (Nominees had to adhere to "scientific principles"—a term vague enough to mean just about anything—and be recognized as leaders in their fields.)[14] Though some came from humble backgrounds, nearly all held university degrees in natural science. They even tended to look alike. Attendees' typical uniform included a white shirt, a conservative suit, and a slight paunch. In early photos, they could be easily mistaken for a group of industrialists—a far cry from the whip-cracking, khaki-clad heroes found in dime novels and B-movies.

For all their lip service about cross-border cooperation, members of the IUDZG embodied a stunted definition of "international." Of the eighteen attendees of the 1935 conference, only one—Julian Huxley—came from outside mainland Europe. The first American, Roderick MacDonald, director of the Philadelphia Zoo, joined the following year, and the Union did not contain a single member from Africa, Asia, Australia, or South America.[15] The heart of zoo country, as far as the IUDZG was concerned, stretched from the eastern United States to the Adriatic, with Germany as its spiritual center.

Union members would have likely claimed that zoo men outside Europe and North America simply lacked the status and credentials to gain admission. But there is a darker explanation. Like their nineteenth-century forebears, European zoo men tended to see the world through a distinctly colonialist lens, dividing it up between *nations* (where exotic fauna are caged, displayed, and studied for scientific edification) and *colonies* (where wild animals and wild people existed in a state of nature). If they discussed the colonial backdrop of the zoo at all, it was to lament what might happen when the artifice of empire disappeared and zoos had to look elsewhere to fill their cages. Writing in 1913, the head of the Bronx Zoo, William T. Hornaday, offered up what would become a common sentiment among Western zoo directors: "The gorilla and the chimpanzee are so well protected by the density of their jungles that they never can be exterminated—until the natives are permitted to have all the firearms that they desire! When that day arrives, it is 'good-night' to all the wild life that is large enough to eat or wear."[16]

Above all else, zoo directors' particular brand of internationalism was bound up in a sense of collective identity. Working at a zoo was not simply a career—it was a calling, an obsession, a way of life. Zoo families contended with similar problems (an escaped leopard, an outbreak of influenza) and gloried in similar triumphs (the birth of an endangered rhino, the construction of a new aviary). No doubt this helps explain zoo leaders' reluctance to let politics stand in the way of personal relationships. Whatever their misgivings about German zoos' ubiquitous swastikas and Rome's zoological booty from Ethiopia, for instance, IUDZG members saw themselves as part of an exclusive club, bound together by profession, by inclination, and by the unique character of their lives.

Gatherings of Zoo Men

The highlight of the IUDZG calendar was its annual conference. Lasting nearly a week, meetings more closely resembled family reunions than staid, professional gatherings. In August 1936, just as Hitler's Olympics thundered to a close in Berlin, the group met in Cologne. About two-thirds of the attendees (and their wives) were native Germans; the rest came from as far away as Rotterdam, Basel, and Warsaw. Most had known each other for years—if not personally, then by reputation. Their host, Dr. Friedrich Hauchecorne, the forty-one-year-old director of the Cologne Zoological Garden, had started his career as an assistant to Lutz Heck in Berlin. Others' ties stretched back to the early 1920s, when zoos across central Europe began to reconnect after years of stagnating war.[17]

During the day, Hauchecorne led behind-the-scenes tours of the Cologne Zoo, highlighting its outstanding collection of birds of prey. Lutz Heck screened a short film about his recent trip to North America (he was hoping to breed European wisents with American bison). Meanwhile, attendees read papers on such varied topics as rearing baby gorillas and improving veterinary care. Much of the time, however, industry matters took a backseat to the meeting's unspoken aim: cementing bonds of friendship throughout the upper echelons of the zoo world. When they weren't downing steins of beer, the motley group of "zoo men"—a term that persisted well after World War II—visited historic monuments, schmoozed with local dignitaries, and inspected natural history museums up and down the Rhine Valley.

In 1937, the Union held a six-day conference in Munich, where Heinz Heck proudly discussed his efforts to "back-breed" extinct animals. The following year, the group convened in Amsterdam, home to the Royal Natura Artis Magistra Zoo, known as Artis. Its magnetic director, Armand Louis Jean Sunier, was the epitome of the modern zoo man: educated, cosmopolitan, with the mind of an academic and a showman's flair for promotion. Born in Baarn in central Holland in 1886, Sunier earned his doctorate in biology in 1911; he then sailed to the Dutch East Indies, where he worked at a fishery and eventually served as chairman of the Royal Physical Society of the Netherlands Indies. In 1922, Sunier returned from the tropics and took up work as a curator at the National Museum of Natural History in Leiden. Five years later, at the age of forty-one, he landed his dream job as director of Amsterdam's aging zoo.[18] Although Artis remained perpetually short on funds, Sunier managed to keep the creditors at bay. Bald-headed with a brushy mustache and a wide, genial face, Sunier became something of a national icon, famous for his hands-on approach to the animals in his care. A promotional film from the late 1930s shows him stroking a caged tiger as if it were little more than an oversized house cat.[19]

When the IUDZG conference opened on May 23, 1938, Europe was in a state of turmoil. Little more than two months after German troops

Figure 4.1. Artis Zoo director Armand Sunier (*left*) and A. F. J. Portielje (*right*) with the zoo's first gorilla, Japie, two years before Amsterdam hosted the 1938 conference of the International Union of Directors of Zoological Gardens. In later years, Japie would share a wall with people trying to evade German detection by hiding in the zoo. Courtesy of the Archives of the Royal Zoological Society Natura Artis Magistra.

marched into Austria, Hitler had turned his eye toward Czechoslovakia and beyond. Yet, as they assembled that Monday morning, the roughly fifteen zoo men tried their best to tune out political matters. Over the following days, President Kurt Priemel and company conducted association business and debated the latest advancements in the field. They visited the Colonial Institute, where Dr. Kurt Kramer dazzled the audience with his X-ray snake studies and discussed the "muzzle and claw" epidemic sweeping Europe. But they also made sure to set aside plenty of time for recreation. On Tuesday, participants and their wives spent the afternoon on a water-taxi tour of Amsterdam Harbor, followed by a formal dinner at the Amstel Hotel. The next day they boarded a bus to the beach town of Noordwijk, world famous for its sand dunes and bulb fields. On the final day of the conference, the group ate lunch at the zoo restaurant, then drove to the Naardermeer nature reserve—a wide, shallow lake lined with reed-beds and forest—just southeast of the city. As they paddled over beds of lily pads, scanning the skies for colonies of terns and cormorants, none could have predicted what was to come: their exhibits smashed by falling bombs; their animals looted by invading armies; their staffs debased, starved, and killed. On that summer afternoon at least, some of the world's leading zoo directors took solace in the belief that, even in an age of national antagonisms, the brotherhood of zoo men would not falter.[20]

It would be nearly a decade before the International Union of Directors of Zoological Gardens met again. In the intervening years, zoo men from across Europe—and around the globe—would find themselves cast, willingly or not, on opposing sides of the most destructive war the world had ever known. Some would encounter each other again in new roles: occupier and occupied. A few would become heroes, celebrated as paragons of resistance; others would be vilified, their professional reputations permanently tarred by collaboration and greed. One would die by his own hand. And the international fraternity of zoo men would be tested in ways few thought possible.

However, the leaders of the zoo world did not need to wait until the bombing of Rotterdam or the invasion of Russia to glimpse the perils awaiting them in the next war. All they had to do was read the latest headlines from Spain.

5

A Dress Rehearsal in España

From the start of the Spanish Civil War in July 1936, outsiders viewed it as the opening stage of a much larger struggle: a "rehearsal," in historian Paul Preston's words, of the war soon to envelop mainland Europe.[1] On one side were the Nationalists, a loose coalition of monarchists, right-wing military officers, conservative Catholics, and fascists led by Generalissimo Francisco Franco and backed by Adolf Hitler and Benito Mussolini. On the other, the Republicans: a popular-front army of socialists, anarchists, and communists, whose calls to democracy and universal brotherhood attracted leftist volunteers from around the world. In many eyes, the war functioned more as a symbol than anything else: it was an ideological drama of good versus evil, progress versus reaction, the power of the many versus the dictatorship of the few.

Within the tightly knit community of zoo directors and professionals, the Spanish Civil War represented a kind of living nightmare, a vision of their worst fears come to pass. In Barcelona and Madrid, Spain's two major zoological institutions endured relentless bombing attacks, food shortages, and sharp declines in visitors. To many outsider observers, the question wasn't how long Spanish zoos could survive the onslaught. The question was whether they should even try.

La Casa de Fieras and the Citadel Park Zoo

Prior to the outbreak of the civil war, few would have suspected that Spanish zoos might ever attract the world's attention. In many respects,

Madrid's *Casa de Fieras* and the *Parc Zoològic de Barcelona* mirrored the poverty and isolation of Spain itself. In the 1930s, crossing the Spanish border would have felt like stepping back into an earlier era—a time when the Catholic Church controlled the schools; when illiterate peasants wielded "Stone Age harrows, sickles which had not changed since the Bronze Age, threshing-boards like those described in the Old Testament, ploughs such as were depicted on ancient Greek vases."[2] Although Spain's cities, especially Barcelona and Madrid, were bastions of revolutionary politics, little of their progressive thinking trickled down to the cities' zoos. In a three-volume history of zoos published in 1912, the French zoologist Gustave Antoine Armand Loisel devotes little more than a paragraph to Spanish zoos, dismissing Madrid's animal collection as *"peu importante"* (unimportant).[3]

He was right to do so.

Though the origins of the Madrid Zoo date back to the eighteenth century, for much of its life it had been little more than a small, royal menagerie. Devastated by Napoleon's invasion in 1812, the animal collection was later moved to the eastern edge of Retiro Park, a large, landscaped garden only a short walk from the city center. In 1868, when the Glorious Revolution ousted Queen Isabella II, the zoo was opened to the public, and—after several decades under private management—the Madrid city council took permanent control of the facility in 1918. Such changes did little to improve the lives of the zoo's residents. At a time when other European zoos were experimenting with "barless cages" and open enclosures, the *Casa de Fieras* seemed stuck in the previous century. Cages were tiny (some animals barely had enough room to stand upright or pace back and forth). Madrid's polar bears spent their days perched on blocks of rough concrete above a moat of dirty water. Yet this was the lap of luxury compared to the zoo's most iconic building, the two-story *Leonera* (or "lion's den"). While the top floor was reserved for the royal family and their guests, the lower level housed lions, tigers, and other large felines in cramped, identical cells—a perfect architectural metaphor for the zoo's philosophy of human over beast.

The Barcelona Zoo was little better. It opened on September 24, 1892, in the former grounds of the 1888 Universal Exhibition in the Ciutadella, a seventy-acre park not far from the Mediterranean.

The city council purchased much of its early collection from a cash-strapped banker who kept a private menagerie at his nearby estate. The five-acre zoo was insignificant by the standards of the day, and many animals were crammed into wire enclosures and crude metal cages. Throughout the first decade or so, the zoo raised money through public auctions. In 1896, it sold "seven Great Danes, ten wild boar, two Murcia-Granada goats," and more than a thousand eggs.[*] Two years later, it auctioned off two adult lions, Bluton and Micci, as well as three lion cubs, an assortment of dogs, various small livestock, and fifteen "5-kilo containers of fat" from horses slaughtered to feed the carnivores. In April 1927, the zoo began to charge admission (twenty-five cents per ticket), and it beefed up security measures to curb harassment from patrons, who were known to throw lit matches at the animals. Four decades after its founding, however, the Barcelona Zoo continued to struggle. The low point came on December 21, 1935, when a female leopard managed to escape through a hole in her enclosure. Nearly a day passed before she was finally recaptured.[4]

Empty Bellies and Falling Bombs

When the civil war began in July 1936, Spanish zoos initially attempted to carry on as usual. Only a day before Nationalist army officers staged their rebellion, a hippo in Barcelona gave birth to a calf, an event so rare that it made news around the world.[5] Later that September, Barcelona's local commission on natural sciences ordered the zoo director, Ignasi de Sagarra, not only to draw up plans for additional animal parks and nature reserves aimed at protecting native species, but also to design facilities for a new zoo on Montjuïc, a prominent hill in the city.[6] Yet it wasn't long before zoos began to feel the pinch of wartime restrictions.

The most pressing issue was a lack of food, a problem zoo animals shared with millions of their human counterparts. With Nationalist forces controlling the country's richest farmlands, the Republican strongholds of Barcelona and Madrid soon lacked the resources to

---

[*] Besides exhibiting several breeds of dogs, the Barcelona Zoo also hosted a twice-weekly dog market, where owners could register their animals for sale.

feed their swollen populations.[7] In Barcelona, the Catalan government launched *la batalla de l'ou* (the battle of the egg), a scheme to induce urban residents to raise chickens at home. Desperate gourmands smoked dried lettuce (instead of tobacco), made "ersatz fries" from discarded orange peel, and scoured the streets for stray cats and dogs, which—when blackened or baked into a casserole—could be passed off as rabbit or lamb.[8] Cookbooks published during the war years enjoined Republicans to welcome their limited diets in a spirit of patriotic sacrifice. In *Menús de Guerra*, one cookbook author wrote, "War imposes restrictions on us that we need to accept as our moral duty."[9] Moral duty or not, wartime hunger often proved deadly. Avitaminotic diseases such as pellagra ran rampant, and nearly 2,500 people died from malnutrition in Madrid alone by 1939.[10]

At a time when many people subsisted on meals of lentils (dubbed "resistance pills"), sweet potatoes, and meatless gruel, zoo animals ranked near the very bottom of the hierarchy of need—below soldiers, below children, below even those who refused to take sides.[11] Zookeepers did what they could to keep hunger at bay. Staff at Madrid's *Casa de Fieras* gathered goldfish from local parks to feed the pelicans (fish was reserved for hospital patients) and scavenged the front lines for dead horses, dodging bullets to haul the bloated corpses back to the zoo grounds. By early 1937, however, food shortages had taken a heavy toll. In Madrid, a hippo named Pepe broke out in a rash after eating chicken feed, while a pregnant giraffe at the Barcelona Zoo eventually died after keepers were forced to cut her rations of barley and milk.[12]

On top of their own dietary woes, zoos also had to contend with the threat of hungry soldiers in search of a quick meal. In January 1937, the United Press reported that fighters stationed in Madrid had machine-gunned a zoo warthog named Willie and served him with parsley and seasoning.[13] An Englishman in the International Brigades echoed the story, telling a Brisbane newspaper in 1938: "I doubt whether there is one animal left in the Madrid Zoo. Most of the soldiers long since realize that there lay a potential source of food. During my stay, I tasted some bear. It was not bad at all, like sweet pork."[14]

From abroad, it was difficult to separate fact from fiction. Veterans were known to exaggerate, and press coverage skewed toward the sensational. George Orwell, who fought as part of the left-wing

POUM militia in 1937, recalled sardonically, "The fighting had barely started when the newspapers of the Left and Right dived into the same cesspool of abuse. We all remember the *Daily Mail*'s poster: 'REDS CRUCIFY NUNS,' while to the *Daily Worker* Franco's Foreign Legion was 'composed of murders, white-slavers, dope-fiends and the offal of every European country.'"[15]

Closer to the battlefield, the state of zoos was often clouded by what historian Antony Beevor calls the "hysterical relationship with the truth" that infected wartime Spain. Neither side was immune to exaggeration, particularly when it came to dramatizing the barbarism of the enemy. American journalist Virginia Cowles encountered an especially strongly held (and demonstrably false) zoo rumor on a visit to Salamanca, a Nationalist stronghold near Portugal. Republican militiamen were "feeding right-wing prisoners to the animals" in the Madrid Zoo, she was told. And only a closet "red" would think otherwise.[16]

In the fall of 1936, Spanish zoos received their first taste of a more spectacular threat: aerial bombardment.[17] Prior to the 1930s, the idea of using airplanes to terrorize European cities, let alone their zoos, would have struck most observers as the stuff of science fiction. In May 1899, four years before the Wright brothers' flight at Kitty Hawk, delegates to the first International Peace Conference at The Hague signed a five-year ban prohibiting "the launching of projectiles or explosives from balloons, or by other new methods of similar nature."[18] The ban was extended in 1907, and Article 25 of the fourth Hague Convention specifically outlawed the "bombardment, by whatever means, of towns, villages, dwellings, or buildings, which are undefended."[19] But such measures carried little weight, especially among those who imagined themselves victorious in future conflicts. During World War I, the fledgling *Deutsche Luftstreitkräfte* (German Air Force), using a combination of zeppelin airships and heavy bombers, carried out more than fifty air raids on the English mainland, killing some 1,400 people. (Although the London Zoo was not bombed, the grounds were periodically littered with spent shrapnel from antiaircraft guns perched on nearby Primrose Hill.)[20] "No longer can areas exist in which life can be lived in safety and tranquility, nor can the battlefield any longer be limited to combatants," wrote Italian air theorist Giulio Douhet in his 1921 book *Il dominio dell'aria* (The Command of the Air). "On the contrary, the battlefield will be limited only by the boundaries of the nations at war, and all of their citizens will become combatants."[21]

Douhet's theories were put to the test in the skies above Madrid. After Franco's Army of Africa failed to break through Republican trenches, waves of slow-flying Savoia 81 and Junkers 52 bombers—the latter piloted by members of the Luftwaffe's Condor Division—began to pummel the heart of the city. Geoffrey Cox, a twenty-six-year-old journalist from New Zealand, recalled seeing the "black specks" moving across the horizon.[22] Their payload tore through rooftops and reduced buildings to rubble. By late November, the Spanish capital had become, in one reporter's words, "a nightmare of slaughter and living horror."[23] Barcelona was not far behind. Throughout 1937, Italian squadrons based on the Mediterranean island of Majorca periodically bombarded the heart of revolutionary Spain.[24] These attacks would prove to be relatively mild, especially when compared to what was to come. Still, they served as a potent reminder that, in the age of the bomber, nowhere was truly safe.

Initially, the *Casa de Fieras* suffered the lion's share of the bomb damage. Interviewed in February 1937, Vicente Tause, the chief animal keeper, reported that more than a hundred explosives had fallen on the zoo in the previous forty-eight hours alone. During one recent attack, a zebra was so frightened by the deafening sound that it raced madly around its enclosure until eventually hitting a tree and breaking its spine. Press coverage of the air raids typically highlighted what would be a common theme of wartime zoo reporting: the essential innocence of the animals under fire. "To the thundering of the cannons and the rattling of machine-guns," bemoaned an account from the International News Service, "has been added the wails of the panic stricken, half-starved animals who know not what to make of man's carnage."[25]

Later that spring, as the spirit of radicalism reached a boiling point, Barcelona Zoo director Ignasi de Sagarra, scion of an aristocratic family, fled into exile in France, where he'd remain for the rest of the war.[26] His replacement, Antoni Gispert Vila, inherited an institution on the edge of ruin. Gate receipts had plummeted, and the city government had ceased providing financial support. Feeding the animals grew harder by the day, employees protested the lack of a single bomb shelter, and zoo officials fretted about large carnivores escaping in the aftermath of an aerial attack. In early April 1937, the official newspaper of the autonomous Catalonian government announced imminent plans to transfer the zoological collection to France for safekeeping. A few days later, however, the Commissariat of Natural Sciences broadcast that the scheme had been put on hold. Although the zoo was ill prepared to meet the emergency, Barcelona's zoo animals weren't going anywhere, no matter what the future held.[27]

It's worth pausing to ask why Spain's zoos bothered at all. Why go through the trouble of seeking out food and tending to animals injured by bombing? What is the point of watching precious animals die slow, often excruciating, deaths of starvation and disease, knowing that there is nothing you can do to save them? Over much of the next decade, zoo leaders around the world would agonize over these very questions, and time and time again many would come to the same decision: to remain open as long as possible, even if it prolonged the suffering of the beasts on display.

It was partly, zoo leaders would argue, a pragmatic decision. To shut down completely would have meant slaughtering animals that, in many cases, had been raised in the zoo since birth. Nor can we dismiss the personal affection many zoo workers would have felt for the animals in their care. Feelings don't simply fade away at the start of a war; if anything, they grow more intense. In the eyes of political leaders, moreover, closing the zoo—an institution long associated with cheap entertainment for children and families—would have likely felt like a betrayal of their Republican ideals. To be sure, zoos had never played an especially significant role in Spanish society. At best, they represented, in American journalist Martha Gellhorn's words, a "good time, something not exciting or important or grave or memorable but just fun."[28] Even so, zoos were part of the normal life the besieged peoples of Barcelona and Madrid were fighting and dying to preserve.

There's also the fact that humans have a long history of self-interested thinking when it comes to the animals with which they share their lives. As scholar Erica Fudge has shown, people tend to project onto animals what they want to see, ignoring all evidence to the contrary.[29] For decades prior to the start of the Spanish Civil War, dedicated zoo-goers would have learned to overlook the most disturbing aspects of the zoo experience—the cramped cages, the dismal conditions, and the abject misery of many zoo inhabitants. Instead, they would have tried to focus on the positive, even if it meant misrecognizing the emotions, behaviors, and expressions of the animals they'd come to see.

On May 16, 1937, thousands of *madrileños* gathered in Retiro Park for the annual reopening of the Madrid Zoo. The animals were visibly skinny, and the visitors had nothing to give them other than breadcrumbs and tufts of grass. But it was a day of celebration, nonetheless. Half a year after Franco announced the city's impending capture, Madrid was still free—and it still had its zoo.[30]

1938: The Year of Horrors

By the start of 1938, Spain's zoos were in desperate straits. The year began, tragically enough, with the death of Pancho, an elderly elephant at the Madrid Zoo. Since the war's start, Pancho had been restricted to a starvation diet of "coarse black bread." Over time, he grew steadily weaker until, for the last month or so, he struggled to stand. Finally, after a year and a half of "shellfire, nervous shock, cold, and no peanuts," the emaciated elephant died in his cramped, snow-covered pen. As the news spread, zoo staff quickly butchered Pancho's body, eager to convert his remaining fat into "grease" for the war effort.† In Republican Spain, sentimentality was a luxury; even the dead were expected to sacrifice.[31]

In Barcelona, the situation was no better. Between April and July, three tigers, three lions, a pair of black panthers, and a newborn dromedary dropped dead from lack of food. As the year wore on, the list of food casualties continued to add up. A hippo and a polar bear died of

---

† Dismantling an elephant corpse to retrieve the fat is no easy task. Elephants carry much of their fat around the intestines, in the hollows of the eye sockets, and in the large cavities beneath the plantar arches. At the time, the typical fat-removal procedure involved cutting away an elephant's soles to remove the yellow, rubbery substance inside, which would then be boiled. One adult foot could "yield a gallon or more" of "first-class cooking lard." Cuthbert Christy, "The African Elephant: Part III," *Journal of the Royal African Society* 21 (1921–1922): 291–301.

malnutrition. Other animals contracted diseases brought on by famine or were slaughtered to feed the zoo's more valuable species.[32]

All the while, German and Italian bombers terrorized the city. On March 16, at around 10 p.m., six German *Hydro-Heinkel* biplanes launched one of the deadliest air raids yet. Edwin Rolfe, a Jewish American poet who fought in the International Brigades, recalled: "We heard the bombs thudding in the distance—about a mile away—and then the sharper double explosion of antiaircraft shells. The sky was so bright with the moon that we could even see the white puffs of smoke where the antiaircraft shells exploded. Soon the whole horizon behind the buildings was red with the glow of fire."[33] Every three hours, a fresh wave of Italian *Savoia* bombers—seventeen in all—pummeled the city. By the time it was over, an estimated 1,300 people were dead.[34]

The Barcelona Zoo was an easy target for planes heading toward the city center. In April, bomb explosions killed a red kangaroo, a lion, a porcupine, a lesser rhea, and a nilgai (a large, white-footed Asian antelope). On May 2, Nationalist bombs killed the zoo's interim director, Antoni Gispert Vila. Over the next few months, aerial explosives continued to rain down on the zoo grounds. On July 13, four bombs destroyed the ape house and the director's building. The following month, a detonated bomb shattered the jaw of one of the polar bears, while a dromedary bled out after it was hit by flying shrapnel.[35] The attacks left a psychological toll as well. A monkey named Pepe became so aggressive and bad-tempered after an air raid that its keepers decided they had no choice but to destroy him.[36]

On August 13, 1938, the Barcelona Zoo suffered its most devastating blow when it lost its beloved elephant, Júlia. A gift from the exiled sultan of Morocco, Mulai Abdelhafid, the pachyderm arrived with great fanfare from Genoa in May 1915. As thousands of visitors looked on, Júlia was installed in a small Moorish-style "chalet" on the zoo grounds, where she'd spend the next twenty-three years delighting generations of young children. Not that they always reciprocated her legendary affection. According to Manuel Báguena, who spent more than a decade in charge of Júlia's daily upkeep, some boys found dark pleasure in feeding the poor beast oranges containing rocks and bits of broken glass.[37] How exactly Júlia died remains a matter of some dispute. One theory says that she was killed when a shell fragment pierced her skull, another that she died of a heart attack. The communist newspaper *La*

Figure 5.1. Postcard from the early 1920s showing Júlia, an Asian elephant (*Elephas maximus*), in an outdoor cage at the Barcelona Zoo. In 1938, Júlia would be among the most famous zoo casualties of the Spanish Civil War, fueling public speculation about how she met her fatal end. Author's collection.

Humanitat declared that the elephant was seized by depression and lost the will to live. More likely, though, the elephant suffered the same fate as Pancho: starvation, slow, remorseless, agonizing. Near the end, she was so feeble that keepers could not even clean her pen, which meant that—like so many of the war's casualties—Júlia died in her own filth.[38]

When Franco's troops entered Barcelona on January 26, 1939, the zoo was in shambles. Rubble littered the grounds; the air smelled of decay. Remarkably, about three hundred animals, including a few emaciated bears, kangaroos, deer, and apes, had managed to survive the conflict, though their long-term prospects remained grim.[39] In Madrid, conditions were, if anything, worse. By the time Franco's armies took the city on March 26, "enforced fasting" (or starvation) had greatly "streamlined" the zoo's animal stock. Among the final casualties were fourteen zebras, eight endangered Barbary lions, a pair of Spanish wolves, a leopard, a tiger, a panther, and fourteen monkeys. Pipo, the zoo's hippopotamus, had lost two thousand pounds, a third of his prewar body weight. The remaining survivors—as few as twenty-five, by some counts—were so bony and listless they appeared on the verge of death.[40]

Following the Nationalist victory, pro-Franco writers were quick to exploit the zoos' hardships. In February, the Falangist newspaper *Solidaridad Nacional* accused "red separatists" of eating what was left of Barcelona's animal collection. That August, the Barcelona-based *La Vanguardia* leveled a similar charge against "red aldermen" in Madrid, who had saved themselves while the city's animals (and people) starved.[41] One of the most damning critiques came from a foreigner, Henry W. Shoemaker, a noted folklorist and former US ambassador to Bulgaria under Herbert Hoover. (He also was a member of the New York Zoological Society and, for a while, kept a private zoo at his Pennsylvania home.)[42] Writing in the *Altoona Tribune*, Shoemaker charged that "wild-eyed Red agitators" wanted to slaughter Madrid's entire animal collection and replace them with stuffed duplicates from the natural museum. Thankfully, saner minds intervened, and Shoemaker was optimistic about the zoo's future under the Franco regime: with a "lover of wild life and the outdoors at the helm," he predicted Spanish zoos would soon "look like they did before the savage civil war era."[43]

But the start of World War II in Europe a few months later quashed any hope of a quick recovery. Faced with continued shortages of food and supplies, the zoos of Barcelona and Madrid languished until well into the 1950s. Within the zoo community, the Spanish Civil War offered a terrifying reminder of zoo's vulnerability in times of national crisis. More ominous still, the conflict's casualty rolls suggested that the age of total war was finally at hand. Hugh Thomas, author of perhaps the greatest single-volume history of the Spanish Civil War, estimates that, of the war's half a million fatal casualties, fewer than 200,000 were fighters killed in action. The bulk of the dead were noncombatants: Political prisoners massacred by Franco's terror squads. Landowners and religious figures murdered in the name of revolution. Men and women set aflame by falling incendiaries. Children and old people consumed by starvation and disease.[44]

If the Spanish Civil War was any indication, Europe's next great war would be fought over the bodies of civilians—and the continent's zoos were sure to be caught in the crossfire.

PART II

Opening Day Activities

6

Zero Hour

One brisk September morning in 1939, Achille Urbain walked through the grounds of the Vincennes Zoo in Paris.[1] Outside the gates, the streets were a riot of activity. Sirens blared; passersby glanced in and then moved quickly on. There was too much to do. There wasn't much time. He stopped in front of the elephant enclosure and looked inside. No, it was impossible; they were much too big. They'd have to take their chances here under the shelter of their concrete caves, where blankets soaked in hydrosulphite could shield them from the gas. He moved on, from enclosure to enclosure, cage to cage, each time stopping and running his mental calculus. The zoo would have to disperse. But not all the animals could be evacuated. He'd have to choose.

Later, workmen arrived and began loading up the motorized ark with the zoo's prized residents: spotted ocelots like rangy house cats, kangaroos, cranes, the lone giant panda, anthropoid apes, Brazilian macaws whose screeching, according to one observer, resembled the cries of lost women. Giraffes were housed in wooden boxes shaped like the Eiffel Tower and winched onto trucks meant for hauling theater sets. Hippos and rhinos rode uncovered on ten-ton platforms, their thick hide their only defense against falling shrapnel. The caravan passed through the zoo gates and then on toward the train station and then from there . . . only a few people knew. "Somewhere in France." That's what they told the public: somewhere the war would not touch them, somewhere Urbain himself could not go.

That evening, the caravan was followed by a second procession: a funeral march of "*animaux inutiles.*" Foxes, wild boars, jackals, wolves—beasts that could be easily replaced in peacetime, stinking and dangerous and common. In the Jardin des Plantes, near the city center, keepers strangled the poisonous reptiles, preserving their remains in jars of alcohol; at Vincennes, the weapon of choice was poison. Either way, the effect was the same. As for the ones left behind, they were consigned to the worst fate of all. When the air raids came, the leftover animals were to be crated away—locked in cages inside cages—under the cover of concrete. No bombing could free them without killing them. Then again, what was freedom for animals reared to live confined?

World War II in Europe began in much the way it would end: in a torrent of death. In the early morning of September 1, 1939, the German Wehrmacht, tasked with securing *Lebensraum* (living space) for Hitler's thousand-year Reich, invaded Poland. As infantry units poured across the border, Göring's Luftwaffe raced ahead, pummeling Polish defenses and strafing the columns of fleeing refugees. Terror accompanied every step of the German *Blitzkrieg* ("lightning war"). The invading army burned villages and massacred civilians; trailing behind, paramilitary death squads, armed with lists of the condemned, rounded up tens of thousands of Jews, academics, and "dissidents" for immediate execution. All the while, waves of swift-moving JU-87 Stuka bombers laid waste to Poland's cities. By mid-September, German forces controlled the entire country west of the Vistula. The only holdout was the besieged capital of Warsaw, its once elegant boulevards now choked with barricades and retreating soldiers.

For Poland's zoos, the German invasion marked the start of four and a half years of killing, theft, hunger, and hardship. On September 6, a 1,000-pound bomb smashed through the polar bear exhibit at the Warsaw Zoo. Fearing the animals' escape, Polish soldiers shot the bears on the spot and—anticipating the possible liberation of other "dangerous" beasts—quickly turned their guns on the lions, tigers, and a bull elephant. German bombers returned a few days later, blanketing the zoo grounds with explosive shells. Recounted in Diane Ackerman's global bestseller *The Zookeeper's Wife*, the scene was like something out of the book of Revelation:

> The sky broke open and whistling fire hurtled down, cages exploded, moats rained upward, iron bars squealed as they wrenched apart. . . .

Glass and metal shards mutilated skins, feathers, hooves, and scales indiscriminately as wounded zebras ran, ribboned with blood, terrified howler monkeys and orangutans dashed caterwauling into the trees and bushes, snakes slithered loose, and crocodiles pushed onto their toes and trotted at speed.[2]

When the smoke cleared, the zoo's prized mother elephant, Kasia, was dead, as were a pair of giraffes, their bodies mangled by falling shells.[3] Some animals had survived by hiding in their cages; others were found wandering along the banks of the nearby Vistula River.

On September 27, German troops marched into what remained of Warsaw, sealing the zoo's fate. Shortly thereafter, US newspapers published a tidbit about two "Polish refugees" killed by bird hunters near Genoa, Italy. They were storks, each fitted with an iron ring on its leg reading "Warsaw Zoological Garden."[4]

Although the start of World War II sent shock waves through the zoo world, it did not catch European zoos completely unaware. Since the birth of the modern zoo in the eighteenth century, zoo directors had amassed a growing body of knowledge on what to expect during wartime—and how best to plan for survival. During World War I, European zoos had faced widespread privation, staff shortages, even the threat of closure. But few zoo leaders believed that the current world war would look like the last one. Over the previous two decades, aerial bombers had expanded the scope of battle well beyond the front lines. "London is likely to be severely bombed," Zoological Society of London (ZSL) officers declared matter-of-factly in a "private and confidential memo" from May 1939.[5] Future conflicts would most likely resemble the civil war in Spain, where zoos in Republican-held Barcelona and Madrid fell prey to bombardment, siege, and eventual occupation. The head of the Liverpool Zoo did not wait to find out. In 1938, shortly after the end of the Munich Conference, he closed his zoo for good, unconvinced by Neville Chamberlain's promises of "peace for our time." Still, most zoo leaders decided to carry on as best they could.

For their part, British zoos did not wait for war to develop and publicize their contingency measures. In April 1939, the London Zoological Society Council appointed a War Emergency Committee to "formulate plans for immediate and future action."[6] Over the following months, they developed a three-phase strategy designed to maximize their chances of both short- and long-term survival, the effectiveness of which would be debated for years to come.

Phase 1: Prepare for the Worst

The first phase of their preparedness plan began a year earlier as part of a nationwide effort to beef up civil defense. Fearful of the threat posed by Hitler's newly reconstituted Luftwaffe, Parliament passed a series of measures, collectively known as Air Raid Precautions (or ARP), aimed at safeguarding the civilian population. ARP carried out two broad missions. The most important was to coordinate passive air defense and protect civilians from poison gas and falling ordnance. At the same time, the programs served a distinctly propagandistic purpose, extolling the virtues of order, duty, and a stiff upper lip.

Tasked with monitoring every inch of the British skyline, the ARP network relied heavily on volunteers: teenagers, schoolteachers, working mothers, amateur stargazers, disabled vets—anyone who was willing to take a night shift with a gas rattle and a pair of binoculars. The Home Office authorized local leaders to organize rescue parties, treat bomb casualties, set up "emergency communication systems," and remove debris from bombed-out buildings.[7] By 1939, hundreds of thousands of volunteers had trained as air raid wardens, messengers, fireguards, and ambulance drivers. "All this is no war scare," declared one newsreel, "but reasonable preparation against a real danger. To be forewarned is to be twice armed."[8]

Zoos enthusiastically embraced ARP. Their motivations were both practical and strategic. With their thick concrete cells, wrought-iron cages, and round-the-clock security, zoos already resembled miniature citadels. Animal keepers, while not necessarily handy with firearms, had extensive practice corralling stray beasts and, more importantly, rowdy patrons. Plus, civil defense offered boundless opportunities for self-promotion. In London, keepers "taught" George the chimpanzee to stack sandbags; other animals were photographed wearing gas masks and queuing outside air raid shelters—ready to "do their bit" in the looming struggle. In time, zoos became among the most visible exponents of home-front vigilance, reassuring the public that they were prepared for whatever Hitler could throw at them.

In the days leading up to the war, the London Zoo in Regent's Park amassed a mini army of ARP personnel. Of the 250 regular staff, more than eighty volunteered to serve in some defense capacity.[9] Twenty men were trained as air raid wardens; thirty-three were certified in first aid and gas casualty treatment, while nearly a dozen ran firefighting and decontamination drills. When they weren't tending to the cages, animal keepers blacked out skylights, installed strongboxes, and constructed a warren of shelters in strategic locations throughout the park. By September 1939, the zoo's air raid shelters could hold up to a thousand people; by year's end, two thousand, making Regent's Park one of the safest spots in the city. The center of the zoo's security operations was the control room in the basement of the main office. It was equipped with "special telephone units" to communicate with the nearby ARP depot in Marylebone. The ZSL also purchased a village's worth of emergency equipment: whistles, handbells (for ringing the "all clear"), eighty-one civilian respirators, thirty-five steel helmets, pickaxes, white Vaseline, six "collapsible metal ARP stretchers," candles, hurricane lamps, two "A.R.P. Surgical haversacks, and [thirty-nine] pairs of rubber boots."[10]

At times, press coverage of zoos' preparedness efforts bordered on the ludicrous. An article from August 17 assured readers: "Animals at the London Zoo are to have deep air raid shelters. In the event of an emergency all the creatures would be taken from their usual homes and put in small cages or other containers on wheels"—all, presumably, against the backdrop of screaming air raid sirens and exploding bombs.[11]

Exaggeration aside, zoos across Great Britain took their security protocols seriously. At the Whipsnade Animal Park, an open-air zoo outside London, animal keepers dug trenches and patrolled the enclosures with a "small armoury of guns."[12] Further north, staff at the Edinburgh Zoo drilled in the most essential of ARP tasks: leading visitors to shelter. It paid off. On the day the war was declared, Janet Finlayson was working as "assistant lady superintendent" in the catering department. "Within an hour," she recalled later, "the sirens sounded, [and] we got the customers into the cellar. They followed us like lambs."[13]

Figure 6.1. ARP at the London Zoo in Regent's Park. This image from March 1941 shows a pair of kid goats peeking out from an air-raid shelter made of sandbags. Trinity Mirror / Mirrorpix / Alamy.

Phase 2: Women, Children, and Pandas First

The immediate run-up to the war triggered the second phase of the zoo's emergency plan: evacuation. It began in earnest on September 1, 1939. That morning, families of zoo staff, instructed to bring "Hand Luggage Only" and enough food for twelve hours, left central London for Whipsnade Animal Park, the Zoological Society's rural, open-air zoo about thirty-five miles from the city. They were joined, a few hours later, by a selection of the zoo's most "rare and valuable" animals, each handpicked to survive the looming conflict.[14] Not all zoo favorites made the cut. Meng and Moko, the two baby gorillas, stayed behind, as did Buta, the lone okapi. (David Seth-Smith, the curator of mammals and birds, worried that it could break a leg in transit.)[15] Still, the zoo's evacuation list included some of London's most charismatic megafauna: Ming and Tang, the two giant pandas (favorites of cabinet ministers, royals, and commoners alike); Gert, Babu, Boo-Boo II, and Tiny Tim, four of the zoo's collection of chimpanzees; the orangutans, Mary and Franz; Ba-Bar, the baby elephant; and Ranee and Mo Po Ko, two adult Indian "riding" elephants (gifts from Edward VIII and a group of indigenous Burmese Christians, respectively).[16]

Whipsnade had all the makings of a wartime sanctuary. It was big— fifteen times the size of the zoo in Regent's Park—but held little appeal to enemy bombers. Evacuated families lived in army huts; when they weren't in school, children spent their days filling sandbags, learning Morse code, and patrolling the grounds for rubbish. The zoo's location atop a wide plateau overlooking the Dunstable Downs kept it safe from poison gas, which, in the words of one ARP member, tended to "sink, not to come uphill." Even the zoo's iconic "white lion," a 483-foot white chalk hill figure carved into one of the plateau slopes, didn't necessarily pose a security risk.[17] If war broke out, workers planned to cover the lion's head with upturned earth. Then, in an act of scatological subterfuge, they would turn loose the zoo's herd of sheep, Shetland ponies, and slaughter horses, "so that by their feces, urine and food . . . , they will obliterate the white colour, and leave behind a camouflage . . . of yellow brown and green."[18]

The zoo's evacuation efforts unfolded amid the largest planned exodus in British history. Operation Pied Piper was a scheme to relocate schoolchildren, expectant mothers, and the blind from industrial centers—considered the likely target of German bombers—to the countryside. The Home Office justified the plan in pragmatic terms, citing the need to deny the enemy "his chief objects—the creation of anything like panic, or the crippling dislocation of our civil life."[19] On September 1, tens of thousands of boys and girls, many with little more than a gas mask, a carrier bag, and a name card pinned to their coat, waved goodbye to their parents and crowded into designated buses and rail cars. By the time the first wave of evacuations was over, roughly 1.5 million Britons had fled their homes, refugees of a conflict that had barely begun.

In retrospect, any comparison between the London Zoo's modest evacuation efforts and the human drama unfolding across the nation can appear facile. After all, the zoo relocated only a tiny percentage of its animal collection—a pittance when held up against the millions of lives altered by government evacuation programs. Yet both were premised on two underlying and often unspoken articles of faith.

The first was a conviction about where the next war would be fought. Although long-distance airplanes had obliterated the expanse between home front and battlefield, zoo men and government planners believed that certain places lay beyond the range, or at least the interest, of German air power. As the war intensified, both groups' geography of safety shrank until it seemed that nowhere, at least in Britain, was truly safe. In September 1939, however, there was still an expectation that World War II would have boundaries—invisible lines beyond which evacuees could find a semblance of peace.

The zoo and the British government also shared the belief that, when faced with the prospect of mass death, they had every right to designate the most likely survivors. For the government, that meant preserving both the most vulnerable and, in wartime, least useful members of the population. Britain needed children for the future (if only to fight the next war), but they were better off in some faraway village where they wouldn't distract defense workers or their parents. The London Zoo operated from a different set of criteria, filling its mobile ark with celebrity animals. Zoos by their very nature are wedded to ideas of hierarchy and selection. Every day, they calculate which animals to maintain, which ones they hope to acquire, and which ones are no longer worth keeping. In this sense, World War II did not fundamentally disrupt the London Zoo's practice of unnatural selection; the conflict simply drove it out into the open.

Phase 3: Kill Your Darlings

Even as zoo staff marshaled a small number of animals to safety, they embarked on phase three of the London Zoo's war emergency plan: extermination. As early as May 1939, the Committee drew up plans to destroy a small number of animals in the event of hostilities. Over time, the zoo adopted an increasingly liberal approach to animal slaughter, killing hundreds of fish, reptiles, and mammals in the name of human safety and survival.

Zoos' practice of destroying their own animals did not begin with World War II. In 1914, as German armies tore through the Belgian countryside, the Antwerp Zoo decided to shoot thirty-two "dangerous" animals, including several bears, large cats, and venomous snakes. As conditions worsened, zoo staff destroyed additional animals, either because their "value did not justify the cost of maintaining them" or because they proved difficult to feed. Even at the war's end, the Antwerp Zoo "was obliged to slaughter buffaloes, antelopes and other ruminants and sell the meat to butchers in town." The price of hay was simply too high.[20]

In the months leading up to World War II, British zoo leaders and their allies in the press made the case for similar measures. Not long after the Munich Pact, Chester Zoo director George Mottershead reasoned that "the moment might easily have arrived when for sheer safety's sake and human consideration, we would have been called upon to shoot the animals to which we are so attached."[21] Undergirding all talk of animal slaughter, at least in the press, was the fear of animal escape—a prospect that justified the destruction of animals both before and after air raids.[22] On August 26, 1939, the London *Times* assured readers that, although the chances of a large carnivore escaping during an air raid were "so remote to be infinitesimal," the zoo was prepared to take lethal action.[23] Another London paper was less circumspect: "An air-raid might release or maim [the big cats]. In either event the animals would be shot at once."[24]

Not everyone was on board with the zoo's plans. When Julian Huxley told Winston Churchill of the preparations to kill the dangerous animals, Churchill replied, "What a pity. Imagine a great air-raid over the great city of ours—squadrons of enemy planes dropping their bombs on London, houses smashed into ruins, fires breaking out everywhere—corpses lying in the smoking ashes—and lions and tigers roaming the desolation in search of the corpses—and you're going to shoot them!" Others ridiculed the supposed danger posed by escaped animals, particularly during wartime. "At a time of slaughter and the breaking of nations, someone pauses to make certain that nothing inconvenient, in the nature of a snake-bite, happens," an Essex man editorialized in the *Manchester Daily Herald*. "What a small amount of snake to such an intolerable deal of bomb!"[25]

On the morning of September 1, news of Hitler's invasion of Poland reached London. The time for waiting was over. As visitors strolled through the park, pausing occasionally to glimpse the silver

Figure 6.2. Throughout the war years, zoos went to great lengths to warn the public about the "dangers" posed by zoo animals, contributing to the mentality that it was better to destroy certain species rather than risk their escape. This image shows a "monkey family" with their personal cache of sandbags at the London Zoo on August 30, 1939. © Imperial War Museum (HU 102732).

goldfish-shaped barrage balloons floating overhead, keepers in dark uniforms gassed the black widow spiders and beheaded the entire collection of venomous reptiles. Among the dead were ten cobras, a pair of puff adders, three diamondback rattlesnakes, and five Gila monsters—casualties of a hysterical fear of nature that zoos themselves helped manufacture.[26] Still, it wasn't easy, particularly for the executioners. Some of the men had "spent 25 years with reptiles" and were, according to one source, "visibly affected."[27]

Shortly after 11:00 a.m. on September 3, Neville Chamberlain announced that Great Britain was at war with Germany. As staff ushered visitors from the park, the zoo closed for the first time (outside of Christmas) in over a hundred years. The following day, workers began emptying the tanks in the aquarium. They tried to save the most interesting specimens. Some were stored in tubs in the Tortoise House, while the "big Moray eel" was placed in the tank holding the seawater filter.[28] A few native species were released into freshwater ponds or given to local collectors. But the bulk of the zoo's renowned collection was sacrificed "because of the danger from broken glass in the event of an air raid."[29]

All the while, zoo staff decimated their collection. The list of the animals KBO'd (killed by order) might have comprised a zoo in its own right: six alligators, seven iguanas, sixteen southern anacondas, six Indian fruit bats, a fishing cat, a binturong, a Siberian tiger, five magpies, an Alexandrine parakeet, two bullfrogs, three lion cubs, a cheetah, four wolves, and—perhaps most inexplicable of all—a manatee. Zoo records are notably fuzzy about how the animals died (though we can infer that the large mammals were shot). All that's certain is that, between early September and mid-October, zoo staff dispatched more than two hundred mammals, reptiles, and birds—more than would be killed by German bombs over the entirety of the war.[30]

An August 31 memo by David Seth-Smith, curator of mammals and birds, typified the hard logic of the zoo's decisions:

ANIMALS THAT MIGHT BE DISPOSED OF IN THE EVENT OF WAR

Cattle Sheds: Three American Bison, as these can be replaced from
  the Whipsnade herd.
Zebu Cow
Red Deer Stag
2 African Buffalo which can be replaced from Whipsnade.

Antelope House: We are not strong in Antelope and I would not recommend any reduction at present except perhaps in the case of
  one Lechwe ♂.

Lion House: Lions – present strength 9 adult, 2 half-grown males, six
  cubs.
Recommended to dispose of all but 1 pair Indian, 1 pair African
  (Alastair and Patricia) and 1 Indian male and African female
  which are mated.
Tigers – present strength 7.
Recommended to keep 4 – Blang and Sheila, the Siberian ♂ with
  Indian mate.
Leopards – present strength 5.
Recommended retain all.
Jaguars – retain present 2.

Bears: We have in all 24 Bears consisting of 5 Brown, 5 Syrian,
  3 American Black, 3 Himalayan, 4 Sun and 4 Polar.
Recommended to dispose of 2 Brown, 2 Syrian, 1 American Black[,]
  1 Himalayan and 2 Sun.

Dingoes: We have 5 Dingoes of which we might dispose of 3.

Common Wolf: 4, Hybrid Wolves, 5, Indian, 4.
Recommended to dispose of all but 2 of each.
Recommended to dispose of the collection of 10 Common Foxes.

Sea Lions: Present strength 6. If fish becomes scarce it may be necessary to dispose of two or three of these.[31]

Animals that were plentiful (or "easy to replace") were prime candidates for the chopping block, as were those with limited commercial
appeal.[32] Captain W. P. B. Beal, superintendent at Whipsnade, recommended destroying the zoo's herd of Chillingham cattle because they
were "useless and don't breed." Diet played a major role as well. Food
was already scarce, and the situation would only get worse. Animals
that required fresh fruit or fish were, in the eyes of zoo leaders, more
bother than they were worth. Perhaps the most vulnerable—the most
justifiably killable—were animals whose meat value outweighed their
zoological significance. Beal advocated destroying many of Whipsnade's cattle, bison, and deer for "human consumption."[33]

But no zoo animal was truly safe. At the Kursaal Zoo in the resort town of Southend-on-Sea, about forty-five miles outside London, teary-eyed zoo staff shot the entire collection of "dangerous" animals, including a tiger, several hawks and eagles, wolves, bears, and seven lions. The zoo's owner, Frank Bostock, told journalists that he'd been asked by locals to get rid of the beasts. Worth more than 1,000 pounds in peacetime, the collection was now "practically valueless and a liability."[34] Meanwhile, the BBC broadcast a dire notice to pet owners: "If at all possible, send or take your household animals into the country in advance of an emergency. . . . If you cannot place them in the care of neighbors, it really is kindest to have them destroyed." Animal protection groups criticized the government's advice, calling the resulting slaughter "quite unnecessary." But, for the most part, Londoners responded just as ARP leaders might have hoped. Though some chose to do the deed themselves—using a captive-bolt pistol, as the government recommended—most turned their pets over to veterinarians and specially recruited slaughterhouses for euthanasia. By the time the "September Holocaust" was over, some 400,000 dogs, cats, birds, and rabbits were dead.[35]

There is something deeply unsettling about the devaluing of life inherent in such calculations, particularly as it mirrors the genocidal logic that was already beginning to play out across Western Europe. Zoos operated from a mental calculus that suggested that some lives are more important than others—and no animal life is more important than a human one.[36] As the war dragged on, as food supplies grew short and the threat of occupation and bombardment increased, more and more lives came to be viewed as "disposable"—to be sacrificed in the name of some greater good. This is not to suggest that zoo directors or London pet owners were closet Nazis or that they shared Hitler's fantasies of extermination (though some certainly did). Rather, the uncomfortable parallels come from a deeper place, a shared archive of ideas upon which Western culture itself is built. From the Great Chain of Being to nineteenth-century race science, the West has ranked, ordered, and assigned different value to different components of the living world. Zoos were just one manifestation of that legacy; Auschwitz was another; the atomic bomb—a weapon designed to kill enemy civilians en masse to save one's own—yet another.

In many ways, the London Zoo's war emergency plan was just a microcosm of the entire nation's security measures. Like the zoo, the British state invested in civil defense, evacuated a select group of its population, and consigned millions—both animals and people—to an early death. And it was not alone: zoos in Germany and France pursued similar measures, as would, in time, animal parks from the Netherlands to Southern California.

On September 16, the London Zoo reopened to the public. The very next day, the Soviet Union invaded Poland from the east. For zoos across Europe, it was an ominous beginning. And, as Hitler's armies pivoted west toward the Low Countries, France, and the retreating British Army, it was about to get worse. But, in the winter of 1939–1940, Europe's zoos' most urgent danger was not German air power. It was the weather.

7

The Freeze and the Thaw

In the final months of 1939, the greatest threat to European zoos was taking shape tens of thousands of feet above the earth's surface. Over the North Atlantic, torrents of heavy cold air sweeping south from the pole collided with jets of lighter air moving up from the tropics. In most years, such collisions fizzled out as the warm air rose into the upper atmosphere, cooled, and eventually released its moisture back to earth. But in this case—and for the next few winters—the twin jet streams failed to dissipate, building up pressure like two armies amassing along a battlefield. By January 1940, a polar front stretched from Nova Scotia to the Soviet hinterland, plunging Europe into Ice Age conditions. Flocks of birds rarely seen below the Arctic Circle dotted the skies above Hungary and the Netherlands.[1] Ice packs clogged the Danube, while Mussolini's Rome documented the "heaviest snowfall in recorded history," allowing locals to cross St. Peter's Square on skis.[2] In Warsaw, already suffering the effects of a month-long bombardment, the thermometer dipped to −40 degrees Fahrenheit.[3] At such temperatures, liquid mercury freezes solid, and death from exposure can take only minutes.

The zoo world was uniquely susceptible to bitter cold. With few exceptions, zoos in the 1940s continued to rely on exotic megafauna—the more "exotic," the better—to lure in paying customers. In the eyes of European zoo men, no collection was complete without an ark's worth of elephants, lions, and tropical anthropoid apes. That such creatures were highly unsuited for life amid the ashen snowscapes of Helsinki and Hamburg did not matter. When temperatures dropped, the logic went, a thin-skinned kangaroo or cold-blooded crocodile could be secreted into a concrete bunker to await the coming of spring. Even so, winter housing was just the tip of the iceberg. Maintaining food stocks was hard enough in the best of times; during a historically harsh cold streak, feeding a zoo full of hungry bellies was all but impossible. Indeed, winter weather made *everything* at the zoo—cleaning the cages, tending to the sick and dying animals, recruiting staff—exponentially more difficult. This explains why so many zoos choose to hibernate in wintertime, removing all but the hardiest of furbearers from outdoor display.

But the winter of 1939–1940 was a different beast, so to speak. At Whipsnade Zoo, north of London, the cold killed a black rhino and an African elephant. When the ground proved too frozen to bury them, staff burned the carcasses in a pit usually reserved for destroying rubbish. (It took an entire week.)[4] Similar deaths piled up across the continent. In Antwerp, the bitter weather killed an elephant, a hippopotamus, and an okapi—the so-called "forest giraffe" native to the Belgian Congo and virtually unknown to Western science four decades earlier.[5] However, these represented only a fraction of that winter's body count. Walter van den bergh, the Antwerp Zoo's ambitious young director, recounted: "That first winter all the meat-eating animals—the lions, tigers, bears and pumas—60 in all, were shot at the request of the Antwerp authorities" because of a lack of food.[6]

Even Munich's Hellabrunn Zoo, no stranger to subzero temperatures, was nearly overwhelmed. Thick, heavy snow collapsed the roof of the lion cage and sent 200-year-old trees crashing into the deer enclosure. The zoo's director, Heinz Heck, devised experimental techniques to inure some animals to the frigid weather. Several times a day he ventilated the ape cage with air from outside, sending the temperature from 20 degrees Celsius down to −15. The goal was to strengthen the apes' lungs and prevent them from becoming "greenhouse plants" that caught "cold at the slightest draft."[7] Today, Heck's acclimation experiments bear an uncomfortable resemblance to the ghoulish climate "science" performed in Nazi-run concentration camps. Throughout the war years, Josef Mengele and other camp doctors forced prisoners to strip nude and sit for hours in icy water to measure the physiological effects of extreme cold. For men like Mengele, camp prisoners were

Figure 7.1. Staff cleaning up after the flooding of the Prague Zoo on March 22, 1940. Courtesy of Prague Zoo Archive.

little more than human guinea pigs—to be experimented upon, sliced open, measured and weighed, and eventually discarded. In this sense, at the very least, the comparison breaks down: Heck wanted his test subjects to survive.

In March 1940, warming temperatures brought a new set of dangers. As ice-clogged rivers began to thaw, they released torrents of water. In mid-March, the Vltava River, which bisects the Czech capital of Prague, overflowed, carrying logs, dirt, and buffalo-sized chunks of ice into the zoo grounds. The bitterly cold water flooded workshops, destroyed the zoo's heating system, and seeped into the feline pavilion, trapping the lions for two days. Two months later, flooding from the nearby Isar River, combined with the saturated soil from melted snow, overwhelmed Hellabrunn's drainage system, turning walking paths into swiftly running streams. Fish escaped their ponds; ducks and geese were swept away.[8]

Weather aside, many European zoo men remained outwardly optimistic. Outside Poland, already ravaged by twin invasions (Hitler from the west, Stalin from the east), the conflict remained something of an abstraction, a "phoney war" that failed to live up to people's initial fears. As early as February 1940, one Parisian newspaper described the triumphant homecoming of the Vincennes Zoo's "pensioners of quality," a sure sign that the darkest days of the war were already behind them.[9] Zoos inside the Reich, meanwhile, boasted record crowds. In Hitler's adopted hometown of Munich, more than 30,000 "Aryans" spent Easter weekend at the zoo.[10]

In the end, though, the moment of calm was short-lived. That April, German forces launched a two-month campaign to seize control of Europe from the Rhine to the Atlantic. Employing a style of fighting known as *Blitzkrieg*, the Wehrmacht routed the Allies, winning more territory in eight weeks than in four years of trench warfare in World War I. By spring's end, few in the European zoo world held out hope of returning to normal anytime soon. If anything, the onslaught of April–June 1940 was only a preview of the destruction Hitler's forces would leave in their wake.

The "Lightning War" on Dutch Zoos

In common parlance, the concept of *Blitzkrieg* (or "lightning war") refers to the German military strategy of smashing rival forces through a combination of speed, surprise, and coordinated violence. Rather than advancing slowly in large numbers, the goal was to overwhelm opponents with blistering aerial attacks and swift-moving armor (tanks). The concept of shock-and-awing the enemy into submission was not exactly new in 1940.[11] Hindenburg's forces had tried it to some success during World War I before mechanical problems, reliance on horsepower (quite literally), swampy terrain, and—most importantly— French resistance halted their advance. Moreover, as military historian J. P. Harris has rightly pointed out, the *Blitzkrieg* of popular imagination—with its unparalleled speed, its surgical precision, its hints of Nietzschean savagery—is a myth or, at best, an "*ex post facto* rationalization of various aspects of the German approach to war."[12] For all its advocates' talk of orchestrated precision, *Blitzkrieg* was a blunt instrument—more high-powered steamroller than computer-guided missile.

Figure 7.2. Like several zoos, Ouwehand's Zoo in Rhenen was a victim of wartime geography. This advertising brochure (c. 1930s–1940s) highlights the zoo's location atop the militarily significant Grebbeberg, a forested outgrowth overlooking the city and nearby river. Gelders Archief: 1086 – 509 Map Collection of the State Archives in Gelderland, N./. Steendrukkerij "De Maas," Public Domain Mark 1.0 License.

It was a lesson that Cornelis ("Cor") Ouwehand would come to know all too well. Born in 1892, Ouwehand was a Dutch chicken farmer who opened an animal park in Rhenen, about sixty miles east of Rotterdam, in 1932.[13] By 1940, Ouwehand's Dierenpark housed a large collection of animals, including giraffes, tigers, hippos, and elephants. Most spectacular of all was the zoo's float of crocodiles, a thousand strong, which visitors could feed for a small fee.* Unfortunately, like many zoos of the World War II era, Ouwehand's animal park was to become a victim of geography—in the wrong place at unquestionably the wrong time. Throughout the nineteenth and early twentieth centuries, zoo builders sought to construct their "living museums" in city centers where they might add a sense of nature, cultivated and caged though it might be,

---

* Animal fact: a group of crocodiles in the water is called a "float"; crocs on land are a "bask."

to the increasingly smog-choked urban environment. Consequently, by the 1940s, some of Europe's best-known zoos would find themselves located within a bomb's radius of a prime target.

In Ouwehand's case, that target was the *Grebbe Line*, a fortified line of trench works, bunkers, and sluices designed in the mid-eighteenth century to stall invading armies. Ouwehand's Zoo sat atop a steep, forested hill—the *Grebbeberg*—that had been left relatively unprotected. As invasion loomed, the Dutch Army command, worried about the threat of bomb-maddened predators freed by German shells, ordered the destruction of the zoo's large carnivores. With little faith in the marksmanship of the Dutch troops, Ouwehand carried out the grim duty himself, shooting each animal at point-blank range. At the last minute, he decided to spare a female polar bear ("Maxie") that had recently birthed a pair of cubs. The male bear was not so fortunate—or perhaps he was.

On May 10, 1940, Hitler's forces launched *Fall Gelb* (Case Yellow), the simultaneous invasion of Luxembourg, the Low Countries, and eastern France. In Rhenen, zoo staff (the owner included) fled. The following day, German troops stormed the *Grebbeberg*, bombarding the zoo grounds and the surrounding area. When Ouwehand was allowed to return on May 15, following the Dutch capitulation, the zoo resembled a "wasteland." Picking his way through the maze of downed trees and muddy craters, he spotted the remains of buildings still smoldering from German shells. Most tragic of all were the animals— crushed, burned, shell-shocked, dying, dead. Hundreds of crocodiles were buried "under the rubble of their collapsed enclosure." Giraffes lay prostrate, their necks broken after colliding with the walls of their pen.[14]

Elsewhere, the Luftwaffe pounded Dutch cities and shipping yards, unleashing waves of terror not seen since the Spanish Civil War. For staff at Rotterdam's historic animal garden, near the main rail station, it could not have come at a worse time. Founded in 1857, the *Rotterdamsche Diergaard* had been one of the most beautiful zoos of its era, envied for its immaculately manicured grounds and architectural flourishes. Film footage taken in the 1930s reveals a cosmopolitan world seemingly untouched by economic hardship: elegant ladies, decked out in hats and summer fur, feeding zebras by hand; sea lions slip-sliding

Figure 7.3. Maxie and her cubs at Ouwehand's Zoo in 1940. Cor Ouwehand spared Maxie's life in the lead-up to the German invasion—evidence that, even (especially) in desperate times, zoo men still played favorites. Gelders Archief: 458 – 1534 Jacquet Collection, photographer: Jacquet, CC-BY-4.0 license.

atop an enormous artificial rock face; juvenile chimpanzees wrestling on an open lawn to the delight of onlookers.[15] Even so, the Depression took its toll, so much so that zoo leaders decided to start fresh with a new facility in the Blijdorp neighborhood farther to the northwest. In 1939, employees set to work constructing architect Sybold van Ravestyn's fantastic designs for the new zoo, including its centerpiece, the *Rivièrahal* (Riviera Hall), a gargantuan complex of pavilions and exhibit spaces that resembled a cross between a train station, cathedral, and walk-in aviary. By March 1940, some animals had already taken up residence in their new quarters, while others were crammed into temporary holding pens in anticipation of the move.

And then the Germans came.

On the morning of May 12, fire from a German airplane hit the predator house, though none of the animals were injured.[16] The next day, eighteen high-explosive bombs crashed into the zoo grounds, blasting open cages and shredding the animals. Witnesses recalled scenes fit for Dante: antelopes stumbling about, bleeding from open bellies; a recent shipment of young ostriches, their heads and wings ripped from their torsos. At the military's command, the zoo's eminent director, Koenraad Kuiper, shot the large carnivores—panthers, jaguars, lions, tigers, bears—with the exception of a handful of zoo favorites.[17] On May 14, the final day of the German attack, ninety low-flying Heinkel He 111s carpet-bombed the city, setting off a firestorm that killed 900 and reduced much of the old town to rubble. Flames ripped through the zoo's workshops and libraries, destroying 5,000 books. Entering the burning monkey house, a pair of keepers managed to rescue some of the inmates, among them an orangutan, some capuchins, and Josephine, one of the prized chimpanzees. Initially, Josephine was stashed in a café, where she smashed glasses and beat one of the capuchins to death. (She was later transferred to a toilet.) At least one monkey rescuee was locked in a telephone booth; others waited out the inferno from the depths of a beer cellar. A pair of juvenile lions, spared only the day before, asphyxiated in their emergency shelters.

Over the next month, Rotterdam Zoo staff managed to reassemble what remained of their animal collection, staging a grand premiere in Blijdorp that December. In retrospect, it's hard to believe that anything could have survived the Rotterdam bombing, let alone the chaos that followed. Yet the fate of Kuiper's collection mirrored that of all Dutch zoos in at least one important way: it was random. To be sure, individual zoo workers would take heroic steps to rescue the animals in their care. But, in more cases than not, the line between survival and all-out destruction was a matter of luck or historical happenstance. Amsterdam's Artis Zoo escaped the German invasion virtually untouched. Armand Sunier, its director, even resisted calls to destroy his "dangerous" inmates, killing only four poisonous snakes.[18] Over time, the fates of Dutch zoo animals would be decided by their proximity to military targets, the whims of weather, the randomness of human decision-making, and the chaos that would come to define urban war. Overall, though, as the lines between "battlefield" and "home front" disappeared, zoos were simply in the way—collateral damage of a total war.

The Birdman of Clères

With the Belgian surrender on May 28, only one goal remained for Hitler's generals: subduing France. Since the days of Napoleon, France had loomed large in the German military imagination—and not necessarily out of respect. In Hitler's eyes, the nation of Baudelaire and Josephine Baker represented the antithesis of *his* Reich—effete, cosmopolitan, and shockingly degenerate. The fact that France had emerged on top in 1918 was almost too much to contemplate. By taking Paris, Germany would establish itself as the master of continental Europe.

On May 24, with Anglo-French forces in retreat and Rommel's *Panzers* descending upon Paris, French zoos suffered their greatest casualty of the entire war, when more than thirty bombs landed on a château near the small market town of Clères, in Normandy. The property belonged to Jean Théodore Delacour, an ornithologist who, over the course of two decades, had amassed one of the largest private bird parks in the world. Graced with an "encyclopaedic mind" and an appearance "rather like Winston Churchill," Delacour embodied a type once familiar but now all but extinct: the gentleman naturalist.[19] This social type crystalized in the eighteenth and nineteenth centuries, when—driven by imperial glory, a thirst for knowledge, or simple boredom—growing numbers of wealthy Europeans devoted entire lifetimes to capturing and cataloguing nature's wonders.[20] While Charles Darwin was perhaps the prototypical gentleman naturalist, this characterization describes a long lineage of figures including Herband Arthur Russell, the 11th Duke of Bedford (who served as president of the London Zoological Society for more than thirty-five years in the early twentieth century).

Delacour was no mere obsessive. Born in Paris in 1890, Delacour was "crazy about birds" from early childhood.[21] When not yet ten, he convinced his parents to construct an aviary on their lavish country estate at Villers-Bretonneux near Amiens, where he would spend his summers mastering the latest avicultural practices. He would go on to earn a doctorate in biology from the University of Lille, after which he spent decades traveling the globe building his collections and burnishing his reputation as a world-class ornithologist. In the 1920s and '30s, Delacour took part in regular expeditions to French Indochina, Venezuela, and elsewhere, returning with some "30,000 birds and 8,000 mammals" for zoos in New York and Europe.[22] In later years, he would become a celebrity in the tight-knit world of bird keepers, his numerous books still cherished as models of scholarly precision and grace.[23]

Yet no factor had a greater effect on Delacour's life, both personally and professionally, than world war. At the outbreak of World War I, the German Army overran his parents' country estate, only to be pushed back a few weeks later. In 1916, Marshal Ferdinand Foch, the supreme Allied commander in World War I, used the château as his headquarters. Delacour, who was serving in the French Army at the time, later recalled returning home for a quick visit—to check on his birds, of course—"only to find Foch and [his staff officer General Maxime] Weygand discussing the campaign inside the largest aviary."[24] By 1917–1918, Villers had become a "No Man's Land," riddled with trenches and scarred by thousands of fallen shells. When he made it home in 1918, Delacour found nothing but "stumps of trees and crumbling walls and waste. Where the gardens, conservatories and aviaries had been, only tangles of broken steel, glass, and wood remained."[25]

At war's end, Delacour sought a new location to rebuild his collection, finding the perfect spot a year later. Located in a "pretty, narrow valley surrounded by picturesque hills," the estate at Clères looked like something out of a fairy tale: the main house, parts of which dated back to the thirteenth century, sat at the center of hundreds of acres of parkland—space enough for Delacour to indulge his wildest aspirations. Within months, he hired an English gardener and birdman ("always in fashion in France") and contracted a hundred workers to dig a lake and build the new enclosures.[26] Whenever possible, he tried to "keep plants and animals together, in a harmonious whole resembling natural conditions." Most striking of all, his animals seemed to live in "apparent freedom." Gibbons frolicked on artificial islands; free-roaming wallabies hopped across open lawns, while herds of Chinese water deer, muntjacs, and blackbucks dotted the landscape.[27] In February 1939, a fire broke out inside the main house, incinerating Delacour's research library in the process. Even so, at the start of World War II, Clères remained the "last great private collection" of birds and animals on the Continent—a testament to one man's dedication to rebuild in war's wake.[28]

But Delacour's vision would not survive the German invasion. In late May and early June, bombs killed hundreds of birds and mammals, as well as four people. Then German troops looted the park, carting away anything that seemed valuable. Some birds managed to escape in the chaos; others "mixed with different species and were killed in the ensuing fighting," while the "more delicate species" died of trauma or starvation. When a pair of Delacour's colleagues visited Clères that August, only about 1,000 birds remained—and they would be gone soon enough.[29]

A year later, Delacour would publicly reflect on his loss: "To-day practically nothing remains of what I spent the best years of my life creating. Actually, at Clères only a short time ago I possessed everything to which as a child I had looked forward when I dreamed one day of being a naturalist with a great collection of birds and mammals, as well as their skins, and with a comprehensive library devoted to my favourite subjects. It was a dream come true and then, at fifty, I suddenly find it vanished in thin air like a pin-pricked bubble."[30]

To be sure, what happened at Clères—and at Rotterdam and Rhenen—was not necessarily a product of deliberate malice. Göring's Luftwaffe would not have been able to successfully target a zoo (or a cathedral or a beloved historic landmark), even if it tried to do so. But, in many ways, that's the point: as strategies of terror, *Blitzkrieg* and carpet-bombing make no distinctions between "legitimate" and "illegitimate" targets, between military forces and those unlucky enough to be caught in the line of fire. This was the reality facing French leaders: they could surrender or risk the destruction of everything they loved.

Capitulation

On June 10, what remained of the French government fled south to Bordeaux. Four days later, the Wehrmacht marched up the Champs-Élysées like Roman legions. In forcing Paris's capitulation, Hitler had left little doubt about German supremacy in Western Europe. For all their dismissal of Gallic materialism, they now held sway over one of the greatest archives of art and culture in the world. Among the treasures, the capital's two zoos—the Jardin des Plantes and the Vincennes Zoo—would be especially prized, both as tourist spots for vacationing troops and as symbols of the benign nature of the German occupation.

But Jean Delacour would not be there to watch it happen. According to the Vichy minister of the interior, Delacour could not return to Clères without risking arrest. (The Nazis considered his "British associations" to be too dangerous.) So began a months-long trek—to Vichy, Lyons, Algiers, Casablanca, Rabat, Tangiers, and finally Lisbon—in order to secure safe passage overseas. In mid-December, he boarded a passenger ship "crowded with refugees" bound for New York. There to greet him was Lee Crandall, the curator of the Bronx Zoo, Delacour's professional home for the next six years.[31]

In the end, Jean Delacour had become an exile. Yet, for many of Europe's zoo leaders, fleeing was not an option. Instead, they confronted something far more treacherous: occupation.

8

The Rape of the Zoo

In October 1942, about a year and a half into the occupation of Holland, noted ant expert and curator at the Berlin University's natural history museum, Dr. Hans Bischoff, appeared at the Jesuit cloisters at Valkenburg. Asking to inspect Father Schmitz's collection of scuttle flies, the German entomologist announced breezily: "From today on all this belongs to me. I will come and take it. And I want the Wasmann ants, too." The ants in question were the provenance of Erich Wasmann, a former resident of the cloister. In his lifetime, the Tyrol-born Wasmann had amassed the greatest ant collection in the world—412 colonies, thousands of species—which he studiously sorted, pinned, and labeled. When he died in 1931, the celebrated formicologist had gifted his life's work to Schmitz—and now, it seemed, the Germans wanted them.[1]

But there was a problem. In 1940, Schmitz had forwarded Wasmann's ants to the Maastricht museum of natural history, whose curator (herself a noted formicophile) was determined to keep the ants in Dutch hands. On March 5, 1943, Bischoff appeared at the Maastricht burgomaster's office, this time backed up by a member of the SS and bearing a signed letter from the quisling Department of Science, Popular Education and Cultural Affairs. If the mayor did not relinquish the ants, Bischoff threatened, he'd be charged with sabotage. Although sympathetic to the occupation, the politician begged for more time, phoning the head of the Dutch Nazi Party in a final attempt to keep the ants out of German hands. In the end, he reluctantly agreed to surrender Wasmann's collection, but only if Bischoff provided a signed receipt. Excitedly relating the story to the *New York Herald Tribune* the following year, war correspondent and "amateur formicologist" Lewis Gannett declared: "The meanest thing the Germans did in Holland is known in Maastricht as the 'rape of the ants.'"

To be sure, German forces did far "meaner" things than cart away boxes of dead insects. Well before the war began, Adolf Hitler welcomed the chance to occupy, annex, and—when it suited his purpose—liquidate his European neighbors. "State frontiers are established by human beings and may be changed by human beings," he raged near the end of *Mein Kampf*. "The fact that a nation has acquired an enormous territorial area is no reason why it should hold that territory perpetually. At most, the possession of such territory is a proof of the strength of the conqueror and the weakness of those who submit to him."[2] Nazi ideologues spoke openly about their goal of exporting Germany's race laws abroad, and once victorious (for Hitler, that was never a question), they planned to reorganize European economics, politics, and culture into a "New Order" under German control.[3]

Not that all occupied peoples were to be treated the same. In Western European countries like the Netherlands, which was classified as a "Germanic Brother Nation," Nazi administrators encouraged collaboration—at least, at first.[4] Casting themselves in the role of friendly tyrants, the Reich's propagandists hoped to win over the non-Jewish residents of Scandinavia, the Netherlands, Belgium, and France. Nazi plans for Eastern Europe, on the other hand, demanded the starvation and wholesale butchery of millions of people. Hitler authorized a scorched-earth policy in Poland, Ukraine, and Russia, with the aim of turning them into large agricultural colonies for the Reich's soon-to-be-booming population. "Our task is to suck from the Ukraine all the goods we can get hold of," announced newly appointed *Reichskommissar* Erich Koch in September 1941, "without consideration of the feeling or the property of the Ukrainians."[5]

A similar dynamic played out in German-occupied zoos. Indeed, at the risk of generalization, we can divide occupied zoos into two camps: those the Nazis allowed to stay open (the Netherlands, France, Belgium, Czechoslovakia) and those they preferred to wipe from the face of the earth (Poland, the Soviet Union).

Looting the Zoo

For zookeepers, perhaps the most devastating characteristic of the German occupation was looting. Despite its reputation as a nation of zoo-lovers, the Reich's armies and zoo men proved more than willing to ransack foreign animal collections, in some cases stripping them of all they were worth.

Nazi Germany did not invent the practice of pillaging foreign animal collections. Throughout the ancient world, it was commonplace for occupying armies to seize local wildlife as war trophies, a practice that led to some of the earliest collections of exotic animals in recorded history. With the expansion of Roman imperialism, notes zoo historian Vernon N. Kisling Jr., the emperor's legions plundered foreign animal collections, hauling lions, tigers, and elephants back to the capital.[6] Near the end of the eighteenth century, Napoleon's armies returned from defeated Egypt with animals that would serve as the core collection of the Jardin des Plantes. With each conquest, writes historian Louise E. Robbins, "the grasping hands of empire gathered up live animals to be returned to [Paris]. Always justified in terms of public instruction and utility, the living booty also boosted national pride and brought crowds to the Jardin to marvel at the new acquisitions."[7]

The connection between military conquest and zoos reached new heights during the nineteenth century, when agents of European imperialism exported choice human and nonhuman "specimens" back to the continent for study and display.[8] As critic John Berger observes: "The capturing of animals was a symbolic representation of the conquest of all distant lands."[9] In April 1916, *The Daily Standard* drew a direct line between the health of British zoos and the nation's imperial ambitions. In less than a year, it predicted, "the Zoo ought to benefit from the acquisition of the various German colonies, where, it is known there are some uncommon animals not always found in the British colonies."[10] In short, the use of military power to steal, rob, exploit, and scavenge was part of the modern zoo's DNA.

Like ant-thief Hans Bischoff, German occupation forces made no attempt to hide their efforts to raid conquered nations' zoos. This proved to be especially true in Eastern Europe and Russia. German occupiers confiscated nearly all of Kiev's zoo animals, carting them back for exhibition in the East Prussian city of Königsberg.[11] They also stole six "pure-blooded European bison" from the Krakow Zoo, all of which would be killed in bomb attacks on Berlin in 1945.[12] The most infamous case of zoo looting took place in Warsaw, where Berlin Zoo director Lutz Heck, sporting a Nazi uniform, personally supervised the "loan" of the zoo's most valuable animals to Germany. Over the following days, Diane Ackerman reports, crews in trucks quickly emptied most of the cages, "hauling the orphan elephant Tuzinka off to Königsberg; shipping the camels and llamas to Hanover; sending the hippopotamuses to Nuremberg; dispatching the Przewalski's horses to [Heck's] brother, Heinz, in Munich; and claiming the lynxes, zebras, and bison for the Berlin Zoo."[13]

From an economic perspective, zoo thefts amounted to virtually nothing when compared to the untold billions of dollars of plunder—artworks, religious artifacts, rare minerals, clothing, bodies (live and dead), gold coins, jewelry, stocks—sent home to finance Hitler's military ambitions and fatten the coffers of Nazi elites. Viewed ideologically, however, Nazi efforts to loot occupied zoos reflected a broader campaign to invalidate Germany's enemies to the east. "Fascist policy was not only to destroy Polish cities, towns, villages, farms, and factories," observes Leszek Solski, a historian and scientist at Wrocław Zoo, "but also—or perhaps even first of all—to destroy Polish culture and science."[14] In the eyes of German occupiers, the "mongrel" peoples of Poland, Ukraine, and Russia did not deserve to have zoos.[15] Lutz Heck drove this message home in late 1939. Having already swiped the Warsaw Zoo's best specimens, he decided to treat some SS pals to a New Year's Eve shooting party on the zoo grounds—with the caged animals as targets.[16]

"Voor Joden Verboden"

In the West, German forces were less likely to loot occupied zoos (though that happened) than to alter them to reflect the ideology of the Nazi state. Foremost, this involved a systematic campaign to remove Jewish people from public life. Antisemitism was not a by-product of the Nazi worldview; it was a core tenet. Recognizing that many of the nation's Jews were indistinguishable from those with "German blood,"

The Rape of the Zoo   107

the Nazi government employed a variety of legal tactics to make Jews simultaneously hyper-visible in personal appearance—forcing them to wear a "Jewish badge," for example—and invisible within "Aryan" society. In the first six years of Hitler's dictatorship, the Nazi government issued some four hundred ordinances and decrees limiting German Jews' rights, many of which would be exported to the nations now under Germany's control.[17] As early as August 1939, the Czech police directorate in Prague banned Jews from visiting restaurants, swimming pools, and public baths. By the following May, Jews were not allowed to linger in public parks, ride in taxis, keep pigeons, attend the cinema, or seek solace at the nation's zoos.[18]

In the Netherlands, the legal persecution of Dutch Jews followed a similar course. Arthur Seyss-Inquart,* the Reich commissioner for the Occupied Dutch Territories, banned Jewish newspapers in September 1940; the following month, all Dutch civil servants, zoo workers included, were required to fill out forms detailing their family history. People with one or more Jewish grandparents were assigned the legal status of "non-Aryan" and subjected to a host of new antisemitic regulations.[19] After Dutch communists led a sympathy strike protesting German occupation in February 1941, Seyss-Inquart promised violent retaliation. "We will hit the Jews where we find them," he declared, "and whoever takes their side will have to bear the consequences." Over the next year, anti-Jewish violence swept the country, and Jews were forced to wear a six-pointed yellow star—purchased at their own expense, of course—when in public.

While these prohibitions caused distress throughout the country, they proved to be especially traumatic in Amsterdam, home to the nation's largest Jewish community. In February 1941, ominous signs bearing the words *JUDEN VIERTEL JOODISCHE WIJK* ("Jewish Quarter") and *VOOR JODEN VERBODEN* ("Forbidden to Jews") began to appear in the neighborhoods around Artis Zoo. That September, occupying forces issued a new order prohibiting Jewish access to the nation's recreational facilities, including its zoos. Jewish Amsterdammers, many of whom grew up visiting the zoo, pleaded with director Armand Sunier to help lift the ban, but Sunier knew better than to risk

---

* For his crimes in the Netherlands, the Austrian Nazi was hanged at Nuremberg in 1946.

Figure 8.1. This photo, taken at the Hague Zoo on July 30, 1942, shows a formal going-away celebration for 375 Dutch volunteers for the Waffen-SS, evidence that at least some Dutch citizens were eager to support the *Führer*'s battle against Soviet Bolshevism. Photo: John Borrius, National Archives of the Netherlands / Stapf Bilderdienst.

Seyss-Inquart's ire further.[†] Eventually, when Jews were no longer allowed to take part in public life, Artis "thanked" its 335 Jewish members and refunded them half a year's dues—a meager gesture in the face of generations of support.[20]

Perhaps the most famous example of Germany's attempt to "Aryanize" an occupied zoo took place in The Hague. Aryanization typically describes the forced transfer of Jewish assets to "Aryan" owners, usually party members or pro-Nazi foreigners. Yet German occupying forces felt compelled to Aryanize everything they touched. The Hague Zoo fell victim to this mentality in 1943, when the German military decided that the flat sandy coastline surrounding the zoo grounds would be a perfect landing ground for a future Allied invasion. Learning of the zoo's impending closure, zoo staff evacuated the remaining animals (wolves, bears, big cats, bison) to sister zoos across the country.

[†] A few years later, the Nazi-affiliated occupying government of the Netherlands suspended Koenraad Kuiper, the longtime director of the Rotterdam Zoo, and his assistant for protesting the anti-Jewish measures.

Instead of razing the zoo, however, the German occupiers continued to use its main hall as a military cathedral for Dutch recruits preparing to join the Waffen-SS on the Eastern Front.[21]

Everyone Once in Paris

All the while, German occupiers used foreign zoos as a form of recreation—a reward for off-duty troops looking for lighthearted, Reich-approved outdoor fun. Nowhere was this more explicit than in Paris, occupied by the Wehrmacht between May 1940 and August 1944. Not long after settling into his billet at the Hotel Raphaël, author and army captain Ernst Jünger made sure to drop by the Vincennes Zoo, as would numerous German officers and officials in the years that followed.[22] Throughout the occupation, Germany operated a booming tourist industry in the city for soldiers on leave under the policy *Jeder einmal in Paris* (Everyone once in Paris). German soldiers packed Parisian cafés, boozed at nightclubs, and ogled cancan girls late into the night. The Reich's chief propagandist, Joseph Goebbels, saw the defeated French capital as "the soldier's watering hole, his reward, the Wehrmacht's brothel." All the same, military officers worried that Parisian decadence would contaminate the minds, hearts, and *Schwänze* of Hitler's fighting men. Even Philippe Pétain, head of the collaborationist Vichy government, chided Parisians for their hedonism and lack of Christian values.[23]

With this in mind, German propaganda and tourist material regularly touted zoos (along with castles, cathedrals, and nature preserves) as healthy and high-minded alternatives to Parisian sin. The May 1941 issue of *Der Deutsche Wegleiter für Paris*, a "what to see" guide for Wehrmacht soldiers on R and R, is brimming with images of youthful troops touring the city, gazing at Napoleon's crypt, and purchasing German-language newspapers from smiling, beret-topped mademoiselles. One article describes a Sunday visit to the Vincennes Zoo with its well-maintained avenues, comically fat hippo, and families of squabbling monkeys. Readers learn that, during the "war" (as if it were far in the past), all the animals remained in their cages, their cries indistinguishable from the air raid sirens. Now, however, the zoo had returned to its natural state—a place where innocent soldiers and innocent families and innocent children could gather without a care in the world.[24]

Figure 8.2. Propaganda about zoo-loving German occupiers was not limited to Paris. The message on the back of this image (c. late 1941) explains: "In the zoo in Kharkiv. In the Kharkiv Zoo, many animals walk freely. Our soldiers befriended them in a short period of time. A Yak calf." dpa picture alliance / Alamy.

In this sense, zoos were most valuable to German occupiers as a venue for propaganda.[25] A German propaganda film from April–September 1940, *Łódź Becomes Litzmannstadt*, for example, incorporates the zoo into a larger narrative of rebirth and renewal. Before the Germans' arrival, the film implies, Polish Łódź was primitive, dirty, and disreputable. Revitalized under German command, newly named Litzmannstadt, by contrast, is a model of cleanliness and efficiency. As evidence, the film conjures happy images of German soldiers at the zoo and comic scenes of animals at play.[26] In later years, propaganda of this sort would help fuel the "myth of the clean Wehrmacht," the self-serving and demonstrably false notion that ordinary German soldiers treated enemy nations with the respect and kindness they'd expect at home.[27]

Under Occupation

From the perspective of occupied zoos, the German presence was both a constant humiliation and, more immediately, a threat to their daily operations. Despite propaganda-conscious officials' efforts to put a happy face on the occupation, the daily grind of running a zoo—securing food and supplies; retaining workers; keeping up facilities; and, above all else, filling empty cages—became increasingly dangerous . . . and not because of the animals. Zoo directors carried on as best they could, often trying to fly below the Germans' radar. Inevitably, though, leaders of occupied zoos were forced, to some degree or another, to ingratiate themselves with the occupying authorities.

Does that make them "collaborators"? If only it were that simple. Even at the time, collaboration was less an all-or-nothing choice, at least for most people, than a spectrum of responses to an evolving situation. On one end, there were the "quislings," the homegrown SS, those who would betray national allegiances to serve the Reich. Only a smidge less disreputable were leaders like Marshal Philippe Pétain, head of the French Vichy government, who believed (wrongly) that collaboration would "shield" the population from greater repression.[28] On the other side of the spectrum were those who fought the Nazi occupation at every turn. However, in all the occupied nations, the bulk of the citizenry existed somewhere in that murky middle between traitorous *collabos* and iron-willed resistance fighters. For millions across occupied Europe, H. R. Kedward noted in his classic study of wartime collaboration, ideas about national liberation took a backseat to what the "Bretons call 'la chienne du monde'—the malevolent beast of poverty, hunger, and personal or family disaster."[29] In such a context, many chose "internal emigration," losing themselves in books, art, music, and—yes—zoos, in an attempt to shut out the terror.

Indeed, the experiences of the zoos in Prague and Amsterdam illustrate the inadequacy of "collaboration" as a lens through which to evaluate behavior under occupation. At first glance, the Prague Zoo appears to have thrived under German rule. Despite food shortages, it managed to increase its number of animals by about two hundred early in the war, and attendance numbers roughly matched those of the mid-1930s. In 1942, the zoo's new superintendent, Lieutenant Colonel Jan Vlasák, won international fame after he and his wife successfully hand-reared a newborn polar bear, Snow White, in their Prague flat. Early on, he later explained, they bottle-fed the cub up to nine times a day before transitioning her to a diet of breakfast rolls, table sugar, semolina, fresh vegetables, and minced horseflesh.[30] Surely, only a

Figure 8.3. Prague Zoo superintendent Jan Vlasák with the polar bear cub Ilun (or, more commonly, Snow White) circa 1942. Courtesy of Prague Zoo Archive.

collaborator, a bootlicking toady, would be able to afford to spend so much food on so small a bear, right?

Not so fast. Prague Zoo workers had to sign the same loyalty oaths, make the same Aryan declarations, write the same reports to occupying officials, and post the same "No Jews Allowed" signs. We must also remember that German officials liked to trumpet occupation success stories. In the eyes of Hitler's followers, the birth of Snow White was just further proof that the world was better off under Nazi control. In other words, if the Prague Zoo seemed to thrive during the war years, it was only because occupying forces allowed it to happen. At any moment, for any reason, the German occupiers could have decided to box up the most valuable animals and shoot the rest, if only to remind Prague residents who was in charge.

On the outside, Amsterdam's Artis Zoo also appeared a model of appeasement. Maarten Frankenhuis, a former zoo director and author of a history of Artis during World War II, notes that German and Dutch National Socialist organizations frequently celebrated it as an important national resource. Photos of German soldiers on holiday at the zoo proliferated in the Dutch media, and the Department of Public Education and the Arts encouraged zoo-going as a form of *volksopvoeding* (popular education) for adults and youth alike. The *Nederlandsche Volksdienst* (Dutch People's Service), a Nazi-affiliated charity organization, subsidized school trips to the zoo, and in 1944, the Dutch Nazi magazine *Fotonieuws* praised Artis's anti-Jewish vigilance. In public, director Armand Sunier tried to put an upbeat face on the situation—not least because he never knew when the occupation might turn violent. Once, when food supplies dipped, he struck a deal with a nearby Kriegsmarine base to keep its mascot, a brown bear, at the zoo in exchange for leftovers from the base kitchen.[31]

Behind closed doors, however, Artis Zoo defied the occupiers' demands at every turn. Despite prohibitions against hoarding, Armand Sunier stashed barrels of fuel throughout the park to heat the aquarium. At the same time, he refused to allow zoo employees to compromise prewar ethical standards. After a string of thefts, Sunier reminded the staff of their obligations—to the zoo, to the nation, and to their consciences. It's understandable if a hungry man, desperate to feed himself or his family, has to break his moral code, he explained. It was quite another to trespass against the zoo for material gain. Zoo workers had a "social duty" to share in the hunger, cold, and deprivation of their fellow citizens; otherwise, the future of Artis was at risk. Personally, Sunier was "outspokenly anti-German," despite his long friendship with Munich Zoo director Heinz Heck and German animal dealer Christoph Schulz. In a telling indictment of the zoo's new masters, he once told an Artis employee: "Those Krauts love beasts, we love animals."[32]

Reflecting on the United States in the shadow of COVID-19, journalist George Packer wrote: "Invasion and occupation expose a society's fault lines, exaggerating what goes unnoticed or accepted in peacetime, clarifying essential truths, raising the smell of buried rot."[33] From this perspective, Germany's occupation of European zoos did not alter zoo life but unmasked what it had always been. When push came to shove, zoos across occupied Europe clung to the notion that they did more good open than closed, even as the world burned around them. We can say they did it for the "animals' sake"—and that's undoubtedly true to some extent. Two problems, though: first, zoo directors' decision to stay open invariably lent an air of credibility to the occupation, as Nazi propagandists well knew. And second, clinging to the "animals' sake" argument can take us to some very dark places—places in which outwardly embracing racism and hate might seem a small price to pay to save a waddle of penguins.

Like Animals in a Zoo

Reflecting on the Dutch people, Oscar Mohr wrote in the *New York Times* in August 1940: "Their life could be compared to the fate of animals in a modern zoo. There are no visible fences. The animals are supposed to behave as if they were free, within limits. Their keepers are as correct and humane as possible. They even show a certain liking for the inmates of the vast and beautiful garden. The lower animals every now and then forget their new condition. Domestic animals accept the change with inscrutable placidity."[34]

At first glance, it seems an absurd comparison, especially the bit about German occupying forces being as "correct and humane as possible." Flip the metaphor, however, and Mohr's observation is more unsettling still. Visiting the zoo is like playing tourist in a nation under military occupation. Only the sheep accept their captive status—and every zookeeper looks like a Nazi.

9

American Zoos (Finally) Go to War

In May 1941, a crowd gathered in the Bronx for the opening of the zoo's latest exhibit: a dusty artificial "veldt" stocked with a mix of African wildlife. On hand to celebrate was borough president James J. Lyons, a salesman-turned-politician known for his boisterous laugh and irreverent humor. "I only wish we had Adolf [Hitler] here today," he told reporters, gesturing to the collection of man-eating beasts. "I'd put him over there on that island and see what those lions would do to him."[1]

Such talk was sure to ruffle feathers, even in New York City, ground zero of anti-Nazi sentiment in the United States. Although Jews, communists, and other members of the Popular Front had spent years highlighting the threat posed by fascism in Europe, most Americans wanted no part in the latest conflict raging across the Atlantic. Hitler was, by consensus, a deranged lunatic—vain, fanatical, and absurd to the point of caricature—as were many of his Nazi cronies and hangers-on. Still, as late as July 1941, roughly three-quarters of Americans told pollsters they had little interest in taking up arms on the Allies' behalf.[2]

Zoo men were no exception. Whatever their personal feelings, most US zoo directors felt obliged to adopt a posture of neutrality in world affairs. Stories of foreign zoos under fire were heartbreaking, all agreed. But after a decade of crushing economic depression, few in the zoo industry welcomed the prospect of another war and the problems it would inevitably bring. It was far better to focus on matters closer to home, if only to avoid inflaming unwelcome controversy from patrons. Neutrality made sense for practical reasons as well. Staying out of the fight allowed US zoos greater access to global networks of travel and trade—at least when compared to their rivals. On top of everything else, many of the United States' leading zoo men genuinely liked their foreign counterparts, even those who, for whatever reason, hitched their careers to the Nazi bandwagon. Although only a handful of Americans had been invited to join the prewar association of zoo directors, many had decades-long relationships with fellow zoo men on both sides of the Allied-Axis divide.

No one better embodied this combination of personal friendship and professional neutrality than the United States' chief zookeeper, William M. Mann. At first glance, Mann's life resembles something out of Horatio Alger. Born in Montana, he left home as a teenager to join the circus before eventually turning his boundless energy toward academic pursuits—namely, the study of all things entomological. After earning his doctorate at Harvard, he worked at the US Department of Agriculture (USDA), leading bug-hunting trips to Central America and networking with European colleagues. (He also met his future wife, Lucile [Lucy] Quarry, who was working at the USDA's Bureau of Entomology.) Chosen to head the National Zoo in the mid-1920s, Mann quickly transformed Washington into a hub of zoological diplomacy. When he wasn't busy overseeing the zoo's daily operations, Mann hosted foreign dignitaries, oversaw the exchange of animal "gifts," led high-profile collecting expeditions (to British Guiana, the Dutch East Indies, and Argentina), and shared slideshows of his latest adventures at the White House. All the while, he cultivated friendships around the globe and sought to bolster the National Zoo's standing as a neutral authority in an increasingly fractious world.[3]

In 1938, Bill and Lucy embarked on a three-month tour of northern Europe, from Reykjavik to Moscow, with short sojourns to zoos in France and Switzerland. They spent the bulk of their trip in Germany. Much had changed since their last visit, and not, in the Manns' opinion, for the better. Their close acquaintance, the head of the Nuremburg Zoo, had become a Nazi stooge, "more interested in showing us places in town—the hotel where Hitler stayed or the stadium"—than his animal collection, Lucile Mann recalled. When pressed, their "friends in Germany would say, well, of course, they didn't really approve of their children spending so much time in this youth movement, whatever they called it, but that Hitler had done so many wonderful things for the country."[4] Like many Americans who visited Hitler's Reich in the late 1930s, neither Bill nor Lucy had any sympathy for the cult of Nazism that had entranced so many of their foreign counterparts. Mann nevertheless tried his best to separate the abstractions of national politics from the personal and professional intimacies he forged with his foreign colleagues. Right up until December 1941, many of America's zoo leaders clung to the hope that they could have it both ways—support the nation's allies without alienating its future enemies.

For all that, American zookeepers were determined "not [to] be caught napping" if war ever did come.[5] They had two things going for them. The first was that they had experienced a world war before and had survived virtually unscathed. Starting in 1917, zoos across the United States had thrown themselves into the war effort. At the Bronx Zoo, staff hosted recruitment drives and extolled the virtues of military participation. Members of the Red Cross sewed bandages in the lion house, while fresh-faced recruits staged military drills on the main lawn. When night fell, zoo personnel armed with Springfield carbines patrolled the grounds to thwart "civil disorders" and other threats.[6]

More relevant still, American zoo folk had had several years to learn from their foreign counterparts. From 1939 forward, Mann and his contemporaries collected every scrap of info they could, if only to get a head start on future defense plans. The London Zoo proved to be especially important—not only because of Julian Huxley's close ties with several American zoo men, but also because of the global publicity of its various war-related measures. Indeed, throughout the war years, American zoo directors would look at London as both a model and something against which to measure their own fates.[7]

Such was Mann's confidence in US neutrality that, in early 1940, he and Lucy journeyed to Liberia at the behest of rubber magnate Harvey Firestone, whose company leased a million-acre latex plantation in the area.[8] Once a colony for repatriated African American freemen, the West African country was a prime hunting ground for exotic wildlife. Newsreels taken at the time show a lanky-kneed Bill decked out in a pith helmet and shorts, Lucy in cinched trousers—stereotypes of white middle-class adventurers on the hunt. Costuming aside, the expedition bore little resemblance to the "safaris" of Hollywood films or pulp magazines. The first couple of American zookeeping spent days

Figure 9.1. William Mann (*pith helmet left*), cigarette in hand, and Lucile Quarry Mann (*pith helmet right*) during the 1940 Smithsonian-Firestone Expedition to Liberia. Also pictured in this scene are the village's Muslim priest (*far left*); Boima Quaue, a Gola chief (*center*); and Fermetah, the chief's "favorite wife." Smithsonian Institution Archives, Record Unit 7293, William M. Mann and Lucile Quarry Mann Papers, Image No. SIA2009-0984.

trekking from village to village, litter-bearers in tow ("our boys," as Lucy called them), trying to barter for whatever locals had on hand.[9] There were setbacks—false leads, empty nests, and more than a fair share of dead and dying specimens—but this was to be expected. Animal collection was a numbers game, and even the most successful expedition inevitably left a trail of broken bodies in its wake.* Still, Lucy did not hide her contempt when their African hosts came up short. Upon being presented with a "[civet] cat with a broken back and a francolin with a broke leg," she confided in her diary: "These people have no idea of how to catch animals or care for them."[10] (They ate the francolin, nonetheless.)

---

* At one point, Lucy Mann recounted in her diary, an army of fast-moving driver ants invaded the animal holding pen and killed a pair of duikers, a breed of small sub-Saharan antelopes, swarming in the poor beasts' ears and eye sockets and down their throats until the duikers' torsos were completely stiff. The native workers used blow torches to clear the scene. Lucile Mann's Diary, April 7, 1940, 31.

Even in Liberia, the Manns could not escape the war forever. Following the Wehrmacht's invasion of Holland, European colonies across West Africa hardened their borders. Normal levels of political intrigue turned to open hostility. Rumors spread that the Manns had led a "band of Germans to within three miles of the frontier" to provoke an "international crisis."[11] (A doctor in their party happened to be German by birth.) The Americans pleaded their innocence (and, in Lucy's words, wished that "Roosevelt would stop promising aid to the Allies until we get home").[12] Nevertheless, they struggled to find safe passage back to the States. Entering French West Africa on the eve of France's capitulation, they waited for weeks as British ships surrounded Dakar Harbor, checking all boats going in and out. All the while, their living bounty weltered in the equatorial heat. Finally, in midsummer, the Manns managed to gain permission to leave. As their ship steamed out to sea, a large American flag recently painted on its bow, Bill and Lucy could take comfort that the United States was still neutral—but not for long.

Tora! Tora! Tora! (Tiger! Tiger! Tiger!)

On December 7, 1941, American zoo men's dreams of escaping of World War II came to an end. Within hours of the Japanese bombing of Pearl Harbor, news of the attack reverberated across the zoo world, setting off a whir of defense-oriented activity.

Priority number one was prepping their facilities against the threat of aerial bombardment. In San Diego, a few thousand miles to the northeast of Honolulu, workers built makeshift bomb shelters and shielded the zoo's glass snake house behind metal shutters.[13] To protect against incendiaries, Philadelphia Zoo staff assembled firefighting equipment and hauled heavy sandbags into each exhibit building.[14] William Mann, meanwhile, distributed a lengthy set of air raid instructions to all National Zoo employees. If enemy planes were approaching, the zoo's signal system would deliver a "steady blast of horns," warning staff to get to their posts.[15]

Zoos also tried to make themselves as inconspicuous as possible, especially when viewed through an enemy bombsight. Workers in Seattle painted the zoo's boilers, making them virtually invisible (they hoped) to Japanese night raiders.[16] Cincinnati Zoo staff, for their part, installed a "special lighting and communication system to enable its personnel to react quickly in the event of a blackout."[17]

Not surprisingly, the brunt of zoos' security measures was felt most keenly by the animals themselves, their already circumscribed lives made even more so in the name of civil defense. The Bronx Zoo's nightly ritual, for example, included chaining the elephant herd and locking up all big cats in "steel and concrete compartments."[18]

Today, we might characterize many of these efforts as "security theater" designed to project an image of safety to a frightened and paranoid public. In a 1942 interview, William Mann called the National Zoo the "safest place in town," a refrain echoed throughout World War II–era America. The exhibit basements—brutalist caverns often used to store food and tools—formed "natural air-raid shelters," and a seven-foot fence surrounded the property. At night, he joked, the zoo was "so black" that passing enemy planes "may think we're something important and bomb us." (Mann also said he'd been in contact with Julian Huxley, who reassured him that talk of war's danger was overblown.)[19] That same February, Mann joined a local radio show to deliver a similar message. Working from a script, he told the audience: "A bomb big enough to break the walls of a Zoo building would more than likely kill the animals inside. But just in case—we have our guns well oiled."[20]

Locked and Loaded

Mann's comments hinted at one of the most consequential debates American zookeepers would face during World War II: whether to destroy their "dangerous" animals to prevent their escape. The possibility of animal escape is built into the modern zoo and is partly responsible for its appeal. In approaching a caged beast, visitors can experience a charge of fear and danger knowing full well that they are safe. The idea that a stray bomb might set loose a man-eating tiger or a venomous snake changes that calculation. A fugitive animal represents a transgression of the zoo's spatial order—a threat to the fiction of managed and disciplined wildness that zoos seek to offer.[21] "Bombs would be bad enough, or wild animals or big snakes," one nervous DC resident complained, "but having them together sure gives you the creeps."[22] Why not go ahead and eliminate the threat of traumatized zoo animals before it's too late?

It was a question that divided the world of American zoos. Many zoo leaders, like Seattle's Gus Knudson, privately dismissed the hazards posed by escaped animals. Seattle residents faced "more danger from fifth-columnists who might be in our city than from the animals in the zoological park," he reported in 1942. In public, however, Knudson sang a different tune, grudgingly acceding to the philosophy that it was better to be safe than sorry. Citing the threat of "aerial bombardment," staff in Seattle destroyed the zoo's collection of venomous snakes and sawed off the antlers of all male hoofed animals, depriving them of their "fighting weapons."[23] Other zoos made similar calculations, especially in the early days of the conflict. On the theory that a bomb could crack the glass of the reptile house, William Mann decided to evacuate the zoo's collection of venomous reptiles to St. Louis—at least until the coast was clear.[24] As long as America was under threat, the National Zoo would display only "fixed" (defanged) snakes.[25]

Ultimately, most American zoos decided against preemptively slaughtering their animal stock. Their rationales had little to do with animal welfare. Air raid drills notwithstanding, few zoo men believed they were in real danger of enemy attack. Sabotage was always a possibility, but Berlin and Tokyo were half a world away, out of reach of long-range bombers.[26] Others pointed to the experience of the London Zoo, which despite suffering several direct blows had thus far managed to prevent the flight of its man-eating beasts.[27] If anything, the London Zoo's track record suggested that zebras and antelopes—more dangerous to themselves than to humans—were far more likely to flee than the lions, tigers, and bears of public nightmares. Still others in the American zoo community took solace in the irony that many zoos were rendered escape-proof by conditions that, in normal times, made zoo-keeping so onerous. As French ornithologist Jean Delacour explained to reporters in December 1941, New York City's cold winter climate would kill off any poisonous snakes—often the locus of public fears about animal escape—that managed to elude capture.[28]

Above all else, the preemptive killing of their animals struck zoo leaders as a form of professional capitulation to public fear. As they saw it, zoo men were in a constant battle against the ignorance of the visitors, politicians, and city leaders on whom their livelihood depended. It wasn't that long ago that zoos were viewed as little more than menageries, entertainment venues on par with freak shows. For the past half century, the American zoo industry, increasingly led by PhDs of one sort or another, had attempted to claw its way toward scientific and professional legitimacy. Writing not long after Pearl Harbor, the Brookfield Zoo's Robert Bean advised his colleague in Philadelphia to ignore the "foolhardy blast" of zoos' critics.[29] To relent to public pressure now would be a sign of professional cowardice, an admission that the William Manns and Gus Knudsons of the world were little more than the carnival barkers of old, dressed up in fancy titles. If anything, now was the time to hold on to one's animals as long as possible. The National Zoo had already lost four Indian elephants (missing after the Japanese capture of Penang) and one rhino ("stranded" at the Calcutta Zoo) since the Pearl Harbor attack.[30] Who knew how long American zoos would have to make do with what they had on hand?

Nevertheless, US zoos went out of their way to publicize their willingness to do their duty when the time came. In Cincinnati, home of the second-oldest zoo in the country, zoo superintendent John F. Heusser declared that "the Zoo force is prepared to destroy animals that would be a menace if they should get out."[31] The Detroit Zoo organized a "air-strike squad" to kill its captive animals at the first hint of danger, while Floyd S. Young, director of Chicago's Lincoln Park Zoo, promised to destroy all "fierce muscular primates" in the event of an air raid.[32] In Seattle, zoo guards' arsenal of weapons included a "38-Colt revolver, [a] 35-Remington rifle, and shot guns," all of which they planned to use "in case of necessity." The San Diego Zoo, similarly, vowed to halt an "animal stampede" before it got started. Describing the zoo's contingency plans, executive secretary Belle Benchley stressed that each member of the zoo staff "is equipped with a high-powered gun, which he will use if it becomes necessary to prevent danger to the public." The message was clear: if the war ever reached US soil, zoo animals would be among the first home-front casualties.

Racist Zoos and "Moronic Visitors"

Yet bombs were the least of zoos' problems. The start of World War II threatened to shine a spotlight on some of the uglier dimensions of

American zookeeping. The first was US zoos' long and sordid history of racism. Since the late nineteenth century, a small coterie of ideologues, "race scientists," and eugenicists had played an outsized role in shaping the nation's largest zoological collections. Naturalist and white supremacist Madison Grant not only helped found the Bronx Zoo but also authored the 1916 "Nordic" manifesto *The Passing of the Great Race*, among the most influential racist tracts of its time. (Hitler called the book his "bible.")[33] Grant's friend, Henry Fairfield Osborn Sr., president of the American Museum of Natural History and father of longtime New York Zoological Society president Henry Fairfield Osborn Jr., derided Jews, demonized the working class, and singled out the "blue eyed, fair-haired peoples of the north of Europe" for their unique capacity for "leadership," "courage," and "self-sacrifice."[34] Like Edgar Rice Burroughs's *Tarzan* series, zoos imagined a battle between modern civilization—the place where people encounter lions in pulp novels and iron cages—and the "wild," a savage, hostile, unknowable domain inhabited by exotic beasts and primitive (read: nonwhite) people.

As if to drive this point home, many zoos relied upon what public historian Robert R. Weyeneth calls "spatial strategies of white supremacy" to exclude, isolate, and segregate African American visitors.[35] When it opened in 1890, Atlanta's Grant Park Zoo featured a building with separate aisles (and presumably separate doors) for white and Black visitors.[36] Memphis's Overton Park Zoo was for "whites only," except on Tuesdays.[37] In 1939, the Oklahoma City Zoo designated each Thursday as "Negroes' Day." (Prior to that, Blacks were admitted only by appointment.)[38] That same year, officials at the New Orleans Audubon Zoo instructed employees to keep African Americans "moving all the time" (no sitting, no loitering, no congregating in groups) to discourage their attendance.[39]

To be sure, racial segregation was par for the course in the 1940s, especially in the South. Throughout the war years, notes historian Christine Knauer, "the military went out of its way to uphold segregation and to degrade black men and women in any way possible."[40] Indeed, some white visitors complained that the nation's zoos weren't segregated *enough*. In June 1941, Alfred Lawton, the secretary of Senator Ellison D. Smith (South Carolina), wrote a caustic letter to William Mann after his family was seated near a table of African American visitors.

"While it is true that certain high government officials are preaching social and political equality," Lawton ranted, "it still remains a fact that no decent white person is going to eat with negroes."[41] At a time when American propagandists were eager to draw clear and fast lines between the United States and its fascist adversaries, such sentiments proved to be an embarrassment at best, a wartime liability at worst. Yes, German zoos banned Jewish visitors; but, as America's enemies loved to point out, the United States' history of racial discrimination was, if anything, worse by comparison.

The United States' entrance into World War II also renewed concerns about the violent behavior of zoo patrons. All zoos must grapple with vandalism and animal abuse. Locked in their cages, wings clipped, instincts dulled, zoo animals have few protections against visitors bent on wreaking havoc. Sociologists Bob Mullan and Garry Marvin have described vandalism as the logical "end point" of zoo-goers' demand for attention.[42] If you can't catch a monkey's eye, pound on the glass, throw a rock, or toss a lit cigarette into the cage—anything to provoke a response. After all, what good is a zoo if the captive animals refuse to put on a show?

During World War II, American zoo directors noted an uptick in anti-animal violence. Visitor behavior ranged from the casually cruel to the borderline sociopathic. At the Waikiki Bird Park (now the Honolulu Zoo), visitors "poked at the birds with sticks and threw gravel at the tortoises."[43] Seattle's Gus Knudson recounted stories of malicious teens harassing animals with BB guns and "writing obscene words" on zoo property.[44] In Sacramento, vandals at the William Land Park Zoo shot an ostrich with a .22, leaving the animal to die in its pen; while, over the course of three evenings in June 1944, nighttime raiders at the Albuquerque Zoo freed seventy pheasants, set loose four buffalo, sliced the throat of a deer, and tried to cut the chains on the lion cage.[45] Decades later, Lucile Mann recalled with disgust the fate of a London Zoo sea lion that had been shipped to DC for safekeeping only to be stoned to death by vandals. "Why there is vandalism in a zoo I cannot understand," Mann exclaimed in exasperation.[46]

At the time, many observers chalked up such abuse to a rising tide of war-induced juvenile delinquency.[47] With moms working and dads in uniform, American youth were falling prey to a "spirit of recklessness and violence," experts warned.[48] Throughout the war years, the press published lurid stories of teens gone wild—smoking weed, mouthing off to adults, having sex, and getting up to all manner of no good.[49] To a juvenile delinquent looking to cause mischief, a caged lion or exhibited monkey might have seemed an easy target, particularly given public fears at the time. "Certainly our caged animals have to bear enough, what with a loss of freedom and motion, without being subjected to foolishness from wild persons outside the cages," objected one outraged columnist in 1944.[50]

Ernest Untermann was one of the loudest critics of "moronic visitors" to the nation's zoos. Born in Germany in 1881, he came to the United States a decade later and spent his early adulthood as a sailor. Unable (or unwilling) to settle down, he spent time in East Africa, attended the Chicago Art Institute, journeyed to Utah as a mining engineer, and painted images of Jurassic dinosaurs before assuming the role of director at Milwaukee's Washington Park Zoo.[51] A veteran of radical politics (he corresponded frequently with writer Joan London and other members of the interwar Popular Front), Untermann described visitors' behavior as a product of a diseased culture. "The zoo, like the school, has to combat the monkey in man and the false standards of conduct implanted into young minds by fiction writers, movie scenarios, stage heroes and crudely glorified historical characters," he railed, reflecting a disdain for mass culture common among some sectors of the Left. "So we have all sorts of young Buffalo Bills, Kit Carsons . . . Dillingers and Capones stalking the animals in the zoo and putting on airs of injured innocence when caught tormenting and hurting them."[52] In Untermann's mind, zoos functioned as an outlet for cruelty, a stage on which visitors could live out their fantasies of violence with few social repercussions.

Beasts Ablaze

In February 1940, having just left New York en route to West Africa, Lucy Mann flipped on the radio and listened in horror. Amid the constant stream of "British and German propaganda" came a news bulletin about a fire at the winter headquarters of the Cole Brothers' circus near Rochester, Indiana.[53] Unwilling to turn the "man-eating beasts, maddened by fire, loose on an unarmed countryside," the circus's fifty-plus employees could do little more than watch them burn—two tigers, six lions, two black leopards, one hundred monkeys, fifteen antelopes, and a pygmy hippopotamus, "slowly boiled to death in his tank."[54] Two years later, scores of animals met a similar fate during a live performance at the Ringling Brothers' circus in Cleveland. As an audience of five thousand watched in horror, flames swept through the menagerie. Although workers were able to save a pair of prized gorillas, other animals died in agony. "Terrified beasts roasted alive in their cages. Others horribly burned, plaintively waited for keepers, policemen and Coast Guardsmen to end their misery," the Associated Press reported. (One elephant, its skin blackened, had to be shot eight times in the brain before it would die.) By the time it was over, the dead and injured included a small zoo's worth of exotic creatures, "many of them irreplaceable now because of war conditions."[55]

It's tempting to draw parallels between the helpless creatures "roasted alive" beneath the big top and their zoo cousins caged abroad. Both were made unnaturally vulnerable by decisions beyond their control—foremost, the decision to hold them captive in the first place. From the animals' perspective, it did not matter whether their deaths were products of keeper error or a chain of political decisions reaching back decades. Smoke was smoke. Fire was fire.

For what it's worth, World War II–era Americans took some comfort in knowing that the bulk of their exotic animal death came at their own hands and not at the hands of the nation's enemies. Along the vast archipelago of zoos and menageries from Japan to Australia, however, zoo-lovers weren't so lucky.

10

Helpless Gazelles and Beasts on the Hunt

On December 16, 1941, the SS *Manini*, an American cargo ship bound for Auckland, steamed out of Pearl Harbor. Manned by a crew of thirteen merchant marines, and quickly painted gray to camouflage it from above, the freighter joined a convoy heading west, the wide Pacific now a battlefield in a global war. The following day, somewhere east of Guam, a torpedo launched from an Imperial Japanese submarine pierced the ship's hull. As water flooded into the ship's lower passages, the crew raced for the lifeboats. Among the lost cargo was a pair of porcupines from the Toronto Zoo. Natives of Canada's vast forests and facing a future of permanent captivity in New Zealand, they perished like so many in the newest theater of World War II: thousands of miles from home and subject to events beyond their comprehension and control.[1]

The conflict that historians have come to call the Pacific War doesn't easily fit within the popular understanding of World War II. Many in the United States like to think of World War II as a "good war," perhaps *the* "Good War," everything a military conflict could and should be. Frank Capra's 1942 propaganda film *Prelude to War* framed World War II as an epic saga of good versus evil—the "free world" of Boy Scouts and Sunday school versus the "slave world" of Hitler Youth and mass delusion. The story was never quite so simple, of course. Nazi Germany did not have a stranglehold on antisemitism and, for all Churchill's braying about freedom, the British had no interest in extending their airy ideals to the empire's colonial possessions. Under dictator Joseph Stalin, communist forces starved, murdered, or disappeared millions of perceived enemies, and the US armed forces cared more about appeasing racists at home—even the blood banks were segregated—than maximizing their potential to fight Hitler. Despite that, many continue to view World War II as their nation's finest hour: the fascist Axis on the rampage, the Allies in retreat, and the apple pie–eating Americans (or, in the Soviet telling, the selfless volunteers of Mother Russia) saving the day.[2]

The vast tangle of battles, invasions, and retreats that took place in Asia and Oceania, on the other hand, lacked chronological or even geographical fixedness. In 1931, eight years before the Nazi *Blitzkrieg* into Poland, Japanese Imperial Forces occupied Manchuria. Half a decade later, in July 1937, the Japanese military clashed with the Chinese National Revolutionary Army outside of Beijing, the start of a broader conflict. That December, the Japanese Imperial Army took the Chinese city of Nanjing, setting off one of the greatest scenes of mass slaughter in the twentieth century. At a time when Europeans still clung to promises of international peace, Japanese soldiers raped, mutilated, and slaughtered tens of thousands of civilians, dumping their victims' bodies into mass graves. By late 1941, Japanese forces were spread out over thousands of miles and had been fighting for more than a decade. Only Western self-centeredness allows us to cling to the notion that war in the Pacific began on December 7, 1941.

Likewise, much about the Pacific War resists the comforting narratives of occupation and liberation so central to Western memory of the conflict. Outside Mainland China, a nation wrecked by internal conflict, much of Japan's newly conquered empire had been under "alien rule" for decades.[3] East Asia and the Pacific Region was a patchwork of imperial holdings—including the Philippines (held by the United States), Vietnam (then French-occupied Indochina), and Burma, Singapore, and India (all under the control of Great Britain). In time, Japanese propagandists would attempt to sell the war in anti-imperial terms, promising the expansion of a Greater East Asia Co-Prosperity Sphere to ensure "Asia for the Asiatics." The project failed, in no small part because Japanese leaders had little actual interest in sharing the prosperity. Rather, observes John Dower in his classic study *War without Mercy*, "It was the intention of the Japanese to establish permanent domination over all other races and peoples in

Asia—in accordance with their needs, and as befitted their destiny as a superior race."[4]

For all that, the Pacific War is best understood as a cluster of imperial conflicts—between Japan and its Asian rivals, between nascent Yamato imperialism and the self-proclaimed "white man's burden" of European colonial powers, and between Japanese and American ambitions to exercise military and economic control of the Pacific—in which the region's zoos were invariably bound up.

Imperial Holdings

At the start of World War II, many of the zoos in the Pacific Theater were products of the region's centuries-long history with European colonial exploitation. Although royals and elites had always collected animals for amusement, a number of the first Asian and Australian zoos date from the Victorian era (Chennai in 1855, Melbourne in 1857, Saigon in 1864, Lahore in 1872, Calcutta in 1875), when they were introduced to serve as entertainment for colonial administrators and their families.[5] Others opened their gates in the early twentieth century, as members of the overseas establishment sought to recreate Anglo-European institutions. In the minds of the colonial elite of Sydney, Mysore, Bombay, and Perth, no "modern city" was complete without a proper zoo, aquarium, or both.[6] Built to mimic in miniature their counterparts in London and Paris, colonial zoos, to quote critic Randy Malamud, served as both "model[s] of empire (where humanity holds dominion over lesser species arrayed for our pleasure, our betterment, our *use*) and simultaneously as . . . metaphor[s] for the larger, more important imperial enterprises in the sociopolitical hierarchy amid which it flourishes."[7] Put another way, we cannot chalk up the founding of zoos in colonial Asia and Oceania to the abundance of native wildlife. Zoos in French Indochina, British-controlled India, and the Dutch East Indies were just as "foreign" as the people who ran them.

Consider, for example, William Lawrence Soma Basapa's lifelong effort to introduce European-style zookeeping to colonial Singapore. Born in 1893, Basapa grew up as part of the small community of wealthy Indian entrepreneurs and landowners that had immigrated to Singapore in the nineteenth century. In 1922, the self-confessed Anglophile established a private zoo on his one-acre estate. Six years later, he purchased a plot of land at Punggol, a peninsula across the channel from mainland Malaysia, where he opened an expanded zoo to the public.[8] More British than the British, Basapa liked to sport a white suit and neat mustache, and he was known to entertain guests from around the globe. (Albert Einstein dropped by his private zoo in 1922.)[9] Not all foreign visitors appreciated Basapa's attempt to import European zookeeping to the tropics, to be sure. French playwright Jean Cocteau, in 1936, observed sadly that the zoo's recently captured tiger, Apay, had already "learned the obedience that colonial rule demanded."[10]

Nevertheless, the Punggol Zoo quickly became one of the most popular tourist attractions in prewar Singapore. Its collection included both local captures and animals imported from abroad—seals from California, polar bears from Germany, and a cigarette-smoking chimp, among others—many of which Basapa donated to the nearby Raffles Natural History Museum upon their deaths.[11] In the 1930s, Basapa's zoo served as an important hub in the global trade in animals from Southeast Asia. Dubbed the "Animal Man" of Singapore, Basapa hosted William Mann at his home and exchanged animals with counterparts in Australia, British India, and the United States.[12] At the highpoint of its fame, director J. C. "Doc" Cook shot a B-movie adventure on the grounds of Punggol Zoo. Released in 1934, the film was a mishmash of imperialist tropes: man-eating animals, white women in danger, half-naked natives—with Basapa himself featured in publicity shots wrestling a dead python.[13]

No Asian nation embraced zoos more enthusiastically in the run-up to World War II than Japan. The nation's first *dobutsu-en* (zoo), Tokyo's Ueno Imperial Zoological Gardens, was founded in 1882, less than fifteen years after the Meiji Restoration ended two and a half centuries of *sakoku* (self-imposed isolation) from the West. Throughout the late nineteenth century, Japanese leaders rushed to modernize, importing the latest technological know-how to jumpstart their military and industrial prowess. *Sakoku*'s legacies did not disappear overnight, of course. To this day, observes critic and historian Ken Kawata, Japanese zoo culture displays a kind of "outpost mentality," more concerned with acquiring "ABC mammals" (the kind that sell tickets) than cooperating with their international colleagues. "Japan's process of

Helpless Gazelles and Beasts on the Hunt   131

borrowing [from the West] has historically been selective; as in many other fields, zoos' borrowing has been superficial."[14]

One way that Japanese zoos *did* mirror their European counterparts, however, was in their intimate connection to imperial expansion. Following its victory in the Russo-Japanese War of 1904–1905, Japan used its military might to broaden its territorial influence in the region—with the nation's zoos reaping the rewards. Like the National Zoo in Washington, DC, whose collections swelled with the rise of American empire in the Caribbean and the Pacific, Tokyo's Ueno Zoo "expanded together with the nation's reach overseas, offering visitors an increasingly elaborate figuration of Japan's imperial project," writes historian Ian Jared Miller. "As the empire grew, so too the means by which the zoo acquired new specimens."[15] At the start of World War II, Japan had fifteen major zoos at home, along with three overseas—in Taiwan (relinquished to Japan in 1895), Korea (annexed in 1910, though under Japanese "protection" since 1905), and Manchukuo (invaded in 1931). In 1909, Japanese zoo-builders tore down parts of Seoul's Changgyeong Palace, which dated to the fifteenth century, to make room for a new zoo-park complex meant to rival Ueno Park. Taipei's Yuanshan Zoo opened to the public a few years later. Though little more than a series of dome-shaped iron cages and fenced pens, the government-run zoo nevertheless proved popular with citizens, who liked to visit at night to escape the summer heat.[16]

From the very beginning, then, the story of Asian zoos in World War II was primed to look different than in Europe or even the United States. Spread out over thousands of miles, Asian zoos were, for the most part, colonial imports, symbols of the continent's *already-occupied* status.

Feeding Deer Guts to the Carp

In the days following the attack on Pearl Harbor, Hawaii, Japanese Imperial Forces assaulted Hong Kong, Manila, and the Dutch East Indies, forcing the colonial Allied forces into hasty retreat. Popular American military history often leaves the impression that the war in the Pacific was largely a rural, if not amphibious, affair. However, the opening weeks of the war were marked by a series of assaults and sieges on colonial holdings and cities. This meant inevitable civilian casualties and, for zoos, the very real threat of invasion and occupation.

Looking down the barrel of a Japanese takeover, several Southeast Asian zoos followed the British and Dutch examples of preemptively slaughtering their most dangerous animals. Only a week after the Pearl Harbor attack, with Japanese troops moving south into British Malaysia, Tunku Ismail, the son of Sultan Ibrahim of Johor, ordered the destruction of the Johor Zoo's carnivore collection.[17] The following month, a similar scene played out at the Rangoon (Burma) Zoo, located in a park memorializing Queen Victoria. Describing the tense days leading up to the Japanese arrival, British civil servant Leslie Glass recalled:

> Every Japanese air raid increased the steady stream northwards of the city population, and more and more institutions ground to a standstill. One afternoon, I joined in a bizarre and melancholy foray to shoot all dangerous animals in the zoo, as all their keepers had decamped. Tigers, panthers and poisonous snakes were killed and the deer released in the park, except for one which we shot for fresh meat. When we had gutted the poor beast, we threw its entrails into the lake and great fish thrashed and swirled in the course of their unusual meal.[18]

Marching into the colonial outpost a few days later, the Associated Press reported, Japanese occupation forces butchered the giraffes and rhinoceros and attempted to "liberate" the few remaining monkeys and birds, although the "little captives declined the opportunity to escape."[19]

By February 1942, some 30,000 Japanese troops had approached the outskirts of Singapore, home of one of the largest Royal Naval bases. Readying for the Japanese assault, the British military commandeered the grounds of the Punggol Zoo, giving W. L. S. Basapa twenty-four hours to evacuate as many animals as he could. When this proved impossible, soldiers threw open the cages, shooed away the birds and small mammals, and shot the rest. (Basapa never recovered from his loss and died the following year.)[20] On February 15, 1942, more than 80,000 Commonwealth forces surrendered to the Japanese military, a

Australian Arks

On November 15, 1941, a little less than a month before the start of the Japanese Offensive, General Sir Thomas Blamey, commander of the Australian Imperial Force in the Middle East, spoke to a radio station about his recent homecoming: "And to come from that atmosphere and its scenes back to Australia gives one the most extraordinary feeling of helplessness. You are like—here in this country—a lot of gazelles grazing in a dell on the edge of a jungle, while the beasts of prey are working toward you, apparently unseen, unnoticed. And it is the law of the jungle that they spring upon you, merciless."[22] For Blamey, the Commonwealth of Australia was, to use another animal metaphor, a sitting duck, the next inevitable victim of Axis aggression. Over the course of the war, however, many foreigners came to see Australia—with its curious-sounding locals, its relative geographic safety, its agreeable climate, and its well-kept zoos—as an island refuge, just beyond the reach of the war's terrors.

Australia's reputation as a wartime sanctuary began to take shape in the summer of 1940. Eager to safeguard British children from the Blitz, the Children's Overseas Reception Board (CORB) evacuated thousands of youngsters to the far corners of the empire, where (presumably) they could wait out the conflict in relative comfort. In August 1940, one of the most famous evacuee ships, the Polish ocean liner MS *Batory*, left Liverpool on a winding trip around the Horn of Africa to friendly harbors in India, Southeast Asia, and the Australian Commonwealth. Part security measure, part propaganda stunt, the CORB used the voyage of the *Batory* to sell a vision of imperial resilience in the face of Nazi aggression. Onboard the "singing ship," as the vessel was later nicknamed, kids belted out patriotic songs, wrote letters to their parents, and conducted emergency lifeboat drills.[23] At every stop, the young evacuees were led ashore for mandatory ceremonies, mandatory speeches from local politicians, and mandatory fun—all of it faithfully recorded and photographed for public consumption back home. "It was really geared for adults, not kiddies of four," reflected

Figure 10.1. Zoo excursions were a regular part of the itineraries of evacuee children from Great Britain. This photo (c. October 1940) shows a group of English evacuees on a trip to the zoo in Melbourne, Australia. Images such as these, relayed throughout the English-speaking world, helped cement Australia's image as a refuge in a world beset by war. Australia War Memorial.

one passenger years later. "Here we go again, another bus, another cream bun, and another zoo."[24]

When the *Batory* finally reached Port Melbourne after weeks at sea, a film crew from *British Pathé* was on hand to capture the event. The subsequent newsreel depicts the evacuees' journey as a kind of school holiday: all smiling and cheering and giddy excitement. Now "far removed from the horrors of aerial warfare," the narrator reassures us, the children spill down the gangplank—some to their "good-hearted hosts," the rest to (where else?) the nearby city zoo, a playground of normalcy in a violent world. Against a jaunty score, kids ride an elephant, watch a monkey rodeo routine, and frolic in the antipodean sunshine. In case anyone missed the point, the newsreel briefly turns to a well-scrubbed lad holding a metal canister. "It's just my old respirator," he explains. "I don't think I'll need it anymore."[25]

The start of the Japanese Offensive a few months later threatened to undo Australia's reputation as an imperial ark. On February 19, 1942, two waves of Mitsubishi G4M2 bombers—the same type that struck Pearl Harbor—attacked the Northern Territory capital of Darwin, killing roughly 250 people. A few months after that, three Japanese midget subs shelled the Sydney suburbs, piercing the city's veil of invulnerability.[26] Despite such attacks, both Australian and US media promoted the Commonwealth as an ideal spot to rest and recover in between battles. Much like in occupied Paris, where vacationing German soldiers were encouraged to skip the dance halls in favor of more "healthy" amusements, zoos occupied a singular place on the Australian home front. Over the course of the war, more than a million Americans passed through Australia and New Zealand—many with little to do and nowhere to go.[27] After the US military set up a motor camp just outside the Auckland Zoo, uniformed Yanks made up "more than half" of the zoo's Sunday visitors.[28] In September 1942, Taronga Park Zoo's Robert Anthony Patten told a reporter that attendance numbers had exploded since the US arrival. Americans are a "great zoo people," he explained matter-of-factly. "Servicemen of all nations are now the zoo's greatest patrons," outnumbering even children.[29]

Although some locals complained of "isolated cases of drunkenness and disorderly behavior" among off-duty GIs, Commonwealth zoos were happy for both the influx of cash and the boost to their wartime esteem.[30] Australian newspapers published photos of celebrity zoo visitors, including Arthur MacArthur, son of the commander of US Forces in the Far East, and First Lady Eleanor Roosevelt, who dropped by the Taronga Park Zoo before lunching with American casualties of the recent campaigns in New Guinea.[31] Indeed, wartime productions like *Australia Is Like This*, a documentary short produced by the Australian Department of Information and the US Army Signal Corps, made visiting the zoo seem like one of the Commonwealth's national pastimes.[32]

Like their counterparts in North America, Australian zoos were reluctant to destroy their most dangerous (and often most expensive) animal attractions. Early in the war, the Melbourne Zoo announced plans to "put down" its large carnivores, though only in the event of an air raid.[33] The Perth Zoo did the same, instructing keepers to "kill if in doubt about an animal's ferocity," but its director dismissed such measures as unnecessary: "Most animals would be too busy trying to find safety to bother about the public."³⁴ Not all locals appreciated the wait-and-see attitude. "A zoo, however interesting, is undesirable in a congested residential area, even in peacetime," wrote one South Perth resident dismissively in February 1942. "It is a positive menace in time of war. The safety of citizens must be considered before the monetary value of Zoo animals."³⁵

Even so, Australian zoo directors balked at succumbing to public hysteria. Ultimately, the Commonwealth's air raid precautions reflected a mix of hard-nosed practicality, wishful thinking, species preference, and old-fashioned patriotism. If Japanese bombers ever appeared over Adelaide, for example, the plan was to shoot the zoo's lions, tigers, leopards, and jackals; allow the inmates of the Dogs' Rescue Home to ride out the attack in their kennels ("fully protected

Figure 10.2. This publicity photo captures a visibly nervous Eleanor Roosevelt holding Bully the koala at Sydney's Taronga Park Zoo in September 1943. Although not entirely comfortable with the grumpy animal (Bully had left his keeper with visible scratches), the First Lady donned a pair of gloves and gamely did her duty. FDR National Library, United States.

Figure 10.3. A female Red Cross volunteer leads a group of off-duty GIs on a tour of a private zoo in Mackay, Queensland. Photos such as this one helped perpetuate the image of the camera-clicking US serviceman as an innocent abroad, more interested in taking snapshots of local wildlife than sowing his wild oats. Australia War Memorial.

against anything but a direct hit"); and evacuate the residents of the North Adelaide Koala Farm to one of "three different sanctuaries" in the hills outside the city.[36] If only one species could be saved, there was no doubt about which one to pick.

◉ ◉

By early summer 1942, Japanese Imperial Forces controlled vast swathes of the Pacific, from the Aleutian Islands in the far north to New Guinea, Timor, and the Solomon Islands roughly 5,000 miles to the south. In a matter of months, Japan had managed to break the back of Euro-American imperialism throughout much of Asia, occupying British Hong Kong, booting US forces out of the Philippines, and undoing more than a century of Dutch rule in the East Indies.

Within months, the US naval victory at Midway would turn the tide of the war in the Pacific, putting the Japanese on the defensive. Even so, the world's zoo men knew better than to hope for a quick end to the conflict. Still reeling from the war's early years, zoos around the globe settled down to a more familiar battle—against privation, lack of resources, and, above all, perceptions of irrelevance.

PART III

Commissary and Administration (Staff Only)

11

Domestic Worries

On May 30, 1942, Robert Anthony Patten, chief warden of Sydney's Taronga Park Zoo, huddled with his staff, bracing for death. Outside, he could hear a cacophony of sounds: the roar of shells fired from a Japanese submarine, the concussive explosions of depth charges, and the shrieks of caged "Jungle beasts." While keepers tried their best to calm the frenzied animals, Patten debated whether to authorize the slaughter of "thousands of pounds' worth" of lions, tigers, and other potential man-eaters. It was a gamble either way. Pull the trigger now and Sydney risked empty cages until the war's end. Hold off and run the danger of an enemy shell setting loose a bunch of hungry carnivores in an already terrified city. In the end, Patten rolled the dice, and the zoo's venomous snakes and big cats got to live another day, for whatever that was worth. However, as a local reporter noted not long after, the close call with the Japanese sub was the least of Taronga Park's troubles: "The war has brought other problems—the man-power and business worries of the employer, along with the domestic worries, magnified a hundred times, of the housewife."[1]

The start of World War II brought zoos a host of new challenges. Thanks to dwindling capital investment, many zoos had to shelve much-needed building projects, often to the detriment of animal health. Shipping restrictions made it nearly impossible to acquire the charismatic megafauna—the lions, elephants, giraffes—upon which zoos thrived. Zoos that depended on automobile traffic were hit hard by shortages of fuel and tire rubber. Even zoos spared the threat of bombing felt the pinch. In New Zealand, staff at the Auckland Zoo had to stop printing the guidebook because of lack of paper.[2]

142   Chapter 11

Of zoos' many "domestic worries," none provoked more sleepless nights, among zoo staff and their captive wards, than a lack of food. The story of food is central to the history of World War II. Not only did food concerns play a major role in pushing Germany and Japan toward war but, in the words of historian Lizzie Cunningham, the "deliberate starvation of targeted groups became a defining feature of the National Socialist food system."[3] Warring nations devoted vast resources to maintaining adequate food supplies, ramping up their agricultural systems to fuel bodies both at home and in the field. Meanwhile, for untold numbers of people, food became a personal obsession, hunger a near-constant companion. All around the globe, those who weren't fighting spent their off-hours queuing in ration lines, tending their home gardens, and devising creative ways to stretch every calorie. But there was never enough—at least, not in places like Calcutta, Warsaw, Leningrad, and Athens. By the war's end, more than 20 million people had died from starvation, malnutrition, and related diseases—most victims of those who would rob others to feed themselves.[4]

At a time in which every calorie was precious, every spare morsel the possible difference between life and death, zoos found themselves in an increasingly untenable position. To survive, all zoos must acquire fresh food supplies every day, rain or shine, even under the threat of aerial bombardment. Writing in *Popular Mechanics* in April 1943, Wayne Whittaker opined, "A blueprint for feeding a zoo full of mammals, reptiles, and birds from every corner and climate in the world is as intricate as plans for an ocean liner."[5]

He was only slightly exaggerating.

The San Diego Zoo's weekly shopping list included "three thousand pounds of fish, five tons of hay, twelve hundred pounds of various grains and seed, six hundred pounds of stale bread, three boxes of apples, ten stalks of bananas, fifteen crates of carrots, six lug boxes of topless carrots, ten crates of lettuce, fifteen crates of free greens (trimmings from markets), ninety-six quarts of milk, five dozen eggs, fifteen chickens, one hundred mice and rats, one box of grapefruit, three hundred pounds of oranges, one hundred pounds of potatoes," and "four big horses" (to be consumed from eyeball to hoof). While some animals could survive on kitchen scraps, others required fine-tuned diets. Fish-eaters constituted the most expensive animals at the zoo. San Diego's captive navy of seals, penguins, and lesser seafowl consumed an average of 500 pounds of fish daily—feasible enough to obtain in peacetime, practically impossible in an ocean crowded with submarines and gunboats. Adding to the daily burden was providing for all the animals that wanted their dinner to be, if not wriggling, then "freshly killed and fed while still warm and limp." Even in the best of times, San Diego Zoo chefs struggled to keep up with the demand for pigeons, rabbits, frogs, cuttlefish, and other animals required by their meat-hungry predators. The zoo's reptile house featured what amounted to a zoo within the zoo—a nursery for raising mealworms, roaches, rats, and feeder mice. Breeding rats that produced "uniformly large litters" were allowed to endure lives of near-constant pregnancy until the cost of their upkeep outweighed their usefulness as food machines. The others were "sacrificed by nature's law" to the snakes, birds, and other animals the public had come to see.[6]

Even if zoos could somehow afford to pay their grocery bills, locating adequate food supplies was a different matter altogether. Fish, exotic fruits and vegetables, and certain breeds of "living food" had to be imported. During the previous world war, shipping restrictions deprived Allied zoos of stocks of birdseed (previously conveyed from Turkey via Germany) as well as Germany's world-renowned supplies of mealworms ("no other meal-worms were half so mealy or wormy as the German ones").[7] After August 1939, ships of all navies were reluctant to spare precious cargo space for civilian supplies; the thought of risking one's life to import food for banana-hungry monkeys struck most people as lunacy.

No less worrisome, zoos faced a culture of rationing that elevated dietary sacrifice into an act of patriotism. For those on the home front—whether in Germany, the United States, Great Britain, or Japan—rationing was not just a wartime requirement; it was considered an essential element in the war effort. A pamphlet from the US government declared that rationing "had a greater impact on civilian consciousness than any other measure during the war" outside of the draft.[8] At its core, rationing was built on a simple principle: in times of war, scarce resources belonged to those who needed them most. That meant excess food went to the military, not to monkeys.

Against this backdrop, some advocates sought to defend zoos' food consumption. Privately, Carl Hartman, a zoology professor at the University of Illinois, wrote a fellow zoo-lover in 1944:

Museums, arboretums, zoological parks and public aquaria are all marks of civilization. Some would like to remonstrate and say, "Zoo animals eat food." That's true. But cats and dogs do also; indeed they consume 5% of the country's food. And each dog or cat entertains but one family or (very often) a single childless woman. The facts are that zoos and aquaria entertain and edify millions. In my opinion no animal so completely earns its board and care as a zoo animal.[9]

In public, however, zoos struggled not only to locate adequate amounts of nutritious food but also to justify spending it on animals that ranked low in the dietary pecking order—below military personnel, home-front workers, even livestock.

Gardening for Victory

Most zoos adopted a combination of three strategies to deal with the food shortage crisis. The most common involved growing food onsite or collecting it nearby. This strategy wasn't entirely new. All zoos produce at least some of their dietary requirements—typically in a garden or bakery. Moreover, there was a tradition of zoos beefing up their onsite food production in times of crisis. During World War I, the Bronx Zoo converted every spare quarter acre of land into gardens for "war crops." When they weren't patrolling the grounds against German agents and running firefighting drills, staff planted sunflowers, potatoes, beets, turnips, lettuce, and carrots, saving $2,500 in annual food expenses.[10] In London, staff raised "utility animals" (chickens, goats, cattle) and cultivated vegetables in the zoo gardens, some of which they distributed to a nearby hospital to feed wounded soldiers.[11]

With the onset of World War II, the need to plant, grow, and scrounge food spiked. At zoos large and small, staff dug up ornamental gardens and parking lots to make space for crops. Employees of the National Zoological Park in Washington, DC, grew sweet potatoes, corn, and veggies; staff of the Portland Zoo raised thousands of pounds of hay and grain.[12] In Philadelphia, gardeners converted open space into a 26,000-square-foot garden of "potatoes . . . tomatoes, corn, Swiss chard, bush beans, carrots, cabbage, kale, lettuce, spinach, onions,

Figure 11.1. During the war years, many zoos set aside prohibitions against feeding the animals and encouraged zoo-goers to help supplement the food supplies (either from home stocks or from vendors). This 1942 photograph from the National Zoo in Washington, DC, shows a hippopotamus begging visitors for peanuts and other treats. Photo credit: John Ferrell, US Farm Security Administration–Office of War Information Black & White Photograph Collection, Library of Congress, Washington, DC.

and turnips."[13] At the Brookfield Zoo near Chicago, Ed Bean "cultivated all the available land in and around the park and outside the large parking area—amounting to something over 19 acres."[14] During one year, zoo staff grew 21 tons of soybean hay, 3¼ tons of alfalfa, 25 tons of green corn, 90 tons of green soybeans, and 11,320 pounds of pumpkins, for a total savings of $4,000.[15]

In Washington, DC, William Mann cautioned zoo-goers against sneaking animals treats, warning that it was "just as unhealthy for a monkey to eat continually between meals" as it was for human children.[16] But many zoos had little choice but to ask visitors for help. Staff from the Antwerp Zoo went door to door collecting potato peelings in a cart pulled by ponies or llamas.[17] The Dublin Zoo encouraged zoo-lovers to donate "broccoli leaves, old cabbages, small apples and greens."[18] Meanwhile, the London Zoo introduced an ingenious adoption scheme to alleviate the cost of the animals' care. Staff affixed labels to animals' cages, asking private individuals to "adopt" (and thus pay the upkeep for) their "special pets." After only a few months, Londoners adopted more than 180 animals, saving the zoo $1,700 in food costs.[19]

Such schemes were not only good business but also smart politics. Zoos were eager to tamp down public anxieties about the ethics of feeding animals in a time of sacrifice. They routinely stressed that they served food that was "unfit for human consumption."[20] The directorate at the Basel Zoo asked authorities for "goods that were no longer suitable for human consumption, such as spoiled eggs for feeding the bears or horsemeat from deceased animals."[21] In addition to stale bread, broken biscuits, and grass from the municipal parks, the Auckland Zoo served chicken offal, sparrows, condemned beef ("unfit for human food"), and "aged horses."[22] While the San Diego Zoo demanded that all donations be "clean and unpolluted," other zoos adopted a more liberal approach to edibility.[23] The National Zoological Park fed its animals rice that had been "nibbled by rats" and crabmeat that had been "packed under unsanitary conditions."[24] Zoos often depended upon the perceived repugnance of certain foods to stave off criticism that feeding zoo animals represented a waste of precious resources.

Some zoos went out of their way to publicize their wartime self-sufficiency. Stung by criticism during the First World War, the Whipsnade Zoo not only encouraged visitors to bring food from home (including "sugar and buns for the elephants") but also staged public demonstrations of wartime food policy. Lucy Pender, whose father worked at the zoo, gathered grain and cut dry stalks for animal straw; others grew runner beans and root vegetables, planted fields of wheat and barley (elephants plowed part of the land), and raised pigs and sheep to be sold to the Ministry of Supply.[25] Under the supervision of the head gardener of the Zoological Society of London, one Mr. Puddle, Whipsnade boasted two model "victory" gardens of the sort zoo-goers were expected to grow at home. Whipsnade also staged exhibits on keeping bees, rearing silkworms, minimizing household waste, and using agricultural by-products to supplement rationed foods.[26]

Patriotic Diets

Victory gardens helped, but they could hardly account for animals' appetite for exotic foods. Consequently, zoos adopted a second strategy, swapping animals' normal fare for ersatz or "patriotic" diets. To be clear, even in peacetime, zoo animals rarely eat the same foods as their uncaged counterparts. While zoos today purport to mirror the "natural feeding behavior of animals in the wild," zoo diets in the 1940s were "based on tradition and pragmatism as much as anything to do with science."[27] During World War II, most zoos were desperate to find anything, fresh or otherwise, to fill their animals' bellies. At the same time, zoo leaders hoped to win good PR by demonstrating their animals' willingness to swallow hard on behalf of the war effort. Although other zoos' giraffes "flatly refuse[d] to touch anything but mimosa leaves," William Mann publicly bragged that *his* collection of long-necked ruminants switched to a diet of apples, veggies, and hay without complaint.[28]

When possible, zoos tried to substitute in foods that had been sourced close to home. In Chicago, zoo chefs replaced the panda's native bamboo (now impossible to retrieve thanks to the war in the Pacific) with a variety grown in Florida, while the National Zoological Park instituted a "Good Neighbor Policy," importing dried Mexican flies instead of ant eggs from Germany and Japan.[29] As the war dragged on, zoos had to get resourceful. In Munich, keepers fed the apes vitamins and artificial supplements along with local fruits and vegetables; elsewhere, zoos concocted ersatz bananas from a mixture of sweet potatoes and honey.[30] Whenever possible, zoos tried to replicate the taste or appearance of animals' usual fare. At the London Zoo, penguins were fed slivers of cat meat dipped in cod-liver oil; the master feeder at the Hanover Zoo attempted a similar ruse, spraying a cut of zebra thigh with stinking seal oil in hopes it might fool the hungry polar bear.[31]

Zoos were especially eager to locate new sources of animal protein (better known as "meat") to feed their large carnivores. Red meat was a public obsession during World War II. Demand for edible animal flesh skyrocketed, even as government propagandists urged their citizens to swap their sizzling T-bones and steak-and-kidney pies, their wiener schnitzel and pork dumplings, for meatless substitutes. In the

United States, ironically, meat ranked low on many zoos' list of dietary problems. After a decade of economic depression, zoos had grown accustomed to serving cuts of horseflesh, which was cheap, relatively abundant, and—as far as the public was concerned—unfit for human consumption. At Seattle's Woodland Park Zoo, butchers slaughtered horses onsite, feeding the flesh to the animals and shipping the hides to a leather shop to be cured and eventually sold.[32] In Oklahoma City, tigers, lions, and bears went through two horses per week, many of them eighteen-to-twenty-year-old nags.[33]

Outside the United States, it was a different matter. Tokyo's Ueno Zoo, for example, struggled to secure red meat, even though it could usually find fish.[34] Antwerp Zoo staff shot their collection of large carnivores in 1940 when "it was obvious that there was not going to be enough meat available." The following year, Lucile Mann reported, the "last of [Antwerp's] fish-eaters died for lack of food."[35] When fresh meat was unavailable, some zoos stretched their supplies with brewer's yeast, fish oil, and green bone paste.[36] At the Hagenbeck Tierpark outside Hamburg, carnivores were fed organs instead of their usual "juicy quarters of meat."[37] In Rome, wolves and foxes dined on bread boiled with hambones, while the big cats were fed "huge loaves of bread soaked in fresh oxblood," supplemented with the occasional slab of donkey flesh.[38]

As with everything else, zoos relied upon networks of fellow professionals when developing these diets. Although cut off from zoos outside the Reich, German zoo directors carried out a regular correspondence about dietary matters.[39] Similarly, small and mid-sized American zoos often turned to the nation's largest for counsel. In 1942 and 1943, Dan Harkins, the curator of the Franklin Park Zoo in Boston, peppered his peers with questions about extending horsemeat rations, developing grain mixtures for deer, and calculating the daily requirements for elephants. He was especially interested in learning the recipe for "bear bread," a glutinous loaf of bran and whole-wheat flour that was cheap to make and reasonably edible. Without an adequate supply, Harkins worried, his zoo would have to destroy its entire collection of bears.[40]

But zoos did more than swap recipes. They also shared advice on how to assuage public concerns about feeding zoo animals in wartime.

Robert Bean, son of the Brookfield Zoo director, advised colleagues to minimize their use of rationed foods even when they were available. Although the zoo was allowed twenty-five pounds of brown sugar, Bean's keepers used corn syrup and artificial sweeteners instead to demonstrate Brookfield's patriotic bona fides.[41] The National Zoo went so far as to distribute a "stock reply" to other zoos in case they received public complaints about food consumption. It emphasized zoos' use of horsemeat and other foods "not ordinarily used by human beings," such as "weeds, leaves, twigs," and "lower grade hay." It also played up zoos' efforts to raise mice, rats, and worms (staples all) and to collect the "leafy material" typically thrown away at grocery stores. Above all, the National Zoo's reply—and other responses like it—sent the message that zoos weren't competitors in the battle for food.[42] They were allies, models of wartime ingenuity and thrift.

Not surprisingly, zoo directors often used humor to minimize any problems their "war diets" might cause. As William Mann admitted, "There is no stage or screen star as temperamental as a lady lion when you first try to slip her horsemeat as a substitute for her customary slab of beef. Nor are monkeys fooled when you try to serve potatoes masked in honey and palmed off as bananas."[43] Speaking about the "beastial tragedy" at the wartime zoo, Leo Blondin, the circus-performer-turned-superintendent of the Oklahoma City Zoo, opined: "Man may reconcile himself to a rationed diet on the basis of patriotism, but try telling that to the polar bears."[44] One United Press story noted the irony that the "more stupid animals are receiving the best food because they refuse to change their habits."[45]

Superfluous Eaters

Dan Harkins's dilemma hinted at zoos' third strategy for dealing with food shortages: if you cannot feed your zoo's animals, you can always kill them. Selective violence is an essential part of modern zookeeping. All zoos operate according to what Arnold Arluke and Clinton Sanders call a "sociozoologic scale" of animal value: the belief that some animals are worth more than others, depending upon their utility, their perceived intelligence, or some other characteristic.[46] Even in peacetime, a modest-sized zoo might kill hundreds, if not thousands, of some animals ("pests," "food animals," free-roaming strays) in its effort to preserve the lives of a select few. Most of this violence takes place at night or behind closed doors, away from the eyes of animal-loving visitors. That's because the idea of destroying animals, particularly "exotic" ones, tends to strike the public as a kind of betrayal—a smear on the ark image that zoos have spent more than a century trying to cultivate. (The Copenhagen Zoo learned this lesson when, ignoring public outrage, it euthanized Marius, a healthy two-year-old giraffe, in 2014.)[47]

Consequently, zoos often attempted to paint such practices in patriotic terms, emphasizing the need to sacrifice. In October 1942, a zookeeper from Cedar Rapids, Iowa, shot his entire collection of animals, telling the Associated Press, "We don't feel that we can conscientiously keep on buying meat for animals when human beings are limited to a certain amount a week."[48] Many wartime zoo officials reached the grim conclusion that it was better to kill their animal charges (or at least sell them off) rather than risk their slow starvation. In December 1942, Gay's Lion Farm in El Monte, California, shut down after rationing made it difficult to obtain adequate meat supplies.[49]

That same month, Ward R. Walker, director of the zoo in Hershey, Pennsylvania, reached a similar conclusion. Walker pointed to the lack of personnel, the inability to import new specimens, and declining attendance rates because of tire and gasoline rationing. But looming over everything else was a shortage of food. "We cannot, after all these years, resort to the feeding of such foods as moldy bread, soggy sweet rolls, tainted meat, and vegetable cuttings swept off the floor or removed from garbage cans," he explained. The animals would be sold off to other zoos with the hope of repurchasing them in peacetime, though Walker noted that animals with "meat value"—including bison, deer, and elk—would be set aside in case of an "extreme meat shortage" in the community.[50]

Ultimately, all zoos applied a cost-benefit approach to their animal exhibits, weighing the various expenses (food, shelter, etc.) against the payoff in ticket sales and prestige. Early in the war, staff at the Hellabrunn Zoo in Munich decided to thin out "superfluous eaters" to save resources for others.[51] By September 1939, staff had sold, given away, or slaughtered four lions, nine bears, and 150 large herbivores.[52] Staff at the London Zoo made a similar calculation, sentencing some of their less exotic animals to the butcher's table. They sold goats and sheep from Regent's Park to the government's Ministry of Supply; others went to feed the zoo's stock of large carnivores.[53] Writing to a colleague in 1942, Belle Benchley, executive secretary of the San Diego Zoo, expressed a sentiment that was common throughout the zoo world. Faced with shortages of food, she believed it was "foolhardy to bring in rare and valuable animals" only to "have them destroyed" shortly thereafter.[54]

Zoo employees did not relish the thought of killing animals that, in some cases, they had raised since birth—living creatures that recognized their faces, their smell, the sounds of their boots slapping against the pavement. When food supplies ran low, staff snuck table scraps, rummaged through trash bins, even went hungry themselves—anything to forestall the inevitable. Yet, as the war dragged on, more and more zoos decided that their animals were better off dead.

A Hungry World

Most World War II–era zoos proved remarkably adept at withstanding the food crisis, but their three-pronged survival strategy was not a complete success. Crops failed, horsemeat shipments went undelivered, and staffing shortages made the whole feeding process a relentless chore. In Sydney, a prized giraffe died after eating alfalfa that had spoiled in transport. (The zoo's hippo, Sheba, also died after a painful bout of gastroenteritis.)[55] Elsewhere, animals either refused their diets or dropped to dangerously low weights. The Bremerhaven Zoo lost a pair of newborn polar bears, a barnacle goose, a sea lion bull, and several other pinnipeds in the first years of the conflict. Some suffered heart failure after months of malnutrition. The seals died after being served preserved herring, which—while harmless to humans—proved fatal to animals raised on a diet of fresh fish.[56] The situation was even worse in Paris, where the twin pressures of occupation and food shortage emptied a number of zoo cages. According to a report written shortly after liberation, the Jardin des Plantes and the Jardin d'Acclimatation "lost nearly all of their animals during the war." While some were "humanely killed" and others shipped abroad, several

Figure 11.2. Titled "L'Abbatage de l'éléphant" ("elephant slaughter"), this lithograph depicts the most famous wartime zoo killing of the nineteenth century, when besieged Parisians shot and ate several longtime animal residents of the Jardins des Plantes. Invoking a spirit of martial *fraternité*, the illustration's accompanying text assured readers that the elephant's carcass was served to society's "most hungry." In truth, however, much of the zoo's meat harvest wound up in the stomachs of the upper classes. Courtesy of the Musée Carnavalet, Histoire de Paris.

prized animals, including an Indian elephant, died of privation and neglect. Of the survivors, "most of the simians suffered the usual fate of cats and dogs in an enemy-occupied, famished country in wartime—they were eaten."[57]

This final point represented zoos' greatest food vulnerability. Zoo animals not only needed food; in the eyes of a hungry world, they *were* food—better off on someone's dinner table than languishing behind iron bars. During the Prussian siege of Paris in 1870, French gourmands famously raided the nation's zoological pantry, serving up kangaroo stew, elephant consommé, and other exotic delectables in elite banquet rooms across the city.[58] Seven decades later, the restaurant at DC's National Zoological Park began hosting weekly game dinners for wealthy Washingtonians. The idea for the group, known as the Anteaters Association, originated after the zoo's chief chef noticed the "mouths of meat-hungry customers watering as they looked out the window at the animals in their cages." While the rest of the country remained in ration mode, hundreds of zoo-goers paid big bucks to sample buffalo, elk, pheasant, bear, elephant, iguana, even whale (some of the meat freshly harvested on the zoo grounds).[59] For all of that, zoo animals were far more likely to be eaten by their keepers, occupying armies, or—in the war's immediate aftermath—"displaced persons" having endured years of relentless hunger.

In many ways, the story of food at the wartime zoo is a microcosm of larger histories. Zoos' strategies for dealing with the food crisis closely mirrored the propaganda messages espoused by government food agencies. Moreover, the wartime food crisis exposed both zoos' greatest weakness and their greatest strengths. Despite their best efforts, zoos often struggled to carry out their most basic function—to keep their animals alive. At the same time, the food question bound zoo animals and home-front civilians together in a shared community of suffering. During World War II, hunger exceeded the boundaries of class, politics, nation, even species. Many zoo staff came to view zoo animals as members of their own family—if, that is, they were around to take care of them.

12

Zoos without Keepers

In October 1941, two years since the start of the war in Europe, *British Pathé* released a brief newsreel on the latest development at the nation's animal parks. Titled "Ladies Only," it showcased the newly hired female staff at a small zoo in Devon, England, now bereft of its usual flock of male workers. In one scene, a dark-haired woman doles out fish to a waddle of hungry penguins. In another, a teenaged "waitress" in a white smock pushes a slab of ribs (what kind, it's not clear) through the bars of a tiger cage. A final sequence features a somewhat older woman bottle-feeding a baby chimp on her lap. Like other wartime shorts, "Ladies Only" makes women's war work seem like an exciting adventure, a chance to step into roles previously considered for men only. But the newsreel's mocking script undermines its celebratory message. "Yes, they might not be able to keep a secret," jokes the film's male narrator, "but they can keep a flamingo."[1]

"Ladies Only" highlighted a problem that beset all wartime zoos: the need for labor. World War II provoked the greatest migration of workers in history. In less time than it takes for many corporations to open a new factory, tens of millions of workers left their jobs to take places in their nations' war industries. Some went willingly, lured by fat paychecks or dreams of adventure; others were compelled by the threat of prison, death, or public shame.

Whatever their motivations, armies of zoo workers traded their overalls for military fatigues. At the Hershey Zoo in Pennsylvania, nearly all the employees were under thirty-eight years old—the cutoff age for military service. "Hardly a day passed without their being reminded they were employed in nonessential work and they should change immediately," reflected the zoo's director. Those who stayed on "felt they were not patriotic under the circumstances, so the loss of trained men became a serious factor."[2]

The sudden manpower shortage did not affect all zoos equally. In occupied zoos, or in those under regular threat of aerial bombardment, animal keepers might go home one night and never appear again—perhaps because they had been captured, killed, or forced to flee. In June 1941, the Reich's chief zoo-lover Hermann Göring declared it was "absolutely necessary" for zoos to secure their most senior employees, a decision that made it possible to release some former zoo workers from military service.[3] Yet high-flown proclamations did little to solve the problem. At the start of the war, Munich's Hellabrunn Tierpark lost nineteen animal "guards" (keepers) to military service.[4] In Vienna, Tiergarten Schönbrunn was forced to replace its veterinary staff with inexperienced youths, most of whom floundered under the workload. (Later in the war, director Otto Antonius managed to get back some of his most experienced keepers.)[5] The London Zoo encouraged its male workforce to enter civil defense or take up arms—a noble enough gesture but one that left the zoo dangerously short of hired hands.[6]

The same was true for zoos across the United States.[*] In May 1942, the head of the San Diego Zoo complained that only three of the animal keepers had been on the job more than a year.[7] The Bronx Zoo contributed more than sixty staff to the US armed forces.[8] Conditions were nearly as bad at the Brookfield Zoo, which lost so many of its prewar animal keepers (only seven of whom remained as of 1944) that it was forced to shutter its small animal house.[9] One internal report explained Brookfield's labor exodus as a matter of inauspicious geography: "The Park is surrounded by large, new war plants." Although the zoo bumped up its salaries, it was "impossible . . . to meet high wages paid by industry."[10]

---

[*] In December 1944, the magazine of the Philadelphia Zoo related the fates of its former employees: Robert Hudson, a sign painter, had been injured while serving in an artillery battalion. Private Patrick Menichini, the lion keeper, had sustained a chest wound but survived. Fireman Second Class Joseph Hough, a refreshment-stand worker, died at Normandy.

Zoos resorted to a variety of measures to weather the labor crisis. In Munich, Heinz Heck extended the shifts of his remaining workers.[11] Other zoos hired children, cajoled community leaders, or attempted to coax former staff out of retirement. On rare occasions, larger zoos managed to conscript on-duty servicemen into the army of zoo workers. In the summer of 1942, while waiting to be shipped out to fight, Henry Hooper spent a week hauling pig "slather" in Regent's Park, scooping the soupy mix of urine and feces into metal barrels before dumping it out on the London Zoo's vegetable garden.[12] Many zoo directors hoped to survive by hiring temporary workers—ex-carnies or circus veterans who didn't mind cleaning cages and scooping rhino dung at low pay. Unfortunately, they struggled to attract prime candidates. After losing several experienced keepers to the war effort, Sydney's Taronga Park Zoo was forced to hire "men who in some cases had never before seen anything more exotic than a sparrow."[13]

Captive Workers

It wasn't long before German zoos began to experiment with a new solution to the manpower shortage: they enlisted the labor of foreigners. Despite Hitler's paeans to the virtues of the German worker, the Nazi war economy relied almost entirely on outsiders. At its peak in August 1944, more than 7.5 million foreign nationals were employed in the Greater German Reich, including 1.3 million French, 590,000 Italians, 1.7 million Poles, 250,000 Belgians, and 2.8 million citizens of the war-ravaged Soviet Union. Although some of the *ausländische Arbeitskräfte* [foreign workers] came of their own accord, most were POWs or slaves—men and women who could be worked to death (often literally) with no compensation and little concern about safety or health. According to historian Ulrich Herbert, the wartime policy of *Ausländereinsatz* [foreigner deployment] "instituted a functional national hierarchy based on national criteria: Germans on top, foreigners underneath, graded from the French above all the way down to the Russians at the bottom. Here was a Nazi vision of the future, a foretaste of a German-dominated, racially stratified Europe after German victory."[14]

While zoo work never ranked very high on the list of government priorities (the vast majority of foreign workers toiled in agriculture, munitions, and metals), the Reich's zoos nonetheless managed to plug some of their labor holes.[15] The Hagenbeck Zoo replaced departing employees with POWs from France, Czechoslovakia, the Netherlands, and Poland.[16] At the Dresden Zoo, which had lost roughly half of its staff to military service by 1942, the dozen Ukrainian and Russian forced laborers were so hungry they had to scavenge the rubbish bins for scraps of bread.[17] That same year, Lutz Heck returned from a tour of the Białowieża Forest in eastern Poland with six "slave laborers."[18] Later, when British bombers devastated the Berlin Zoo, Heck deployed an army of 700 POWs to help clear the rubble, a practice repeated throughout the Reich.[19] After the war, surviving zoo officials were understandably reticent to discuss their reliance on forced laborers. Those that did either downplayed the practice or went out of their way to highlight the perceived "loyalty" of foreign zoo workers. According to Lorenz Hagenbeck, foreign workers in Hamburg never failed to report to their posts during air raids.[20] Heinz Heck, the prototypical "Good German," liked to recount the bravery of a particular Russian *Zwangsarbeiter* [forced laborer] who risked his life during an especially brutal bomb attack. While the rest of the staff huddled in their shelters, Heck recalled, the unnamed Russian battled a fire in the ape house, eventually saving all the animals inside.[21]

Outsiders, not surprisingly, painted a bleaker picture of the situation. When Corporal Robert G. Hudson, a former member of the Philadelphia Zoo staff, entered the remains of the Nuremburg Zoo in April 1945, he discovered "six old men and several slave-labor Russian families," who told him "they had worked here for three years and been poorly treated." Though technically "liberated," they had stayed on to take care of the animals—not that they had much choice in the matter. Like millions of recently classified "displaced persons," they had spent the war hundreds of miles from home with little contact with the outside world. Things were little better in Munich, where only thirteen Germans and twenty-five "Russian and Polish slave-laborers" had manned the zoo through its darkest hours.[22]

To this day, we know relatively little about the lives of "guestworkers" in Hitler's zoos. Firsthand accounts are hard to come by, and after the war, few German zoo directors were eager to discuss the topic at length. Still, if zoo work mirrored the broader patterns of wartime forced labor, we can make a few broad suppositions. First, we can deduce that workers from Western nations (or from German allies) endured far better conditions than their counterparts from the East, whose lives were "characterized by poor diet, low wages, inadequate housing and clothing, excessively long hours, deficient medical care, cheating by German superiors, abuse and maltreatment, and high mortality."[23] The case of Albert Bourez, author of a memoir about his time at a German zoo, seems to confirm this theory. Born in Pas-de-Calais in 1917, Bourez was wounded and captured at Dunkirk in 1940. Evacuated first to Belgium and later to Germany, he spent five years as a POW, much of it as a zoo worker in the garrison city of Münster, not far from the Belgian border. Compared to other forced laborers under the Nazi regime, Bourez and three fellow French compatriots got off easy. The zoo's director Heinz Randow used his party connections to shield Bourez and his fellow POWS as much as possible. Read today, the memoir comes off as little more than a collection of funny animal stories—curious anecdotes about a side of the zoo the public never gets to see. Yet the upbeat tone of *My Friends in Captivity or The Zoo in Turmoil* (1973) does not fully disguise Bourez's sense of threat—from hunger, falling bombs, or the whims of his captors.[24]

Foreign zoo workers who joined willingly (if grudgingly) also would have had a leg up on those compelled to shovel elephant dung for the Reich. Koenraad Kuiper, for example, could have easily spent the war years laying railroad ties, digging out a mine, or worse. Twenty-four years old when the German Army invaded the Netherlands, Kuiper was captured and held prisoner until the Dutch surrender. Men in his circumstances typically had three potential futures: they could join the Waffen-SS; they could be forced into heavy, often deadly, labor abroad; or they could try to disappear into the netherworld of anti-Nazi resistance. But he was lucky. His father, also named Koenraad Kuiper, was the director of the Rotterdam Zoo and a founding member of the prewar association of international zoo men. He retained many of his contacts in the German zoo world. Eventually, he wrangled his namesake a job with his friend Hermann Ruhe, scion of the world-renowned pet empire and director of the Hanover Zoo.

During the day, Koenraad and six other Dutchmen prepared food, slopped cages, and tended to the animals—all under the gaze of the German patrons. At night, his wife Sara served local takes on hometown classics: ostrich egg omelets, bear's paw soup, turkey with potatoes and applesauce, and an inexplicable concoction called "zoo pudding." But by February 1944, hit on eighty-eight separate bombing runs, Hanover was in rubble, and more than a hundred bomb craters scarred the zoo grounds. When Herr Ruhe moved the remaining animals to his commercial game farm, Koen took a job as a farmworker in the nearby city of Celle. At the war's end, he joined the exodus of thousands of other Dutch citizens—traitors, cowards, heroes, forced workers, concentration camp survivors, profiteers—who had spent the war years laboring for the Reich.[25]

"Girls, You Can Be a Life Guard or Zoo Keeper!"

Outside of Germany, many zoos adopted a second solution to the manpower shortage: they hired women. Today, it is difficult to imagine a zoo without female workers. In the United States, women make up more than 75 percent of zookeepers.[26] Prior to World War II, however, the zoo was governed by a "macho worldview," a belief that animal handling was a matter of muscular force and iron will. The London Zoological Society didn't hire its first female scientist until 1917, when Evelyn Cheesman joined as assistant curator of insects (she left not long after).[27] In fact, zoo-goers between the world wars would have been hard-pressed to find a female animal keeper outside the Soviet Union, a fact noted by William Mann on a trip to Moscow in 1938.[28]

Zoos' reluctance to hire women is somewhat ironic, given that they frequently relied upon the unpaid labor of workers' families, especially the wives of zoo directors. At the height of the Great Depression, women like Warsaw's Antonina Żabińska and Washington, DC's, Lucile Mann more or less functioned as co-directors with their husbands, writing books, attending scientific conferences, and—in the eyes of the press—injecting the zoo with a much-needed dose of feminine charm. A typical profile from the 1940s praised Mann's professional competence, noting how, when accompanying her husband on collecting expeditions, she "not only helped care for the animals but . . . did all of the secretarial work as well." That said, the piece's author seemed more interested in the zoo wife's appearance—she bore a "striking resemblance to movie star Fay Bainter," we're told—than her work on the animals' behalf. The article even included Mann's tips for provisioning cosmetics when out on safari. "You weren't always sure of getting makeup let alone your favorite brand," she advised, harkening back to her earlier career in women's magazines, "so it was always wisest to stock up."[29]

With the start of World War II, male zoo directors were forced to set aside their misgivings about hiring women—at least in the short term. When the Chester Zoo in northwest England lost its male keepers, hundreds of women applied to take their place.[30] By May 1940, it had hired "seven smart girls," teenagers all, to care for the large cats. Before she was put in charge of the lion house, fifteen-year-old Delia McLoughland had only seen lions at the movies; now she was responsible for ten, "four them newly grown." Another recent hire, Helen Moston, a seventeen-year-old from Manchester, abandoned a stint in nursing to care for the zoo's collection of chimpanzees.[31] In November, *Chicago Tribune* readers woke up to the announcement: "Girls, You Can Be a Life Guard or Zoo Keeper!" Desperate to fill manpower shortages, the Chicago Parks District opened one hundred jobs that had previously been restricted to men, including zookeeping. The jobs were considered temporary, but the newspaper promised that female staff would receive the same pay and benefits as the men they replaced.[32]

Many zoos hired women to work with children or small animals, a form of labor that did not threaten gendered assumptions about women's roles as nurturers. Sydney's Taronga Park Zoo lost twelve of its thirteen gardeners, along with several animal keepers, to military service (one former elephant keeper was taken prisoner in Italy, another in Malaya, while the lion and tiger keeper died in the Royal Australian Air Force). To help fill the gap, superintendent Robert Anthony Patten appointed two women, one a former cashier at the zoo, to care for "the zoo's motherless babies in addition to the children's collection of rabbits and squirrels."[33] In 1940, Dublin Zoo director Cedric Flood decided to convert the camel house into a petting zoo, replacing the former inhabitants with kid goats, puppies, lambs, pigs, and lion cubs. Flood hired his daughter, Yvonne Ward, and her half sister, Peggy Shannon, to manage the Children's Corner. As befitting their new status, the women were assigned overalls and given "permission to wear slacks."[34]

At times, zoo publicists highlighted what they perceived as the emotional connections between female keepers and the animals in their care. According to George Mottershead, owner of the Chester

Figure 12.1. A photo of a female zookeeper outside the emu cage at Melbourne's Zoological Gardens (c. 1944). Due to manpower shortages, many wartime zoos did the previously unthinkable: they hired women for the first time. Australia War Memorial.

Zoo, female keepers "will enter a cage with every confidence. They are not afraid of animals and I think this creates a sympathetic feeling between them and their charges."[35] During the Belfast Blitz of 1941, Denise Weston Austin, one of the earliest female keepers at the Belfast Zoo, went a step further. Eager to save her favorite elephant calf (the Royal Ulster Constabulary had already shot twenty-three zoo animals), Austin decided to shelter the young pachyderm in the walled garden behind her home each night, leading it back to the zoo every morning.[36]

To some observers, the idea of a female zookeeper was as exciting (and exotic) as the animals themselves. "A veteran of animal show work," Mrs. George Dittoe made headlines when she "signed up to fill the man shortage" at the San Diego Zoo—finally breaching the "citadel of Men-Only" animal keepers.[37] In January 1942, the *Adelaide Advertiser* breathlessly announced the recent hiring of women to care for animals in the Australian section of the Melbourne Zoo.[38] Speaking at a meeting of the Zonta Club, a women's advocacy group, in 1944,

Lucile Mann reported that women were currently keeping animals in Moscow, London, Sydney, and Seattle—a remarkable change from only a few years earlier.[39]

It's impossible to say precisely how many women donned zoo khaki during World War II. Zoos in Axis countries tended to shy away from hiring women.[40] (Enslaved women were a different matter altogether.) Meanwhile, zoos in the United States and the Commonwealth countries had a tough time retaining female workers, despite the manpower shortages. Zoo work paid poorly and, as female employees were quick to discover, proved to be far less glamorous than other newly opened professions.[41] In the Chicago region, "so much other employment [was] available" that the Brookfield Zoo struggled to hire high school girls to sell refreshments.[42] Even romance might ultimately lead women away from the zoo. In December 1939, the *Daily Express* ran a story on Vera Buck, an eighteen-year-old beauty who met a dashing home officer (and zoological society Fellow) while working as a hostess in the London Zoo's Pets Corner. After a whirlwind courtship, the couple married and moved to Leicester.[43]

Although women's role in freeing men to fight is a central part of many nations' mythologies of World War II, much of what we take for granted about Rosie the Riveter (and her female cousins around the globe) is tinged with nostalgia. In the United States—to cite just one example—relatively "few women took jobs that had been exclusively held by men," and zookeeping was no exception.[44] Plus, older attitudes did not disappear overnight. The case of Jacqueline Sabine is instructive. As historian Daniel E. Bender notes, Sabine seemed to be an ideal candidate for a career in zookeeping. She "boasted impressive qualifications, including undergraduate degrees in botany or zoology." But when she applied for a job at the National Zoological Park, William Mann answered with the "form letter of rejection he sent to all female applicants." For all his wife's help in keeping the ark afloat, Mann would hire women only in the role of secretaries.[45]

Katharina and the Zoo Lady

The experiences of two remarkable zoo women—one American, one German—marked the highpoint of women's involvement in wartime zoo work.[†] Born in 1882, Belle Benchley (née Jennings) had no ambition to enter the zoo world.[46] After divorcing her husband in 1922, and with a son in high school to support, she joined the newly formed San Diego Zoo in 1925. She had no training in business or animal care. In fact, she was only meant to fill in for two weeks while the bookkeeper was on vacation. However, she quickly proved up to the task and more, taking on many of the duties of the zoo's founder, Harry Milton Wegeforth. When he decided to step down as director, he pushed for Benchley to take his place. It was, as he knew, a big step.[47] Eventually, the Zoological Society board agreed and, one year and seven months after her arrival, Benchley assumed the role of executive secretary, making her the first woman in the world to run a zoo.

Not everyone welcomed Benchley's advancement. After a Kodiak bear escaped and was shot dead by a policeman, she received a card "which told me that it was all because I was a woman and incompetent; that if I had been a man in charge of the zoo, the bear would have been lassoed and dragged back into the grotto."[48] (This was in spite of the fact that both the head keeper and the police officer were men.) At her first meeting of the American Association of Zoological Parks and Aquariums, she "was looked upon with a little incredulity by the men and much suspicion by their wives." Indeed, it seemed some people could never fully wrap their heads around the idea of a middle-aged woman running a zoo. Benchley recalled years later, "Perhaps they expected me to stride about ship in high boots, flourishing a 'bull whip' and smoking a pipe."[49]

But if Benchley lacked a "Bring 'Em Back Alive" image, she had other tricks up her sleeve. For starters, she was older than many on the zoo staff, a fact that she used to her advantage. Nearly sixty at the start of World War II, Benchley cultivated a grandmotherly public persona, earning her the nickname the "Zoo Lady" of San Diego. The "rugged, uneducated" men who made up the bulk of the staff treated her with respect—and she them.[50] What's more, the press adored her,

---

[†] At least one other woman led a zoo during World War II. After working as an assistant at the Zoological Institute of the University of Bern, Dr. Monika Meyer-Holzapfel (1907–1995) became the chief administrator of the Bern (Switzerland) Zoo in 1944, a position she held until the late 1960s.

Figure 12.2. The "Zoo Lady" of San Diego, Belle Benchley was executive director of the San Diego Zoo from 1927 to 1953, working both in public and behind the scenes to build a world-class animal collection. Seen here in front of an Oldsmobile and an indifferent elephant in 1940. Credit: San Diego History Center.

in no small part because of her perceived willingness to forgo vanity on behalf of the animals she loved. As she recounted: "I have lost my fear of the press, my personal modesty and my pride, and am now reconciled even to seeing myself in print in ungainly smocks such as no stout women should ever wear and with my hair streaming in what one reporter said was 'no personal style.'"[51] Above all, Benchley had what, in her mind, no zoo man (or woman) could live without: "animal instinct," an ability to forge emotional connections not bound by sex or species.[52] Benchley shepherded the San Diego Zoo through two decades of economic depression and war. In the process, she became a national treasure, her name familiar to the waves of American troops passing through San Diego en route to the Pacific.

Like Belle Benchley, Katharina Heinroth (née Berger) never expected to become the head of one of the world's largest zoos.[53] But that's where the similarities end. Whereas Benchley had little prior interest in animals, Heinroth had grown up with an abiding fascination with the natural world. Born in Breslau (now Wrocław) in 1897, she studied the natural sciences in college, eventually earning a doctorate in 1923. Energetic and ambitious, she spent short stints at public and private research institutions throughout Germany before settling in Berlin with her second husband, Oskar, the acclaimed ornithologist and head of the world-famous Berlin Zoo aquarium.

Heinroth was not content to play the role of supporting wife. During the war years, she met with visiting academics, assumed duties at the aquarium, and shot film footage for scientific research—all the while worrying about the advance of Soviet forces toward her family home in the East. But Heinroth's rise through the ranks at the Berlin Zoo came at a terrible price. In April 1945, as Soviet troops approached the German capital, the Tiergarten's director Lutz Heck fled the scene, leaving the zoo in chaos. Within days, Berlin was overrun, and Heinroth spent a hellish night on the first floor of the aquarium with Oskar, now half-paralyzed from progressive illness and on the brink of death, trying to fend off the assaults of the zoo's occupiers. On May 31, 1945, Oskar died. Katharina tried to follow him, swallowing poison capsules she found in his desk, but they were too old to be effective.

After cremating her husband and burying his ashes on the zoo grounds, Heinroth dedicated every waking hour to picking up the pieces. The zoo's manicured lawns "resembled a lunar landscape," and the stench of tank fuel and exploded munitions was impossible to escape.[54] Thanks to the tireless work of *Katharina die Einzige* ("the one and only Katharina"), however, the zoo managed to reopen on July 1, 1945. (She lettered all the signposts by hand.) That September, the new supervisory board appointed Heinroth the zoo's sole director, the first woman to head a German zoo. By the time she was forced to step down in 1956, the Berlin Zoo had almost entirely recovered from the devastation of the war.

In many respects, the experiences of female zoo workers mirror those of many women in the war. Despite the presence of figures like Benchley and Heinroth, the war did not lead to a gender revolution at the world's zoos. As was the case in so many industries, returning men quickly replaced their female stand-ins. After hiring its first women

Figure 12.3. The first woman to run a German zoo, Katharina Heinroth guided the Berlin Zoo through its recovery in the aftermath of World War II. In this photograph, taken after the war's end, she is giving a side-eye to a pair of orangutans. Courtesy of the Stadtmuseum Berlin.

during the war, the Seattle Zoo didn't hire another for twenty-five years—a pattern replicated across the globe. (Karen Sausman became the first woman to head the World Association of Zoos and Aquariums, in 2006.)[55] While the war temporarily "expanded women's opportunities," its conclusion "brought a return to many conventional limitations."[56] Ultimately, women's current status in zoos has less to do with the examples set during World War II than with the feminization of animal care in general.

In the early 1940s, however, few in the zoo industry gave much thought to the long-term implications of their hiring practices. Instead, they were desperately trying to "do their bit" on behalf of the war effort.

13

Doing Their Bit

In May 1943, Marlin Perkins was desperate. Not yet forty, the energetic director of the Buffalo Zoological Park in upstate New York had been tasked with providing live animals for a series of public exhibits on America's wartime allies. The first two events had gone well enough. The zoo had contributed a tame emu for the public library's South Pacific exhibit, followed by three parrots for a Pan-America exhibit at the Buffalo Historical Society. Next on the schedule was an exhibit on Soviet Russia, a nation rich in fauna though curiously underrepresented in zoos outside Stalin's immediate domain. The future television host thought about crating up a pair of domesticated Bactrian camels, native to the arid steppes of Central Asia, but soon decided they were too large and too smelly for indoor display.[1]

With time ticking down, he dashed off a letter to the nation's chief zoo man, William Mann, in Washington, DC, asking if Buffalo might borrow a few hamsters (possibly the only other Russian animals Perkins could think of). Perkins even promised to throw in some young African porcupines as a bribe if Mann could make it happen. On May 21, a box containing four fuzzy rodents left Washington in an express shipment. Technically, Buffalo's newest residents weren't Russian—they were Syrian hamsters, a fast-breeding variety frequently "used for medical research"—but Mann assured him they were close enough.[2] A month later, Perkins wrote with an update. The hamsters, now seventeen in number, "stole the show." As Mann had predicted, no one cared (or even recognized) that the Buffalo Zoo had fudged the truth. All that mattered was that the zoo had done its bit.[3]

As both men well understood, the greatest threat to most wartime zoos was not an occupying army or wayward bombardier. It was a perception of irrelevance.

Since their emergence in the early nineteenth century, modern zoos have waged a never-ending campaign to justify their existence. All too often, they can seem like frivolous entertainment—the stuff of "child's play"—an impression amplified by the theme-park atmosphere that continues to characterize even world-class zoological parks. To combat such associations, early zoo supporters celebrated their institutions as emblems of civic pride. Today, zoo publicists are more likely to tout the zoo as an indispensable response to ecological disasters. Even so, for many people, zoos belong to a class of inessential (and, hence, disposable) institutions to be shuttered at the first hint of real danger.

The onset of World War II, not surprisingly, triggered an avalanche of anti-zoo commentary in the press. Detractors continued to grumble about the costs, their earlier complaints now cast in the language of wartime necessity. In 1940, an Australian union president protested that the nation spent more money on the upkeep of animals than on unemployed workers—a sign of just how far out of whack the nation's priorities had become.[4] The following year, the mayor of Brisbane, Australia, himself a zoo supporter, declared that "nobody would be justified in using money or labor" on revamping the zoo, not when the nation faced such dire threats from abroad.[5] At the heart of such thinking was the idea that wartime societies needed to put people first; animals, especially those kept only for amusement, were a distant second, if that.

At the same time, a vocal contingent of animal lovers renewed charges that zoos were barbaric—bad for the human visitors and even worse for the furred and feathered residents. In August 1942, Laura Rawstorn of Kirkland, Washington, wrote the Seattle city council about conditions at the Woodland Park Zoo. Even as the United States was "fighting [a war] for freedom and liberation," Seattle's zoo resembled something one "expected to find in the cruel dark ages." Animals that had evolved to live wild in nature were "confined, without occupation of any kind, to pass the whole of their dreary lives away in tiny, cement-and-iron, evil smelling dens, without sun or moon, or any natural blessing." Rawstorn claimed to be "speaking for a lot of poor creatures that cannot speak for themselves." Ultimately, she reserved her greatest wrath for the people of Seattle, who "allow and take pleasure in such unnecessary torture." Only "Morons" would pay good money to visit Woodland Park's tableau of animal suffering, she seethed. The most the animals could hope for would be a quick death by Japanese bomber.[6]

Expensive, difficult to maintain, dangerous to humans, and—to some, at least—inescapably cruel, zoos struck many observers as a wartime liability. Wouldn't it be better, as one Washington, DC, resident suggested, to melt down all zoo cages for scrap metal?[7]

Patriotic Zoos

In fending off their critics, World War II–era zoos' first line of defense was to rally around the flag, adopting the imagery and ideology of the wartime state. Working hand-in-hand with military officials, zoos in Allied and Axis countries hosted fundraising drives, blanketed their grounds with propaganda, and staged displays of martial pomp and circumstance. Zoos from Vienna to Berlin celebrated "Wehrmacht Days" (German Army Days) for injured and off-duty troops.[8] In Maidstone, UK, politicians used the lion cage as a backdrop for their war savings campaigns.[9] In addition to its normal attractions, the Cincinnati Zoo displayed captured military paraphernalia, including an engine from a German Messerschmitt; the Toronto Zoo, meanwhile, boasted patriotic rallies featuring, among others, the world-famous singing Dionne Quintuplets.[10]

Zoo advocates made a point of extending this spirit of patriotism to the animals themselves. Writing in the *New York Times* in December 1939, Sylvia Lucas offered a typically upbeat take on the can-do spirit of Britain's zoo animals. Faced with cutbacks in food and fuel, the London Zoo "enlisted" its captive inhabitants to ready the nation for war: llamas and camels carried "food supplies to the other animals and sandbags to the air-raid shelters"; Shetland ponies drew messenger carts throughout the city; elephants plowed land for crops.[11] Trained chimpanzees, it seems, were especially prone to patriotic showboating— not that they had much choice in the matter. Although zoo chimps had some degree of agency (they could bite, snarl, climb, refuse to eat, throw feces, spit on visitors, and generally make a nuisance of themselves), they had little power to refuse their keepers' wishes.[12] In Detroit, chimps decked out in military uniforms were filmed shooting toy guns at caricatures of Hideki Tojo.[13] The San Diego Zoo circulated photos of Georgie "weighing his own toy, a rubber tire, as he was about to 'turn it in' to the scrap rubber drive."[14] Hank, a chimpanzee in Chicago, was known to deliver a "Bronx Cheer" (what today we might call a "raspberry") when he heard Mel Blanc's rendition of "Der Führer's Face."[15]

No zoo animal better illustrates the fusion of wartime propaganda and zoo patriotism than Ming, the London Zoo's prized panda. Dubbed the "Shirley Temple of the Animal World" by the *Daily Mail*, Ming was a true media superstar, his anthropomorphized image reproduced on toys, postcards, brooches, and countless magazine covers.[16] Early in the war, zoo staff had evacuated the panda to the relative safety of Whipsnade, but his rural exile proved short-lived. In April 1940, with the aim of boosting home-front morale, the London Zoo announced Ming's imminent return to the capital. Newsreel coverage showed the panda in various wartime pursuits: stalking around his cage wearing an air raid helmet, holding a Union Jack between his paws (he liked to gnaw on the wooden stick), and entertaining members of the women's division of the Royal Canadian Air Force.[17] Later posters depicted Ming as an exemplar of Churchillian vigor, ready and willing to brave war's dangers alongside his human counterparts. In the hands of zoo propagandists, Ming was less a flesh-and-blood animal than a model citizen, eager to do his part in the war effort.[18]

Still, efforts to brand individual animals (or entire species) as die-hard partisans carried a risk. Zoos hoped to boost visitors' affection for their favorite animals, but *not so much* that they'd question the virtue of the beasts' lifelong confinement. Even celebrity animals had no control over their daily lives. After his heroic return to inner London, Ming spent his days on a bare concrete pad with only iron bars to separate him from a pride of lions on one side and chattering crowds of humans on the other. Zoo men wanted to have it both ways, publicizing cartoonish theatrics of animals' war sentiment while (wink-wink) acknowledging that it was all just a big joke. But holding "dumb"

Figure 13.1. Helmet in paw, with his identity card and ration coupons stuffed under his arm, a smiling Ming the panda returns to London after his rural retreat at Whipsnade Zoo. © Imperial War Museum (Art.IWM PST 18851).

(unspeaking) beasts in captivity was one thing; caging would-be patriots was something else entirely.[19] If zoo animals had the wherewithal to knit stockings, fill sandbags, don face masks, and wave the national standard (as zoo publicists liked to claim), how could zoos justify holding them captive?

Figure 13.2. Designed by famed illustrators Lewitt-Him, this poster is an advertisement for the London Zoo's "Off the Ration" Exhibition, which was part of a Ministry of Agriculture campaign to boost wartime food production. The kangaroo appears unfazed by the fact that it is leading the smiling pig, chicken, and rabbit to their certain deaths. © Imperial War Museum (Art.IWM PST 8106).

In early 1943, Arthur M. Greenhall, director of the Portland Zoo, was forced to confront this thorny issue head-on. After the zoo acquired a bald eagle that had been rescued six hundred miles out to sea, the local paper called for a national movement to free the birds from "hapless captivity." The editor cast the practice as an affront to American ideals:

> we shame ourselves as a free people, who claim the eagle as the emblem of our liberties, when we hold the bird in sorry prison like any felon or common fowl of the air. . . . The eagle, the bald eagle, specifically, and the great race of eagles more liberally, is the American totem, the visualization in life of the national ideal and purpose—freedom and fearlessness. If we degrade the bird by bars, forbidding it to soar into the windy sunshine, the epitome of liberty, what have we done to our spiritual natures?

The editorial did not dismiss the idea of zoos altogether. "Something of course might be said for the other animals we have caged for our pleasure and instruction and for the children to poke with sticks," its author granted with barely veiled hostility. But sentencing *these* beloved creatures to death-by-cage was a national insult. As for the need to educate Portland's kiddies: "A stuffed eagle would serve quite as well, cost less to keep, and experience none of the torments."[20]

These were alarming sentiments—and not simply as they pertained to eagles in wartime. Zoos' entire educational mission rested on the theory that nothing could replace people's experiences with *living* animals. This was what distinguished zoos from natural history museums—that indescribable spark of empathy and recognition, that ineffable feeling of wildness, that zoo advocates claimed could only be found in zoos (or in nature). If stuffed animals were just as good (or better than) their breathing-eating-shitting counterparts, it was that much more difficult to justify zoos' existence. Sensing the threat, Greenhall wrote William Mann for advice. Mann, typically, counseled the Portland Zoo director to ignore such complaints. Eagles can live half a century in captivity, he assured his colleague. Besides, "if an animal or bird will not live happily in confinement, its life is always short." By Mann's logic, zoo captivity could never be cruel; if a caged animal is alive, then ipso facto it must be happy.[21]

Healthful Amusements

Besides wrapping themselves in the flag, World War II–era zoos sought to brand themselves as "healthful" amusements, the ideal antidote to the crude (and morally corrupting) entertainments often frequented by soldiers on leave. For many nations, World War II represented a dangerous breakdown in social order. Old rules of behavior eroded, even in places relatively safe from the conflict's worst effects. Among the generation that would fight, and inevitably die, in World War II, public scolding about the dangers of sex and excess drinking carried little weight—not when death could be just around the corner. This was more than a question of public morality, as warring armies well knew. A soldier hospitalized because of venereal disease or a drunken accident was just as incapacitated as a man wounded on the battlefield. Plus, many nations clung to the fantasy that, for all the war's bloodshed and horror, *their* troops remained fundamentally innocent—clean of body and pure of heart. In this sense, zoos framed their contributions in both restorative and prophylactic terms, helping to heal the already injured while buffering the innocent against the moral hazards of wartime life.[22]

As early as October 1938, Tokyo's Ueno Zoo offered free admission to invalid veterans of the campaign in Nanjing, their traditional white kimonos and hats distinguishing them from the rest of the zoo-going public.[23] Other zoos quickly followed suit, throwing open their doors, albeit sometimes selectively, to men and women in military uniform. In January 1940, Lord Richard Onslow, the president of the Zoological Society of London, announced that troops and their wives would be admitted at half price, with the wounded allowed in for free. (On Sundays, everyone in uniform got in for free.) Such changes were remarkable given the London Zoo's century-long history as a private institution with only limited access. Still, the peer believed they represented a "good sample of the public spirit and patriotism" of the zoo society.[24] The San Diego Zoo limited its free admissions to trainees under officers' supervision, a compromise meant to prevent the zoo from being overrun by drunken recruits. In the first month of 1941, more than 2,700 sailors and 560 army troops visited the zoo, numbers that would grow throughout the war years.[25]

Zoos' benefits weren't confined to those in uniform. According to advocates, zoos performed a distinctly therapeutic purpose, calming

Figure 13.3. Two young sailors pose before the lion cage at the San Diego Zoo. Although Belle Benchley and others promoted zoo visits as healthy alternatives to seedier forms of R and R (e.g., getting drunk, visiting prostitutes), US service members nonetheless found plenty of ways to get into trouble on their trips to the zoo. Credit: San Diego History Center.

the nerves of a war-weary public. A visit to the London Zoo, remarked one observer, offered a "feeling of escape into a saner and more agreeable world."[26] Alex Downs Jr., writing in *Fauna*, the publication of the Philadelphia Zoological Society, agreed. "There is no place like a zoo, to help mend shattered nerves and give new incentive to those who have suffered man's inhumanity to man," he mused, deploying a common mixture of pop psychology and philosophizing.[27] In Berlin, Lutz Heck struck a similar chord, citing the numerous letters he'd received that testified to zoos' unique value. "In my view, occupying oneself with the animal world is the best way to lead a healthier life," he asserted confidently, "and in particular to balance out the demands of the fight."[28]

Describing the "Defense Activities" of the San Diego Zoo in February 1942, director Belle Benchley offered a characteristically upbeat account of zoos' contributions to "public morale." At a time of social upheaval, with off-duty war workers and service personnel swarming into the nation's cities, the zoo provided "clean," carefully supervised recreation. Benchley talked up the benefits of zoos on young visitors in particular. After spending time at a zoo, "tense and jittery children" returned to school "relaxed and thinking of something whole and normal." Unlike movies and radio stories, which she claimed were "bound to be built upon war plots and tragedies," the zoo offered kids a chance to escape their wartime worries and "get out to nature." The logic behind such sentiments was somewhat incongruous (and not just because of the unnaturalness of the zoo as an institution). No zoo could fully separate itself from the war's effects. Indeed, the more zoos tried to display their patriotic sentiment, the more publicly they announced their defense plans or studded their grounds with bomb shelters and armed guards, the more difficult it became to convince the anxious public that everything was "business as usual." Still, Benchley and other zoo advocates would not be dissuaded. In her mind, the zoo remained the "most wholesome form of constructive entertainment to be found in the city."[29]

Read today, such arguments can appear absurdly naïve, particularly against the backdrop of the war's unfathomable suffering. There is a quality of *protesting too much* to many zoo defenses, especially those written by zoo employees such as Benchley. And yet, they reflected a dawning consensus about the importance of the "home front" in an age of total war. On all sides of the conflict, propagandists agreed: World War II would be won on the battlefield but not without the support and mental hardiness of people at home. R. J. Dunham, president of Chicago's Parks District, which oversaw the Lincoln Park Zoo, among other properties, insisted that park workers played an "essential" role in the war machine. "We are helping to make the men and women in war work healthier, more active, more full energy," he declared not long after the Pearl Harbor attack.[30] Zoos, parks, community gardens, and other outdoor spaces provided recreation, which was critical if nations hoped to convert pent-up civilian energies into victory in the field or at sea. For this reason alone, one British writer asserted, "a scientific menagerie is as essential to national welfare as art or literature, and can no more be dispensed with, if a people is to win through, and successfully reconstruct its normal life, when at last the 'Cease Fire' sounds."[31]

War Work

On top of boosting morale, zoos engaged in various forms of "war work" aimed at translating their firsthand knowledge—about animal welfare, environmental dangers, and the like—for military use. As their supporters liked to point out, zoos were experts in the tricky practice of keeping things alive, the bare requisite of any successful military. Every zookeeper was a veteran of a daily battle against hunger, disease, and decay. Zoo scientists and animal wranglers tended to be well acquainted with living, at least temporarily, in arctic, tropical, and desert climates. Beyond their expertise, zoos cultivated a culture of worker pluckiness that mirrored the DIY spirit celebrated in wartime propaganda. Frequently underfunded and understaffed, many zoos had little choice but to "make do," whether that meant jury-rigging a temporary cage, rationing medical supplies, or sacrificing some animals in order to keep others. In short, the world's zoo professionals saw themselves as vital wartime resources if military leaders had the wherewithal to use them.

Zoos' most visible war work came in the form of educational displays.* Some of these were little more than propaganda (in Tokyo, for example, zoo staff offered detailed information about nations recently conquered by the Japanese Imperial Army), but many zoos' contributions had a decidedly utilitarian bent.[32] In the spring of 1940, the London Zoo hosted a large "war utility exposition" designed to teach city-dwelling Britons how to stretch their food budgets. Zoo staff and government workers built model backyard farms and provided hands-on advice about raising rabbits, milking goats, keeping silkworms, and killing vermin.[33] Elsewhere, zoo workers mobilized their expertise in such diverse fields as tropical disease and animal pathology. In New Jersey, staff from nearby zoos in Staten Island and Philadelphia toured USO clubs and YMCAs with joking demonstrations of various reptiles. (Among other lessons: rattlesnakes displayed an "American attitude of striking only in self-defense of liberty.")[34] The Bronx Zoo distributed books on natural history to US troops in the Pacific. The zoo also staged a "Lost in the Jungle" exhibit, designed by its world-renowned

---

* At the war's end, staff at the Moscow Zoo received the Red Banner of Labor for exhibits on animal husbandry, their school and hospital outreach programs, their work to breed mice for vaccine research, and their efforts to raise chickens to feed Moscow workers.

Department of Tropical Research, to teach zoo-goers how to survive if stranded in jungle terrain. The exhibit attracted some 230,000 visitors in 1943 alone. It was a special favorite of men in uniform, who reportedly spent hours copying down its instructions by hand.[35]

Not that all zoos' war work was meant for public consumption. In the Bronx, William Beebe converted his deep-sea bathysphere into a kind of underwater laboratory, testing depth charges, shark repellents, and the viability of "parasitized fish" as emergency food rations.[36] His colleague, Dr. Christopher W. Coates, relocated from the aquarium at Coney Island to the lion house at the Bronx Zoo, conducted top-secret experiments with electric eels.[37] Working with a military lab, the Philadelphia Zoo milked snakes to develop various anti-venoms for use in the Pacific.[38] The National Zoo did the same, displaying one group of anonymous blotchy olive snakes in a glass cage beneath a sign that read "recent addition." Only at the war's end did Washingtonians learn the truth: the mystery serpents were in fact venomous habu (*Protobothrops flavoviridis*) collected during the battle of Okinawa and flown to DC as part of a classified program to develop anti-venom.[39]

In a few cases, zoo staff even entered the field (and not simply as soldiers). In 1944, William Mann embarked on a tour of the Solomon Islands, at one point landing with the troops at Bougainville, to report on sanitary and dietary conditions in New Caledonia. Armed with a four-page questionnaire, he toured latrines, evaluated the effectiveness of insecticides, and quizzed troops about whether they preferred powdered or liquid milk (liquid proved to be a clear winner). While Mann might have been an unlikely agent for such an assignment, few civilians had his experience living in tropical climates, battling mildew and disease, and trying to satisfy the dietary requirements of large numbers of disgruntled eaters.

For individual soldiers, zoos' most important contributions to the war effort had nothing to do with spreading propaganda or carrying out experiments. Some troops saw the zoo as a place to escape the drudgery of wartime life, at least for an afternoon. According to one correspondent, Australian "Diggers" flocked to the Cairo Zoo during their off-hours—it was free, shaded (in a largely unshaded city), and the smell of the zoo's gum trees reminded them of home.[40]

Others saw the zoo as an impartial arbiter of the sort rarely found in military culture. Throughout the war, soldiers wrote their hometown

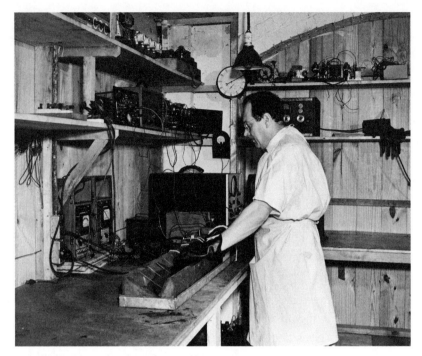

Figure 13.4. Once described by *Time* magazine as the "New York Aquarium's inquisitive tropical fishman," Christopher Coates spent part of World War II conducting nerve gas experiments using electric eels. © Wildlife Conservation Society. Reproduced by permission of the WCS Archives.

zoos asking them to settle the kinds of bets that inevitably arose among bored young men. *Are white crows real or are they just a myth?* (They're real.) *Is the Kodiak bear the largest member of the bear family?* (It is, though some experts disagree.) In May 1945, an American soldier stationed in the Marianas asked William Mann to put to rest a five-day argument: *Do boa constrictors strike their victims and then squeeze them to death? Or does it happen the other way around?* (According to Mann, the great snakes first bite and then coil around their prey; however, it happens so rapidly that "it seems like one movement.")[41]

For the world's zoo men, answering soldiers' letters was the least they could do to help the war effort. More than that, they hoped to instill in troops a love of wild animals—and zoos!—for decades to come. In some respects, zoos' wartime contributions were no different than those of other venues of popular amusement. Film studios, public parks, museums—they too mixed entertainment, propaganda, and education to "do their bit" in World War II. Zoo leaders buoyed the public with thrilling tales of courage under fire, even as they sought to distance their institutions from the worst of the war's horrors. In a 1941 article, "The Zoo's Peace Aims," writer James Fisher drew a distinction between zoology, which he associated with future abundance and goodwill, and the dehumanizing "sciences of the present."[42]

Nevertheless, the wartime zoo industry—in the United States, Britain, Germany, and elsewhere—willingly set aside its pretenses of scientific objectivity in the name of nationalist obligation. As one American zoo leader declared not long after the United States' entry into the conflict:

> War of the kind we are now waging raises problems that would hardly be conceived in peace time and the answers must be sought in fields that normally have little to do with the cataclysm of war. Lines of research that might have been cited as examples of "pure science" found themselves suddenly on the other side of the fence— "practical," rather than "pure," science. By some twist of war's necessities, some of the most theoretical considerations were adaptable to pressing practical endeavors.[43]

This logic would lead zoo men to sacrifice animals in the name of military experimentation and apply their hard-won knowledge to the practical endeavor of national defense. It was also the same logic that would justify doctors' participation in the Holocaust and physicists' development of the atomic bomb.

But that was still in the future. As the war entered its darkest years, conditions at wartime zoos reached new lows—in a Soviet Union under siege, a starving Japanese empire, and a German nation blown apart from above.

PART IV

Carnivore Encounters

14

Sacrificial Lambs

In October 1942, after more than a year of deadly siege, a plane took off from Leningrad en route to Moscow. Among the passengers were thirteen monkeys from the world-famous Physiological Institute, whose former director, Ivan Pavlov, had achieved global fame (and, in some quarters, scorn) for his experiments on animal conditioning. According to a *New York Times* story, Pavlov's simian disciples were impeccably mannered—some even took to looking out the window as the plane bumped and rattled toward its destination. After more than an hour of dodging German fighter planes and antiaircraft fire, the flying menagerie set down in the Soviet capital. Institute staff unstrapped the monkeys from their seats and transported them to the Moscow Zoo. Theirs was not a future of public display, however. The thirteen monkeys were fated to die for "experimental purposes"—sacrificed, like untold animals before them, in the name of wartime science.[1]

During World War II, Allied and Axis governments demanded sacrifice—and they weren't shy about letting their people know:

> . . . If I call the Wehrmacht, if I now demand the German people to sacrifice, and if necessary, I demand to sacrifice everything, I have the right to do so. Because I am ready today, as I did in the past, to bring any personal sacrifice. (Adolf Hitler)[2]

> "Give 'em the stuff to fight with . . ." SACRIFICE FOR FREEDOM! (American propaganda poster)[3]

The Red Army has a stern struggle before it against a crafty, cruel and still formidable enemy. This struggle will require time, sacrifice, the exertion of all our efforts and the mobilization of all our potentialities. (Joseph Stalin)[4]

Out of the depths of sorrow and sacrifice will be born again the glory of mankind. (Winston Churchill)[5]

At their most idealistic, references to sacrifice elevated the simplest acts—sharing a car, eating a meatless meal—into expressions of civic virtue. Sacrifice was unpleasant; it implied suffering, but suffering for a reason, a higher good. If ordinary folks were willing to give up something now, the logic went, they had a chance to earn something more valuable down the road (namely, victory). According to wartime leaders, people's willingness to sacrifice was the difference between survival and defeat. What, if anything, could be more important than that?

It's only fair to view references to wartime sacrifice with a healthy dose of cynicism. Even in the most democratically minded nations, the poorest and most vulnerable frequently had to bear the brunt of government demands for fresh bodies. In a testament to the ancient principle of "old men start wars, young men fight them," millions of military-age youth were called upon to risk life and limb on their elders' behalf. Wartime governments weren't afraid to use scare tactics when making their appeals, either. This was especially true in authoritarian regimes, where those who refused to fall in line faced social exile, prison, or worse. In this sense, government talk of sacrifice was often little more than euphemism—a way to sugarcoat policies aimed at squeezing the most from war-addled citizens.

Yet, as the story of two nations' zoos shows us, the line between high-minded selflessness and naked propaganda was not always clear-cut. In Joseph Stalin's Soviet Union, besieged zoo-lovers forfeited precious calories to save zoo animals from the indignity of starvation. Faced with the imminent threat of aerial attack, Japanese authorities called on the nation's largest zoo to make the ultimate sacrifice: destroy its most charismatic (and potentially hazardous) megafauna to shock and inspire the Japanese people. At first glance, the fates of Soviet and Japanese zoos in the darkest days of World War II seem to send diametrically opposed messages about humans' obligations to

Sacrificial Lambs   187

the animals they keep. Step back a bit further, however, and the politics of zoo sacrifice appear far messier (in all possible ways) than initial appearances might lead us to believe.

Making Soviet Zoos

When the war in Europe began in August 1939, the Soviet Union was, at best, a middling player in the zoo world. Although Russian aristocrats had collected wild animals for display since the Middle Ages, the nation's first zoo, the Moscow Zoological Gardens, did not open until 1864, nearly forty years after the London Zoo and two decades after its counterpart in Berlin. The following year, the nation's second zoo was founded in St. Petersburg, where it was popular with military officers stationed nearby. In 1890, German-Russian landowner Friedrich Falz-Fein established Russia's third major zoological collection on his nearly 250,000-acre estate in Kherson Oblast near the Black Sea. Specializing in hoofed mammals native to the region, Askaniya Nova (New Ascania) kept ostriches, wisents, saiga antelopes, kangaroos, wildebeests, and Przewalski's horses in fenced-in pens open to the elements.[6] Czar Nicholas II was so impressed by Falz-Fein's "oasis on the steppes" that he elevated him to nobility in 1915.[7] Despite such accolades, the first generation of Russian zoos were plagued by debt, mismanagement, and political instability, making it all but impossible to keep up with their European cohort.

That started to change after 1917. The Bolshevik Revolution breathed new life into Russia's zoos, even as it sought to remake them in the state's image. Government edicts placed zoos under the "direct supervision" of local bureaucrats (who reported to bosses in Moscow), ensuring a decidedly top-down model of institutional control. Zoos were expected to practice and promote "Soviet science," specifically a form of modified Darwinism shorn of its "reactionary" elements.* Stalin's agricultural advisors also wanted zoos to develop a program of "practical zoology" to benefit the enormous *kolkhozy* (collective farms)

---

* Hostile to talk of natural selection, the new "scientific biology" held that humans can bend the natural world to suit their interests. "We must not wait for favours from Nature," botanist and apple breeder I. V. Michurin declared darkly. "Our task is to wrest them from her." Trofin Denisovich Lysenko, "The Situation in the Science of Biology" (1948).

in eastern Russia and Ukraine.[8] Zoos would continue to entertain the masses, of course, but moving forward, they had an additional mandate to provide real-world solutions to problems facing the Soviet people.

Flush with ideological purpose, Soviet zoos began a rapid turnaround. After years of financial mismanagement and disrepair, the Moscow Zoo expanded and modernized its facilities. In 1930, the renamed Leningrad Zoo became the first Soviet zoo to breed polar bear cubs, a rare achievement at that time. Perhaps the greatest about-face occurred at Askaniya Nova. When the Revolution began, Falz-Fein fled to Germany (his elderly mother, who refused to leave, was executed by Red Army troops), and the Black Sea estate fell into disrepair. In the years that followed, however, Askaniya Nova was rebuilt as a combination zoo, nature preserve, cattle breeding station, and research center focused on hybridizing and acclimatizing domestic animals from the region.[9] All told, more than ten new zoos opened in Soviet territory between 1919 and 1941.[10]

But state control brought its own set of problems. As historian Leszek Solski explains, "To become a director, or to keep any other kind of important position in a zoo, required not only appropriate qualifications . . . but one also had to be a member of the Communist Party."[11] Unlike in Europe and the United States, where zoo men often prided themselves on their independence and adventurous spirit, Soviet zoo directors had to maintain a high degree of "ideological vigilance." When the People's Commissariat for Internal Affairs, the home-front security force better known as the NKVD, arrested a Moscow Zoo employee as a "class-alien element" in October 1941, for example, members of the zoo collective reproached the zoo's director for failing to halt the infiltration of "spies and saboteurs."[12] (The jailed employee was inexplicably back at work a few weeks later.) At the same time, Soviet zoo directors remained somewhat estranged from their peers in the West. Not one belonged to the prewar IUDZG, and exchanges with zoos outside the USSR were comparatively few and far between.

The Hippo of Leningrad

On June 22, 1941, Germany launched Operation Barbarossa, Hitler's long-planned invasion of the Soviet Union. More than 150 German divisions poured into the Balkans, Belorussia, and Soviet-occupied

Figure 14.1. Two German soldiers at Askaniya Nova in Ukraine in 1941. Sueddeutsche Zeitung Photo / Alamy.

Poland. By mid-October, Hitler's forces had bombed, burned, and bulldozed their way to roughly sixty miles from Moscow.

Zoos in sectors overrun by German troops proved to be ripe pickings. In the Ukrainian capital of Kiev, invading forces followed a playbook they'd used in Poland: the best, they confiscated for shipment back home; the rest, they either ate or left to suffer slow deaths from hunger and disease. Askaniya Nova met a similar fate. After several years under German occupation, Wehrmacht troops proceeded to loot the zoo reserve, sending the best (and most valuable) specimens back to Germany. Never short on excuses, Berlin Zoo director Lutz Heck would later claim he had been trying to "save" the animals, particularly the endangered Przewalski's horses. (Göring himself wanted one of the stocky horses for his personal forest preserve.) If so, Heck failed miserably. By one historian's reckoning, "nearly 70 percent of [the animals] transferred from the eastern front died in German zoos and wildlife parks from aerial bombardment or deprivation."[13]

In Moscow, the effects of the invasion were more immediate and no less lethal. Before the first German crossed the border, the Moscow

Zoo's newly appointed director, Trofim Burdelev, evacuated two shipments of animals with disastrous results. One, destined for Stalingrad, simply disappeared from the record. The other, which included an African elephant (Nona), a rhino (Mari), and several big cats, survived a two-thousand-kilometer train trip to Sverdlovsk only to be refused help by the locals.[†] Fearing an aerial attack on the Russian capital, Burdelev authorized staff to euthanize the zoo's collection of venomous snakes, polar bears, and other large carnivores. He was just in time: on July 22–23, 1941, more than five hundred phosphorous bombs hit the zoo, the first of a number of similar, and increasingly deadly, episodes.[14]

The zoo's problems weren't limited to falling bombs. Overwhelmed, the Moscow municipal government cut funding when the zoo needed it most.[15] Unable to secure adequate food supplies, zoo workers, now 98 percent women, cobbled together whatever they could, often replacing foreign citrus with blander, less nutrient-dense grains sourced from nearby. Always aware of their larger obligations, employees and volunteers raised poultry (to feed the war effort) and taught homeworkers to breed white mice, guinea pigs, and Angora rabbits for vaccine testing and various military applications. (The rabbits' fur, historian Tracy McDonald tells us, was used to line soldiers' gloves.) All the while, the zoo's veterinary staff fought an unbroken battle against infection, disease, and decay, the effects of which were impossible to ignore.[16]

Farther to the west, in the port city of Leningrad, the German invasion turned hunger into a weapon of war. By September 1941, German troops had encircled the city, cutting off all access except for the "Road of Life," a precarious transport route across the ice of Lake Ladoga. With the onset of winter, temperatures plummeted, and manual workers' allotments of cabbage and bread—a mix of rye flour, chaff, and whatever else bakers could find—dipped to the equivalent of 700 calories per day. (Nonmanual workers and kids received far less.)[17] People consumed anything they could get their hands on: wallpaper paste, linseed oil, boiled leather soup, wood shavings, joiner's glue

---

[†] As a result, most of the animal evacuees died of starvation—a chilling reminder that while people might be willing to sacrifice for *their* zoo, they might not be willing to help someone else's.

(which contained "proteinaceous material"), soggy bread fried in paint thinner, cologne, tooth powder.[18] Eventually, writes historian Todd Tucker, some people "descended into a rare kind of hunger, a hunger that tested even the most fundamental taboos."[19] Pets disappeared from homes, and whispers of cannibalism spread among the most desperate.

The Leningrad Zoo had not waited to take evasive action. In August 1941, staff evacuated eighty of their most precious animals—tigers, polar bears, black panthers, an adult rhinoceros, and a tapir (in appearance, a cross between an elephant and a wild pig)—to the Volga river city of Kazan, some 1,200 kilometers to the southwest.[20] (The evacuation train vanished on the return to Leningrad in 1944. The fate of the animals onboard is unknown, but it's not hard to guess what happened.) That same month, the director dispatched a band of soldiers to shoot the large predators (tigers, wolves, lions) as a precaution against falling shells.[21] They did not have to wait long. On September 8, the day the Siege began, a bomb landed on the elephant house, collapsing the roof. Trapped beneath the rubble, her lungs crushed and wailing in pain, Betty, the star Asian elephant, became one of the first martyrs of the Blockade years—a symbol of the life that Hitler wanted to destroy.[22]

The Leningrad Zoo's greatest challenge, it will come as no surprise, was meeting animals' unrelenting demand for nourishment. Early on, employees scavenged the corpses of horses, invented new recipes for rat flesh, and gathered plants and berries in the countryside. The following spring, zoo staff planted cabbage, oats, turnips, and new grass for hay. In an attempt to win over picky carnivores, cooks stuffed hollowed-out rabbit and guinea pig skins with a mix of grass, cabbage leaves, and discarded vegetable matter, which were then boiled in water, slathered in fish oil, and flavored with a few drops of blood.[23] On occasion, keepers even shared their own meager rations with the animals, giving away precious calories when they needed them most.

No figure exemplified the zoo's spirit of sacrifice more than Yevdokia Dashina. With hundreds of Leningrad residents dropping dead of hunger every week, Dashina was tasked with caring for the zoo's prized hippopotamus, Beauty, who had been brought to the city in 1911. It's an understatement to say that hippos are ill suited to life on the snowy Baltic. They evolved over the last million or so years to live in the warm, muddy rivers of sub-Saharan Africa. Unless exposed to heat and moisture, their thick, mucus-covered skin will dry and crack into pus-filled blisters. Adult hippos also require up to a hundred pounds of food per day, preferably fresh, to maintain their massive bulk—a burden for any zoo in peacetime, an impossibility in a famine. Most days, all Dashina could muster at feeding time was a mix of grass, leftover plant pulp, a few meager vegetables, and about thirty kilograms of "steamed sawdust," a fraction of Beauty's normal fare but far more than most Leningrad families could hope to enjoy. Rain or shine, Dashina made daily trips to the Neva River for fresh water, which she transported in a large barrel atop a wooden sled. After heating it over an open fire, she ladled the water over Beauty's skin, which she'd then massage with camphor oil.[24] It was dangerous, tedious, backbreaking, and often invisible work, exacerbated by Dashina's own slow starvation. Against impossible odds, Beauty survived the Blockade, not dying at the zoo until 1951.

Given the circumstances, starving Leningraders might have easily abandoned the zoo as a peacetime luxury, butchering its inmates for the valuable calories their meat and sinew would provide. If ever a city could be forgiven for raiding the zoological pantry, it would have to be Leningrad in 1941–1944. And yet, in perhaps the most famous example of wartime rationing of the modern era, Leningraders kept their knives at bay.

So, we ask again: Why did they do it? Why at a time when hundreds of people were dying of hunger daily would Leningrad Zoo staff risk so much to save a group of animals? And why would Leningrad residents allow them to do so?

The simplest answer is that it was their job. Staff had a personal, professional, and patriotic duty to care for the zoo as best they could— and, in a time of national crisis, that would have been all the justification they needed. But that's not the only reason. In a culture that celebrated (and, to some degree, demanded) "maternal self-sacrifice," the female keepers would have felt doubly obligated to give everything to save those in their care.[25] The campaign to save the zoo animals from starvation also reflected official propaganda, which shifted over the course of the war from defending party ideology to defending "Mother Russia" (its land, its institutions, its inhabitants).[26] Leningrad residents were determined to keep the cultural and scientific life of the city alive. To do less would be to admit defeat.

Ultimately, the most convincing explanation is that Leningrad residents empathized with the zoo animals. They knew what it meant to be mad with hunger and trapped in a cage not of their making. More than any other event before or since, the Siege threatened to unmask Leningrad residents' basest selves and ugliest appetites. "Starvation tends to reduce us to a primitive, 'dehumanized' state in which our only concern is to find food," historian Darra Goldstein observes in her account of the Siege. "Under such conditions so far beyond our everyday understanding of 'alienation,' when one's very self [is] undone, it [is] difficult to care about anyone other than oneself."[27] And yet, at this moment, in the worst conditions imaginable, enough people did just that—they cared about the needs of others.

Patriotic Hunger

Even as the citizens of Leningrad waged war against starvation, news of a different sort of zoo sacrifice was beginning to emerge in Japan.[28] After a wave of Japanese victories early in the war, the tide had turned in dramatic fashion. On April 18, 1942, the Doolittle Raid marked the first American air attack on the main island, puncturing the myth that Japan was somehow out of reach of US air power. By that summer, propaganda messages began to shift from exhortations of victory to warnings about the battles yet to come. No one dared predict defeat. Even the most optimistic Allied commanders knew it would take years to secure the Japanese homeland militarily. But, if the Imperial Army had any chance at victory, Japanese leaders reasoned, it would require a level of commitment thus far unmatched among all the warring nations.

Higher-ups at Tokyo's Ueno Zoo had prepared for this turn of events. One year earlier, newly installed acting director Saburō Fukuda ordered the killing of four "surplus" bears in an effort to stretch resources. That August, the zoo submitted a "general plan" outlining what steps to take in case of an emergency. Like the London Zoo's wartime security measures, it divided Tokyo's animal holdings into categories from most to least dangerous and provided detailed instructions about how to dispatch them in the event of an air raid. Ever conscious of public opinion, Fukuda and his staff hoped to avoid gunplay, which they feared might traumatize visiting families. Instead, the preferred means of execution was a fast-acting poison such as cyanide or strychnine nitrate—something that could put down a five-ton elephant without the noise, mess, and expense of blowing its brains out.[29]

On August 16, 1943, Fukuda received word that Shigeo Ōdachi, Tokyo's governor-general, had decided that the time had come to put the "general plan" into action. Although slaughtering the zoos' dangerous inmates was initially justified as a security measure, Ōdachi had a different agenda: to shock war-weary Tokyoites into a renewed commitment to the struggle. In his memoirs, former zoo director Tadamichi Koga, who had taken temporary leave from the zoo to teach at Tokyo's Army Veterinary School during the war, recalled receiving the news:

> At the time I felt "Oh, finally things have come to this." . . . When [Ōdachi] returned to the motherland to become governor of Tokyo and saw the attitude of the people, he seems to have felt keenly that he had to open the people's eyes to the fact that this was not the way to go, that war was not such an easy affair. And Ōdachi chose to give the people the warning not by expressing it in words, but by the disposal of the zoo's wild beasts.[30]

In one decisive blow, the governor-general hoped to transform the people's love of animals into hatred for their enemies. Preventing escapes was the pretext; reanimating Tokyoites' fighting spirit, the point. Look at what they made us do. Never doubt our commitment to sacrifice and suffer.

From the start of the killing spree, however, Fukuda and his staff proved to be ambivalent about how much they wanted the public to see. In late August, signs about "construction work" went up around the zoo, though workers made little effort to disguise their deadly mission. As historian Freddy Litten, author of several works on the "great zoo massacre," points out: "Killing the animals was meant to become known to the public anyway, otherwise it would not have fulfilled its propaganda purpose."[31] The first to die, on August 17, were a pair of bears, both poisoned with strychnine provided by the Army Veterinary

School. Four days later, after poison failed to get the job done, keepers got creative, stabbing one brown bear to death and strangling another bear with a rope while it slept. (Presumably, it woke up in time to have the life choked out of it.) Less than a week later—I cannot fathom why—Ueno Zoo staff decided to kill a rattlesnake by forcing a piece of heated wire into its head, which was subsequently fashioned into a kind of subcutaneous noose. When the snake refused to die, they eventually decided to put it out of its misery . . . after sixteen hours. Perhaps the most gruesome pair of executions took place on August 29. That day, employees strangled the zoo's remaining polar bear, already weakened from starvation, with a wire and beat an American bison to death with a pickaxe and a hammer. All told, twenty-four animals— including leopards (poisoned, strangled), a sun bear (poisoned), a python (decapitated), another polar bear (starved), and a leopard cub (poisoned)—died in the first round of propaganda killings, sacrificed to harden the people's hearts for the struggle ahead.[32]

On September 2, the metropolitan government notified the media about the recent "disposal" efforts at Ueno Zoo. Two days later, the zoo held a memorial service to honor the animals' sacrifice. Hundreds of Tokyo-area schoolchildren attended, as did several top government administrators, the governor-general included. Speaking to a Tokyo newspaper, zoo director Fukuda repeated the official line on the zoo killings: "At a time of decisive battle, this is actually an unavoidable measure that must be taken. . . . [The animals] went to their deaths to let the people know in silence about the unavoidability of air attacks."[33]

Of all the animals on the zoo's kill list, none provoked greater outpourings of sympathy than the three elephants, Jon (male), Tonki (female), and Hanako (female). Although Ueno's pachyderms were among the zoo's most valuable—and popular—living attractions, Fukuda's superiors considered them a hazard to visitor safety. Even before the zoo killings, park staff had removed Jon from public display, chaining him in his pen for weeks on end. (He was said to be too aggressive toward his keepers.) Then, on August 13, in consultation with his boss in the Tokyo parks office, Fukuda pulled Jon's food and water. Tonki and Hanako were placed on starvation diets a little more than a week later, left to suffer in agony as their bodies slowly began to shut down. After twelve days, Jon stopped breathing, but the female elephants clung to life for weeks. In fact, on the date of the memorial service, Hanako and Tonki remained very much alive, literally a stone's throw from the lines of schoolchildren, their emaciated bodies hidden behind vertical sheets of striped bunting.[34]

We don't have to project ourselves into the minds of Jon, Tonki, and Hanako to know that their torment was immense. Without food, the elephants would have faced a host of symptoms: loss of fat and muscle, apathy, skin lesions, irregular heartbeat, and eventually total organ failure. Starvation is a relatively common cause of death for aged, wild elephants that can no longer feed themselves once their teeth have worn away. But that was not the case here. On September 11, more than two weeks after zoo staff last fed her, Hanako collapsed in her cage. Tonki hung on two weeks longer, all the while performing tricks in a feeble attempt to coax food from her keepers. Finally, after a month of bewildering hunger, the last of the Ueno three died as she had lived: helpless against the whims of her keepers.

The Politics of Zoo Sacrifice

When confronted with these stories, it would be easy to lean into national stereotypes. The moral drama of the Leningrad Zoo gels with the idealized vision of Soviet fortitude in the Great Patriotic War. As early as the 1940s, Stalin dubbed Leningrad a "hero city," a model of collective bravery in the face of impossible odds. Historian Anna Reid has called the effort to preserve the Leningrad Zoo one of the few "specks of light in a vast darkness," emblematic of ordinary people's willingness to put others' lives above their own.[35]

The propaganda killings at Tokyo's Ueno Zoo, by contrast, fit a distinctly Japanese understanding of patriotic sacrifice. As Litten points out, the animal's state-imposed martyrdom aligned with the celebration of *gyoukusai* (shattering like a jewel), the death-with-honor mentality associated with banzai attacks.[36] Mayumi Itoh, author of a book on Japan's wartime zoo policy, agrees, arguing that "no country conducted as nationwide and systematic a disposal of zoo animals as Japan."[37] Other nations killed their zoo animals, certainly. But only in Japan was the highest level of government so willing and eager to use animal death to inspire its people.

That being said, we shouldn't lose sight of the similarities between the two nations' responses. Soviet zoos, like their Japanese counterparts, were more than willing to destroy "dangerous" or excessively expensive animals when it suited their purpose. Moreover, from the very beginning, popular memory of both nations' zoos was filtered through the machinery of state propaganda. To this day, accounts of the Moscow and Leningrad zoos often exemplify socialist realist tendencies to cast all war-related efforts in a heroic light. As early as 1944, Russian literary critic Lidiya Ginzburg noted a kind of self-imposed amnesia among her fellow Leningraders.[‡] Instead of dwelling on the acts of desperation and cruelty, people constructed an "aggregate feeling that they had remained in the city, suffered, patiently endured, that they had not feared death, that they had continued to work and to participate in the course of life."[38]

Plus, it's important to compare like for like. If we're going to celebrate the grit of Soviet zookeepers, we must also acknowledge that Japanese zoo staff had little choice in the matter. Just as in Stalin's Soviet Union, Japanese zoo staff lacked any power to buck the system. Higher-ups blocked all attempts by Fukuda to send the elephants out of the city where, presumably, they would have posed less of a threat in an air raid. I have little doubt that Leningrad's zookeepers would have done the same as their Tokyo counterparts if Stalin's government had demanded it. In the end, though, it doesn't really matter *why* specific animals died. What matters is that they did. For every Beauty the hippopotamus, many more perished in bombing raids, were butchered for meat, contracted hypothermia, and starved to death. The triumph of the Leningrad Zoo obscures the broader landscape of animal suffering in wartime Soviet zoos.

In time, both nations' zoo stories would be folded into public myths about the war and its meaning. The "rescue" of the Leningrad Zoo animals came to symbolize the spirit of sacrifice that is central to state memories of the Great Patriotic War. Even after the city was renamed

---

[‡] An optimistic reporter told Americans in 1943: "I have seen none of the neurotic types described by novelists of the last war's 'lost generation.' Everybody here knows why he is fighting and is ready to fight on." Even the Leningrad Zoo's lone tiger wasn't complaining, though it was now a "vegetarian." Henry Shapiro, "100,000 Died in Leningrad Siege; People Fought Off 300,000 Nazis," *New York Times*, June 29, 1943, 6.

St. Petersburg, the zoo would retain its Soviet-era name as a testament to the heroism and selflessness of the zoo staff. Meanwhile, generations of Japanese schoolchildren would grow up learning about Tokyo's elephant patriots. First published in 1951 and later expanded into a picture book in 1970, Yukio Tsuchiya's *The Pitiful Elephants* reframes the animals' deaths through an anti-militarist lens. At the climax, the book shows the dead elephants' distraught keeper—fists clenched, arms raised—screaming toward the sky: "Stop the war! Stop the war! Stop all wars!"[39] But make no mistake: Jon, Hanako, and Tonki did *not* die because of "the war" (or even the generic "all wars"), as much as I sympathize with the keeper's peace-minded sentiments. They died because Japan was losing, and one Tokyo bureaucrat hoped that this might help turn the tide. Decades after the war, the elephants' deaths continue to be molded to rewrite history and cast their keepers' actions in the best light possible.

That, however, was in the future. In the fall of 1943, the long-awaited threat of destruction from above had finally started to hit home.

15

Bombing the Zoo

It is the summer of 1943, and a German zoo is under attack. Heavy-explosive bombs tumble down from above, smashing into buildings. Shrapnel tears through wood, reduces brick walls to rubble. As bursts of flak pockmark the sky, smoke from burning fires blankets the ground in suffocating haze. Amid the chaos are sounds of terror and pain: whimpering, howling, roaring, trumpeting, screeching. Then come the tremors, stomach-turning in their implications, like those of an earthquake reaching its peak. Furious with terror and rage, the elephants have broken free from their cages. And they want their revenge.

If this sounds like a scene from a movie, that's because it is. Filmed on location at Munich's Hellabrunn Animal Park, *Panik* tells the story of Peter Fanger, a German *Großtierfänger* (large animal catcher) in East Africa. At the onset of World War II, he returns home, taking up a job as an animal keeper at the zoo. In the film's climax, an air raid allows several elephants to escape their cages and rampage through the zoo grounds. The film's director, Harry Piel (who also starred), had started production in 1940, shooting footage off and on over the next few years. A veteran of more than a hundred films, he had hoped the film would meld Frank Buck–style action and home-front melodrama.

But by 1943, the film's subject matter seemed to hit a little too close to home—literally. Despite Piel's impeccable Nazi credentials (he had joined the party a decade earlier and his films were SS favorites), Reich film policy promoted escapism, not ripped-from-the-headlines realism. In October of that year, Joseph Goebbels banned the film from

Figure 15.1. Unseen during the war years, Piel's film was eventually released as *Gesprengte Gitter—Die Elephanten Sind Los* (Broken Bars—The Elephants Are Loose) in 1953. In the United States, the film went by a punchier, albeit no less ominous, title: *Elephant Fury*. Everett Collection, Inc. / Alamy.

future release. The Nazi film board didn't want to send the message that Germany was vulnerable to aerial attack. As it turns out, they were right to be worried.[1]

Instinctively, many people feel a sense of revulsion at the thought of dropping bombs from an airplane.[2] There is something about it that seems categorically unfair, the very opposite of the macho courage espoused in recruiting ads and pro-war pageantry. During World War I, front-line troops railed against the presumed cowardice of those who did their killing at a distance. And yet, for all our misgivings, we've come to accept aerial bombardment as an inevitable, albeit sordid, fact of modern warfare. In countries like the United States, launching missiles from airplanes—or, more likely, unmanned drones—is often promoted as a more humane alternative to putting troops in "harm's way." (The same cannot be said for those on the other end of American gun sights.)[3] For all the noble talk about avoiding "collateral damage," few nations have been able to resist the lure of aerial bombing if they've had the chance to deploy it. During World War II, the Western Allies dropped 2.7 million tons of bombs on Europe alone, obliterating whatever pretense was left about the line between military and civilian life.[4]

For World War II–era zoos, aerial bombing represented an existential threat on several levels. In their efforts to ward off fears of animal escape, some zoos took the drastic step of preemptively destroying some of their most precious possessions, something that could not be said of other scientific and cultural institutions. (London's National Gallery, as a point of contrast, did not decide to torch its collection of Turners and Monets at the first blare of air raid sirens.) The experience of bombing forced both workers and visitors to grapple with the zoo's founding fiction: that humans can control the animals they cage. Above all else, though, the threat of aerial bombing transformed the character of war for millions of civilians, zoo folk among them.

Within the war's opening seconds, the race to obliterate homefront populations from the sky was well on its way, bringing some of the continent's oldest zoos squarely into the crosshairs.

From *Blitzkrieg* to the Blitz

In 1939–1940, as we've already seen, the bulk of zoos' bomb damage resulted from the *Blitzkrieg*, the German military strategy of using coordinated air and armor attacks to overwhelm enemy forces.[5] Zoos caught in the path of such assaults faced the threat of total obliteration. The Warsaw Zoo, for example, was pounded for nearly a month in the opening weeks of the war. During one raid, writes Diane Ackerman: "Some animals, hiding in their cages and basins, became engulfed by rolling waves of flame. Two giraffes lay dead on the ground, legs twisted, shockingly horizontal." Of the living: "The monkeys and birds, screeching infernally, created an otherworldly chorus backed by a crackling timpani of bullets and bomb blasts."[6]

Following Hitler's victories in the Netherlands and France in April–June 1940, European zoos faced a different threat: strategic bombing.[7] Closely associated with the concept of "total war," strategic bombing refers to the use of sustained aerial bombardment—months, possibly years, on end—against an enemy's war-making capabilities, both material and human. The goal of strategic bombing was not necessarily to soften up a target in the lead-up to immediate invasion, though that was often a long-term objective. Rather, it was designed, according to Royal Air Force Marshal Hugh Trenchard (sometimes dubbed the "patron saint of air power"), to destroy an enemy's "means of resistance" and weaken its "means to fight."[8] This meant, above all else, targeting cities and, inevitably, the people who lived in them. At their most optimistic, advocates of strategic bombing argued that protracted urban bombardment could break a nation's fighting spirit, its willingness to carry on amid the daily traumas of random and seemingly relentless violence. For this reason, some of the doctrine's founding fathers favored a different, though no less euphemistic, term: "morale bombing."[9]

Morale bombing moved from theory to reality in autumn 1940 with the start of the Blitz, perhaps the longest and deadliest campaign of aerial warfare to that time. From early September to mid-November 1940, German bombers pounded British cities over fifty-seven consecutive nights, killing and wounding tens of thousands of civilians. By the end of the Blitz the following year, the number of civilians killed, seriously wounded, or missing was close to 150,000.[10]

The London Zoo's first taste of the Blitz came on September 17. The sound of the exploding shells sent waves of panic through the captive animals. A young giraffe named Boxer was so frightened it fell dead of a heart attack; several antelopes met similar fates, killed not by the explosives themselves but by the terror they engendered.[11] Little more than a week later, on the night of September 27, the zoo endured its second round of bombings. High-explosive bombs damaged the rodent house, the civet house, and parts of the north gate. Amid the chaos, a zebra and an ass escaped to the nearby neighborhood of Camden, where they were recaptured the following day. That same night more than thirty incendiaries dropped onto the zoo grounds. In retrospect, perhaps the most shocking aspect of the episode was how *little* damage was done. Located at the north end of Regent's Park, less than three miles from the Cabinet's underground war rooms, the London Zoo could have easily fallen victim to a misguided bombing run.

Figure 15.2. In 1942, English painter Carel Victor Morlais Weight produced an oil canvas of the zebra's escape; the painting was purchased by Britain's War Artists' Advisory Committee, a government agency devoted to documenting the nation's wartime experiences, and eventually donated to the Manchester Art Gallery at the conflict's end. Credit: Manchester Art Gallery, UK, © Manchester Art Gallery / © Estate of Carel Weight.

In this, the animals at the London Zoo were remarkably lucky (those, that is, who weren't killed by their keepers in the war's early weeks).

The same was true for the inhabitants of the UK's smaller zoos. Although no British zoo experienced anything comparable to the destruction suffered on the Continent, even a single errant bomber could cause irreparable harm. In October 1940, a German plane dropped four bombs on the Chessington Zoo in southwest London after mistaking it for a nearby army camp. One hit the penguin enclosure; another smashed through the roof of an underground bunker and killed four people, including a ten-year-old boy.[12] The following month, the *New York Times* noted efforts to study animals' "behavior under fire" at the Maidstone Zoo, a private zoo located in the "invasion corner" of southeast England. At the sound of antiaircraft fire, one of the zoo's emus reacted so violently that her keepers thought she might "kill herself against her cage." Two chimps were known to "stamp and shriek at the sound of the siren," while a twenty-year-old elephant responded to antiaircraft barrages by rushing inside her house. But these were the "exceptions," the report explained. For the most part, Maidstone's collection of elephants, kangaroos, zebras, and yaks were said to have affected an air of blithe disinterest, showing "no reaction to the most violent air activity or anti-aircraft fire."[13]

Today, it is tempting to dismiss such reports as little more than wishful thinking or, more likely, propaganda. Facing the terror of German bombers, newspapers and government publications promoted an idealized vision of British society characterized by a willingness to carry on at all costs.[14] Although the myth of Britons' shared "Blitz spirit" has been widely debunked, British zoos' experiences in 1940–1941 showed it would take more than a few near misses to knock them out of action. (Had Göring's bombs landed a few yards to the left, a few to the right, the story would likely have been different.) Describing the mood in Regent's Park in mid-November 1940, one sympathetic writer struck an air of understated confidence: "Hitler's bombs cause a certain amount of damage . . . and a considerable amount of inconvenience, but they have not destroyed the morale or the routine of its inhabitants, animal or human."[15] If anything, months of bombing, at the kingdom's zoos and elsewhere, only hardened British resolve to strike back in kind.

German Zoos in an Age of Total War

German zoos' experiences with strategic warfare proved to be far bloodier than those of their British counterparts. Given the scale of the bombing campaign waged against the Reich, this should hardly be a surprise. The Royal Air Force alone dropped a "million tons of bombs" on German towns and cities, killing 600,000 people in the process.[16] Politicians and military leaders justified such attacks as military necessity. In the race to defeat Hitler, the logic went, the Allies needed to destroy the German war machine before it reached the battlefield. Munitions factories, oil refineries, supply depots, workers' housing units—if it contributed to the German war effort (and what didn't?), it was a legitimate target. Yet beneath this façade of strategy was a barely concealed desire for blood. Sir Arthur "Bomber" Harris, chief of the British bomber command, made this point without equivocation: "Those that loosed these horrors upon mankind will now in their homes and persons feel the shattering strokes of just retribution."[17] In Harris's mind, killing civilians (and destroying the places they lived, worked, and played) was not an unfortunate by-product of the Allied Bomber Offensive over Germany; it was the point.[18]

Some of the earliest zoo casualties came in the far northwest of the country. Near an important *Kriegsmarine* base on the North Sea, the area around the Bremerhaven Zoo was hit several times as early as December 1939. In one especially tragic incident, a mother polar bear became so terrified by the unfamiliar sound of firing flak that she killed her two newborn cubs.[19] The Berlin Zoo's "baptism of fire," in Lutz Heck's words, followed in 1941, when six "five-hundred pounders" crashed into the antelope house.[20] The next year, Munich's Hellabrunn Zoo was hit with three 235-kilo bombs. According to eyewitnesses, the animals remained relatively calm throughout the ordeal.[21]

Reflecting on the 1941 raid, Heck feigned moral outrage that "a zoological garden with its innocent animals could be seriously considered as a target for bombs."[22] (This was coming from a man who was all too happy to plunder the bombed-out zoos of the Reich's rivals.) But Allied bombers did not intentionally attempt to destroy specific zoos, no more than they tried to hit specific museums, churches, or historic landmarks. Even in the best conditions, targeting remained something of a crapshoot. Tens of thousands of feet up, cities resembled clusters of light, cut through by patches of shadow and dark. In reaching their destinations, bombers traced the paths of rivers, followed targeting flares, calculated distances and location by hand. A bomb dropped from directly overhead would follow a parabolic path and land miles away. The survival of any individual zoo animal (or any individual human, for that matter) was often a result of geography, weather conditions, or simple dumb luck.

The turning point, for both German zoos and the Reich as a whole, came in 1943. Starting that summer, the Allies launched the deadliest and most destructive aerial campaign in history. The first casualty was Hamburg, a major transport hub and home to the world-renowned Hagenbeck Animal Park. Around 1:00 a.m. on July 27, 1943, Allied aircraft dropped "ten thousand tons of high-explosive and incendiary

Figure 15.3. While zoo directors routinely complained about being "targeted" by enemy bombers, this was rarely, if ever, the case. Eagle-eyed bombardiers would have had a difficult time picking out a zoo from the rest of the environment, particularly if it was surrounded by green space such as a forest or a city park. In this aerial photograph, taken in the lead-up to Operation Market Garden in September 1944, Arnhem's Burgers' Zoo is barely distinguishable from the rest of the landscape. Resembling (to my eye, at least) a Dalmatian puppy, the zoo can be seen near the center of the photograph—just to the left of the road leading north from town. Gelders Archief: 409 – 1560 Second World War photo collection, Public Domain Mark 1.0 license.

bombs" on the residential neighborhood of Hamburg-Mitte. Within minutes, W. G. Sebald writes, "a firestorm of an intensity that no one would ever before had thought possible arose. The fire, now rising thousands of meters into the sky, snatched oxygen to itself so violently that the air currents reached hurricane force."[23] Code-named Operation Gomorrah, the Allies' multiday campaign to incinerate Hamburg inaugurated a new type of war—war as annihilation. According to historian Jörg Friedrich, "Annihilation occurs when nothing can continue to exist in a certain place. . . . As if thrown through a revolving door, 4.5 square miles of Hamburg found itself in a room for three hours not where life dies—that always happens—but rather, where life is not possible, where it cannot exist."[24]

Over the following days, forty to fifty thousand people died in the flames—burned, suffocated, eviscerated, melted into non-existence—along with tens of thousands, possibly millions, of pets, domesticated animals, and other nonhuman inhabitants of the city.[25] Parts of Hagenbeck's Tierpark, though spared the worst of the firestorm, were reduced to rubble. Hundreds of animals were killed, including twenty-five who were burned alive in a railway car en route to Vienna. Of the survivors, some had to be shot because of the severity of their injuries; others "died from licking traces of phosphorus from the fire bombs." Terrified by the sound of the air raid sirens, Hagenbeck's seals swam wildly in their pools until drowning from exhaustion.[26]

In the aftermath of the Hamburg attack, German zoo leaders decided to evacuate some animals to "safe" zoos they hoped were beyond the reach of Allied bombers. The Berlin Zoo shipped several of its most "Germanic" animals—aurochs, European bison (wisents), and Przewalski's horses—to an enclosure in the Schorfheide, a forest preserve near the Polish border where Göring kept a hunting lodge. In August 1943, Lutz Heck stepped up his evacuation campaign, sending "irreplaceable animals or whole collections" to zoos in far eastern Germany and beyond.[27] Otto Antonius, director of the Schönbrunn Zoo in Vienna, actively recruited donations from other Reich zoos.[28] Yet such efforts amounted to too little, too late. By early autumn, the killing range of British and American air power stretched deep into the Reich. More than that, Anna-Katharina Wöbse and Mieke Roscher point out that last-minute evacuations "meant extreme stress for the animals and the destruction of routine and family ties."[29] Of Schönbrunn's numerous "animal guests," only one—a male giraffe named Rieke—was returned to Berlin at the war's end.[30]

Fires in the Tiergarten

The most destructive zoo bombing of 1943 took place on November 22–23. Over the course of two nights, 750 RAF Lancaster bombers turned the Berlin Zoo, the world's largest, into a hellscape of death and destruction. As detailed in Lutz Heck's memoir, the attack began shortly after 7:15 p.m. Not long after the air raid sirens began to blare, RAF Pathfinders lit up the zoo grounds with phosphorescent flares (known in Germany as "Christmas trees"), which drifted down on small parachutes. The first wave of bombers followed shortly thereafter. Incendiaries crashed through the roof of the world-famous elephant pagoda, trapping its residents inside. A few minutes later, a mine exploded against the pagoda's eastern wall, collapsing its iron frame and burying the elephants in a pile of burning rubble. Over the next half hour, bombs demolished the deer house and blanketed the grounds in flame. One bull hippo was so crazed with fear that it refused to leave its burning cage. By the time zoo staff managed to drag the animal to safety, the hippo's "hide had been burnt away on one side, and six days later it succumbed to its injuries."[31]

The following morning, zoo staff assessed the wreckage. By one count, bombs had damaged more than fifteen buildings, some beyond repair; corpses littered the zoo grounds. With every passing minute, the toll of the dead grew longer: seven elephants; fifteen small monkeys; six large cats (three lions, two tigers, and a "lion-tiger bastard"); a pair of giraffes (one on the verge of giving birth); a lone rhinoceros, its thick hide unmarked by the flame. (It had died from a "pulmonary rupture" caused by the high air pressure that accompanied the bombs.)[32] In the course of a single evening, nearly 600 animals had been killed, fully one-third of the zoo's collection from the day before.[33]

If the attack had ended there, November 22, 1943, would have been the single deadliest day in zoo history. But RAF bombers returned the next evening as well, seeding the Tiergarten with explosive shells. Minutes into the attack, an air mine crashed through the glass dome of the aquarium; it landed in the crocodile hall, a large artificial landscape made to resemble a tropical river. The explosion rocked the building, sending torrents of water pouring from the shattered tanks. Future zoo director Katharina Heinroth, who had taken shelter a floor below the crocodile enclosure, described the scene: "In the light of the flashlights, we saw some crocodiles bleeding from their nasal holes. Two or three of the animals still lived and whipped the ground with their huge tails." Only at daybreak, though, was the extent of the damage fully revealed. The aquarium, unrivaled only the day before, lay in ruin. Of the building's 750 inhabitants, only a dozen still lived, the vast majority having been killed by the deadly combination of explosive bombs and icy temperatures.[34]

Finding Meaning in the Rubble

In the days, months, even years, that followed, both survivors and onlookers sought to frame the November zoo bombings to suit their interests. A December 1943 account struck what would become a familiar note, praising the heroism of the German staff, detailing the scale of the animal destruction, and declaring: "The slaughter of innocent and helpless creatures deeply stirred the human heart."[35] Lutz Heck's accounts of the events were especially self-serving. In his autobiography, Heck makes little effort to atone for his Nazi past. Instead, he places both himself and his staff in the role of innocent victims, as blameless for the disaster—"a blow by Fate," in his words—as the animals themselves.[36] In her own recollections, Katharina Heinroth does not feign *total* ignorance to the political realities in Germany. (Unlike Heck, she acknowledges the 700 POWs used to clear out the post-bombing rubble.) However, she too tends to view the events of November 22–23 as a tragedy beyond human reckoning.

Viewed today, we might derive additional meanings from the zoo wreckage. While the bombing was undeniably destructive, it was not a "blow by Fate." The zoo bombing is better understood as a product of moral relativism cast in the dehumanizing language of pragmatism and revenge. At the beginning of World War II, many political leaders continued to pay lip service to the idea that bombing civilians lay outside the bounds of wartime decency. In 1939, US president Franklin

Roosevelt famously criticized the "inhumane barbarism" inherent in bombing nonmilitary populations.[37] For FDR and other global leaders, targeting civilians evidenced a profound degree of cruelty—a final Rubicon that, once crossed, would forever discredit the myth of "civilized" warfare. This attitude, we now know, would be one of the war's first moral casualties (though it was far from the last).[38] If anything, the annihilation of the Berlin Zoo, like that of Hagenbeck's Tierpark a few months earlier, was but a preview of what was to come. Over the following year, similar scenes played out across the Reich's zoo world, from Frankfurt (wiped out in a single night in March 1944) and Leipzig (December 1944) to Dresden (February 1945).[39] In the logic of strategic bombing, zoo animals—like houses, churches, hospitals, historic landmarks, and schools—were fair game for destruction.

Above all, the bombings in Berlin and elsewhere remind us, once again, of zoo animals' inherent vulnerability, both under fire and otherwise. Faced with unfamiliar and artificial environments, and long deprived of the skills necessary to find food and shelter, even nature's most ingenious predators can easily succumb to accidents, starvation, and violent death. The very act of caging exotic animals in zoos primes them for wartime victimization, not least because it increases the likelihood that they will be bombed in the first place. From this perspective, then, Heck, Heinroth, and their colleagues on both sides of the Allied-Axis divide bear far more responsibility for zoos' wartime death tolls than any air force commander.

16

The Mask of the Chimpanzee

Once upon a time:

> A Belgian boy was ordered to report to the Nazi labor service. His uncle, an employee at a local zoo, suggested a way out: A large chimpanzee had just died, and the boy could wear its skin and take its place until the Gestapo gave up its search. . . . One day his mother came to the zoo to visit him, and he showed her some of the tricks he had learned. But, alas, while performing on a trapeze he lost his grasp and went flying over the bars into a cage of lions. His mother screamed. One of the lions went over to her and said, "Contain yourself, madam. Do you want to give us all away?"[1]

It's a familiar premise but a good joke, nonetheless. During World War II, people really *did* turn to the zoo to avoid Hitler's minions. Besides, people like stories about tricksters, rebels—Davids willing to stand up to (or, at least, outmaneuver) the world's would-be Goliaths. Tales of stealthy double agents and iron-willed freedom fighters circulated widely throughout the war years, and for good reason. Against the backdrop of fascist cruelty, those who resisted Hitler (or any tyrant, for that matter) were held up as heroes. At a time when it was easier to keep your head down, they stood up, pushed back, and—when the time came—ran for cover.

Following the defeat of Nazi Germany, formerly occupied populations in France, the Netherlands, Belgium, and elsewhere wore their collective resistance as a badge of honor. To hear the postwar pronouncements of liberation-leader-turned-president Charles de Gaulle and others, virtually all French people said *non* to the Nazi regime, in heart if not in words. Historians Saskia Hansen and Julia Zarankin have called antifascist resistance the "founding myth" of the Dutch nation, a "unifying memory that creates a sense of solidarity and national identity."[2] In this telling, resisting the Nazis was the norm; collaborating, the traitorous (and decidedly un-Dutch) exception.

In truth, postwar governments tended to exaggerate ordinary people's active resistance to German rule—and it's easy to understand why. Focusing on resistance allowed recently occupied peoples to minimize, if not ignore entirely, their willingness to accede to occupation-era policies, particularly those aimed at their Jewish neighbors. Resistance narratives also provided a way for both individuals and, indeed, entire nations to blot out (now) shameful memories of the recent past. Although an estimated 90 percent of the French people either willingly collaborated with the German occupation or were too scared to do anything about it, postwar ideologues promoted a different story, one in which Vichy-controlled France was seething with pro-Resistance sentiment from the occupation's opening hours.[3] Today, we recognize that this version of wartime resistance was largely a myth—part deliberate obfuscation, part wishful thinking, part psychological compensation— that allowed countries to avoid reckoning with their complicity with Nazi terror. The upside is that tales of antifascist resistance appear even *more* heroic because we now know just how rare they were.

To be sure, resistance was never an all-or-nothing affair in World War II. Much like the dreaded C-word (collaboration), the concept of resistance would be applied to a broad range of actions, allegiances, and affinities—from visible exhibitions of protest to imperceptible, even unconscious, demonstrations of moral outrage. At one extreme, some resistance groups waged all-out guerrilla war against occupying forces. No tactic was off the table, even if it was sure to provoke harsh reprisals. After British-trained Czech commandos assassinated Reinhard Heydrich, the acting Reich Protector of Bohemia and Moravia and a chief architect of the Final Solution, in 1942, Hitler unleashed his wrath on the small village of Lidice, considered a hotbed of anti-Nazi sentiment.[4] On June 10, 1942, members of the Nazi *Grüne Polizei* (green police) and intelligence services executed all men age fifteen or older on the spot; nearly 150 of Lidice's women and children were murdered in extermination camps. The Nazis even slaughtered the villagers' pets and looted the graveyard. Was it worth it to kill the notorious "Butcher of Prague"? It's impossible to say. What *is* clear is that the antifascist resistance refused to cede the right to use violence to Hitler and his murderous thugs.

The Resistance of Zoo Men

Zoos' involvement in anti-German resistance tended to fall on the opposite side of the spectrum. Instead of making a violent splash, zoo men preferred to keep their resistance activities hidden. This might be as simple as allowing organized resistance groups to use zoo facilities. A sympathetic zoo manager in Marseilles, for example, permitted members of the French Special Forces to use a bear cage to train with high explosives. The cage was divided in half—the bears on one side, the presumably nervous commandos on the other.[5]

Other zoo workers and associates went further, using their day jobs to help fund clandestine activities. Occupied Prague spawned several such figures. Barely in his twenties at the time, the budding ornithologist Veleslav Wahl played an active role in the Czech resistance, helping funnel vital information to the government in exile. The zoologist, explorer, and noted Czech car enthusiast Jiří Baum joined the resistance after more than a decade of adventures around the globe. In 1931, he and a friend, sculptor František Foit, drove a modified Tatra 12 motorcar from Alexandria to Cape Town, stopping along the way to visit pyramids, snap photos, and collect insects for the National Museum.[6] Returning to Prague just before the German invasion, he was a familiar face at the zoo, where he liked to photograph the animals. All the while, he led a secret life as a member of several left-wing anti-Nazi groups. Working alongside his sister Anna and wife Růžena, Baum used his camera skills to copy stolen papers and document war atrocities. In 1943, Baum was arrested—not for his resistance activities, but because he was a Jew. He was sent to the Warsaw ghetto and died the following year at the age of forty-four.

He wasn't alone. We now know that several prominent zoo directors used their positions to further the cause of anti-Nazi resistance.

Case in point: Achille Urbain—Great War veteran, scientist, and director of Paris's Vincennes Zoo during the German occupation. As the most prominent figure associated with the zoo, Urbain recognized that even the slightest suspicion of Free French sentiment could endanger not just his life but the lives of every animal in his care. To protect the zoo (or, at least, keep it under his watchful eye), he'd have to make some kind of pact with both the German occupiers and the Vichy authorities. Indeed, unlike his counterparts at the nearby Musée de l'Homme, a hotbed of opposition, Urbain often seemed more concerned with preserving the status quo than antagonizing the occupiers. Yet he refused to rat out a resistance group caught stealing from the Natural History Museum, where he also served as director, and protected a colleague accused of pinching some coal. Urbain doctored employees' CVs to shield them from the dreaded *service du travail obligatoire* (compulsory work detail). He also looked the other way when his daughter, Geneviève, borrowed the museum truck to smuggle food and transport German-born Jews to the Free Zone. Though always professional, he responded to Vichy police with an obvious air of repugnance. In perhaps his most visible show of defiance, he refused to hang a picture of collaborationist prime minister Philippe Pétain in his office. (His excuse? It was poorly framed.) Small stuff, for sure. Urbain's sympathetic biographer describes him as, at best, a minor player in the resistance cause. Nevertheless, even so-called passive resistance reminded the German occupiers that they weren't welcome—and never would be.[7]

Recognized as "Righteous Among the Nations" by Yad Vashem, Israel's official Holocaust memorial, Jan and Antonina Żabiński transformed the ruins of the Warsaw Zoo into a den of underground activity. A lieutenant in the Polish Home Army, the armed wing of the government in exile, Jan used his position with the Warsaw Parks and Gardens Department to transmit messages to Jews inside the ghetto. Eventually, the couple sheltered some three hundred "guests" (mainly, Jewish refugees) trying to flee Nazi terror. According to Diane Ackerman, "German-speaking Jews who looked Aryan received false identity papers and sailed smoothly through"; others stayed for months, even years—hidden in closets, under floorboards, and in the ramshackle cages. The fact that most of the zoo's animals had been killed or looted in the early days of the war proved a mixed blessing. While the Żabińskis did not have to spend their days gathering food and slopping cages, the lack of visitors often made it difficult to camouflage their activities. If discovered, all involved in the operation would have faced torture and execution. But Jan and Antonina felt they had a moral duty to protect their neighbors. Explaining his wife's courage, Jan told a reporter: "It wasn't that she identified with [animals], but from time to time she seemed to shed her human traits and *become* a panther or a hyena. Then, able to adopt their fighting instinct, she was a fearless defender of her kind."[8]

A Refuge in Amsterdam

If Antonina Żabińska was a panther, Amsterdam's Armand Sunier was more like a sheepdog—genial on the outside but willing to risk everything to save his flock. Over the course of the war, Sunier and Artis Zoo staff managed to hide between 200 and 300 people from German authorities. Most were young zoo personnel hoping to avoid the *Arbeitseinsatz*, the program of compulsory labor instituted throughout the German-controlled territories. Sunier used every bureaucratic trick in the book to slow the process, routinely forging special work permits classifying each of his employees as "indispensable." Fluent in German, he managed to shield Cor Wiers, Artis's lion keeper, for several years, before the young man was finally forced to abscond to the hayloft above the Predator House. When Rudolf Polak, the zoo's seventy-two-year-old entomologist, was sent to a Dutch concentration camp, the ever-loyal zoo director continued to advocate on his friend's behalf, ensuring that Polak was placed on a list of high-profile prisoners. It worked. In 1945, Sunier received news that Artis's bug expert was living in Switzerland, the beneficiary of an exchange with the neutral Swiss.[9]

At times, Sunier and Artis staff secretly housed as many as twenty people in the zoo's buildings and cages. In the winter, when the temperatures dropped, some of the zoo's human residents took shelter in the cattle shed, buffeted by the warmth (and smell) emanating from the animals' bodies. Others preferred to sleep in the reptile house, one of the few buildings with heat. In September 1944, twenty-four-year-old sculptor Arie Teeuwisse spent several nights in the polar bear cage. He and his bunkmates (all youth evading German authorities) slept on wooden slats covered with straw and spent long hours gambling for pennies. Skilled at making and repairing weapons, resistance fighter Henk Blonk sought refuge at the zoo on several occasions. Once, in 1942, the former zoo volunteer spent a few lonely weeks in the wolf enclosure. Another time, he hid out in an empty chimpanzee cage, where cockroaches nibbled at his eyebrows and a curious gorilla named Japie followed his every move through a hole in the wall. During the day, Blonk sometimes recognized members of Amsterdam's Jewish community pitching in around the zoo, but he dared not acknowledge them. "It is the safest for all parties," he explained later. "You can't tell what you don't know."[10]

Artis's location in the heart of Amsterdam added to the risk. The zoo was popular with German visitors, especially off-duty soldiers. Stationed in the nearby Colonial Museum, the notorious *Grüne Polizei* could drop by at a moment's notice. So-called because of the color of their uniforms, the "green police" used fear, violence, and murder to enforce Hitler's vision of law and order. Looming over all other threats (quite literally) was the Hollandsche Schouwburg, an elegant stone theater that sat diagonally opposite the zoo's main gates. In July 1942, the Gestapo converted the building into a holding pen for Jewish Amsterdammers en route to the concentration camps. For thousands of men, women, and children, the road to Auschwitz and Sobibor began just across the street from the Artis Zoo. The theater was a daily reminder of why there could be no slip-ups. Even an offhand comment, Sunier understood, could bring the forces of the occupation crashing down on the zoo. For this reason, he tried to keep the zoo's resistance activities on a strict need-to-know basis. Only the grandfatherly Sunier, by all appearances a caricature of Dutch accommodation, knew the whole truth.[11]

Amsterdam's zoo staff had plenty of reasons to defy their German occupiers—anger, revenge, patriotism, and sheer obstinacy, to name just a few. Perhaps the simplest explanation is that they did it to save their friends and neighbors. It's true that most of the people hiding at the zoo happened to be employees seeking to avoid forced labor abroad. But Sunier's staff also risked imprisonment and, likely,

The Mask of the Chimpanzee   217

execution to save the children of local merchants, student agitators, and, according to rumors, even a few downed Allied pilots.

At the same time, Artis's resistance activities undoubtedly stemmed from the zoo's decades-long connection to the most visible targets of Nazi terror: the city's Jewish population. Nestled in the Plantation District, a dense neighborhood of parks and gardens on the outer edges of the city's *Jodenbuurt* (Jewish Quarter), the zoo held a special place in the lives of the city's Jewish residents. Generations of Jewish youth grew up at the zoo—visiting with their families as toddlers, returning with their high school sweethearts, and eventually introducing the zoo to their own children.[12] Van Schalkwijk, an animal keeper who spent more than half a century working at the zoo, once recalled helping a group of Jewish boys escape a band of German soldiers. Without hesitating, he led them to the zoo's "monkey island" exhibit, placed a wooden plank across the water, and hurried the boys to the other side. By the time the soldiers appeared, the youth were safely hidden inside the hollow rock face.[13]

Other Jewish Amsterdammers lived at Artis for months on end. The fifth child in a working-class Jewish family, Hartog W. was smuggled into Artis after Dutch fascists raided his home and arrested his parents and siblings. (He never saw them again.) Bleaching his hair blond, he passed most days helping his Christian cousin, Andreis, who worked as an animal keeper. At night, he slept on a rough cot in the zoo's birdhouse with only a horse blanket and his clothes to protect him from the subzero temperatures. During the Hunger Winter of 1944–1945, when German blockades led to famine conditions in the occupied Netherlands, he survived on meager rations of carrots, onions, and bread baked from discarded pig feed.[14]

Nearly sixty years old when she went into hiding, Duifje van den Brink spent more than four years at the zoo. When the zoo was open, she liked to give self-guided tours (in German) and sit on a bench opposite the monkey cages, chatting to anyone who happened to wander by. The German officers who frequented the zoo were none the wiser. In the end, unlike Anne Frank (hiding little more than a mile away), her brother Mozes (murdered at Auschwitz), and three-quarters of the country's Jewish population, Duif van den Brink survived World War II—thanks to the courage and human decency exhibited by Armand Sunier and Artis Zoo staff.[15]

Hiding in Plain Sight

As it turns out, the zoo often proved an ideal place for resistance fighters, concentration camp escapees, Jewish refugees, and other victims of Nazi tyranny to camouflage their activities. Zoo architecture encouraged surveillance, but it was arranged to focus viewers' attention away from themselves and toward the animals on display.[16] Zoos were also one of the few places in occupied Europe where a person could loiter for hours at a time without attracting undue attention. Plus, as generations of secret lovers (and, according to Hollywood, spies) can attest, the garden design favored by many World War II–era zoos provided ample chances to duck down a shady path for a moment of privacy.

Lotte Strauss describes using the zoo for just such a purpose in her memoir. In October 1942, the Gestapo arrived at her Nuremberg apartment, declaring that the twenty-nine-year-old was to join her parents for "resettlement" in the East. Recognizing her danger, she managed to slip away and join her future husband in Berlin, where they hid in a cellar before escaping to Switzerland in May 1943. "Whenever Herbert and I had time on our hands," she recalled, "we went to the zoo at the Joachimsthaler Strasse, in the center of West Berlin. It was a famous zoo with many buildings in a large park. Later on, when we had separate hiding places and came from different directions to meet in town, we frequently met at the zoo at the elephant house. . . . When the weather was inclement, and it had become colder, we added visits to the aquarium." Entering the zoo, Strauss felt as "safe as wearing a magic hat." Hitler's ideologues could rant about how to spot a Jew, but without a Star of David pinned to her chest, she blended into the crowd unnoticed. Besides, Strauss believed the Gestapo would never think to check a place so brazenly public and so obviously forbidden to her kind.[17]

For resistance hero Benjamin Miedzyrzecki, the zoo offered a temporary asylum from what Polish historian and Holocaust victim Emanuel Ringelblum called the "psychosis of fear" felt by Jews trying to evade discovery.[18] Born into a Zionist and Orthodox household in February 1918, Miedzyrzecki grew up in Warsaw, finishing high school not long before the Wehrmacht attacked his country. In 1940, he joined the Jewish underground, where he helped found a lending library for children trapped in the ghetto. In late 1942, now posing as a Christian named Czeslaw Pankiewicz, the blond-haired and blue-eyed youth escaped to "Aryan" Warsaw, living behind a false wall in an attic above a sausage factory. Over the following year, he constructed a web of hiding places across the city and worked with his recruiter and future wife, Vladka, to smuggle weapons and supplies into the ghetto.

In the daytime, when it was too risky to sneak back into his hideout, Miedzyrzecki spent many idle hours at the local zoo, where Antonina Żabińska had managed to cobble together a small menagerie. These visits offered him temporary solace from the nauseating anxiety and hatred that he'd come to associate with his fellow humans. "I developed a terrible fear," he recounted to an oral historian decades later:

> I also developed a sense of recognizing dangers faster than anybody else. My antennas were tune . . . tuned much more . . . uh . . . delicately, to delicate . . . uh . . . more. But what was . . . what I remember from those days . . . that practically every human being which had the human feature walking on the streets freely was mine enemy. Possible I passed through the street and I passed through people which were righteous people and maybe they had in their own house hiding Jews or doing other good deeds, but to me when they had the human features, he became . . . he . . . he was a part of the human race. He was my enemy.

Around zoo animals, however, the paranoia evaporated. "It could have been even a tiger," he said. "I was not afraid." Surrounded by creatures more vulnerable than himself, he felt a buffer of safety, even as he was forced to feign indifference to the suffering of his people. His brother shot, his sister and her husband deported to Treblinka, Miedzyrzecki managed to survive the war, eventually moving to the United States and changing his name to Benjamin Meed. But he never forgot his long hours loitering in the remnants of the Warsaw Zoo, the one place in the city where he did not have to fear the faces that met his gaze.[19]

The Zoo at Heart Mountain

Stories of resistance, whether violent or passive, tend to overshadow the seemingly unremarkable ways that millions of people responded to the traumas of World War II. The fact is, many civilian survivors neither took to the barricades nor shattered under psychological pressure in the face of brutal occupation. This explains why growing numbers of researchers have turned their attention to *resilience*, a concept used to describe the mechanisms individuals (and groups) use to cope with prolonged periods of hardship and stress. Resilience is more than a character trait or something that can be achieved through sheer power of will. It's the product of a complex interplay of brain chemistry, personality, societal expectations, historical context, and more.[20]

One factor known to have a demonstrable effect on people's ability to withstand adversity is exposure to animals. Human interactions with animals have been shown to lower blood pressure, reduce stress, promote higher coping abilities, and kindle feelings of empathy. Engaging with animals also stimulates the hypothalamus to release oxytocin, a hormone associated with "trust, social skills, positive self-perception, generosity, and [decreased] depression."[21] Of course, a brief zoo visit is no substitute for the kinds of support provided by Antonina Żabińska or Armand Sunier. The health benefits of pet ownership, moreover, only seem to apply to *some* people *some* of the time.[22] Nevertheless, for those experiencing trauma, lacking well-defined support structures, or (like Benjamin Miedzyrzecki) having abandoned their faith in humanity, collecting and caring for animals can provide a sense of purpose and stability at a time when the world seems upside down.[23]

Outside of occupied Europe and Japanese-controlled Asia, few groups experienced a greater sense of betrayal and dislocation than Americans of Japanese ancestry.[24] About two months after the attack on Pearl Harbor, President Franklin Delano Roosevelt issued Executive Order 9066, which mandated the immediate removal of some 120,000 Japanese American citizens and permanent residents from their homes along the Pacific coast to one of ten inland incarceration camps. When pressed, government officials justified the decision in the euphemistic language of "public safety," though some were happy to say the quiet part out loud. "All Japanese [should] be put in concentration camps," thundered Idaho attorney general Bert Miller at a meeting with War Relocation Authority officials in April 1943. "We want to keep this a white man's country."[25] Given only a week to dispose of a lifetime's possessions, many people arrived at their destinations with little more than a suitcase and the clothes on their backs. (Tellingly, white neighbors were all too happy to snap up Japanese Americans' homes, businesses, and belongings for pennies on the dollar.)[26] When Aiko Yoshinaga, then a senior at Los Angeles High School, disembarked at what would become Manzanar War Relocation Center, near Death Valley, in April 1942, the camp was little more than a dusty collection of empty barracks. "The only thing that was in the 'apartments' when we got there were army metal beds with the springs on it, and a pot-bellied stove in the middle of the room," she recalled. "It was the barest of the bare."[27] Barbed-wire fences prevented camp residents from leaving, and guards armed with machine guns stood at the ready. Incarcerated at several facilities, including one at a former horse stable at a California racetrack, future *Star Trek* actor George Takei recalled: "I was old enough by then to understand the camp was something like jail, but could not fully grasp what we had done to be sent there."[28]

In the arid wastes of northwest Wyoming, Heart Mountain Relocation Center played host to more than 10,000 men, women, and children, many of whom had been forced to abandon their pets back home. Although nearby municipalities would sometimes drop off unwanted litters of cats and dogs at the camp, "traditional" pets were often hard to come by. Not surprisingly, many animal-loving incarcerees were forced to improvise. In 1943, Arthur Ishigo, a proto-hippie who liked to walk around shirtless in the winter, tamed a male magpie and kept a small rattlesnake in a wooden cage. One boy, Ken Suo, raised homing pigeons in the vent of his barracks, while his friend Akira Yoshimura adopted a baby sparrow that had broken its wing.[29] In the rush to "evacuate," nine-year-old Shigeru Yabu had no choice but to give away four pets: a dog (German shepherd mix), a yellow Japanese canary, a miniature turtle purchased at the San Francisco World's Fair, and a goldfish.[30] Once settled at Heart Mountain, he quickly amassed a new menagerie, including an ant farm, a lizard, a horned toad, and a salamander that he found frozen in a canal. (With his father's help, he chipped the salamander out of the ice and thawed it out in a bowl.)[31] At one point, Shig even had a pet tapeworm, which he kept in a Coke bottle filled with water.[32]

A US War Relocation bulletin from September 1942 announced that "colonists" at Heart Mountain had started their own camp zoo made up of animals—rattlesnakes, gopher snakes, rabbits, kangaroo

Figure 16.1. Taken by Estelle Peck Ishigo, this photograph shows a shirtless Arthur Ishigo and his dog at Heart Mountain. One of his animal cages is visible on the far-left side of the image. Estelle Ishigo Photographs, Collection No. 10368, box 1, folder 1, American Heritage Center, University of Wyoming.

rats, horned toads, mice, chipmunks, bats—caught on the grounds. The collection was housed at Heart Mountain's rec hall, the hub of social activity. Its head (and likely sole) caretaker, Clarence Matsumura, would later help liberate Dachau concentration camp as a member of the famed 442nd Regiment of Japanese American troops.[33] Although Matsumura likely came up with the "zoo" idea as a joke, he was not the only one to do so.[34] Prisoners fashioned similar makeshift menageries at other camps, including Manzanar, where the county health department had banned individual ownership of birds and other companion animals. With permission from authorities, members of the camp museum staff constructed a small petting zoo for children at the edge of one of the residential blocks.[35]

It hardly needs saying that the animal collections in places like Heart Mountain and Manzanar offered few of the amenities found at professional zoos. Even the zoo at Buchenwald, with its bear mountain, would have seemed an architectural wonder when compared to the wire-and-mesh animal cages in the United States' concentration camps. To the people *oohing* over the baby gophers and *ahhing* over the bantam hens, however, the psychological payoff would have been much the same. According to historian Albert Marrin, Japanese Americans went to great lengths to "create a sense of structure and normality" inside their barbed-wire prisons. Much like other leisure activities (baseball games, sumo matches, Saturday-night dances), keeping animals would have "helped them feel they were in control of their own lives"—and the lives of others.[36]

The experience of forced removal and confinement left some incarcerees with a heightened sense of empathy for their animal companions. If there were to be dogs and cats at Heart Mountain, artist Estelle Peck Ishigo, one of the few people not of Japanese ancestry held at the camp, wanted to make sure they received proper care. In 1944, she not only wrote the American Kennel Club for films about canine upkeep but also petitioned the state of Wyoming to start an in-camp branch of the humane society. (The state commission wrote back informing her that Wyoming had abolished its Department of Child and Animal Protection in 1929.)[37]

My recent correspondence with two brothers formerly incarcerated at Heart Mountain also suggests a dawning unease about captivity of any sort. Decades afterward, Hiroshi Hoshizaki continued to be haunted by an episode in the rec hall zoo: "One day when I was in there I noticed that there was a small mouse in the cage with the rattlesnake. The snake was at one end of the cage and the mouse was at the other end. The snake was just calmly sitting there eyeing the mouse while the poor mouse was trembling with fear. It's hard to imagine what it feels like when you know you are about to be eaten."[38] His older brother, Takashi, one of sixty-three men at Heart Mountain convicted for refusing military service, had a similar realization after watching a group of children beating a snake for seemingly no reason. Seeking help, the sixteen-year-old carried the injured animal to a "guy that had a number of animals in captivity" (presumably, Clarence Matsumura). But the children's cruelty left him shaken, as did the sight of the birds, rabbits, and other creatures visible through the wire mesh. "He had an owl, poor thing in a small cage," Takashi Hoshizaki recalled, perhaps reflecting on the nearly three years he would spend at Washington's McNeil Island federal penitentiary. "Was sorry to see how it looked at me."[39]

Even Shig Yabu came to second-guess the ethics of keeping wild animals captive. One day, on a bet, he and a friend aimed their slingshots at a nearby magpie nest. The next thing they knew, a baby bird had tumbled to the earth. Immediately sorry, Shig carried the bird (later known as "Maggie") back to the barracks in his T-shirt, where with his mother's help he nursed it back to health. In time, Maggie became a camp celebrity, entertaining visitors by mimicking wolf whistles and whatever profanity the older kids happened to utter in the bird's hearing. In the warmer months, Maggie would pay house calls on Shig's neighbors, hopping from stairway to stairway on its clipped wings.[40]

From the beginning, however, Shig had felt a vague sense of apprehension about introducing Maggie to life at Heart Mountain: "The irony of this bird was that [it] was like any other internee. We were forced into camp behind the barbed wires, that magpie bird went between the barbed wire, went in just like an internee." Even if he managed to save the bird, Shig understood, Maggie would be too "domesticated" to return to the wild. Sadly, Maggie did not survive Heart Mountain. In October 1945, a few weeks before his family was expected to leave the camp, Shig Yabu awoke to find the bird at the bottom of the cage, its eyes wavering. That night, he went to bed hoping that the next day would be different, that Maggie would be "another internee like the rest of us." But the bird was dead. Shig buried Maggie with her toys and his T-shirt beneath a homemade cross. Later, a friend speculated that "Maggie served the Heart Mountain internees by entertaining, being one of the internees, and all of a sudden, when people started to depart, felt that her mission, her job is completed, she no longer was needed."[41]

Perhaps—or perhaps this is just what they needed to tell themselves, to give Maggie's death some kind of meaning. In this respect, at least, Shig Yabu was not unique. As the end of the war neared, people around the globe were compelled to look to the future and tally up everything they'd lost.

17

Beastly Liberations

On the morning of March 30, 1945, a flatbed truck rattled into the once busy neighborhood surrounding Tokyo's Ueno Zoo. In the back, a blindfolded Raymond "Hap" Halloran felt every bump in his aching, emaciated body. Like millions of men of his generation, Halloran had entered the military not long after Pearl Harbor, eventually serving as a navigator on a B-29 bomber. On January 27, 1945, his eleven-man crew took off from Isley Field on Saipan for the 1,500-mile flight to bombard an aircraft factory in the Tokyo suburbs. Not far from the target, Halloran's B-29 started to encounter flak. When the nose section of the plane exploded, he bailed out at 27,000 feet. He hit the ground stunned to be alive. Within minutes, a "mob of civilians" had closed in around him, beating him with metal poles until he lost consciousness.[1] Imprisoned by the Kempeitai, Japan's notorious secret police, Halloran was placed in a four-by-six-foot cage for sixty-seven days straight. By the time he was let out, he'd lost more than ninety pounds.[2]

Now, here he was: shivering, black with grime, skin running with sores, taken who knows where for God knows what. Pulled to his feet, he was hustled past rows of animal enclosures, most empty. Finally coming to a halt, Halloran was stripped naked and placed inside an abandoned lion cage, where he was bound to the iron bars. "The rear door to my cage was closed and locked," he recalled. "I was alone. I was on exhibit in the lion cage. The vultures were foreboding as I viewed my future[;] I found myself screaming at the vultures. They did not move. The monkeys chattered and departed." Not long after, visitors started to arrive. Some jeered (he was the enemy, after all), though the young airman also recognized a sense of "compassion and empathy" on their faces.[3] Perhaps they too could imagine themselves naked and caged, defenseless for all to see. Or perhaps something different kicked in, a nagging recognition that, all too soon, Japan would have to answer for its wartime actions.

Decades later, Halloran continued to reflect on his brief stay at the Ueno Zoo. "The military may have wanted to show the people an example of B-29 flyers; that they were not super beings," he speculated, still haunted by the ordeal. Whatever his captors' motivations, Hap Halloran came to view his time in the lion cage as the "ultimate test," one that nearly broke him.* "Strapped to the bars for exhibit purposes; naked, cold and in pain I almost gave up. When your dignity dissipates your ability to fight to live becomes marginal."[4]

When considering the past, it's easy to see inevitabilities, as if the march of history is fixed along an unchanging and unchangeable path. Today, we know that World War II ended in 1945. We know the Allied powers were victorious. And we know that the war's final days would be viewed as much as a beginning as an end.

For Hap Halloran and everyone else living through the final eighteen months of the war, however, the ultimate outcome would have seemed anything but certain. Although the Wehrmacht had failed to bring Stalin to heel, Hitler's citadel still presented a daunting challenge to Allied war planners. The fate of Japan's Greater East Asia Co-Prosperity Sphere was pretty much sealed. But there was a big difference between uprooting defensive positions in the South Pacific—a key part of the United States' "island-hopping" strategy—and forcing Japan's military government to admit final defeat. That could very well take a full-scale invasion of the Japanese Home Islands, a campaign that promised to drag on for months, even years, against a desperate population with everything to fight for and nothing to lose. The Allies were still committed to "total victory" in 1944 and 1945, but what if the

---

* Halloran experienced nightmares about his experience for decades. They only began to dissipate when he returned to Japan with a CBS television crew in 1984. Before his death in 2011, he visited the country on more than ten separate occasions to try to come to terms with his past traumas. Jun Hongo, "War Trauma Leads to Efforts to Reconcile," *The Japan Times*, April 30, 2008.

war had dragged on two, three, even five years longer—what kind of negotiated peace would they have been willing to stomach then?

Ever the optimists, zoo directors in the United States entered 1944 with a clear sense of what the future would bring. That March, the San Antonio Zoological Society distributed a list of more than fifty animal species it was hoping to acquire: black leopards, great gray kangaroos, concave-casqued hornbills, hippopotami (one male pygmy, one female Nile), and female Himalayan bears, to name just a few.[5] Other zoos sketched designs for new exhibits, penciled in orders for (re)building supplies, and talked up their postwar plans—all they needed was the official victory announcement.

But most of the world's zoos, particularly those between London to the west and Tokyo to the east, enjoyed no such luxury. Zoo work, at its core, is a matter of repetition—the daily grind. Each day is different: there are births and deaths; new visitors stream in, old visitors stream out; there are the rare days when zoos acquire new animals, the ones rarer still when they open new exhibits. Overall, however, zoo life involves doing the same thing (feeding, watering, cleaning, opening, closing) at roughly the same time every day over and over again. This is why the war made life at the zoo so arduous: it disrupted the daily rhythm. It made everything—preparing food, messing out cages, keeping up with repairs—that much more difficult. And, as time wore on, things began to break down. Meals came late or not at all; cages went unrepaired; workers left, not to be replaced. The temporary fixes, the experimental rations, the jury-rigged and patched-together living quarters— all the things that worked well enough in 1939, 1940, 1941, 1942, and 1943—increasingly stopped working. And, of course, the world's zoos were getting emptier by the day, cages once crowded with exotic wildlife replaced with domestic livestock, military mascots, or nothing at all.

The tragic final months of Caesar, a male African forest elephant, illustrate how any disruption, especially in wartime, can lead to fatal results. The Düsseldorf Zoo had purchased Caesar from Firma Ruhe, one of the world's leading animal dealers, in 1939. Four years later, to shield their star attraction, the zoo shipped Caesar to the Silesian border city of Breslau. The move unsettled the elephant. In May 1944, in a fit of nervous aggression, Caesar chipped off a piece of his right tusk. A month later, he smashed apart his enclosure; that August, he injured his tusk once again—only this time, he exposed the nerve, leading to bleeding and excruciating pain. Breslau staff tried their best to patch him up, but medicine was difficult to come by. As the days grew colder (and Germany's war situation worsened), correspondence with the Düsseldorf Zoo, which was responsible for Caesar's medical bills, broke down. Finally, in December 1944, someone at the Breslau Zoo picked up a gun and put Caesar out of his misery. Nothing about the elephant's death was preordained. It took a multitude of factors—the move from Düsseldorf, the strange faces and surroundings, the paucity of supplies, the radiating pain of a twice-cracked tooth—to send him to an early grave.[6]

A Giraffe Named "D-Day" and the Zoo Too Far

On June 6, 1944, a giraffe at the San Diego Zoo gave birth to a calf. Keepers named it D-Day in recognition of the launch of the American, British, and Canadian assault on the beaches of Normandy, France.[7] In the eyes of millions of people across the continent, the attack was more than the kickoff for the final push toward Berlin. It represented the promise of "liberation." In the United States, we're used to seeing the liberation of Europe as the nation's finest hour. To this day, American leaders invoke the visual imagery of liberation—women throwing flowers, children cheering, handmade stars-and-stripes blowing in the breeze—when trying to sell military adventures.

But liberation had a far uglier side as well. In her study of American GIs in liberated France, historian Mary Louise Roberts notes, "Even after civilians were reassured that freedom—and the Americans—were there to stay, shock took a huge toll on the population."[8] Allied liberators brought with them many things: guns, condoms, food (with which to barter), stereotypes (about who needed to be liberated in the first place), and, more often than not, a sense of entitlement about what they were owed for their trouble. The undoing of four-plus years of German rule also unleashed a tidal wave of pent-up anger and shame, much of it aimed at punishing those perceived as cozying up to the occupying forces.

The liberation of Antwerp by British forces in September 1944 sparked a series of public rituals designed to humiliate the onetime occupiers. In addition to shaving the heads of women accused of sleeping with the enemy, angry citizens rounded up German soldiers and suspected collaborators and sequestered them in empty zoo cages—a symbol of just how far they had fallen and an acknowledgment of zoos' obvious resemblance to prisoners' "holding pens." Film footage shows uniformed men in various states of unease. Some appear to be chatting to themselves; others are lying prostrate on the straw-covered concrete floor, making little effort to maintain any sense of military demeanor. Unlike most zoo cages, theirs is open—but there is nowhere to run, no reason to hide.[9] As much as anything else, "liberation" was a matter of spectacle. It was about showing, in no uncertain terms, that the war (*their* war, at least) was over—and what better place to do that than the zoo? Indeed, British forces eventually took charge of the zoo grounds, setting up a barracks on the main lawn and turning the reception area into a dance hall.[10]

The Soviet deliverance of Eastern Europe, starting around the summer of 1944, hinted at a different future for recently occupied zoos. "In Poland, Hungary, Germany, Czechoslovakia, Romania, and Bulgaria," writes historian Anne Applebaum, "the Red Army's arrival is rarely remembered as pure liberation. Instead, it is remembered as the brutal beginning of a new occupation."[11] Enraged by the deaths of loved ones and hungry for revenge, Soviet forces wanted blood—and they were willing to kill everyone and destroy everything in their path. In Poland, after German soldiers shot the Poznan Zoo's large carnivores and ungulates, Soviet bombs finished the job, leaving only 176 animals alive at the war's conclusion. Not long after entering Prague in May 1945, Soviet troops replaced German signs at the zoo with Russian ones, which would remain until the end of the Cold War half a century later. But that wasn't close to the worst of it. During the war, an employee at the zoo, Veleslav Wahl, led a resistance group and fought in the Prague Uprising in 1945. For his efforts, Wahl was awarded the Czechoslovakia military cross, though it could not save him in 1950, when he was arrested and executed for anticommunist activities.[12]

The story of Burgers' Zoo testifies to the two-sided nature of the Allied campaign to free Western Europe from Hitler's armies. Located near the Dutch city of Arnhem, just across the Rhine River from Germany, the privately owned animal park was better off than most,

Figure 17.1. Captured German soldiers in the lion's cage at the Antwerp Zoo in September 1944. © Imperial War Museum (BU 558).

though that wasn't saying much. Although the zoo's director, Reinier van Hooff, convinced the German authorities to take a hands-off approach to the zoo's operations, food and fuel were always in short supply. In 1942, a number of the zoo's tropical birds literally froze to death (some had to be cut from the ice) because the zoo lacked the coal to heat their cages. When the local German commander decreed that sea fish were too valuable to spare, van Hooff tried to feed his seals and penguins a freshwater diet, only to watch them die a few days later.

The zoo's fate took an unexpected turn in September 1944, when Allied forces launched Operation Market Garden with the goal of establishing a bridgehead across the Rhine into the Reich.[13] For more than a week, British and American planes pounded the city center; thousands of terrified refugees fled north. However, van Hooff and his family refused to leave—not when it meant abandoning their few remaining animals to starve or be eaten. During the day, van Hooff scoured the grassy banks of the Rhine for dead cattle, which he butchered in full view of both armies. At night, the family crowded into a beet cellar beneath the zoo's main barn, their only shelter against the exploding bombs and falling flak. Seven decades later, van Hooff's son Jan, who grew up to become an acclaimed primate biologist at Utrecht University, continued to be haunted by memories of the zoo's most pitiful resident: a hyena whose entire lower jaw had been sheared away by a piece of shrapnel. "I put pieces of meat in his throat, in that open hole," he recalled. "That hyena *lovvved* me, because every day, when he was hungry, he couldn't eat himself. He was waiting for me."[14] In December 1944, Burgers' Zoo faced a different kind of test when armed German soldiers showed up with orders to destroy the "less precious predators." Only by using their bodies to shield the wolf and bear cages were the van Hooffs able to stay the executions.[15]

By the following spring, the greatest threat to Burgers' survival came from Allied bombers, whose flight path to Berlin ran just past the zoo gates. One day, with the forces of liberation rapidly closing in, van Hooff grabbed a pail and some plaster, and climbed a ladder to the roof of the park restaurant. On the side tilted toward the south, he and Jan painted the words "SAVE OUR ZOO" in large letters; on the opposite end, he added a message for the pilots stationed at *Fliegerhorst Deelen*, a German-occupied airbase a few miles to the north: "SPAREN SIE UNSERE TIERGARTEN." It was a long shot. Still, he hoped someone might see it—someone who understood that, despite everything that had happened in the war, certain places were worth sparing.

Unfortunately, his plea went unheeded. On April 2, 1945, Allied bombers followed an unexpected trajectory, circling around the zoo before coming back from the other side. When it was over, van Hooff and his family emerged from their makeshift bunker and logged the dead: four tigers, several adult lions, and a polar bear.[16] Less than two weeks later, Allied troops liberated Arnhem for good. Reinier van Hooff's war finally was over, but he could not help but reflect on everything they had lost: fourteen lions, two polar bears, a pair of elephants, hyenas, peccaries, most of the residents of monkey island

Beastly Liberations 233

(also destroyed), zebras, camels, endangered Caspian sheep, rare cattle, and twenty species of pheasant—all gone. In the following months, other animals would die or disappear, including van Hooff's beloved St. Bernard, Caesar.

Zoos in Fortress Deutschland

For zoos in the Greater Reich, the final year and a half of the war were characterized by fear, hunger, anxiety, and death. Throughout 1944, Allied air forces ratcheted up their nightly assaults on German cities, killing hundreds of thousands in the process. In March 1944, Royal Air Force (RAF) bombers destroyed the Frankfurt Zoo, killing 90 percent of the animals in a single night.[17] In July, Munich was hit, forcing the Hellabrunn Zoo to shut its doors until further notice.[18] Vienna's Schönbrunn Zoo managed to escape four years of war virtually unscathed—that changed in February 1945. Seventy bombs crashed into the zoo grounds, destroying the elephant house, the reptile building, and several storage facilities. Roughly 800 animals died, including a bull rhino (Toni) and an Asian elephant (Nelli). As a unit of Hitler Youth helped clear the rubble, the zoo's director, Otto Antonius, published reward notices in local newspapers in an attempt to track down missing birds.[19]

Starting on the night of February 13–14, 1945, with Allied leaders growing increasingly impatient to bring the war in Europe to a decisive close, the campaign to bomb Hitler into submission marked a new milestone. In four coordinated raids, hundreds of RAF and US heavy bombers pummeled the city of Dresden, a center of arts and learning sometimes called the "Florence of the Elbe." The resulting firestorm killed some thirty thousand people, destroyed 85 percent of the buildings, and reduced much of the urban core to ash. One of the most frequently cited accounts of the experience of the Dresden Zoo comes from Otto Sailer-Jackson, a zookeeper who was on duty at the time.[20] Sixty-one years old, Sailer-Jackson was in his office around 9 p.m. when he heard the alarms start to blare. The scenes that followed haunted him for the rest of his life:

> The elephants gave spine-chilling screams. Their house was still standing, but an explosive bomb of terrific force had landed behind it and lifted the dome of the house, turning it round and putting it back

on again. The baby cow elephant was lying in the narrow barrier-moat on her back, her legs up to the sky. She had suffered severe stomach injuries and could not move.[21]

At the hippo enclosure, he found the corpses of three of the massive beasts pinned to the bottom of their pool beneath chunks of iron debris. But the worst was yet to come. Reaching the great apes house, Sailer-Jackson came across a gibbon whose hands had been torn away in an explosion. As the zookeeper approached, the gibbon held out its bloody stumps, as if begging for help. Years later, Sailer-Jackson reported, the image of the gibbon's facial expression was burned into his brain. In that terrifying moment, however, all he could do was try to put the gibbon out of its misery.[22]

The effects of the bombing on the zoo were staggeringly horrific—on that, there can be no argument. Yet it's important to pause before taking this account (any account of wartime zoo atrocities, for that matter) at face value. As Mustafa Haikal and Winfried Gensch, authors of a well-received history of the Dresden Zoo, point out, some parts of Sailer-Jackson's retelling verge on exaggeration, if not outright invention. The gibbon story in particular is almost *too* grotesque, as if it were specifically designed to tug at the heartstrings. There is a rich tradition of weaponizing animal suffering for emotional and political manipulation. Indeed, to this day, commentators on both the far left and white-identity right periodically cite Sailer-Jackson's bombing narrative to hammer home their arguments (in the former case, about the evils of war and speciesism; in the latter, about the fate of German innocents in World War II).[23]

After Dresden, few in the German zoo industry held out any hope for victory. The only question was whether they could survive the violence and chaos of the Reich's final days. For workers at the Breslau Zoo, the answer came that same February, when Soviet troops encircled the city. The previous August, Adolf Hitler had declared Breslau, just across the border from Poland, a *Festung* (fortress) to be defended to the last man standing. (Women, children, and old people were told to leave.) For more than two months, Red Army artillery shelled the area, lobbing more than seventy explosives and incendiaries into the zoo grounds. Long considered a sanctuary, the place other wartime zoos sent their prized possessions, the Breslau Zoo was not the target of the Soviets' fury. It just happened to be located near a strategic river crossing, and that was enough to ensure its destruction. Falling bombs smashed through buildings, exposing their residents to the frigid air outside. In late February, a juvenile pygmy hippo and a manatee cow froze to death on consecutive nights. Not long after, zoo staff made the fateful decision to destroy all the "dangerous animals." Starting with the large predators, a Wehrmacht special commando shot the tigers, lions, leopards, bears, and hyenas. Then, on March 30, it was the four elephants' turn; the only difference was that their keeper, not the commando, pulled the trigger.[24]

The following month, Soviet forces began the final push to take Berlin. The ensuing battle, fought street by street, block by block, transformed the world-renowned Tiergarten into a pit of destruction.[25] As a thirteen-story flak tower, built on the zoo grounds, covered the sky in flame, Soviet troops en route to the Reichstag leveled everything in sight. When it was over, future zoo director Katharina Heinroth proclaimed that the grounds resembled a "lunar landscape." Upon entering the monkey house, Konstantin Simonov, a Soviet war correspondent, discovered the corpses of three SS soldiers, as well as the mutilated body of Pongo, Berlin's famed gorilla, "who was slain with stab wounds in the chest."[26] Workers did what they could to comfort the zoo's ninety-one animal survivors—down from more than three thousand in 1939—but the task was enormous. Many of the animals were starving, and the air stank of decomposing corpses. Some of the zoo dead were either too large (or too far gone) for burial. A brown bear was cremated in its cage, while zoo staff used axes to chop up the rotting body of Rosa, a massive hippo killed by a shell fragment. With ruptured landscapes and a "futile minority" of surviving inhabitants, concluded British writer Ivor Montagu, the Berlin Zoo mirrored the "rubble-strewn chaos of the whole city outside."[27]

The Alligator at Nagasaki

Even as Allied forces were starting their final bloody push to Berlin, American bombers, facing increasingly little resistance from Japanese air defenses, flattened cities and terrorized the civilian population.

Near midnight on March 9–10, 1945, against the lurid backdrop of exploding flak, the first wave of low-flying B-29s, each loaded with 6,000 pounds of napalm and other inflammable liquids, appeared in the skies above Tokyo. The resulting conflagration, swept by superheated wind (1,800 degrees Fahrenheit), devoured everything in its path. Canals boiled, and oxygen was sucked from the air, so that people died, reporter Masuo Kato observed poetically, "like so many fish left gasping on the bottom of a lake that has been drained."[28] The deadliest bombing of the war, the attack killed 100,000 Tokyoites and left a million others without housing.[29] In the days that followed, nearby residents dropped off thousands of bodies at the Ueno Zoo, which had readied 7,600 coffins for burial. When that proved inadequate, the zoo ordered 10,000 more.[30]

Although the zoo survived the firebombing structurally intact, the writing was on the wall. In late March, right around Hap Halloran's inauspicious stay in the empty lion cage, Ueno Zoo officials decided they had no choice but to destroy the two remaining hippopotami, six-year-old Maru and his mother Kyōko. The method, as with the elephants, was to be starvation. Keepers halted their daily feedings and drained the water from the hippos' pool. Maru lived for fourteen days, his skin cracked and bleeding from dehydration; his twenty-seven-year-old mother held out for nearly two weeks longer, finally succumbing to the effects of hunger on April 24. They weren't the Japanese zoo world's final war casualties. Indeed, throughout the summer of 1945, zoo animals across the country would continue to die—from malnutrition, falling bombs, forced starvation, and anxiety brought on by the screams of air raid sirens.[31]

Whatever hope was left died on August 6, 1945, when the United States detonated an atomic bomb equivalent to some fifteen kilotons of TNT on the city of Hiroshima. Three days later, on March 9, a second, more powerful bomb was dropped on Nagasaki—the most recent and, one hopes, the last atomic weapon deployed in wartime. The combined blasts killed upward of 200,000 people and sentenced untold others to lifetimes of mental anguish. White hot and blindingly bright, the bombs' thermal flash charred skin, burst eyeballs, and stripped flesh from bone. Corpses, blackened and twisted like naked marionettes, melted into the ground. Some of the blast victims were vaporized entirely—every molecule in their being instantly and irrevocably erased. In the months and years to follow, thousands died from the effects of high-dose radiation poisoning, including elevated rates of leukemia. Though few fully grasped it at the time, the dropping of the A-bombs inaugurated a new era in humans' relationship with the natural world. More than the terror bombings of Dresden and Hamburg, more than the man-made famines of Ukraine (1932–1933) and Bengal (1943), Hiroshima and Nagasaki offered a glimpse of how the world as we know it might come to an end.

It's somewhat fitting, then, that neither of the target cities had a proper zoo at the time. The zoo, for better or worse, is a product of a time when big-N Nature was a mystery, unknowable and incomprehensible. It was larger than us—something that we might snatch pieces of, bring home for exhibition, but never fully bend to our will. The A-bomb signaled a transition to a different age, the full implications of which we're still grappling with today.

Nevertheless, the testimony of one fifteen-year-old *hibakusha* ("survivor of the bomb") offers a powerful reminder of zoos' lingering power to affect our attitudes about the place of animals in humans' unnatural world. Michie Hattori was taking shelter near the rear of a cave when the bomb exploded over Nagasaki.

> A searing hot flash accompanied the light that blasted me. For a second I dimly saw it burn the girls standing in front of the cave. They appeared as bowling pins, falling in all directions, screaming and slapping at their burning school uniforms. I saw nothing for a while after that.

Partially blinded, her body racked with pain, she picked her way toward her school, barely comprehending the horror of her surroundings.

> My classmate Fumiko scampered about 50 meters ahead of us. When I looked up to see why she was calling, I saw her pointing to a large form on the ground.
>
> "Look over there," she shouted. "It has escaped from the zoo. It's an alligator." It lay in our path to the school, so we approached with caution. Fumiko found a rock.

She drew back the rock above her head as she approached the creature. Then, Fumiko froze in her tracks, screaming hysterically. I ran to her side. The face looking up at us from the crawling creature was human. . . . I could see it pleading for something—probably water. No clothes or hair were visible, just large, gray, scalelike burns covering its head and body. The skin around its eyes had burned away, leaving the eyeballs, huge and terrifying. Whether male or female I never found out.[32]

Ours is not the place to judge the actions of a schoolgirl on the day her entire world was turned to hell. And yet, there's something telling about young Fumiko's actions in this moment. Her first instinct was to kill—to strike the "alligator" dead. Perhaps she'd heard too many stories about what would happen if zoo animals ever broke free. Perhaps she thought she was doing her patriotic duty, protecting her fellow residents from the threat of a man-eater on the loose. Or perhaps—and I think this is more likely—Fumiko wasn't thinking at all. She was reacting on gut instinct. An "alligator" was out of place. It was uncaged. It was a threat. And it needed to be destroyed.

Zoos send many messages, but the most consequential is that wild animals and humans belong to separate worlds—one in "nature," the other in civilization; one in captivity, the other looking in from the outside. In this sense, at least, Fumiko's reaction was not only understandable; it was exactly what zoos had been cultivating in one way or another since the war began.

18

KZ Zoo

In April 1945, Captain Derrick Sington's armored jeep wheeled past lines of soldiers and into a muddy clearing. He'd heard rumors of the place—the Bergen-Belsen concentration camp—so gruesome they staggered the imagination. But as he passed through the wooden gate and tried to comprehend the scale of the suffering, Sington was reminded of a more familiar sight: a zoo. "On the left of the thoroughfare stood row upon row of green wooden huts, and we came into a smell of ordure—like the smell of a monkey-house," he recalled. At the sound of the approaching jeep, "a strange simian throng" of prisoners crowded the barbed-wire fence, and "sad blue smoke floated like a ground mist between the low buildings." Sington concluded, "I had tried to visualize the interior of a concentration camp, but I had not imagined it like this."[1]

The liberation of the concentration camp network in 1945 shattered whatever hope was left of a benevolent world. Though not everyone understood what they were seeing, what we today call the Holocaust—the murder of more than six million Jews, political prisoners, Roma and Sinti peoples, disabled people, and homosexuals—revealed modernity's murderous potential: the capacity of the state to produce death on an industrial scale. The response to the Holocaust has varied, from an unwillingness or inability to comprehend what had happened to probing questions about the ideas, the cultural mechanisms, the systems of thought that made it possible.[2] Nevertheless, the responses of Derrick Sington and countless others like him raised unsettling questions: What should we make of the fact that, seeing the horrors of the Nazi

Figure 18.1. Members of Lt. General George S. Patton's 3rd Army, XX Corps, inspecting the emaciated corpses of prisoners at the Buchenwald concentration camp on April 11, 1945. The empty bear enclosure is clearly visible just on the other side of the barbed-wire fence. Photo: Ardean R. Miller, US Signal Corps, April 18, 1945 | National Archives, Washington.

prison-state, many early witnesses immediately thought of zoos? And if concentration camps resemble zoos—can we ever visit a zoo again?

Not Quite Human

In a sense, the story of the zoo and the Holocaust is yet another extension of the Nazis' hierarchical view of the natural world. Just as Nazi ideologues viewed evolution as a "process of perpetual improvement through 'survival of the fittest,'" they drew sharp distinctions between nature's supposed winners (violent, "pure," willing to take what's theirs) and the species and peoples destined for extinction.[3] This helps explain why, when Nazi leadership introduced restrictions on animal research not long before the war's end, groups like the Hygiene Institute of the Waffen-SS turned to concentration camp prisoners for their medical experiments. For many SS doctors and medical researchers, there was little difference between incarcerated Jews (often considered little more than human lab rats) and the dogs, rabbits, and mice upon which they usually operated.[4] In concentration camps, spaces specifically designed to strip prisoners of their sense of self, the categories "animal" and "human" frequently blurred, both in practice and in rhetoric. Nazi scientists, when conducting hypothermia tests, would re-warm victims with "physical contact with animals or women." At Dachau, one of the former guards—blond, tall, the embodiment of Aryanism—was asked by a reporter: "'How could you do this to these people?' 'They're not people,' the soldier sneered. 'They're animals.'"[5]

The rhetorical link between animals and Jews, the primary target of Hitler's Final Solution, played an important role in legitimating the Holocaust in the eyes of its perpetrators. There was a long history of equating Jews with animals (pigs, dogs) and disease, one amplified by Nazi propagandists.[6] Hitler referred to Jews as a "pack of rats," while "an SS propaganda booklet, *The Subhuman*, described all peoples of the 'East' as 'animalistic trash, to be exterminated.'" Russians were "unrestrained beasts." Even the animals owned by Jews were viewed as "racially contaminating," as if their proximity to Jewishness made them incompatible with racially pure herds.[7] Indeed, references to animals proliferated throughout the concentration camp (KZ) system, from the *Tonnenadler* [rubbish-bin eagles], a term used to describe desperately hungry inmates who plundered rubbish dumps, to the *Singende Pferde* [singing horses], gangs of "Jewish inmates forced to sing while hauling heavily laden wagons."[8]

But calling the prisoners animal names was one thing. Hitler's human victims were *treated* like animals—herded into camps, stripped and shorn, worked to death, shot, slaughtered, and starved. Charles Patterson, author of a book on animals and the Holocaust, notes that the "use of animal terms to vilify and dehumanize the victims, combined with the abominably degraded conditions in the camps, made it easier for the SS to do their job, since treating prisoners like animals made them begin to look and smell like animals."[9] And killing animals was easy. It was normal. If Jews were treated like animals, the logic went, then that's what they were—what other possibility could there be?

This line of thinking was not unique to the architects to the Holocaust. Worried that, with the eradication of Europe's Jews, the

Figure 18.2. Antisemitic cartoon (c. 1926) showing a caricature of a Jewish man displayed in a zoo cage. The text reads: "Class 13. Predatory animals with elongated snouts that stink. Germany's most dangerous predator (Cain) Habitat: Galicia and Zion (Palestine) Diet: Mainly garlic, onions, and matzahs." Beyond reinforcing antisemitic stereotypes, such images sent a message that Jews were to be treated like animals. US Holocaust Memorial Museum, courtesy of Dottie Bennett.

"younger generation" might fail to grasp the "repellent nature that the Jew gives in everyday life," one Frankfurt pharmacist suggested building a "roomy cage next to the monkey cages at the zoo." As he wrote in *Der Stürmer*: "In one part of this cage, a Jewish family will be displayed with the typical Jewish attributes: flat feet, crooked nose, curly black hair, hunchback posture, thick lips, half-closed eyes, heavy eye lids; in the other part of the cage, there will be a family whose appearance will not appear Jewish."[10] In the Nazi mind, Jews did not belong in polite society; they needed to be corralled, studied, exhibited for public edification, and ultimately exterminated.

Lutz Heck's *Lebensraum*

Such attitudes inevitably bled into the zoo world, which by the war's start was stocked with a fresh cohort of Nazi ideologues, party members, fellow travelers, and hangers-on. Although the bulk of German zoo folk were not actively involved in the systematic mass murder of Jews, they were nonetheless willing to take advantage of the situation. Consider, for example, Nazi prohibitions against Jewish participation in public life. Zoo leaders did not quit in disgust when Jews were banned from visiting their institutions. Nor did they raise much of a stink in the mid-1930s when the two remaining Jewish members of the Berlin Zoo board, Georg Siegmann and Walter Simon, were ousted in favor of "ardent Nazis." Both men were eventually arrested and shipped off to concentration camps, yet Germany's zoos carried on as if the nation's Jewish population, hundreds of thousands strong prior to Hitler's rise, did not exist and never had.[11]

German zoos were equally happy to take advantage of their connections to Nazi higher-ups to pad their collections with plunder from the Reich's occupied territories. Here, Berlin Zoo director Lutz Heck proved to be especially culpable. Like his good friend Hermann Göring, the elder Heck brother fantasized about turning the Białowieża, a thickly forested area on the frontier of Poland and Belarus, into a large game reserve populated by genetically back-bred animals from Germany's mythic past. For Heck, German eastward expansion offered an "unprecedented opportunity to reshape the landscape," which he believed languished in "'inferior' Slavic hands."[12]

But before Heck and company could start the rewilding process, the locals had to go. In this way, notes writer Michael Wang, the Nazi "dream of a wilderness untouched by human hands helped justify the murderous campaigns carried out under the banner of Germanization."[13] In 1941, Heck applied to the *Deutsche Forschungsgemeinschaft*, a Nazi-affiliated research foundation, for a grant to research the effects of the future rewilding efforts on local flora and fauna.[14] All the while, German forces carried out one of the most sustained efforts of human extermination in history, emptying the landscape of its non-Aryan inhabitants.

The Zoo at Treblinka

The familiarity of the zoo made it a potent weapon in Nazi efforts to camouflage the destruction of Europe's Jewish population. Nowhere was this more evident than at the killing center of Treblinka.[15] Located in a forested region northwest of Warsaw, *SS-Sonderkommando Treblinka* was constructed in 1942 with the sole aim of murdering as many people as possible. Everything about the camp was a lie. The camp's train station was designed to resemble an ordinary railway depot—a temporary stopover before resettlement farther east. The reception area was decorated with flower beds, and guards dressed as medical "orderlies" stood by to help sick passengers disembark. The deception continued, even as men, women, and children were told to abandon their luggage and hurry on to the bathhouse. Separated by sex, stripped nude, their heads shaved, the condemned were finally forced to turn over their documents and valuables. "The spell of illusion was broken at this point," wrote the Soviet reporter Vasily Grossman in 1946. "Here . . . ended the anguish of uncertainty that had kept the people in a fever from hope to despair, from visions of life to visions of death."[16] No longer concerned with maintaining any sort of false hope, guards force-marched their naked victims down a sandy avenue—beating and whipping them as they went—until they reached the gas chambers. At its heart, reflected Richard Glazar, one of only a handful of prisoners to escape the camp, Treblinka was a "huge freshly polished, painted trap, purely for swallowing up more human beings."[17]

In the spring of 1943, camp commandant Franz Stangl decided to freshen up the camp's inviting façade with the construction of a zoo. Kurt Franz, a baby-faced sociopath whose cruelty stood out even in Treblinka, selected a site between the SS mess hall and the barracks of the Ukrainian guards. Once completed, "Zoo Corner" housed pigeons, squirrels, foxes, and other small animals.[18] Decades later, while serving a life sentence for mass murder in a Düsseldorf prison, Franz Stangl remembered the zoo with fondness. "We had any number of marvelous birds there," he mused to journalist Gitta Sereny. "An expert from Vienna designed it for us."[19]

More than a source of recreation for officers and staff, Treblinka's animal collection is best understood as part of what Sereny dubbed the "whole macabre fakery" of the camp—just one more bit of stagecraft to distract from the horror.[20] There is some irony in this. All zoos, to some degree or another, engage in their fair share of visual trickery. With their carefully manicured landscapes, trompe-l'oeil cage scenery, and artificial "environments," modern zoos aim to create the illusion that they aren't zoos at all. They are portals to another world—a world where animals willingly put themselves on display for our entertainment. At their most deceptive, zoos tell the story that wild animals are better off in human hands, where they are safe from the inevitable cruelties of the natural world. Considered this way, Stangl and his Nazi cohort seemed to be taking a page out of the zoo playbook. To borrow a phrase from Nazi war criminal Franz Suchomel, the Treblinka zoo was part of a "beautification strategy," a means of distracting from the camp's murderous purposes.[21]

Still, it bears asking: Who *exactly* was the zoo meant to fool? Not the prisoners, the "living corpses" (Grossman's term), the soon-to-be dead. Passing from the train platform to the gas chambers, their fields of vision carefully managed and screened, most prisoners would not have been able to see the zoo, let alone take the time to ponder its significance. The zoo's illusion of normalcy was meant to assuage the camp's permanent inhabitants (the administration, camp guards, members of the SS), to offer a kind of psychological barrier against the horrors of their own making. Stangl said as much to Sereny. As a rule, we're better off ignoring the words of ex-Nazis, particularly those eager to explain *their side* of the story. Still, Stangl admitted his need to deny what they were doing at Treblinka: "I repressed it all by trying to create a special place: gardens, new barracks, new kitchens, new everything; barbers, tailors, shoemakers, carpenters. There were hundreds of ways to take one's mind off it; I used them all."[22] Including a zoo.

On Zoos and Metaphor

The most powerful relationship between zoos and the Holocaust came at the level of metaphor. According to James Geary, author of a popular book on the influence of metaphorical language, metaphor allows us to "experience and think about the world in fluid, unusual ways." We use metaphors to draw connections between the "utterly strange and the utterly familiar," to translate the incomprehensible into the language of the everyday.[23] The Holocaust was awash in metaphorical language and logic. Life in the KZ system was "hell," the barely living inhabitants "zombies." Both survivors and witnesses described the camps as "slaughterhouses," drawing an explicit connection between the industrial destruction of animals and Hitler's Final Solution. As German philosopher Theodor Adorno famously put it, "Auschwitz begins wherever someone looks at a slaughterhouse and thinks: they're only animals." For the perpetrators, metaphor made the Holocaust thinkable, doable, defendable. For the millions trapped in the KZ system, metaphor made camp life survivable, if only briefly.

Over time, the zoo emerged as one of the most potent metaphors for framing the concentration camp experience and viewing those who endured it. This was certainly the case among Allied liberators, who often used "zoomorphic" language to make sense of what they were seeing. Historian Mark Celinscak has argued that liberators' frequent use of animal-related terminology served as a kind of psychological shield: "To view the survivors as something other than human was a way to protect the soldier against thinking that it was possible that this could also happen to them."[24] But references to zoos, stockyards, and animal pests also had a more ominous effect. Odette Rosenstock, who survived both Auschwitz and Bergen-Belsen, recalled how the camp inmates had "disappointed our liberators." For all their attempts at comprehension, the British troops at Belsen "understood nothing about it; it seemed to them that they were looking after a zoo inhabited by savage beasts, with dominant species and the mass of the dying, an antediluvian zoo where it was as natural to dominate as to die."[25] Confronted by the scenes of corpses and barely living prisoners, Derrick Sington and other Allied troops wound up resorting to the same kind of dehumanizing thinking as the Nazis.

The zoo metaphor was even more pervasive among the victims of Nazi violence. According to the testimony of some Jewish survivors, the feeling of being in a zoo began as early as the 1930s, when Nazi administrators began to cordon off urban Jews from the rest of the population. Recalling the debased atmosphere of life in the Łódź ghetto after the German invasion of Poland in 1939, Paula Biren explained: "It was like a zoo, it was animalistic. We lived, not a human life. . . . developed a numbness, a dreamlike state . . . the putting on of a shell. You hope you survive. You fight for survival."[26] Some ghetto residents used metaphors of zoo life to describe the effects of surveillance, of being constantly on display. Amalie Petranker Salsitz remembered a particularly humiliating practice in the Polish city of Stanislav, where German officers and their wives liked to tour the ghetto gawking at the Jewish inhabitants.[27] In her diary, twelve-year-old Tamar Lazerson noted a similar experience in the Kovno ghetto, which held nearly 30,000 Jews in the Lithuanian capital: "Yesterday, an excursion of Hitler Youths came to the workshops. They came as if to a zoo, to look at the Jews at work. For them it is a joke!"[28]

This sense of being an animal trapped in a zoo was amplified further in the camps themselves. With their barbed-wire fences, open sewage pits, and squalid shelters, many camps bore a striking resemblance to rundown zoos—a fact that was not lost on prisoners. Moreover, everything about camp life was calculated to reduce inmates—physically, mentally, ethically—to the status of animals. The testimony of Carola Stern Steinhardt speaks to the depths of Nazi efforts to dehumanize camp prisoners. Arriving at Auschwitz at age seventeen, Carola Stern Steinhardt was stripped, tattooed, and deloused—all under the gaze of SS supervisors. Once she was released into the general population (Steinhardt worked as a "beautician"), the teenager's life was a daily litany of terror and humiliation. "You looked like an animal," she recounted decades later, explaining how camp guards liked to sic their dogs on prisoners for sport. Sick with typhoid, and no longer able to control her bowels, she was eventually evacuated to Ravensbrück and then Malchow, where she subsisted on a diet of water and potato peels. There she spent the final days of the war observing a nearby camp of English POWs: "It was just across from the camp we were in. They were also laying around, like, you know, like, like dead animals. You know, when you go to a zoo and sometimes those animals look like tranquilized, that's what we all looked like. We were just either waiting to die or being liberated. Something had to happen to us, we couldn't go on anymore."[29]

Survivors' metaphorical connection to zoo animals did not dissipate overnight. Freed in a swap for German POWS, Polish-born Rose Warner (née Luft) eventually made her way to a quarantine facility in Sweden. Yet even there she remained highly attuned to her diminished status. Weekend visitors "look[ed] at us like monkeys in a cage, because we were something to them like they never saw," she told a historian.[30] Ruth Reiser felt something similar upon her return to her hometown of Prague. "You feel nobody can ever understand what you went through," the Theresienstadt survivor explained. "So they look at you a little bit like from somebody from a zoo."[31] A native of Horochow, Poland, Charlene Schiff (née Shulamit Perlmutter) spent much of the war hiding in the woods near her hometown. Eventually liberated by Soviet troops, she immigrated to the United States in 1948, hoping to put the terrors of the war years behind her. But she could never fully shake her sense of being an outsider. In the eyes of her new neighbors in Ohio, Schiff remembered, "I was regarded as a—like in a zoo, what do you call it, when there's something strange or different. I was not regarded as a—a regular human being."[32] For survivors like Schiff, the zoo offered a metaphor for the seemingly unexplainable experience of being stripped of her humanity.

If Concentration Camps Resemble Zoos, Does That Mean . . . ?

But if concentration camps resemble zoos in the eyes of survivors, what does that imply about the world's animal collections? Does the metaphor suggest a preexisting ambivalence on the part of Holocaust survivors—a recognition that the zoo represented something far less innocent than an "ark in the park"? Do zoos and concentration camps share the same philosophical underpinnings, the same logic of oppressor and oppressed? Does zoo-going prime visitors to engage in acts of cruelty and humiliation of the sort endured by Tamar Lazerson and Rose Warner? Put simply, if concentration camps are like zoos, can we ever look at zoos the same way again?

This is dangerous territory. To those who view the mass murder of Europe's Jews as a singular event, unrivaled in its lethality and scale, playing fast-and-loose with Holocaust analogies risks trivializing the Final Solution's epic horror. This is especially the case when it comes to animals. Tom Regan, author of a groundbreaking treatise on the ethics of animal liberation, once hinted at the pitfalls of such comparisons: "Do we dare speak of a *Holocaust for the animals*? May we depict the horror they must endure, using this fearful image of wanton inhumanity, without desecrating the memory of those innocents who died in the death camps?"[33] Scholar Karen Davis chalks up hostility to such thinking to "thousands of years of teaching that humans are superior to animals in all respects."[34] Even so-called animal lovers will often bristle at the suggestion that—in visiting a zoo or stopping off for a cheeseburger—they might be inhabiting the same immoral universe as those who carried out Hitler's genocidal vision. Finally, we need to entertain the possibility that "like an animal in a zoo" was little more than a cliché, a bit of conventional phrasing that signified a general sense of diminished status. As one writer later opined, "Yes, the Nazis treated us like animals, maybe worse than animals. But it's just an expression we use."[35] To read anything more into the phrase is to miss the point.

Yet discounting the zoo metaphor comes with its own risks—not least, the danger of ignoring survivors' own takeaways about comparative suffering. For some victims of Nazi terror, the only moral response to it was a kind of radical empathy, a willingness to assign ethical value to the lives of all creatures, human and animal alike. Such was the view of journalist Edgar Kupfer-Koberwitz, whose 1,800-page diary of his time at Dachau remains one of the definitive first-person accounts of life in Hitler's prison-state. A staunch vegan, Kupfer-Koberwitz explained: "I eat no animals, because I don't want to live on the suffering and death of other creatures, for I have suffered so much myself, that I can feel other creatures' suffering, by virtue of my own." Kupfer-Koberwitz drew a direct link between his own experiences and the banal, often taken for granted, violence meted out against the animal kingdom. "As long as animals are confined in cages," he argued, "there will be prisons as well—for incarceration must be practiced and learned, in a small scale, inwardly and outwardly."[36]

Alex Hershaft, who survived the Warsaw ghetto as a child and later immigrated to the United States, made a similar connection while visiting a slaughterhouse in 1972. "I noted with horror the striking similarities between what the Nazis did to my family and my people, and what we do to animals we raise for food," he recounted, "the branding or tattooing of serial numbers to identify victims, the use of cattle cars to transport victims to their death, the crowded housing of victims in wood crates, the arbitrary designation of who lives and who dies."[37] An environmental consultant by profession, Hershaft founded the Farm Animal Rights Movement (FARM), the United States' first grassroots organization to promote veganism and animal rights, in the early 1980s, and he has spent decades fighting on behalf of social justice—for humans and for animals. "Oppressing animals is the gateway drug to oppressing humans," he told an audience of New Yorkers in 2016. "As a survivor, I have made a choice. I have chosen against silence. I have chosen against oppression. I have chosen life."[38]

A similar sense of moral outrage runs throughout the work of Nobel Prize–winning writer Isaac Bashevis Singer, arguably the foremost literary advocate of animal compassion in the postwar era. The son of a Hasidic rabbi, Singer grew up in a Yiddish-speaking quarter of Warsaw; in 1935, he managed to immigrate to the United States, escaping the worst of the Nazi terror. However, the ethical questions posed by the Holocaust would come to inform much of his literary output. Among animal advocates, Singer is perhaps best known for opening the door to Holocaust comparisons. "In relation to [animals]," he wrote in 1968, "all people are Nazis; for the animals, it is an eternal Treblinka."[39] In his 1972 novel *Enemies, a Love Story*, Singer uses Holocaust imagery to describe his protagonist's visit to the Bronx Zoo, at the time vying for the title of the world's best. In the eyes of Herman Broder, a Polish survivor of the Holocaust, the zoo was little more than a prison: "The air here was full of longing—for deserts, hills, valleys, dens, families. Like the Jews, the animals had been dragged here from all parts of the world, condemned to isolation and boredom." Over the past decades, increasing numbers of zoo critics have followed Singer's lead, using Holocaust-inspired references to disparage especially despicable animal collections. Indeed, among certain detractors, the concentration camp has emerged as *the* most powerful rhetorical weapon in the war against zoos.[40]

In the end, the Holocaust would pose a challenge for postwar zoos that was different than the immediate privation and destruction. More so than any other aspect of World War II, Nazi Germany's embrace of genocide would undermine claims of European civilization and call into question any attempt to manipulate life, human or otherwise, for political ends. To critics, the world's zoos—with their iron cages, their rituals of seeing and being seen, their rankings of valuable and expendable life—bore a striking resemblance to the architecture of Hitler's slave state. The Holocaust made so much about the zoo suspect, not least the ideology of dominion upon which all zoos depend. Never again would it be quite so easy to justify using violence in the name of "science," incarceration in need of economic good, exploitation in the name of entertainment. Even today, the Holocaust casts a shadow over the world's zoos, if only in more people's willingness to see themselves in the roles of the caged.[41] This, ultimately, is Holocaust survivors' greatest gift to humanity—and it is why so many people find zoos intolerable.

In 1945, however, zookeepers had more pragmatic concerns. After more than half a decade of war, they wanted to restock their arks, rebuild their cages, and restore their reputations on the world stage.

PART V

Future Exhibits

19

Brave Zoo World

How can we measure the cost of a war?

We can tally expenses paid and monies lost. We can take stock of ruined buildings, polluted rivers, land seeded with unexploded bombs. We can count corpses and try to calculate the lives shortened by hunger, injury, and disease. And we can try to weigh the intangible legacies—the nightmares, the lost faith, the sadness and horror and rage.

By all these measures, World War II was the most devastating conflict in modern history. More than seventy-five million people perished—ripped apart on the battlefield, buried under concrete, incinerated in bombing raids, murdered in concentration camps, brutalized and left for dead. Tens of millions were left homeless. In Germany, Allied bombs destroyed more than 3.6 million apartments, one-fifth of the entire rental stock. In Great Britain, people spent the night in Underground tunnels; Warsaw residents slept in makeshift shelters and holes in the earth.[1] Even as the Allies trumpeted their victory, writes historian Keith Lowe, "waves of vengeance and retribution washed over every sphere of European life."[2]

Meanwhile, the dual threat of bitter cold and hunger continued to loom large. Wrote the London *Sunday Observer* in late 1945: "Europe is threatened by a catastrophe this winter which has no precedent since the Black Death of 1348."[3] In postwar Germany, food rations fell to starvation levels, and intestinal disease ran rampant.[4] Unable to procure food, observed novelist Sandor Marai, "most Budapest inhabitants became as skeletally thin as the sketches of the human structure found in anatomy books, without any flesh or fat." The situation in postwar Japan was no better. Utterly defeated, the people of the Rising Sun were advised "how to prepare meals from acorns, grain husks, sawdust (for pancakes), snails, grasshoppers, and rats."[5]

The devastation went far deeper than rubble-filled streets, skeletal cathedrals, and weakened bodies. In March 1945, the *New York Times* dubbed Europe "The New Dark Continent," a place where "universal famine had made personal morality an irrelevance."[6] The English poet Stephen Spender, who served as part of the Allied Commission in postwar Germany, agreed. After a tour of Cologne, he wrote: "The ruin of the city is reflected in the internal ruin of its inhabitants, who, instead of being lives that can form a scar over the city's wounds, are parasites sucking at a dead carcass, digging among the ruins for hidden food."[7] American writer John Dos Passos, increasingly in the thrall of anticommunist fervor, described a Europe on the brink of chaos: "The entire fabric of a million little routines has broken down. No one can think beyond food for tomorrow. Money is worthless. Cigarettes are used as a kind of lunatic travesty currency." Summing up his view, he concluded grimly: "All we have brought to Europe so far is confusion backed up by a drumhead regime of military courts. We have swept away Hitlerism, but a great many Europeans feel that the cure has been worse than the disease."[8]

The misery was not confined to humans. Throughout the war years, some animal advocates had tried to raise alarms about the dangers facing the world's wildlife. "Bullets are no respecters of persons—nor of animals," observed one zoo-loving GI at the time. "Now that the entire world is engulfed in the most deadly and far-reaching combat in history, animals of many kinds are seriously threatened." Jean Delacour's prediction was no less ominous. "Unless Allied and Japanese authorities take very strong steps to check it," he warned, "it is certain that quantities of big game will be destroyed by the troops."[9] However, such concerns went unnoticed. In the race for victory, both sides deployed an arsenal of pollutants, toxic chemicals, and soon-to-be trash (shell casings, cigarette butts, rubber tubing, food wrappers, syringes) with little thought to the environmental costs. Animals were burned alive in bombing raids, drowned in oil slicks, poisoned by industrial runoff, crushed beneath tank treads, or hunted to near extinction. In some cases, it would take decades for species to return to their prewar natural habitats; in others, they never would.

Writing in the Philadelphia Zoo magazine in June 1945, US Sgt. Robert Robinson described the Ardennes Forest, scene of the Battle of the Bulge, as all but devoid of large game. Except for the occasional rabbit, "deer seem to be all that is left of this once-great redoubt of European wildlife." West of the Rhine, once-prosperous farms lay in ruin. "The cattle are dead or untended, the chickens have vanished with the coming of the infantry, and the horses romp loose on the flat fields, their little groups shying away from sudden sounds of passing convoys." At one point, the sergeant reported, the sound of approaching trucks scared a lone buck into breaking cover, setting off a shooting spree as soldiers up and down the line tried to pick it off. "The frightened animal made a dash across the clearing with the tracers weaving a pattern about him as he went, and he vanished into the woods—unscathed. So there is at least one deer left in Naziland." Nevertheless, the animal-loving Robinson was despondent. "This is a stinking war," he seethed. "I want to come home."[10]

The Ark in Ruin

The situation at the world's zoos was equally dire. After five years of hunger and deadly fighting, countless zoo cages lay empty. Of the surviving animals, hundreds perished in the war's immediate aftermath, victims of malnutrition, bitter cold, and theft. As with everything about the conflict, the traumatic effects of the fighting fell unevenly across the zoo world. Zoos in Australia, for example, not only missed the routine air attacks but benefited from a steady stream of US GIs on leave. After surviving the early days of the Blitz, the London Zoo in Regent's Park remained open throughout the remainder of the war. Visiting the Rome Zoo in August 1944, US Staff Sgt. Paul M. Daniel, a member of the Junior Zoological Society of Philadelphia, remarked that the collection had "withstood the war quite well," no doubt because Rome was "one of the very few European cities to be spared intensive bombing."[11] Zoos located in the remnants of Hitler's Greater Reich were not so fortunate. The zoo in Warsaw, ground zero of Nazi rapacity, did not reopen until September 1948.[12] The Budapest Zoo, emptied of all animals, was reduced to staging exhibitions of local wines and automobiles to make ends meet.[13]

In newly occupied Germany, the fate of individual zoos was partly determined by the quirks of geography. Germany had been divided into four zones, each under the control of a different Allied power: the Soviet Union, Great Britain, the United States, and France. In principle, all four occupiers agreed to abide by a set of rules. In practice, however, they tended to display markedly different attitudes toward the newly conquered German people—and vice versa.

Leadership at Munich's Hellabrunn Zoo adopted a welcoming attitude toward their Yankee overseers. After retreating Wehrmacht forces attempted to stall US tanks by blocking a major bridge with a tramcar, the zoo's director, Heinz Heck, used an elephant to remove the obstruction, physically and symbolically welcoming the Americans' arrival. The only German zoo man who never joined the Nazi Party, Heck had always enjoyed friendly relations with his counterparts in the United States. Not surprisingly, US forces allowed Hellabrunn to resume operations only a few weeks after the German capitulation. Justifying the decision, an American PR officer drew a distinction between innocent bystanders and die-hard Hitlerites. Munich's zoo animals weren't Nazis, he mused—why should they be punished?[14]

In Berlin, talk of recovery took a backseat to the more pressing task of clearing debris. In the final days of the war, fighting between Soviet troops and retreating Germans had reduced the zoo to a wasteland. "Its terrain was no longer identifiable as that of a zoo," notes historian Gary Bruce. "Bomb craters, fallen trees, rubble piles, and the charred shells of trucks and tanks had replaced the elegant pathways and exotic buildings."[15] Now in the British zone of occupation (the capital city was also divided four ways), the Berlin Zoo struggled to find adequate supplies to feed its ninety-one remaining inhabitants. Volunteers spent hours going door to door begging for potato peels and other scraps, and sympathetic Red Army veterinarians donated dead horses to supplement the zoo's meager meat supplies. Eventually, Katharina Heinroth began giving monthly tours to the higher-ups in the British occupation authority, pointing out the greatest sources of need. Colonel Robert Nunn, a British officer who pulled a number of strings on the zoo's behalf, saw the zoo as a "symbol of recovery" in

Figure 19.1. In this apocalyptic scene from 1945, two uniformed policemen survey the devastation at Berlin's Tiergarten. Photo credit: bpk Bildagenturm / Bundesarchiv / Friedrich Seidenstücker / Art Resource, NY.

a city dominated by death.[16] Nevertheless, when the Berlin Zoo reopened its gates on July 1, 1945, it was a skeleton of its former self—its cages vacant, its boulevards piled with rubble, its grounds bursting with the corpses of humans and animals alike.

The experience of Hamburg's Hagenbeck Tierpark testifies to the fragile political status of all German zoos after World War II. Located on an important outlet to the North Sea, the port city had been targeted numerous times during the war. Surveying the damage, British Lieutenant Philip Dark observed: "As far as the eye could see, square mile after square mile of empty shells of buildings with twisted girders scarecrowed in the air, radiators of a flat jutting out from a shaft of a still-standing wall, like a crucified pterodactyl skeleton."[17] Among the few institutions to escape the inferno, the zoo at one time housed a camp for slave laborers for the shipbuilder Blohm+Voss. When British authorities arrived on May 5, 1945, they converted the camp into an assembly center for "displaced persons," a bureaucratic term applied to the millions of forced laborers, concentration camp victims, and refugees dispersed across the rotting corpse of Hitler's Reich. Against

Figure 19.2. Leon Waszczuk is doused with DDT (anti-vermin chemicals) shortly after his arrival at the No. 17 Displaced Persons Assembly Center at the Hagenbeck Zoo in Hamburg. Credit: © Imperial War Museum (BU 6633).

the backdrop of open cages, children and adults were issued registration cards, doused with anti-lice powder, and readied for repatriation (if, that is, their home countries still existed). In the first four weeks alone, more than 68,000 people from twenty-six different nations (including 33,043 Russians, 102 Chinese, and 1 American) passed through the "Zoo Camp," unwilling visitors in a nation that had threatened to hold all of Europe captive.[18]

As in Munich, Hagenbeck Zoo leaders went out of their way to cozy up to the new occupiers. The zoo loaned out two of its trained Indian elephants, Kiri and Many, to clear debris. Newsreels at the time joyously captured scenes of the chained "animal collaborators" wading through rubble and pulling out massive chunks of iron with their muscular trunks.[19] Yet no amount of good publicity could disguise the enormity of the task at hand. It would take years to restore Hagenbeck's famed exhibit spaces to their prewar condition. Many of the zoo's most prized animals had been evacuated to the east, only to be killed in the final weeks of the war. Others in Lorenz Hagenbeck's personal collection were sold for pfennig on the mark to Scandinavian circuses to offset the cost of German "war damage."[20] Above all else, zoo staff struggled to keep up with the daily demand for fresh food.

In April 1947, British authorities took the rare step of removing the zoo's top animals for safekeeping. Given the scarcity of the animals, noted the London *Times* approvingly, "it becomes ever more important

Figure 19.3. Hagenbeck Zoo elephants Kiri and Many using their brute strength to move a bombed-out car in 1945. © Imperial War Museum (BU 11449).

both to protect, where possible, the surviving wild stocks and to avoid unnecessary wastage among captive specimens."[21] The Hagenbeck Zoo, the British contended, lacked the resources to adequately care for its animals. Thus, they needed to be removed for their own good. The first consignment (including an Indian elephant, a pair of hippos, a polar bear, and other assorted creatures) arrived by ship from Hanover in April. They were accompanied by L. M. Flewin, overseer of mammals at Regent's Park, who had been coordinating the transfer.[22] In all, some forty-five animal exiles left Hamburg for London.[23] For an already defeated nation, humiliated and impoverished, the move smacked of paternalism at best, rank punishment at worst. At the very moment that German zoos were assailing the world with plaintive requests to help rebuild, British ships were further emptying their coffers.

For all their differences, zoos of the former Reich had one thing in common: they were forced to grapple with the devil's bargain they had made with Adolf Hitler. During the 1930s and well into the war years, when Nazi power was in its ascendency, German zoo men jockeyed to win favor with Hitler and his toadies. With the war's end in sight, Otto Antonius, director of Vienna's Schönbrunn Zoo, decided to commit suicide rather than live with the shame of defeat. As Soviet troops closed in, the fifty-nine-year-old shot his wife Margarethe before turning the gun on himself—a fitting end for a man who did everything to live up to the Nazi ideal.

Most of his former Reich colleagues, however, sought to distance themselves, both ideologically and geographically, from the Nazi regime. Fearing retribution from the Soviets, Berlin Zoo director Lutz Heck fled the city in the final days of the war, leaving his underlings to clean up the mess. Eventually, he turned himself in to US authorities, eager to whitewash his reputation as Hermann Göring's favorite zoo man. Other zoo directors fell victim to the campaign of *Entnazifizierung* (denazification) that swept postwar Germany. By denazifying German society, Allied leaders wanted to cleanse any taint of pro-Hitler sympathy. Former party members were stripped of their positions and, in some cases, forced to stand trial for their wartime actions. Munich's Heinz Heck was required to provide a list of zoo personnel who had joined the Nazi Party.[24] In 1946, the director of the Breslau

Zoo was dismissed following the forced expulsion of German citizens in newly reshaped Poland.[25]

Conditions in postwar Japan were equally stark. Cut off from the European zoo network, Japanese zoos had to make do with what they had, which wasn't much. Most zoo cages stood empty. Across the entire country, only a handful of large zoo animals (three elephants, four giraffes, a single chimpanzee) remained alive. With millions on the brink of starvation, feeding zoo animals was a distant afterthought. To offset the human famine, staff converted unused zoo grounds into farms for growing potatoes, while would-be zoo-goers were encouraged to bring food from home. (A visitor could gain admission with a few stalks of celery or some pumpkin seeds.)[26] Despite such measures, animals continued to starve. Even the Ueno Zoo's collections of Inner Mongolian camels lost their humps—a sure sign, zoo director Tadamichi Koga told the press, of dangerous malnutrition.[27]

Like everything else in the defeated nation, Japanese zoos depended upon the good graces of the American occupiers for their daily survival. On August 15, 1945, Emperor Hirohito had asked his people to "bear the unbearable and endure the unendurable" by accepting surrender. In return, the Supreme Commander for the Allied Powers (SCAP) promised to help Japan rebuild as a US-friendly Western ally. In July 1946, the United Press reported that workers from Ueno Zoo purchased 550 pounds of potato peels and other food scraps from SCAP kitchens daily.[28] The following year, Australian journalist Peggy Warner wrote that most of Ueno's animals appeared on the brink of death. A pair of black swans paddled listlessly in a "stagnant pool," and the kangaroos were so emaciated that they could barely hop. The "saddest sight," in Warner's eyes, "was a painfully thin black and white cat who lived in the monkey island. The sides of the island [were] too steep . . . so the cat spen[t] its days in the pit, with two monkeys and a pig."[29]

Not surprisingly, the US occupation brought its fair share of problems. Although SCAP had a vested interest in winning over the defeated Japanese, there was no question who was in charge. In Kyoto, US engineers received "permission" from the new mayor to turn roughly one-third of the zoo into a motor pool for SCAP vehicles. Zoo officials protested, accusing the Americans of taking advantage of the political

Figure 19.4. Woodcut by renowned printmaker Kōshirō Onchi of Tokyo's Ueno Zoo from December 1945, less than six months after the Japanese surrender. Much like the actual zoo, the image is strikingly devoid of life, with only five people and one animal—a seal—in view. Rijksmuseum, Amsterdam.

confusion to ram through the project. But, like so many institutions in postwar Japan, the zoo had little choice in the matter.[30] Over time, the Kyoto Zoo became a popular destination for GIs to bring prostitutes.[31] The message was not lost on the locals. After surviving the war structurally intact, the Kyoto Zoological Gardens (and by implication the entire nation) could be reduced to whatever the American occupiers needed it to be.

The American Century of Zookeeping

The mood was very different across the Atlantic, where the end of World War II ushered in a period of renewed optimism in American zoo circles. In August 1945, *The Billboard*, a popular magazine covering the entertainment industry, offered a typically upbeat assessment of the war's legacy for American zoos. Detailing ongoing plans to renovate the Brookfield Zoo, the magazine explained: "Plastics, glass and other materials developed during the last few years are being tested for use in post-war construction." In the zoo of the future, "Apes, now confined behind bars, will be housed in a building made of plastic such as is used in plane turrets."[32] In the minds of American zoo folk, the introduction of Plexiglas and other war-related materials would translate into a new type of zoo—hyper-visible, intimate, transparent in its confinement—more in keeping with the television age. (They also thought two-inch acrylic would protect valuable animals from humans' respiratory diseases.)[33] Writing to Belle Benchley in May 1946, Seattle's Woodland Park Zoo director Gus Knudson forecast "great things in the years to come." With a flourish typical of postwar American finger-pointing, he added: "The zoo situation in this country is wonderful compared to the situation in Europe—but that is what Europe gets for having a war."[34]

By 1947, triumphalism about the looming American century of zoo-keeping reached a fever pitch. That November, a reporter for the Associated Press announced a "brave new postwar world" for America's zoo animals. No longer overshadowed by the "great collections" in Rotterdam, Antwerp, London, and Berlin, US zoos were now the "world's best." As architects sketched plans for the latest "ultramodern" enclosures, more than 230,000 wild birds and animals reached American ports—two to three times the number from the year before. Not even the increasingly chilly Cold War threatened to stem the tide of recent arrivals. Hinting at a future of zoological détente, the reporter gushed: "Russia's animals are ready to join the peace loving and vetoless communities of their American furred and feathered comrades. The Soviet government has just sent United States zoos a list of animals it is ready to sell."[35]

Compared to their overseas counterparts, American zoos were also better equipped to deal with the skyrocketing animal prices. The German-born animal dealer Henry Trefflich chalked up the spike to the cost of shipping, which "more than doubled" the prewar rates. He likewise attributed the price hikes to African and Indian animal merchants looking to exploit zoo-hungry foreigners. "Tigers jumped from $1,200 to $3,500 a pair," he complained. "Leopards that were $600 went up to $1,800. Before the war an elephant from India cost $1,200, which covered freight and insurance." After the war, that same elephant would go for $2,200 in Calcutta—shipping and handling not included.[36]

After years of going without, American zoos were itching to snatch up fresh specimens, even at inflated costs. Well before the war's end, some US zoos amassed significant war chests for restocking efforts. In April 1945, the Milwaukee Zoo set up a fund to replace animals that had died during the war years. By that August, it had collected more than $15,000, including a $10,000 pledge from Pabst Brewing Company to bring a panda to Wisconsin.[37] Zoo men outside the United States cried foul, blaming American excess for driving up prices. But there was little they could do. This was never clearer than in 1948, when the Bronx Zoo ponied up $8,700 for the purchase of a single platypus, the first of its kind exhibited on US soil. Walter van den bergh, the director of the Antwerp Zoo, remarked in visible frustration: "That is more than I have to spend in a year." Van den bergh put the blame squarely on his US counterparts: "You Americans have spoiled the world market. . . . You have too much money."[38]

Restocking the Postwar Zoo

When it came to restocking their collections, zoos had several options. The first—and, for most zoos, the least feasible—was to mount an expedition. Since their emergence, Western zoos had relied on animal-collecting expeditions to Africa, Southeast Asia, and elsewhere to fill their cages. In the decade prior to World War II, animal collectors like Frank Buck spun romantic stories about intrepid white adventurers plundering exotic locales for rare and exciting wildlife.

Within the first half decade after the war, the London Zoological Society sponsored (or directly benefited from) half a dozen animal-collecting expeditions to India, Egypt, the British Cameroons, the Falklands, Ceylon, and other imperial outposts. One zoo employee returned from British Guiana with twenty-eight reptiles and fish, ninety-five birds, and fifty-seven mammals, including sloths, monkeys, and tapirs. A second came from Singapore with a shipment of orangutans, Malay bears, and pythons.[39] Other European zoos looked to their African and Asian colonies to replenish their decimated collections as well. In 1948, Achille Urbain, director of the Vincennes Zoo in Paris, said he was waiting for a large shipment of gorillas, elephants, and monkeys from the French Cameroons.

"In one stroke," Urbain announced, "we shall restore the glories of this zoo."[40]

The center of much of this collecting fervor was sub-Saharan Africa, all of which (except Liberia) remained under European colonial control. In 1946, Bruce Brown, secretary of Sydney's Taronga Park Zoo, embarked on a 10,000-mile lorry journey through Rhodesia, Kenya, Uganda, Tanganyika, the Belgian Congo, and South Africa in search of fresh specimens. Like most animal collectors of his era, Brown relied on locals to do much of the dirty work. He also used his extensive contacts at zoos in Pretoria and Johannesburg to fill his living larder. Still, animal-collecting remained dangerous work, particularly to those tasked with keeping their precious stock safe from curious predators. "We lost a sentry at the Kampala camp one night," Brown explained to an Australian newspaper. "He was snatched by a lion, though we were only two miles from town."[41] Brown returned home the following year with a trained elephant, a beer-drinking chimpanzee, a rhino, six cheetahs, and three lion cubs—all part of the first large consignment of African animals to reach Australia since the war's end. Having spent nine months in Africa, Brown waxed poetic about the impact of European colonialism on the Continent: "There is now no longer 'a dark continent,' and the part we once called 'darkest Africa' has been traversed by lovely motor roads since the war. It is now quite the usual thing to drive through the country, especially through the animal sanctuaries, and see antelopes and other animals grazing quite near. Lions seem to be the only animals that have never become accustomed to passers-by."[42]

However, few believed that such ventures were the answer to zoos' problems. Animal-collecting expeditions were notoriously expensive, in terms of both money and the large numbers of animals killed in the pursuit of zoo-worthy specimens. On his return trip from Africa, Bruce Brown's floating menagerie consumed eighty pounds of fresh meat per day (they kept chickens to feed the cheetah cubs) along with heaping rations of corn, millet, sugarcane, and greens.[43] Besides food costs, zoos had to foot the bill for insurance in case animals died or—as was all too common—were washed overboard. Plus, expeditions were slow. Munich's Hellabrunn Zoo did not receive its first large shipment of African animals until September 1950. The following July, an even larger consignment of African wildlife left Mombasa for a five-week journey to Genoa and eventually Munich. Valued at approximately 75,000 DM, Hellabrunn's latest inhabitants included four giraffes, eight antelopes, seven lions, twelve cranes, and an elephant—the first to reach Germany since Hitler's defeat.[44]

A better solution was to use captive breeding programs to repopulate zoos. During the war, a number of high-profile zoos made headlines by developing novel techniques for cultivating animal births. In 1944, Nazi propagandists trumpeted the birth of an African elephant at Hellabrunn Zoo as a landmark achievement in breeding and "hereditary education." (It was killed in a bombing raid.) By war's end, many zoo leaders believed that successful breeding programs were central to any effort to protect endangered species. With euphemism typical of the era, Robert MacMillan explained the significance of zoo breeding programs this way: "The reason there are plenty of animals for the public to marvel or shudder at is . . . because of Love, which in its natural course brings baby hippos, lions, bears and suchlike to the zoos without anybody having to chase them down in the jungle."[45]

Captive breeding proved especially successful in the United States. Even before war was declared, several major US zoos had begun to cultivate extensive breeding programs, allowing them to maintain vast collections, despite wartime travel restrictions. Describing a rash of births at the Brookfield Zoo in September 1944, *Life Magazine* pronounced, "Brookfield's multifarious births exemplify the solution U.S. zoos have found for their problem of wartime maintenance. Since exotic importations from Asia, Africa and even South America have been curtailed by lack of safaris and shipping space, zoomen have been encouraging intramural procreation. Single males and females are shipped from zoo to zoo for breeding purposes, or swapped outright as needs arise."[46] Thanks to technology and careful planning, American zoos had no need for international travel. They could reproduce zoo-worthy megafauna from the safety of US soil.

Any solution to postwar zoos' animal problem would inevitably involve a fair amount of barter and exchange. Zoos had always relied on other zoos to acquire animal stock and get rid of unwanted or redundant specimens. However, in the aftermath of World War II, such transactions became more important than ever. Zoos large and small sent out feelers to their fellow animal collectors. The Antwerp Zoo acquired two ostriches in a trade for a pair of lion cubs, themselves the offspring of a lioness gifted from London and a male lion purchased on the cheap from a circus in Luxemburg.[47] In late 1949, Sydney's Taronga Park Zoo negotiated a deal with Paris's Vincennes Zoo for two baby gorillas (worth between £1,400 and £1,500 each). In return, Vincennes received a shipment of rare and highly prized Australian fauna.[48]

Not surprisingly, American zoos assumed an especially public role in helping to restock the war-depleted zoos of Europe and Asia. Like the architects of the American century, US zoo men believed they had a special mission to help their foreign counterparts recover from the war's devastation. Within a year of the conflict's end, zoos in the United States sent shipments of animals to former enemies and allies alike, a gesture that went a long way toward confirming the United States' global leadership in zoo circles. In many cases, such shipments resulted from intimate connections between communities in the United States and abroad. In May 1948, three dozen Chicagoans flew to Czechoslovakia to visit family members (most of whom they hadn't seen in over a decade). Accompanying them on the United Airlines flight were four baby alligators—gifts from the Brookfield Zoo to the Prague Zoological Garden.[49] Similarly, Salt Lake City's Hogle Zoo was motivated to donate animals to Japan because of a relationship forged with Japanese Americans held at a nearby internment camp during the war years.[50]

Atomic Livestock and the End of Nature

On July 1, 1946, an atomic bomb exploded 500 feet above the South Pacific. The first of a series of US nuclear weapons tests since the war's end, the blast lit up the sky in blinding white light. In the seconds to follow, a towering plume rose toward the heavens, its shadow rolling across the crystal waters of Bikini Atoll like a black wave. Among the few survivors that day was a fifty-pound spotted Dutch-China hog dubbed "Pig 311," one of 3,000 animal test subjects placed on target ships anchored near the blast site. Some of the pigs and goats had their hair snipped to resemble GI buzz cuts; others were slathered in skin lotion or draped in makeshift uniforms to test their protection against radiation. Pig 311 was said to have been "locked in the officers' head (toilet)" of a captured Japanese light cruiser at the time of the explosion.[51] After she somehow managed to escape the sinking ship, Pig 311 was picked up hours later in a nearby lagoon. The AP tried its best to debunk the story, claiming that the floppy-eared stoat was most likely "AWOL" on the day of the A-bomb test.[52] Still, the initial story stuck, and Pig 311 was shipped first to the Naval Research Institute at Bethesda, Maryland, and then on to the National Zoo, where she spent the rest of her short life. No longer a living approximation of human flesh, Pig 311—along with Goat 311 and three coconut crabs found at Bikini the next year—was a celebrity, a symbol of survival in the atomic age.[53]

Although the onset of a new Cold War threatened to shatter the zoo world's fragile peace, many zoo leaders were initially reluctant to ramp up tensions with rivals across the Iron Curtain. Even as Joseph McCarthy raged against the "Red Menace" infecting American society, US zoo men like Theodore Reed and William Mann used their diplomatic skills to maintain an open dialogue with their Soviet-backed counterparts, exchanging information, participating in captive breeding projects, and sponsoring international conferences on the future of wildlife. The same proved true around the world, where the press frequently characterized zoo animals as international ambassadors of peace and goodwill.

Typical was the story of the *Dmitry Donskoy*, which in 1950 became the first Russian ship to enter the harbor of Sydney, Australia, since the end of World War II. After dropping off a consignment of ammonia sulfate farther to the north, the merchant vessel had arrived to pick up 5,000 tons of wheat bound for Cairo.[54] However, this fact was immediately overshadowed by press coverage of a gift given to the ship's captain: a small female Queensland wallaby named "Mickey" (after Mickey Mouse). Once onboard, Mickey lived in a handmade pouch in the captain's quarters (directly beneath, it turns out, a portrait of Stalin). Eventually, the nature-loving sailor hoped to acquire a male wallaby to give to the Leningrad Zoo, whose lone kangaroo had been killed during the war.[55] Press accounts highlighted the feelings of cordiality between the Russian shipmaster and his Australian guests. At a moment of fraught global tensions, there was "no iron curtain" aboard the *Dmitry Donskoy*, recalled one journalist. Instead, the captain "toasted the visitors in Russian liqueur, and offered them long, strong Russian cigarettes."[56]

Despite such gestures of friendship, the fate of Cold War zoos was by no means certain. In December 1951, with US troops locked in a bloody stalemate in Korea, Henry Fairfield Osborn Jr., then president of the New York Zoological Society, used his monthly *Animal Kingdom* editorial to deliver a blistering critique of communist expansion: "The Soviets have constructed a one-way street carrying a constant and immense traffic of ideological power, of threats, and of fear. Its cargoes are unloaded the world over, irresistibly influence the economy and cultures of every country." A longtime advocate of international cooperation, Osborn nonetheless pledged to enlist the zoo in the "struggle" to contain Soviet influence at home and abroad.[57]

In divided Berlin, ground zero of Cold War posturing, the city's two zoos weren't just rivals—they were ideological enemies.[58] When the East Berlin Zoo announced its intention to become the largest zoological park in the world in 1954, the US State Department urged zoological societies to donate to its West Berlin counterpart. (From a geopolitical perspective, it was vital that the communist zoo didn't take the "lead.")[59] Political paranoia did not help matters. Although many zoo leaders were eager to rebuild prewar trading networks, Cold War governments often had strict rules about doing business across the Iron Curtain. After the last of the United States' stock of large pandas died in the early 1950s, a policy against trading in "enemy goods" made it impossible to import a replacement.[60] It would take Nixon and Mao's "panda diplomacy" of the 1970s to break the embargo—fully three decades after Pan-Dee and Pan-Dah arrived via Pearl Harbor.

The Cold War represented just one of zoos' long-term problems. Western zoo leaders and animal dealers also worried about losing their claim on the most zoo-worthy wild creatures. Although most European powers clung to the illusion that they could hold on to their prewar colonies, zoo leaders saw rising anticolonial sentiment in Africa and Southeast Asia as a direct threat to their future interests. "It is undeniable that the sudden granting of political independence in a tropical territory, of which one has seen several recent examples, can constitute a very real danger to the survival of certain particular vulnerable species," announced Artis's Armand Sunier in 1952.[61] Used to having

Figure 19.5. Despite an upswing in anti-imperial sentiment in the aftermath of World War II, zoos remained popular with Western militaries tasked with maintaining their nations' colonial possessions. Snapped during the Indonesia War of Independence, this photograph from 1947 shows an armed Dutch soldier momentarily squeezing the finger of a caged chimpanzee at an Indonesian Zoo. Photo: Harry Steggerda, National Archives of the Netherlands / DLC.

untrammeled access to the Global South's jungles and savannahs, zoo folk fretted that newly emancipated governments would be unwilling to part with their animal resources—at least, not without a price hike. At their most hysterical, Western zoo leaders and conservationists predicted that, without the disciplinary hand of European colonialism, leaders in newly independent nations would exterminate their local wildlife, with little thought to the long-term consequences.[62]

Newly liberated nations did indeed assert themselves. Reflecting in 1974, writer Bernard Livingston declared:

> So-called Third-World countries—the animal-supplying countries—have taken over management of their own affairs. The Frank Bucks, Trader Horns and assorted "bring-'em-back-alivers" who plundered native wildernesses under the guise of zoological research have, for the most part, been booted out of Africa together with the colonial administrators who issued export permits and native safari boys at

ten cents a day. . . . Even a prestigious, government-supported zoo would today find it politically impossible, as well as financially unfeasible in the era of soaring costs, to mount a large-scale collecting expedition.[63]

Most ominous of all, zoos were forced to confront a future of rapid, potentially world-ending, environmental destruction. Many in the industry viewed the decade surrounding World War II as a tipping point in humans' relationship with the natural world. For the first time, writes historian R. S. Deese, *Homo sapiens* became the "decisive power in determining the future direction of life on earth," for good or ill.[64] The most obvious danger came in the form of atomic weapons, which threatened to render the globe virtually unlivable. Soon, the United States and Soviet Union had developed hydrogen bombs a thousand times more destructive than those dropped on Hiroshima and Nagasaki. By the 1980s, the Cold War rivals had produced more than 60,000 nuclear warheads, enough to kill all sentient life on earth many times over.[65] But even a small-scale nuclear conflict could inflict irreparable damage to the world's ecosystems, unleashing global famine and sending countless animal species to early extinction.[66] In the eyes of critics, global annihilation by nuclear war was not just possible—it was all but inevitable.

If mass death by nuclear destruction was bad, mass life by rapid population growth posed its own environmental risks. Decades before the publication of Paul and Anne Ehrlich's 1968 bestseller *The Population Bomb*, members of groups like the Conference on Science and World Affairs warned that the "exponential growth of human populations and the accompanying industrial, agricultural, and scientific activities" were pushing some plant and animal species to the brink of extinction.[67] Much like today, doomsayers directed much of their alarmism toward newly independent peoples in Africa and Asia—in other words, those *least* responsible for the destructive growth of industrial society. Even so, the numbers were difficult to ignore. Between 1950 and 1987, the global population doubled from 2.5 to 5 billion people.[68] (We recently topped 8 billion.) At that rate, critics warned, not even another world war could "solve" the "man pressure" problem. "Two world wars killed between them perhaps 50 million people," figured British zoologist Colin Bertram in 1963. "That's the world's net increase of a mere 400 days." The only solution, in Bertram's mind, was fertility control—doing unto humans what zoo men had long done to reduce the number of excessive or unwanted animals in their stock.[69]

Faced with such threats, zoo leaders increasingly rallied behind a new vision of the zoo predicated, above all else, on the goal of species preservation. The best kind of zoo, noted one British observer hopefully in April 1947, would not be a "mere raree-show, not even only a collection of scientific specimens, but an institution, which, properly handled and developed, may preserve for prosperity much that the world is in grave danger of losing."[70] Zoos alone could not halt humans' destruction of the natural world. They could nonetheless offer the globe's endangered species a metaphorical life rope. "If wild habits are destroyed," London Zoo director C. G. C. Rawlins proclaimed in 1977, "zoos may become the last refuge of many species."[71] Charles R. Schroeder, director emeritus of the San Diego Zoo, agreed: "I can find no reason for optimism about the future of wild animals in nature." Nor was he confident that zoos held all the solutions for endangered animals. As a "last resort," however, they were far better than the alternative. Looking to the future, he concluded, "The modern zoo is indeed the 21st century Ark—and it needs our support."[72]

The most momentous step in rebuilding the fleet of postwar zoos came in September 1946, when seven European zoo directors met in Rotterdam to reestablish the International Union of Directors of Zoological Gardens (IUDZG). Under the leadership of Armand Sunier, the revamped IUDZG resolved to promote "zoological research in the widest sense" and protect the world's fauna from extinction. At first, membership was limited to zoo directors from Allied or neutral nations (German zoo folk, in other words, were strictly *verboten*). But old hostilities eroded quickly, and in 1950, the IUDZG invited three German zoo directors to join. The following year, based on the personal recommendations of colleagues in Germany and the United States, Tokyo's Tadamichi Koga became the first member from a nation outside Europe and North America.

Early on, the day-to-day workings of the postwar IUDZG tended to focus on pragmatic concerns—organizing conferences, exchanging the latest and greatest trade secrets, and serving as a professional hub. Over time, the organization (renamed the World Association of Zoos and Aquariums in 2000) shifted much of its institutional energy toward tackling the threat of wildlife extinction. Members supported initiatives to curb wildlife trafficking, petitioned national governments to protect endangered species, and collaborated with groups like the International Union for Conservation of Nature on wildlife relief projects.[73] Above all, the association touted the zoo as a potential bulwark against the twin terrors of unsustainable population growth and atomic age destruction. "The more zoos, the better it is for the human race," William Mann, the "zoo-keeper's zoo-keeper," told a reporter in the 1950s.[74] Indeed, at their most ambitious, advocates saw the zoo as a one-stop shop for addressing the alienation and violence of the modern age.

The Radiant Prison of Light

In June 1948, a contingent of zoo folk—William and Lucy Mann, Philadelphia Zoo director Freeman Shelly, the Bronx Zoo's Lee Crandall, and wartime ex-pat Jean Delacour—left Washington, DC, en route to the annual IUDZG meeting in Paris. As an act of symbolism, the trip was meant to put a bow on the war years—to show, once and for all, that World War II was over and that it was time to move on. For the Manns in particular, who had embarked on a similar excursion a decade earlier, it offered a chance to reconnect with old friends. Arriving in London before traveling on to Germany, Switzerland, and the Low Countries, Mann saw plenty of evidence of continued suffering. Food rations remained low, and signs of malnutrition were impossible to ignore. Some facilities, including Delacour's bird sanctuary at Clères, required total rehabilitation. After the French ornithologist had been forced to flee, the Wehrmacht used the area around his home as a launching pad for V-weapons. Explosive misfires pockmarked the grounds and killed hundreds of caged birds, including an "almost priceless collection of Siberian cranes." As a parting gift, German troops ate Delacour's prized geese.[75]

Overwhelmingly, however, the mood was upbeat. Everywhere they went, the Manns were "greeted like lost kin," one reporter noted, their buoyant pronouncements breathlessly relayed around the zoo world. The London Zoo, William Mann told reporters, had "made a magnificent comeback. Its buildings and grounds have been repaired and somehow it has managed to keep up its fine collections."[76] Mann came to a similar conclusion after visiting Heinz Heck in Munich. Heck, who burst into tears of joy upon seeing his visitors, described watching a US fighter plane dive-bomb the zoo, machine-gunning an American buffalo. Nevertheless, he was enthusiastic about how far his zoo park had come since the war's end.[77]

The highpoint of their tour was in Antwerp, where the party inspected a radical new set of birdcages designed by the zoo's director, Walter van den bergh. Instead of physical bars, the birds were constrained by beams of brilliant fluorescent light. Drawing upon experiments in animal psychology, van den bergh discovered that, given the choice, the birds would not venture past the "radiant prison of light" into the dark beyond.[78] Though impressed, Mann wanted to see further evidence. London Zoological Society superintendent George Cansdale, for his part, worried that van den bergh's design would not fly in Regent's Park. (Apparently, he thought sticky-fingered Londoners would be more likely to steal the birds than admire them.) Nevertheless, Antwerp's barless birdcage seemed to embody all the promise of the post–World War II era: technological progress, the conquest of brains over brawn, humans' capacity to will nature to do its bidding.

At the time, however, at least some observers saw in van den bergh's contraption a glimpse of something darker: the all-too-human preference for the "illusion of freedom" instead of the "real thing." Hitler had exploited this disposition. During the postwar years, others would too—psychologists, fearmongers, Cold War hawks, would-be politicians, cult leaders, marketing gurus. In an age of A-bombs and species collapse, would we resign ourselves to mental prisons, seemingly secure from the dangers outside? Or would we have the courage to reach for something more—a world beyond illusion and artifice? Charles Murphy, a writer for *Life Magazine*, wondered at the birds' seeming willingness to stay in their place: "Isn't there a single rebel in the entire bird kingdom?" Finally, he spotted one, a lone white-crested Himalayan jay. Making its way toward the edge of its spectral captivity, the bird "peer[ed] wildly into the dark and then leap[t] into space"— evidence that, no matter how ingenious, no zoo can fully contain the wildness of the natural world.[79]

EPILOGUE

Baboon or Bear?

In the years after the Deluge, the Bible tells us, Noah left the ark behind and took up work as a farmer. One day, after imbibing a bit too much wine from his vineyard, he passed out "uncovered" in his tent (these were the days before underwear), only to be discovered by his son Ham. Once sobered up, Noah promptly cursed Ham for telling his brothers about what he'd seen, as if the act of relaying the naked truth of the ex–zoo man's compromised state was a sin beyond forgiveness.

I can't help but think there is a metaphor here for what this book has tried to accomplish and how some in the zoo world might receive it. Zoo advocates, as a rule, don't like it when outsiders shine a light on their nether regions. (Who does?) When asked to consider past traumas, zoos are far more likely to stress the ingenuity of the staff (and the stoicism of the animals) than the kind of ethical complexities I have tried to raise in these pages.

Many contemporary zoos favor what might be described as the mannequin and monument school of public history, a mode of remembrance aimed at repackaging history's worst horrors into family-friendly amusement. At the Leningrad Zoo, visitors can tour a small exhibit dedicated to life under the Blockade. Highlights include donated photographs, a collection of veterinary instruments, and a model set of workers' living quarters complete with an ottoman, a stove, and a handmade rocking horse, all designed to highlight the zoo staff's tireless dedication to their duties.[1] Tokyo's Ueno Zoo still honors its animal martyrs in a small stone memorial, its smooth edges and elegant design offering little hint of the horrors inflicted on Jon,

Figure E.1. Meant to resemble a World War II bunker, the Prague Zoo's "historical corridor" is built into a disused mineshaft on the zoo grounds. Courtesy of Tomas Adamec, Prague Zoo Archive.

Tonki, Hanako, and others. The Prague Zoo's memorial efforts, meanwhile, resemble something out of a second-rate children's museum. Unveiled in 2014, the "historical corridor" allows visitors to glimpse the insides of a makeshift bomb shelter built into a former mining tunnel. It's better than nothing, I suppose, but the display does little to shed light on the zoo's collaboration, forced or otherwise, with German occupiers.[2]

Unsurprisingly, zoos in the former Third Reich have been reluctant to own up to their wartime past. For decades after the war's end, Germany's zoos tended to downplay their complicity in Hitler's war machine. Despite efforts to denazify German society, former party members continued to work throughout the upper echelons of the German zoo world. Although Lutz Heck was never able to recover his post, the Berlin Zoo nonetheless honored him with a memorial bust following his death in 1983. (When pressed, the zoo added a small informational plaque about Heck's Nazi past in 2015.) For years, Berlin Zoo officials refused to entertain the notion that it had defrauded Jewish shareholders during the Nazi era, despite mounting evidence to the contrary.[3] Indeed, well into the twenty-first century, German zoos treated their Nazi ties as a kind of unspeakable taboo, better forgotten than confronted in the light of day.

After decades of stalling, leadership at the Berlin Zoo finally took the first baby steps toward acknowledging the zoo's shameful history. In 2011, the zoo unveiled a small bronze plaque on the antelope house acknowledging what critics had known all along: "Under National Socialist rule, [Jewish shareholders] were discriminated against, persecuted, deprived of their rights, and dispossessed. . . . As Jews, they were refused entry to the Berlin Zoological Garden. In sadness and unending memory."[4] The zoo also contracted Holocaust scholar Monika Schmidt of the Center for Research on Anti-Semitism in Berlin to prepare an in-depth report detailing the zoo's complicity with the Nazi regime.[5]

Such measures are important, even if they are decades too late. But it's hard to take German zoos' moral awakening seriously, particularly given their fierce reluctance to own up to their past actions.[6] As recently as 2000, Berlin Zoo CEO Hans-Peter Czupalla told an assembled group of insiders: "The Zoo that you see today, no Jewish citizen has contributed anything to it. It was rebuilt by a new generation. I say this without pathos and without pride. It is simply a fact."[7]

Perhaps the twenty-first century's most powerful meditation on the relationship between the zoo and Nazi terror arrived in the form of a children's play. Produced first as a German radio drama before its 2015 stage premiere, Jens Raschke's prize-winning *What the Rhino Saw When It Looked on the Other Side of the Fence* tells the story of a young Siberian bear's arrival at the zoo in Buchenwald concentration camp. The other animals—Mama and Papa Baboon, Mr. and Mrs. Mouflon, and Marmot Girl—seem happy enough, but the bear has questions about his new home: Who are the zebra-colored "stripes" living on the other side of the buzzing fence? Why does the air reek of killing? And what did a former resident, a rhino, see before his unexpected death? Keep your head down, Papa Baboon tells him. Asking questions will only cause trouble. Yet the bear will not listen. He needs to know what happened, even if he meets a similar fate.[8]

Raschke has spoken openly about his desire to use the play to introduce children to the horrors of the Holocaust. But *What the Rhino*

Saw is so much more than that. Told from the perspective of caged animals, it is a fable about precariousness, about lives held hostage by forces beyond their control. It's also a model of the kind of cross-species empathy that's desperately needed in the twenty-first century. If animals can acknowledge the suffering of humans, it seems to suggest, why can't we do the same for them? Above all, Raschke's play is a philosophical drama about how to exist in a world filled with violence and injustice. Do we look away from society's problems, or do we face them head-on? Which is better—to live like a baboon or die like a bear?

◉ ◉

In many ways, zoos' tendency toward self-congratulation has failed to mask the many obstacles they continue to face. Since the dissolution of the communist bloc in the 1990s, the threat of nuclear Armageddon has been replaced by sporadic outbreaks of localized violence, with zoo animals large and small caught in the middle. The breakup of the former Yugoslavia in 1992 transformed the Bosnian capital of Sarajevo into a hellscape. Arriving at the Sarajevo Zoo in October 1992, *New York Times* reporter John F. Burns discovered only one animal still alive: a tick-infested female black bear, barely strong enough to "stand upright against the rusting bars of her cage." After six months of siege, the zoo's main building resembled a charnel house, with "cage after cage . . . littered with the carcasses of lions, tigers, leopards and pumas." Burns found that some of the late survivors had consumed the corpses of their former cage mates "before they, too, succumbed to hunger."[9]

A similar fate befell the inhabitants of the Kabul Zoo. The withdrawal of Soviet fighters at the end of the Cold War sparked fierce internal fighting in Afghanistan. After securing the capital, newly victorious Taliban fighters commandeered the Kabul Zoo, eating the deer, shelling the aquarium, and destroying many of the captive animals. By the start of the US-led invasion in late 2001, most of the cages at the Kabul Zoo remained empty after years of drought and instability. One exception was that of Marjan, a malnourished one-eyed lion who had been blinded years earlier after a Taliban fighter tossed a grenade into his pen. To many observers, particularly in the United States, Marjan's scarred visage was a symbol of the barbarism of America's newest enemy. Donations poured in from across the world, and rebuilding the

Figure E.2. On September 1, 2021, nearly twenty years after the United States' thwarted invasion of Afghanistan, armed Taliban fighters tour the Kabul Zoo. Credit: Andrew Quilty.

zoo—and restocking it with animals—soon became a focal point of the US civilian mission in the region.[10] As commitment to the war waned, however, so too did global interest in the fate of Afghanistan's zoo animals. Today, after more than two decades of violent conflict and with the Taliban back in charge, the Kabul Zoo is pretty much what it has always been: an animal prison, outdated, inhumane, and deadly.

Even as I write this, the global news is flooded with horror stories from Israel's invasion of Gaza, a conflict that threatens to turn the Palestinian territory into a mass grave. After Hamas militants attacked a music festival on October 7, 2023, killing more than a thousand people, vans from the Israel Nature and Parks Authority evacuated "dozens" of exotic captives (lemurs, iguanas, meerkats, emus, and more) from kibbutzim on the Gaza border.[11] Since that time, Saeed Al-Err of Sulala Animal Rescue has provided social media with near-daily updates on the fate of Gaza's millions of starving, displaced, and traumatized animals.[12] But with famine and disease at nightmare levels, it's hard to imagine a future for Gaza's animals—and its zoo animals especially. In November 2023, Al Jazeera English reported that Gaza's largest zoo, once home to one hundred species, had been "reduced to rubble." During a temporary ceasefire, zoo workers found smashed cages littered with corpses, some so dehydrated they looked like they'd been chewed up and shat out as bits of fur and bones. The few survivors ran madly in their pens, consumed by fear, or waited dazed and starving for death to come.[13] Many months on, conditions were, if anything, worse, with no end in sight.[14]

◉ ◉

Moving forward, the largest existential threat to the future of zoos is climate change (and all the problems that will inevitably accompany it). Global climate change threatens to alter life on the planet and kill untold billions of birds, mammals, fish, insects, and reptiles in the process. A 1998 poll of four hundred scientists found that "70 percent believe the Earth is in the midst of one of its fastest mass extinctions, one that threatens the existence of humans as well as the millions of species we rely on."[15] Since that time, warnings about the dangers of anthropogenic (human-induced) extinction have only gotten louder. In her Pulitzer Prize–winning *The Sixth Extinction*, writer Elizabeth Kolbert predicts the current extinction event will "continue to determine the course of life long after everything people have written and painted and built has been ground into dust and giant rats have—or have not—inherited the earth."[16]

Unlike the biblical flood, climate change will not wash away the world's problems. If climate scientists are correct (and I believe they are), the twenty-first century promises to be more violent, more deadly, more characterized by mass suffering than the previous one. According to reporter David Wallace-Wells, a global temperature rise of four degrees Celsius "would mean that whole regions of Africa and Australia and the United States, parts of South America north of Patagonia, and Asia south of Siberia would be rendered uninhabitable by direct heat, desertification, and flooding." The United Nations predicts upward of 200 million climate refugees by 2050—more if one includes those pushed from their homes by the violence and civil unrest that global climate shifts will cause. Meanwhile, large chunks of the globe's green spaces are under attack from fire, wind, ice, water, and paralyzing heat. In 2017 alone, Wallace-Wells points out, wildfires burned through "more than 12,400,000 acres—nearly two thousand miles made soot."[17]

To their credit, the world's zoos have spent decades gearing up for this crisis. That's meant, above all else, prioritizing captive breeding as the best means of sustaining vulnerable creatures. In 1971, the *New York Times* ran a story on Catskill Game Park, a 1,200-acre facility set up to shelter extremely rare and threatened animals for future sale. According to its director, Heinz Heck, the latest in a line of Heck men to take up the zoo trade: "Every zoo now has a duty and obligation to breed animals. And to bring animals and people together so that people can learn to care."[18] The world's zoos, advocates point out, have developed cutting-edge techniques in conservation science and genetic research; they've also sought to translate laboratory research into practical tools for preserving the world's ecological wealth.[19] At a time when many people continue to deny the possibility of climate disruption, zoos have embraced this opportunity to educate visitors about what can (and should) be done to halt its progress. According to a recent study, institutions accredited by the Association of Zoos and Aquariums "fund over 2500 conservation projects in more than 100 countries and spend on average $160 million on conservation initiatives annually."[20] Meanwhile, with the creation of Species Survival Plans in the 1980s, zoos continue to champion the "ark model" of managing endangered wildlife.[21] Even as the world burns, floods, suffocates, and changes, the thinking goes, zoos will serve as reservoirs of wild creatures.

◉ ◉

Will it work? Will zoos, Noah-like, be able to steward the world's wildlife into a post–climate change future?

Yes . . . perhaps . . . in a technical sense.

I don't expect to read headlines about the death of the world's last tiger, lion, or elephant in my lifetime. Zoos will no doubt maintain living populations of many large land animals, even if (or, more likely, after) they have gone extinct in nature. And, in some cases, zoos will be able to stall what often feels inevitable. In December 2023, the International Union for Conservation of Nature downgraded the scimitar-horned oryx from "Extinct in the Wild" to "Endangered" after zoos and breeding facilities in the United Arab Emirates, the UK, and the United States succeeded in reintroducing a small population of the desert antelopes to Chad's Ouadi Rimé-Ouadi Achim Faunal Reserve. "The initiative is a glowing example of what can be achieved to save Africa's wildlife if we all pull together and combine our conservation efforts," declared Tim Woodfine, chief executive officer of Sahara Conservation.[22] But this will not be possible for all critically endangered creatures. The clock is ticking on the northern white rhinoceros (only two remain—both female), and many "extinct in the wild" species won't have a viable home to which they can return.[23]

There's another problem: Noah had the luxury of ignoring much of the world's biomass—the fish, mammals, crustaceans, and other creatures that, presumably, did not need to hitch a ride aboard the ark. (In reality, a sudden torrent of fresh water large enough to cover all the world's landmass would wreak havoc on ocean saline levels, leading to widespread die-offs of aquatic wildlife.) This is not an option for today's aquariums. Thanks to rising ocean temperatures, growing numbers of whales, sharks, and other marine species are forced to abandon their traditional territories, many already fragile because of centuries of pollution, overfishing, and human traffic. Nature will adapt, as it always does. Still, it's not hard to imagine a future without narwhals, blue whales, great white sharks, and giant squid, none of which can survive in captivity.

But even *if*—and that's a big if—zoos can house all the most threatened species, we cannot take animals' survival for granted. Critics charge that "zoos and aquariums in fact do very little for biodiversity conservation and that any promotion as a legitimate conservation organization is a cynical appeal to justify an anachronistic and exploitative kind of institution."[24] It's easy to forget that, for every animal housed in a state-of-the-art biopark, countless others spend their entire lives in roadside tourist traps and amusement parks. Twenty-first-century zoo animals are just as vulnerable to the effects of social disruption, economic collapse, and violence as their counterparts were during World War II. In 2016, more than fifty animals starved to death at the Caricuao Zoo in Caracas, Venezuela, victims of a national crisis brought on by plummeting oil prices.[25] That same year, more than two hundred animals at a zoo in Khan Younis, Gaza, met a similar fate in the aftermath of a bloody seven-week conflict between Israel and Palestinian militants. (The zoo owner filled the empty cages with stray dogs and the mummified corpses of animals that had died, much to the outrage of the international media.)[26] For all the hand-wringing on social media, many people continue to view zoo animals as expendable—too expensive, too dangerous, or simply too inhuman to be worth the effort.

It bears asking: What *exactly* is the point of preserving animal life in zoos? Is the end goal to repopulate wild species, either by returning them to their previous habitats or introducing them to new ones? Or do we want to hold on to animals for the same reasons we always have—because we can?

For critics like the Jewish feminist writer Aviva Cantor, it's the latter. "Zoos, despite all the best efforts of progressive curators and educators, most often resemble prisons or the mental asylums one visited in the 17th and 18th centuries for an entertaining Sunday afternoon," she explained in 1983. "Children learn that it is all right to capture and pen an animal up for life as long as humans are entertained or 'educated' by the spectacle."[27] Because zoos favor the exotic and crowd-pleasing above all else, they can't necessarily be trusted to make the best decisions about which animals' welfare to prioritize. (As of 2017, the world's zoos held more than 3,000 of Lutz Heck's back-bred cattle—beasts that would not have come into existence were it not for the Nazi zoo man's Wagnerian fantasies.)[28] This is why frequent zoo-goers will encounter the same handful of animals at nearly every zoo they visit, despite the fact that other, less charismatic creatures might be in greater need.

Zoos face another problem, one that makes them especially ill suited to take the lead on climate change and its violent aftereffects. As so many have noted, the consequences of climate change are not distributed equally across the globe.[29] Despite the fact that the richest nations, such as the United States, have contributed the most to fossil fuel emissions, the worst of the fallout is being felt by the world's poorest people—those who, in centuries past, bore the brunt of Western imperialism, those whose resources have been picked over by Western companies, whose lands have been "opened up" to Western exploitation, whose bodies have been broken laboring in Western plantations and digging through the earth for the minerals upon which technological society depends. For all their advancements (and the best zoos *are* miles better than they were a century ago), zoos have not been able to fully separate themselves from their roots in imperial exploitation. Although zoo-goers are less likely to encounter explicitly imperialist language, today's zoos continue to sport their fair share of "native villages" and oriental motifs. The birth of the modern zoo coincided with the greatest effort to steal the land, resources, freedom, and bodies of non-Western peoples of the past thousand years. Few zoos, if any, have tried to grapple with that history, let alone atone for it and make reparations. As humans look toward a future of global catastrophe, contemporary zoos can offer very little to the billions of humans likely to suffer the most—other than to keep a select group of animals safely ensconced behind moats and bars, concrete and artificial greenery, for the world's richest, most privileged peoples to enjoy and ignore at their leisure.

Zoos counter that the upsides far outnumber the negatives. Exposing animals to humans, defenders point out, has all sorts of benefits. In addition to breeding animals, zoos cultivate a sense of human obligation to wild creatures. How many of us can still remember the first time we came face to face with a lion, an orangutan, a harem of seals? (I can.) Such encounters, even through several inches of Plexiglas, are critical if we hope to promote cross-species empathy in future generations—or so we are told. On this front, however, zoos have a decidedly mixed record of success. One lesson of World War II is that empathy for animals was often a local matter. Yes, some people were willing to sacrifice for *their* zoos, but little evidence suggests that this translated into a greater commitment to the natural world.

In many respects, the story of how zoos survived World War II is one of triumph. At a time of privation, violence, and social turmoil, a surprising number of zoos managed to make the best of a dreadful situation. Whether occupied or under fire, zoo directors often went to great lengths to save the bulk of their animal collections. Already skilled in the hard work of pinching pennies, they stretched food budgets, devised new animal breeding techniques, and tried to put on a happy face to the public. Not all the world's arks survived the storm. Either on their own initiative or at the insistence of government forces, zoos destroyed thousands of their own animals. Nevertheless, many zoos could take pride that, in a time when millions of people died, they did their bit to shelter the war's most vulnerable populations, both animal and human.

I am deeply uncertain about the future of the world's zoos, particularly in light of climate change. In writing this book, I know that I've developed a case of low-grade "compassion fatigue," the psychological burnout often experienced by those in the care professions.[30] I'm also pessimistic about Western countries' willingness to do their part to tackle the problem. I'm not a climate "Doomist"—not yet, at least. Doomists believe that humans have already passed the point of no return and that we're better off preparing ourselves for the inevitability of a hotter, wetter, less hospitable Earth.[31] I just think it will take radical action—and a lot of suffering, human and animal—to set us on a better course.

If I have any hope, it's because I am angry—and because others are too. Take Lawrence Anthony. When the owner of South Africa's Thula Thula Game Reserve arrived in Baghdad not long after the start of the US invasion in 2003, he admittedly understood very little about the "politics" of the Iraq War. All he knew is that he could help alleviate the suffering of the Baghdad Zoo's remaining animals, many near death from starvation and lack of water. The more time he spent picking up the pieces, however, the more enraged Anthony became. "This was to be our stand. This was more than just a zoo in a war zone," he later wrote. "It was about making an intrinsically ethical and moral statement, saying: Enough is enough. You just can't say to hell with the consequences to the animal kingdom." Ultimately, Anthony's time in Baghdad forced him to confront what he described as "mankind's near-suicidal relationship" with the natural world: "The most crucial lesson I learned in Baghdad was this: If 'civilized' man is capable of routinely justifying such blatant abuse of trapped wildlife, what of the other unseen atrocities being inflicted on our planet?"[32]

Few of us will know what it's like to help traumatized zoo animals in an active combat zone. But I hope we can all appreciate Anthony's sentiment: we are collectively damning animals, both captive and free, to lives of suffering and degradation. If that doesn't make you mad, I'm afraid it's probably too late.

One thing is clear: if zoos are to survive this century's conflicts, they must abandon the ark metaphor. Faced with the threat of catastrophic climate disruptions, the world does not need a fleet of life rafts designed to help choice species through a metaphorical forty days and forty nights of tumult. Rather, we require a strategy for surviving a climate indefinitely altered. At the very least, we must ask tough questions about whether the upsides of zoos outweigh their obvious drawbacks, including the physical and mental distress endured by captive species.

The world's zoos—and the animals they hold—face an uphill battle. Still, if World War II teaches us anything, it's that zoo folk are canny survivors and that many, no doubt, are itching to take up the fight.

Acknowledgments
of a Recovering Zoo-Lover

I am at heart a recovering zoo-lover. Growing up in the 1980s, I visited every zoo I could. Big, small, old, new—it didn't matter. If there were animals (especially the small, fuzzy mammalian kind), I wanted to see them. My love of zoos continued into adulthood. While a grad student at the University of Minnesota, I liked to unwind at the Como Park Zoo, a small urban menagerie located near my St. Paul apartment. By then, however, I could not escape a gnawing sense of guilt thinking about the creatures I'd come to see. To this day, I can't shake the memory of one of the zoo's polar bears robotically swimming from one Plexiglas wall to the other—again and again and again—as if he were trying to stretch every inch of space from his confinement. I eventually learned that zoologists refer to such repetitive behavior as *stereotypy*. It's generally regarded as a sign of maladaptation to under-sized or barren artificial environments. Over time, I visited the zoo less and less. What was once a source of pure pleasure now left me feeling guilty.

Writing this book, I logged countless hours watching zoo animals. I spent the night in the Prague Zoo, toured elephant houses in Wisconsin and Berlin, wandered unaccompanied through the Bronx Zoo before opening hours, waded through zoo archives (sometimes with a rabbit, quite literally, nibbling around my feet), and spoke at length with the men and women who have made zookeeping their livelihood. In all my travels, zoo workers have been extraordinarily generous with their time, despite some early reservations about my intentions. Much like the people who inhabit this narrative, twenty-first-century zoo folk tend to be true believers, and they are willing to work long hours, in tough conditions, often with relatively little pay to do what they do. Some, I have no doubt, would be willing to die for the creatures in their charge, and they are committed to the idea that "good zoos" represent our last best chance to ward off future animal extinctions.

But the more I think about zoos, the less I'm convinced that their upsides outweigh their shortcomings—not, at least, in their current form. Spend any time at a zoo (and I mean *any* time) and you will be forced to confront their not-so-subtle messages that some animals matter more than others, and humans matter most of all. This was never clearer to me than during a research trip to the Jardin des Plantes in central Paris. Entering the zoo's vivarium one chilly spring morning, I saw what looked like an empty storage space. Paint flaked from the walls, the bare concrete floor was painted a muddy brown, and a few pieces of wilted lettuce sat in a plastic dish. Amid all this depressing emptiness was a single small tortoise—this in a zoo founded in 1794, a zoo once populated with animals from Napoleon's conquest of Egypt, a zoo just a short walk from the Pantheon and the Sorbonne. Here, in the City of Light, this tortoise was afforded little more than the rusty glow of a space heater.

It's a minor episode, I know. And yet, it's telling. For all the hype about "immersive exhibits" and "activity-based designs," many zoo animals spend their lives in environments little changed since the nineteenth century.

Despite all this, I remain deeply sympathetic to the zoo community, both past and present, who have devoted their lives to caring for their fellow living creatures. At a time when so many of us would rather ignore the threats of global warming and climate change, zoo workers recognize that whatever damage we do to the planet, humans won't be the only victims.

On this note, I wish to acknowledge the following individuals and institutions, without whom (and which) this book would not have been possible.

For their sincerity: the archivists, librarians, and administrators at the National Zoo (Washington, DC), the New York Zoological Society (Bronx Zoo), the Brookfield Zoo (Chicago), the Oklahoma City Zoo, the

Woodland Park Zoo (Seattle), the Milwaukee County Zoo, the Philadelphia Zoo, the London Zoological Society, the Prague Zoo, the Berlin Zoo, the Hagenbeck Zoo, the Wrocław Zoo, and Buchenwald concentration camp.

For their professionalism: the California State University Archives, the University of Wisconsin Archives, the Oklahoma State University Library, the Australian War Memorial, the US Holocaust Museum, and the Library of Congress.

For their generosity: Koenraad Kuiper, Herman Reichenbach, Gerhard Heindl, Carla Owens, Zuzana Karlíková, Miroslav Bobek, Leszek Solski, Johanna van Niewstadt-van Hooff, Kerry Prendergast, Nigel Rothfels, Mary Kazmierczak, Beth Frank, Mark Norris, Klaus Gille, Carl Claus Hagenbeck, and many others.

For their willingness to share their stories: survivors of the Heart Mountain Incarceration Camp, including Shig Yabu, Sam Mihara, Hiroshi Hoshizaki, and Takashi Hoshizaki.

For their constructive criticism: the anonymous peer reviewers of this manuscript.

For their hard work on the book's behalf: everyone at the University of Chicago Press, especially Andrea Blatz, Lindsy Rice, and Marianne Tatom.

For their encouragement and support: Ryan Hediger; Tracy McDonald and Dan Vandersommers; Jimmy Bryan Jr.; Susan Nance and Jennifer Marks; my colleagues at Oklahoma State University, especially my writing partners, David Gray and Sarah Griswold; my present and former department/program heads, Stacy Takacs, Brian Hosmer, and Laura Belmonte; members of the OSU History Department Writing Group; and my extended family.

For their belief in this project (even when I had doubt): Elise Capron and Timothy Mennel.

For their inspiration: Pyg, Simon, Charlie, Hilo, and Pullo.

This book is dedicated to my wife, Jenny.

Notes

Prologue

1. This account of the SS *President Coolidge* and the pandas at Pearl Harbor is woven together from several sources, including James F. Lee, "Ship Offered Safe Passage after Attack at Pearl Harbor," *Honolulu Star-Advertiser*, December 2, 2012; "Hawaii's Wounded Return," *Mail* (Adelaide, SA), February 21, 1942, 6; "Excerpt from Oral History of LT Ruth Erikson, NC," *Naval History and Heritage Command*, September 21, 2015, https://www.history.navy.mil/research/library/oral-histories/wwii/pearl-harbor/pearl-harbor-attack-lt-erickson.html; John Tee-Van, "Two Pandas— China's Gift to America," *Animal Kingdom* 45, no. 1 (January 1942): 3–18; Colin Schultz, "How an American Missionary Helped Capture the First Panda Given to the U.S.," *Smithsonian Magazine*, August 18, 2014, https://www.smithsonianmag.com/smart-news/how-american-missionary-helped-captured-first-panda-given-us-180952369/.

2. "Pandora Dies at Zoo," *New York Times*, May 14, 1941, 23; "Animals: A Szechwanese Dies," *Time*, May 26, 1941.

3. Tee-Van, "Two Pandas—China's Gift to America," 5.

4. "Zoo Gets Pandas; Debut Is Formal," *New York Times*, December 31, 1941, 19.

Introduction

1. Henry Fairfield Osborn Jr., Report of the President, Forty-Ninth Annual Report of the New York Zoological Society (New York: New York Zoological Society, 1944), 3–4.

2. Lord Zuckerman, "The Rise of Zoos and Zoological Societies," in *Great Zoos of the World: Their Origins and Significance*, ed. Solly Zuckerman (Boulder: Westview Press, 1980), 16.

3. On human ascendancy and control of the natural world, see Keith Thomas, *Man and the Natural World: Changing Attitudes in England 1500–1800* (New York: Penguin Books, 1984).

4. Hillary Hanson, "Van Packed with Kangaroos, Wallabies Escapes Shell-Shocked Kharkiv Zoo," *HuffPost*, March 29, 2022.

294 Notes to Pages 4–11

5. AP, "Lion and Wolf Safely Evacuated from Zoo in War-Torn Ukraine," NBC News, March 23, 2022.

6. Peter Singer, "Moral Progress and Animal Welfare," *Project Syndicate*, July 13, 2011, https://www.project-syndicate.org/commentary/moral-progress-and -animal-welfare; Ambassador Matthew Rycroft, "How a Society Treats Its Most Vulnerable Is Always the Measure of Its Humanity," June 18, 2015, https://www.gov.uk /government/speeches/how-a-society-treats-its-most-vulnerable-is-always-the -measure-of-its-humanity.

7. Zoo animals are not the only nonhuman creatures uniquely susceptible to war and other unnatural disasters. See Leslie Irvine, *Filling the Ark: Animal Welfare in Disasters* (Philadelphia: Temple University Press, 2009).

8. Brian Massumi, *What Animals Teach Us about Politics* (Durham, NC: Duke University Press, 2014), 82.

9. This is, admittedly, a far from scientific estimate. Countless zoo animals die every day from disease, old age, accidents, and so on. Moreover, zoos, especially at this time, didn't always agree on what counted as an "animal." Monkeys, lions, hippos, alligators—for sure. But what about common birds? Goldfish? Insects? All the miscellaneous creatures that inevitably make their homes in zoos, whether keepers want them there or not? Add these in and zoos' World War II death tolls would no doubt skyrocket. Still, I wanted to convey *my* sense of how many broadly recognizable "zoo animals" (leopards, zebras, chimpanzees, crocodiles, buffaloes, eagles, kangaroos, rattlesnakes, and so forth) likely perished because of factors directly related to the war, such as starvation, occupation, bombing, and safety killings.

10. Elisabeth Leigh, "Almost Human," *West Australian* (Perth, WA), September 3, 1938, 4.

11. Margo DeMello, *Animals and Society: An Introduction to Human-Animal Studies* (New York: Columbia University Press, 2012), 272, 269.

12. Over the past few decades, scholars have amassed an extensive body of literature on the history, evolution, and social function of zoos in the modern world. Useful starting points include Harriet Ritvo, *The Animal Estate: The English and Other Creatures in Victorian England* (Cambridge, MA: Harvard University Press, 1987); Vernon N. Kisling Jr., ed., *Zoo and Aquarium History: Ancient Animal Collections to Zoological Gardens* (Boca Raton, FL: CRC Press, 2001); Nigel Rothfels, *Savages and Beasts: The Birth of the Modern Zoo* (Baltimore: Johns Hopkins University Press, 2002); and Tracy McDonald and Dan Vandersommers, eds., *Zoo Studies: A New Humanities* (Montreal: McGill-Queen's University Press, 2019).

13. Quoted in Lucile Q. Mann, "Post War Developments in European Zoos" (c. 1945), p. 2, folder 5, box 10, RU 7293, Smithsonian Institution Archives, Washington, DC (hereafter SIA).

14. For a nuanced reflection on Levi-Strauss's famous claim that animals are "good to think with" (*bonnes á penser*), see Marjorie Garber, "Good to Think With," *Profession* (2008): 11–20.

15. Rothfels, *Savages and Beasts*, 175; Ben A. Minteer, Jane Maienschein, and James P. Collins, *The Ark and Beyond: The Evolution of Zoos and Aquarium Conservation* (Chicago: University of Chicago Press, 2018).

Notes to Pages 15–17   295

Chapter 1

1. "Animals and Suicide," *Telegraph* (Brisbane, Qld.), September 2, 1932, 6; "Animals Cause Suicide Debate in London Zoo," *Shamokin Daily News* [PN], August 26, 1932, 5.

2. Quoted in "Animals and Suicide"; for a similar view, see "Zooicide?," *The Cromwell Argus*, April 24, 1933, 2.

3. "Tragedy in a Zoo," *Daily Mercury* (Mackay, Qld.), July 16, 1932, 6.

4. Laurel Braitman, *Animal Madness: How Anxious Dogs, Compulsive Parrots, and Elephants in Recovery Help Us Understand Ourselves* (New York: Simon and Schuster, 2014), 159–60.

5. "Sulking Tigress Goes on a Hunger Strike," *New York Times*, July 21, 1930, 11. "Rochester Zoo Has Suicide Run," *St. Cloud Times* [MN], September 2, 1930, 11; "Monkey Looks Once, Then Takes Fatal Jump," *Palm Beach Post*, July 6, 1939, 10.

6. "Crocodile's Suicide," *The World News* (Sydney, NSW), September 13, 1933, 4.

7. Tangiwai, "Men and Monkeys," *Auckland Star*, March 21, 1933, 6.

8. "Do Animals Commit Suicide?," *Mirror* (Perth), August 6, 1932, 6.

9. Eric Baratay and Elisabeth Hardouin-Fugier, *Zoo: A History of Zoological Gardens in the West*, trans. Oliver Welsh (London: Reaktion Books, 2004), 216.

10. Derek Wood with Robert Mannion, *A Tiger by the Tail: A History of Auckland Zoo 1922–1992* (Auckland: Auckland City, 1992), 50.

11. "Reduction of Salaries," *Recorder* (Port Pirie, SA), September 10, 1930, 1.

12. "Zoo Acquisitions," *West Australian* (Perth, WA), February 21, 1931, 10.

13. Jesse C. Donahue and Erik K. Trump, *American Zoos During the Depression: A New Deal for Animals* (Jefferson, NC: McFarland, 2010), 12.

14. Andrea Friederici Ross, *Let the Lions Roar! The Evolution of the Brookfield Zoo* (Brookfield, IL: Chicago Zoological Society, 1997), 59.

15. "A Zoo Grows Its Food," *New York Times*, March 22, 1931, XX5.

16. "Soviet Raises Ostriches for Meat in Moscow Zoo," *New York Times*, November 5, 1933, N3.

17. On power and spectacle at the American circus, see Janet M. Davis, *The Circus Age: Culture and Society under the American Big Top* (Chapel Hill: University of North Carolina Press, 2002).

18. "Elephants at Antwerp Zoo Beg for Coppers to Buy Food," *New York Times*, August 28, 1932, E3.

19. "Saggio musicale di elefanti allo zoo di Berlino," June 16, 1937, Giornale Luce B113, https://patrimonio.archivioluce.com/luce-web/detail/IL5000024027/2/saggio-musicale-elefanti-allo-zoo-berlino.

20. According to historian Harriet Ritvo, early zoos' use of animal spectacle was more than mere entertainment; rather, it provided reassuring evidence that "humankind had conquered the animal kingdom." Harriet Ritvo, *The Animal Estate: The English and Other Creatures in the Victorian Age* (Cambridge, MA: Harvard University Press, 1987), 224.

21. Twenty-first-century zoos continue to rely upon interactive animal spectacle to entice visitors, including scheduled feedings, dolphin and sea lion shows, and exhibitions of trained apes. Once, while visiting a prominent German zoo, I watched as a small crowd was invited to hand-feed a trio of elephants. It would have been

dangerous (for the visitors, I mean) were it not for the fact that the elephants were chained to the ground.

22. "Zoo Ball," *British Pathé* (1937), https://www.youtube.com/watch?v=1PpYB cuJZho.

23. William Cadwalader, president of the Philadelphia Zoological Society, claimed that zoos could not sell off unwanted animals because of the "depression in the animal market." "Closing of Zoo Is Feared," *New York Times*, October 7, 1932, 23.

24. "Animals Go Begging at Park Zoo Auction," *New York Times*, June 23, 1932, 23.

25. "Waco Will Sell Zoo to Feed Poor," *New York Times*, May 8, 1932, E6.

26. "Beaumaris Zoo," *Mercury* (Hobart, Tas.), May 19, 1932, 8.

27. "Perth Zoo," *Daily News* (Perth, WA), December 8, 1930, 6.

28. Quoted in Donahue and Trump, *American Zoos During the Depression*, 4.

29. Edith A. Waterworth, "Municipal Extravagance," *Mercury* (Hobart, Tas.), March 10, 1931, 6; "Letters to the Editor," *Telegraph* (Brisbane, Qld.), December 3, 1936, 14.

30. Letter to the Editor, *The Pittsburgh Press*, July 30, 1931, 12.

31. P. E. Moreton, "Misery in the Zoos," *New York Times*, October 9, 1930, 26.

32. "Mr. Semple and the Zoo," *Evening Post*, June 18, 1932, 10.

33. Lord Zuckerman, "The Rise of Zoos and Zoological Societies," in *Great Zoos of the World: Their Origins and Significance*, ed. Solly Zuckerman (Boulder: Westview Press, 1980), 11.

34. On Zuckerman's life from birth to the end of the Second World War, see Solly Zuckerman, *From Apes to Warlords* (New York: Harper & Row, 1978).

35. Lord Zuckerman, "The Rise of Zoos and Zoological Societies," 11, 15, 16–17, 17.

36. Donahue and Trump, *American Zoos During the Depression*, 4, 76–77, 76, 84.

37. Ritvo, *The Animal Estate*, 207.

38. Wilson Chamberlin, "Are Zoos Inhumane?," *St. Louis Post-Dispatch*, May 17, 1937, 20.

39. On the lives and careers of the Huxleys, see Alison Bashford, *The Huxleys: An Intimate History of Evolution* (Chicago: University of Chicago Press, 2022).

40. R. S. Deese, *We Are Amphibians: Julian and Aldous Huxley on the Future of Our Species* (Oakland: University of California Press, 2014), 109.

41. Ronald W. Clark, *Sir Julian Huxley, F.R.S.* (London: Phoenix House, 1960), 82.

42. Julian Huxley, *Memories* (New York: Harper & Row, 1970), 232.

43. Huxley, *Memories*, 232.

44. "Zoo's Value in Education," *The Times* (London), August 5, 1936, 9.

45. Deese, *We Are Amphibians*, 117.

46. "The Pets Corner: Professor Huxley Introduces Animal Playmates for Young Visitors at London Zoo" (1935), *British Pathé*, https://www.youtube.com/watch?v=hFmCJ1ahq38.

47. J. Barrington-Johnson, *The Zoo: The Story of the London Zoo* (London: Robert Hale, 2005), 114.

48. "Criticism of Zoo Changes," *The Times* (London), April 30, 1936, 9.

49. Lorenz Hagenbeck, *Animals Are My Life*, trans. Alec Brown (London: Bodley Head, 1956), 144.

50. Patricia A. Morton, *Hybrid Modernities: Architecture and Representation and the 1931 Colonial Exposition, Paris* (Cambridge, MA: MIT Press, 2000), 3.

Notes to Pages 24–30   297

51. Baratay and Hardouin-Fugier, *Zoo*, 129.

52. Quoted in Baratay and Hardouin-Fugier, *Zoo*, 129.

53. Georges G. Toudouze, "Les Coulisses Du Zoo," *Lectures Pour Tous* (1934), 24.

54. Thierry Antione Borrel, "Achille Urbain (1884–1957), Le Premier Director of the Parc Zoologique de Paris," *Bulletin Académie Vétérinaire France* 167, no. 4 (January 2014): 337–38, 342–43. Armand-Henry Flassch's account of the 1935 expedition appeared as *De la brousse au zoo: carnet de route de l'expedition Urbain au Sahara, en A.O.F., en A.E.F. et au Cameroun* (Paris: Payot, 1938).

55. According to Baratay and Hardouin-Fugier, the Rome Zoo was "produced, 'ready to visit,' by Carl Hagenbeck, who provided everything from plans to construction, from animals (282 mammals, 682 birds and 56 reptiles) to the director, Theodor Knottnerus-Meyer, his scientific advisor." Baratay and Hardouin-Fugier, *Zoo*, 249.

56. Quoted in Piers Brendon, *The Dark Valley: A Panorama of the 1930s* (New York: Knopf, 2000), 30.

57. Giulia Guazzaloca, "'Anyone who Abuses Animals Is No Italian': Animal Protection in Fascist Italy," *European History Quarterly* 50, no. 4 (2020): 669, 678, 673.

58. Spartaco Gippoliti, "A Contribution to the History of Zoos in Italy up to the Second World War," *International Zoo News* 44, no. 8 (1997): 461–62.

59. To view documentary newsreels about the zoo renovation, see "Costruzione di nuovi spazi per gli animali dello zoo di Roma," September 1934, Giornale Luce B0562; "Lavori d'ampliamento del Giardino Zoologico," April 10, 1935, Giornale Luce B0657; "Continuano i lavori al Giardino zoologico," August 5, 1935; and "Nuove strutture dello zoo Giornale," June 12, 1935, Luce B0692. All can be found at http://www.archivioluce.com/archivio/#n.

60. "Loss of Abbi Addi Denied," *New York Times*, December 29, 1935, 1.

61. "War on Rats Opens in Park Zoo Sector," *New York Times*, November 25, 1931, 6.

62. "War on Rats Opens in Park Zoo Sector."

63. "Lethal Toast Rids Park Zoo of Rats," *New York Times*, November 26, 1931, 32.

64. Earl Chapin May, "To the Zoos Has Come a New Deal," SM19.

65. "Audubon Zoo, Monkey Hill—New Orleans, LA," *The Living New Deal*, https://livingnewdeal.org/projects/audubon-zoo-monkey-hill-new-orleans-la/.

66. "Como Park Zoo Improvements—St. Paul, MN," *The Living New Deal*, https://livingnewdeal.org/projects/como-zoo-gates-st-paul-mn/.

67. Daniel E. Bender, *The Animal Games: Searching for Wildness at the American Zoo* (Cambridge, MA: Harvard University Press, 2016), 188.

68. Earl Chapin May, "To the Zoos Has Come a New Deal," *New York Times*, February 10, 1935, SM19.

69. "Zoo Visitors Here Setting Records," *New York Times*, November 17, 1935, N1.

70. Milton Bracker, "Al Smith Talks about Sundry Animals," *New York Times*, August 25, 1935, SM8.

71. "New Zoo Opens, Al Smith Gets Job as Honorary Night Superintendent," *New York Times*, December 3, 1934, 1; "Smith Visits Zoo, Feeds His Charges . . . ," *New York Times*, April 18, 1935, 25.

72. "Smith Now 'Agent' for Prospect Zoo," *New York Times*, May 10, 1935, 23.

73. "'Dear Haile's' Lions Accepted by 'Al,'" *New York Times*, November 21, 1935, 25.

74. "War in Ethiopia Hard on Zoos," *The Decatur Daily* [IL], October 30, 1935, 19; "World Zoos Will Feel War Effects," *Palladium-Item* (Richmond, IN), October 11, 1935, 1.

298 Notes to Pages 30–36

75. Walter Duranty, "Spoilage of Food Disturbing Soviet," *New York Times*, October 5, 1937, 10.

76. "Economies in Japan," *Mercury* (Hobart, Tas.), December 29, 1937, 4.

77. "National Revolution," *Time*, March 13, 1933. On the death of Adele Langer and her sons, see "3 Chicago Deaths Blamed on Nazis," *New York Times*, August 5, 1939, 6; see also "Exile's Escape," *Akron Beacon Journal*, August 5, 1939, 6; "Death Leap of 3 Refugees Laid to Persecution," *Chicago Tribune*, August 5, 1939, 10; and "Refugee Mother Leaps to Death With 2 Children," *Middleton Times Herald* (Middleton, NY), August 4, 1939, 1.

Chapter 2

1. Neal Walter Fortner, *Hermann Göring's 1935 Photo Album: A Contradiction of Humanity*, 2nd ed. (Middletown, DE: Lulu.com, 2014), 51–54.

2. Nancy H. Yeide, *Beyond the Dreams of Avarice: The Hermann Goering Collection* (Dallas: Laurel Publishing, 2009); see also Lynn H. Nicholas, *The Rape of Europa: The Fate of Europe's Treasures in the Third Reich and Second World War* (New York: Vintage Books, 1995).

3. "Lion Cub Is Given to Reich Minister," *New York Times*, July 9, 1933, 2.

4. Gary Bruce, *Through the Lion Gate: A History of the Berlin Zoo* (New York: Oxford University Press, 2017), 160.

5. Bruce, *Through the Lion Gate*, 35–39.

6. Bruce, *Through the Lion Gate*, 227.

7. Arnold Arluke and Boria Sax, "Understanding Nazi Animal Protection and the Holocaust," *Anthrozoös* 5, no. 1 (1992): 7.

8. "Law on Animal Protection" (Appendix 1), in Boria Sax, *Animals in the Third Reich: Pets, Scapegoats, and the Holocaust* (New York: Continuum, 2000), 176, 177.

9. Quoted in Arluke and Sax, "Understanding Nazi Animal Protection," 8.

10. References to Hitler's vegetarianism and love of animals appeared frequently in contemporary accounts of his life. Even at the time, however, critics outside the Reich viewed the *Führer's* pronouncements on the topics with suspicion. See, for example, "Vegetarian Society Objects to Calling Hitler Vegetarian," *Chicago Tribune*, February 7, 1939, 1.

11. Quoted in Arnold Arluke and Clinton Sanders, *Regarding Animals* (Philadelphia: Temple University Press, 1996), 148.

12. Arluke and Sax, "Understanding Nazi Animal Protection," 18.

13. Albert Speer, *Inside the Third Reich*, trans. Richard and Clara Winston (New York: Bonanza Books, 1982), 97.

14. Frank Uekoetter, *The Green and the Brown: A History of Conservation in Nazi Germany* (Cambridge: Cambridge University Press, 2006), 31–32.

15. Leonard Moseley, *The Reich Marshal: A Biography of Hermann Goering* (New York: Doubleday, 1974), 179.

16. Charles Patterson, *Eternal Treblinka: Our Treatment of Animals and the Holocaust* (New York: Lantern Books, 2002), 126, 125.

17. Stewart Lee Allen, *In the Devil's Garden: A Sinful History of Forbidden Food* (New York: Ballantine Books, 2002), 233.

18. Patterson, *Eternal Treblinka*, 128.

19. Speer, *Inside the Third Reich*, 128, 129.

20. Quoted in Patterson, *Eternal Treblinka*, 128.

21. Sven Tetzlaff, "Tierliebe und Menschenhass," in *Genutzt—geliebt—getötet: Tiere in unserer Geschichte*, ed. Lothar Dittmer (Hamburg: Körber-Stiftung, 2001), 18–24.

22. Patterson, *Eternal Treblinka*, 124.

23. Max Horkheimer and Theodor W. Adorno, *Dialectic of Enlightenment: Philosophical Fragments*, ed. Gunzelin Schmid Noerr, trans. Edmund Jephcott (Stanford, CA: Stanford University Press, 2002), 210.

24. Arluke and Sax, "Understanding Nazi Animal Protection," 23.

25. Patterson, *Eternal Treblinka*, 126.

26. Colin Goldner, "75 Jahre 'Nazi-Zoo,'" *Humanisticher Pressedienst*, May 5, 2014, https://hpd.de/node/18482.

27. Joseph Goebbels, *Tagebücher 1924–1945* (1st ed. 1992, 3rd ed. 2003) (Munich: Piper Verlag, 1992/1999), III:101; II:567; II:561; III:101.

28. Goldner, "75 Jahre 'Nazi-Zoo.'"

29. Evelyn Gottschlich, "Wiedereröffnung und Zerstörung (1928–1945)," in *Nilpferde an der Isar: Eine Geschichte des Tierparks Hellabrunn in München*, ed. Michael Kamp and Helmut Zedelmaier (München: Buchendorfer Verlag, 2000), 136.

30. Mustafa Haikal and Winfried Gensch, *Der Gesang Des Orang-utans: die Geschischte des Dresdner Zoos* (Dresden: Sächsische Zeitung, 2011), 87; Kai Artinger, "Lutz Heck: 'Der Vater der Rominter Ure': Einige Bemerkungen zum wissenschaftlichen Leiter des Berliner Zoos im Nationalsozialismus," *Der Bär von Berlin. Jahrbuch* (1994): 125–38, https://www.diegeschichteberlins.de/geschichteberlins/persoenlichkeiten/persoenlichkeitenhn/491-heck.html.

31. Bruce, *Through the Lion Gate*, 158.

32. Gerhard Heindl, "Otto Antonius—ein Leben für Zoo und Wissenschaft. Erinnerunger anlässlich seines 125. Geburtstag und 65. Todestags," *Der Zoologische Garten* 79 (2010): 229.

33. Gerhard Heindl, "Otto Antonius—ein Wissenshaftler als Tiergärtner," in *Otto Antonius: Wegbereiter der Tiergartenbiologie*, ed. Dagmar Schratter and Gerhard Heindl (Wien: Braumüller Verlag, 2010), 59, 52–58.

34. Quoted in Bruce, *Through the Lion Gate*, 157.

35. Bruce, *Through the Lion Gate*, 155–60; Artinger, "Lutz Heck."

36. On the Hecks' attempts to back-breed aurochs and other extinct European game, see Frank Fox, "Jews and Buffaloes, Victims of Nazi Pseudo-Science," *East European Jewish Affairs* 31, no. 2 (2001): 82–93; Scott Weidensaul, *The Ghost with Trembling Wings: Science, Wishful Thinking, and the Search for Lost Species* (New York: North Point Press, 2002), 187–213; Michael Wang, "Heavy Breeding," *Cabinet* 45 (Spring 2012), https://www.cabinetmagazine.org/issues/45/wang.php; Sandra Swart, "Zombie Zoology: History and Reanimating Extinct Animals," in *The Historical Animal*, ed. Susan Nance (Syracuse, NY: Syracuse University Press, 2015), 54–71; Clemens Driessen and Jamie Lorimer, "Back Breeding the Aurochs: The Heck Brothers, National Socialism, and Imagined Geographies for Non-Human *Lebensraum*," in *Hitler's Geographies: The Spatialities of the Third Reich* (Chicago: University of Chicago Press, 2016), 138–57; and Harriet Ritvo, "Visualizing Extinction: Harriet Ritvo in Conversation," in *Animals, Plants and Afterimages: The Art and Science of Representing Extinction*, ed. Valérie Bienvenue and Nicholas Chare (New York: Berghahn Books, 2022), 77–90.

300　Notes to Pages 41–48

37. Lutz Heck, *Animals, My Adventure*, trans. E. W. Dickes (London: Methuen & Co., 1954), 129.

38. Heck, *Animals, My Adventure*, 144.

39. Heck, *Animals, My Adventure*, 154.

40. Quoted in Arluke and Sax, "Understanding Nazi Animal Protection," 10.

41. Artinger, "Lutz Heck." On the mini-zoo, see Bruce, *Through the Lion Gate*, 181; on the makeup of the Olympic Village, see Barbara J. Keys, *Globalizing Sport: National Rivalry and International Community in the 1930s* (Cambridge, MA: Harvard University Press, 2006).

42. Frederick T. Birchall, "Goebbels Denies Intent to Use Games for Propaganda Purposes," *New York Times*, July 31, 1936, 13.

43. Artinger, "Lutz Heck."

Chapter 3

1. Eugen Kogon, *The Theory and Practice of Hell: The German Concentration Camps and the System Behind Them*, trans. Heinz Norden (New York: Octagon Books, 1979), 54.

2. *The Buchenwald Report*, trans. David A. Hackett (Boulder: Westview Press, 1995), 33.

3. On the development and evolution of the Nazi concentration camp system, see Nikolaus Wachsmann, *KL: A History of the Nazi Concentration Camps* (New York: Farrar, Straus & Giroux, 2015).

4. Quoted in Gedenkstätte Buchenwald, ed., *Buchenwald Concentration Camp 1937–1945: A Guide to the Permanent Historical Exhibition*, compiled by Harry Stein, trans. Judith Rosenthal (Wallstein Verlag, 2004), 25.

5. Gedenkstätte Buchenwald, *Buchenwald Concentration Camp*, 35.

6. Deputy Judge Advocate's Office 7708 War Crimes Group European Command APO 47, *United States v. Josias Prince zu Waldeck et al.* (Case No. 000-50-9), Review and Recommendations of the Deputy Judge Advocate for War Crimes, November 15, 1947, 5–9.

7. *United States v. Josias Prince zu Waldeck et al.*, 9; Kogon, *Theory and Practice of Hell*, 155, 159.

8. David Rousset, *The Other Kingdom*, trans. and with an introduction by Ramon Guthrie (New York: Reynal & Guthrie, 1947), 15.

9. *United States v. Josias Prince zu Waldeck et al.*, 11.

10. Gedenkstätte Buchenwald, *Buchenwald Concentration Camp*, 43.

11. Nicholas Fox Weber, "Deadly Style: Bauhaus's Nazi Connection," *New York Times*, December 23, 2009, 27.

12. Thomas Stange, "Den Tieren geht es gut," *Jungle World*, April 16, 2015.

13. *The Buchenwald Report*, 42, 131.

14. Commander's Order No. 56 dated 8 September 1938 (Extract), Buchenwald Historical Archives.

15. To mold them into good Nazis, Koch ordered the men under his command to attend "clan evenings" and withdraw from church membership. He also required staff to eat communal meals on Sundays, a ritual designed to "practice fellowship with the entire nation." Koch, quoted in Gedenkstätte Buchenwald, *Buchenwald Concentration Camp*, 39.

Notes to Pages 48–57   301

16. Stange, "Den Tieren geht es gut."

17. Commander's Order No. 56 dated 8 September 1938 (Extract), Buchenwald Historical Archives.

18. Command from Karl Koch (August 22, 1939), Buchenwald Historical Archives.

19. *The Buchenwald Report*, 129.

20. *The Buchenwald Report*, 131, 149, 150.

21. Quoted in "Buchenwald Trial," *Kalgoorlie Miner* (WA), April 15, 1947, 5.

22. Transcription of the letter from Hans Bergmann to the SS Obersturmführer Rödl, October 8, 1939; source: Thüringisches Hauptstaatsarchiv Weimar, BWA Signature NS 4 Bu 102, Film 8 3.4.2, Buchenwald Historical Archives.

23. Kurt Dittmar, *Eine Bären-jagd im KZ Buchenwald. Tragi-komisches Idyll* [A Bear Hunt at KZ Buchenwald: A Tragicomic Episode] (Gotha, 1946), 6, 10, 12, 16. A copy can be found in the historical archives of Buchenwald concentration camp.

24. Dittmar, *Eine Bären-jagd im KZ Buchenwald*, 20, 22, 24, 26, 29, 28, 30, 36, 34.

25. Fontenoy's visit to Sachsenhausen was part of a seven-part behind-the-scenes look at the "truth" of the Nazi prison-state. See Jean Fontenoy, "La Vérité sur un camp de concentration," *Le Journal*, on April 4, 5, 7, 8, 9, 10, 11, 12, 1939.

26. Kogon, *Theory and Practice of Hell*, 49.

27. *The Buchenwald Report*, 123.

28. Frank Van Vree, "Indigestible Images: On the Ethics and Limits of Representation," in *Performing the Past: Memory, History, and Identity in Modern Europe*, ed. Karin Tilmans, Frank van Vree, and J. M. Winter (Amsterdam: Amsterdam University Press, 2010), 270.

29. Rousset, *The Other Kingdom*, 41.

30. Stange, "Den Tieren geht es gut."

Chapter 4

1. Glenda Sluga, *Internationalism in the Age of Nationalism* (Philadelphia: University of Pennsylvania Press, 2013), 63.

2. Kiran Klaus Patel, *The New Deal: A Global History* (Princeton, NJ: Princeton University Press, 2016), 40.

3. Sluga, *Internationalism in the Age of Nationalism*, 64.

4. Hans Dieter Schäfer, quoted in Barbara J. Keys, *Globalizing Sport: National Rivalry and International Community in the 1930s* (Cambridge, MA: Harvard University Press, 2006), 40.

5. Edwin Black, *The Nazi Nexus: America's Corporate Connections to Hitler's Holocaust* (Washington, DC: Dialog Press), 17–49.

6. Charles Patterson, *Eternal Treblinka: Our Treatment of Animals and the Holocaust* (New York: Lantern Books, 2002), 97–100.

7. R. Jeffrey Stott, "The Historical Origins of the Zoological Park in American Thought," *Environmental Review* 5, no. 2 (Autumn 1981): 52–65. The zoo's role as a showcase of national status was not limited to the West. As Ian Miller has shown, Japan's first modern zoo, which opened its gates in 1882, was designed to serve a similar purpose, validating "Japanese claims of membership in the international community of civilized humanity" (Ian Jared Miller, *The Nature of the Beasts: Empire and Exhibition at the Tokyo Imperial Zoo* [Berkeley: University of California Press,

302   Notes to Pages 57–66

2013], 273). See "Didactic Nature: Exhibiting Nation and Empire at the Ueno Zoological Gardens," in *JAPANimals: History and Culture in Japan's Animal Life*, ed. Gregory M. Pfludfelder and Brett L. Walker (Ann Arbor: Center for Japanese Studies, 2005), 273–313.

8. Nigel Rothfels, *Savages and Beasts: The Birth of the Modern Zoo* (Baltimore: Johns Hopkins University Press, 2002), 183.

9. Rothfels, *Savages and Beasts*, 114.

10. Eric Baratay and Elisabeth Hardouin-Fugier, *Zoo: A History of Zoological Gardens in the West*, trans. Oliver Welsh (London: Reaktion Books, 2004), 251.

11. Julian Huxley, *Memories* (New York: Harper & Row, 1970), 231–32.

12. On the precursors to the IUDZG, see Heinz-George Klös, "100 Jahre Verband Deutscher Zoodirektoren," *Bongo* 13 (1987): 3–35; Heinz-George Klös and Herman Reichenbach, "Verband Deutscher Zoodirektoren," *Encyclopedia of the World's Zoos*, vol. 3, ed. Catherine E. Bell (Chicago: Fitzroy Dearborn, 2001), 1288–90; and Laura Penn, Markus Gusset, and Gerald Dick, *77 Years: The History and the Evolution of the World Association of Zoos and Aquariums* (Gland, Switzerland: WAZA, 2012), 18–21.

13. Quoted in "Project Häppchen," *Gorilla: Magazin Der Zoologische Gesellschaft Frankfurt* 1 (2004): 2.

14. Kurt Priemel, "Der 'Internationalen Verband der Direktoren Zoologischer Gärten' unde seine zweite Jahrestagung in Köln a. Rh. (17. Bis 20. VIII. 1936)," *Der Zoologische Garten* 9, no. 5 (1937): 48.

15. Klös and Reichenbach, "Verband Deutscher Zoodirektoren," 1289.

16. William T. Hornaday, *Our Vanishing Wild Life: Its Extermination and Preservation* (New York: New York Zoological Society, 1913), 187.

17. On the 1936 annual IUDZG conference, see Priemel, "Der 'Internationalen Verband der Direktoren Zoologischer Gärten,'" 47–51.

18. P. Smit, "Sunier, Armand Louis Jean (1886–1974)," *Biografisch Woordenboek van Nederland*, http://resources.huygens.knaw.nl/bwn1880-2000/lemmata/bwn2/sunier.

19. "Artis-film," December 31, 1937, Nederlands Instituut voor Beeld en Geluid, https://openbeelden.nl/media/956837/Artisfilm_HD.en.

20. Priemel, "Die fünfzigste Jahrestagung des 'Internationalen Verbandes der Direktoren Zoologischer Gärten' in Amsterdam," *Der Zoologische Garten* 10, no. 5 (1939): 230–32.

Chapter 5

1. Paul Preston, *The Spanish Civil War, 1936–39* (New York: Grove Press, 1986), 4.

2. Piers Brendon, *The Dark Valley: A Panorama of the 1930s* (New York: Knopf, 2000), 360.

3. Gustave Loisel, *Histoire des Ménageries de l'Antiquité a Nos Jours*, vol. III (Paris: Octave Doin et Fils, 1912), 109.

4. ZOOXXI, *History of the Barcelona Zoo* (Thematic Report), April 2015, 3–5, 6, 10, https://zooxxi.org/en/2015/04/29/history-of-barcelona-zoo/.

5. "A la señor hipopótomo le had nacido un hijo," *Ahora* (Madrid), July 16, 1936, 11.

6. Emili Pons, *El Parc Zoològic De Barcelona: Cent anys d'història* (Barcelona: Edicions 62, 1992), 123.

Notes to Pages 67–70   303

7. Maria Paz Moreno, "Food Fight: Survival and Ideology in Cookbooks from the Spanish Civil War," in *Food and Communication: Proceedings of the Oxford Symposium on Food and Cookery 2015*, ed. Mark McWilliams (London: Prospect Books, 2016), 276.

8. Anthony Beevor, *The Battle for Spain: The Spanish Civil War 1936–1939* (New York: Penguin, 2006), 332; Sergio C. Fanjul, "Madrid's Hungry Years," *El País*, April 2, 2015.

9. Moreno, "Food Fight," 280.

10. Fanjul, "Madrid's Hungry Years"; Beevor, *Battle for Spain*, 168.

11. Fanjul, "Madrid's Hungry Years."

12. "Beasts in Madrid's Zoo Ferocious in Terror of Continuous Bombing," *Evening Review* (East Liverpool, OH), March 1, 1937, 12; John Darma, "Tinned Fruit for Monkeys Tragedy in Spanish Zoo," *Shepparton Advertiser* (Vic.), February 17, 1937, 2; Pons, *El Parc Zoològic De Barcelona*, 124.

13. "Soldiers Eat Hog from Madrid Zoo," *El Paso Herald-Post*, January 15, 1937, 1.

14. "Franco's Belated Cup of Coffee," *Telegraph* (Brisbane, Qld.), February 1, 1938, 7.

15. George Orwell, *Homage to Catalonia* (Orlando, FL: Harcourt, 1980), 65.

16. Beevor, *Battle for Spain*, 242. For a joking response to the rumor that "veterinary unions" are feeding the children of well-heeled fascists to the lions at the Madrid Zoo, see "Epilogo de Granollers," *¡Campo libre!*, June 8, 1938, 7.

17. On the development of aerial bombing, see Sven Lindquist, *A History of Bombing*, trans. Linda Haverty Rugg (New York: The New Press, 2001).

18. "Prohibiting Launching of Projectiles or Explosives from Balloons (Hague, IV, 1)," in *Treaties and Other International Agreements of the United States of America 1776–1949*, compiled by Charles I. Bevans, vol. 1: *Multilateral 1776–1917* (Washington, DC: GPO, 1968), 270.

19. "Laws of Customs of War on Land (Hague IV)," in *Treaties and Other International Agreements*, 648.

20. L. R. Brightwell, *The Zoo Story* (London: Museum Press, 1952), in "A Gardener Named Banks, Britain's First Air Raid Casualty 24 December 1914," December 24, 2014, World War Zoo Gardens Project, https://worldwarzoogardener1939.wordpress.com/2014/12/24/a-gardener-named-banks-britains-first-air-raid-casualty-24-december-1914/.

21. Giulio Douhet, *The Command of the Air*, trans. Dino Ferrari (1942; reprint, with a foreword by Richard P. Hallion; Washington, DC: Air Force History and Museums Program, 1998), 9–10.

22. Geoffrey Cox, *Defence of Madrid: An Eye Witness Account from the Spanish Civil War* (1937; Dundedin, NZ: Otago University Press, 2006), 79.

23. Quoted in Brendon, *Dark Valley*, 383.

24. Beevor, *Battle for Spain*, 377.

25. "Beasts in Madrid's Zoo Ferocious in Terror of Continuous Bombing," 12.

26. Carolina Martin, "Ignasi de Sagarra ie de Castellarnau (1880–1940)," *Museo Nacional de Ciencies Naturales* (2006), http://www.tagis.pt/uploads/4/7/9/5/47950987/ignasi_sagarra.pdf.

27. Pons, *El Parc Zoològic De Barcelona*, 124, 128; see also "Barcelona Zoo Animals May Be Moved to France," *The Guardian*, April 6, 1937, 11.

28. Martha Gellhorn, "Zoo in Madrid," in *The Heart of Another* (New York: Charles Scribner's Sons, 1941), 123.

29. Erica Fudge, *Animal* (London: Reaktion Books, 2002), 25–65.

30. "Visitors to Madrid Zoo Have No Food for Animals," *New York Times*, May 17, 1937, 4.

31. "Madrid Zoo Elephant Dies, Casualty of War," *Indianapolis Star*, January 5, 1938, 5; "Death of Pancho," *Time*, 31, no. 7 (January 17, 1938): 25.

32. Pons, *El Parc Zoològic De Barcelona*, 126.

33. Edwin Rolfe to Leo Hurwitz (March 17, 1938), in *Madrid 1937: Letters of the Abraham Lincoln Brigade from the Spanish Civil War*, ed. Cary Nelson and Jefferson Hendricks (New York: Routledge, 1996), 426.

34. Hugh Thomas, *The Spanish Civil War*, 3rd ed. (New York: Harper & Row, 1986), 807.

35. Pons, *El Parc Zoològic De Barcelona*, 126, 121.

36. V. Del. O., "La Metralla Fascista y Los Animals," *Umbral* (Valencia), August 20, 1938, no. 40, 15.

37. Del. O., "La Metralla Fascista y Los Animals," 15.

38. Pons, *El Parc Zoològic De Barcelona*, 123. The heart attack theory is mentioned in Del. O., "La Metralla Fascista y Los Animals," 15.

39. Pons, *El Parc Zoològic De Barcelona*, 129.

40. Henry W. Shoemaker, "This Morning's Comment," *Altoona Tribune* (Altoona, PA), July 4, 1939, 4; "War Reduces Pipo the Hippo," *St. Louis Post-Dispatch*, April 18, 1939, 1.

41. Pons, *El Parc Zoològic De Barcelona*, 132.

42. "Seen from the Hilltop by a Casual Observer," *Kane Republican* (Kane, PA), October 23, 1931, at *Dr. McCleery Lobo Wolves Digital Archive*, http://www.mccleery wolves.com/.

43. Shoemaker, "This Morning's Comment," 4.

44. Thomas, *Spanish Civil War*, 926–27.

Chapter 6

1. This vignette is based on "L'Arche de Noe a Roulettes," *Le Matin*, 5 heure, September 12, 1939, 1–2; Merry Bromberger, "Le Zoo s'en va en pièces détachées," *L'Intransigeant*, sixieme derniere, September 12, 1939, 1, 3.

2. Diane Ackerman, *The Zookeeper's Wife: A War Story* (New York: W. W. Norton & Co., 2007), 61.

3. Ackerman, *Zookeeper's Wife*, 61.

4. "Incidents in European Conflict," *New York Times*, October 2, 1939, 2.

5. "Actions to be Taken in Wartime," May 6, 1939, folder 54, London Zoological Society (ZSL).

6. *Reports of the Council and Auditors of the Zoological Society of London for the Year 1939* (Bungay, Suffolk: Richard Clay and Company, Ltd., 1940), 4.

7. British Library of Information, *Air Raid Precautions* (c. 1941), 1; original held in the Ward M. Canaday Center for Special Collections at the University of Toledo, https://utdr.utoledo.edu/islandora/object/utoledo%3A5367.

8. "A.R.P. Air-Raid-Precautions" (1938), *British Pathé*, https://www.youtube.com /watch?v=OJPyEtwUqZw.

9. "A.R.P. for Snakes and Lions," *The Times* (London), August 26, 1938, 8, issue 48394.

Notes to Pages 81–88   305

10. J. Fisher, "Air Raid Precautions, September, 1939," copy in folder 54, ZSL.

11. Quoted in C. H. Keeling, *They All Came into the Ark: A Record of the Zoological Society of London in Two World Wars* (Clam Publications, 1988), 129.

12. Craven Hill, "Zoo Animals Would be Shot in an Air Raid," *The Evening Standard*, September 3, 1939.

13. Janet Finlayson, "From Edinburgh to UNRRA and After—Part 1," *WW2 People's War*, February 24. 2005, www.bbc.co.uk/history/ww2peopleswar/stories/20/a3712420.shtml.

14. "Zoo Evacuation in Event of War," *The Daily Telegraph and Morning Post*, August 25, 1939, clipping in ZSL.

15. Sydney Moorhouse, "War Time and the Zoos," *The Boy's Own Paper*, August 1940, 483; David Seth-Smith, "Report of the Curator of Mammals and Birds to the War Emergency Committee," December 6, 1939, folder 54, ZSL.

16. Keeling, *They All Came into the Ark*, 131.

17. "Whipsnade Zoo's Giant Hillside Lion Makeover Completed ," *BBC News*, March 20, 2018, https://www.bbc.com/news/uk-england-beds-bucks-herts-43459229.

18. "A. R. P. Whipsnade," October 4, 1939, folder "ZSL—Reports etc. regarding War Emergencies and Bomb Damage," ZSL.

19. The Lord Privy's Seal Office, *Evacuation Why and How?*, Public Information Leaflet No. 3, July 1939.

20. Roland Baetens, *The Chant of Paradise: The Antwerp Zoo: 150 Years of History* (Tielt: Lannoo, 1993), 104.

21. Quoted in June Mottershead, with Penelope Dening, *Our Zoo* (London: Headline, 2014), 163.

22. See "The Zoo Opens Again," *The Times*, September 16, 1939, 5, issue 48412; Sydney Moorhouse, "War Time and the Zoos," *The Boy's Own Paper* (August 1940): 383; "The Animals in the Zoo Don't Mind the Raids," *The War Illustrated*, November 15, 1940, 526.

23. "A.R.P. for Snakes and Lions," 8.

24. "Zoo Danger Would Be Killed," *The Star*, August 26, 1939.

25. K. R. Banning, "Dangerous Animals," *Manchester Daily Herald*, September 15, 1939.

26. Keeling, *They All Came into the Ark*, 131. Sources vary about how many poisonous reptiles were killed that day. See Mayumi Itoh, *Japanese Wartime Zoo Policy: The Silent Victims of World War* (New York: Palgrave Macmillan, 2010), 122.

27. "Thinning Out at the Zoo," *The Times*, September 9, 1939, 6, issue 48406.

28. G. M. Vevers, "Report on the Aquarium to the War Emergency Committee," September 8, 1939, folder 54, ZSL.

29. *Reports of the Council and Auditors of the Zoological Society of London*, 6.

30. "List of Animals Destroyed from Commencement of War to October 18, 1939" (c. 1939), ZSL.

31. David Seth-Smith, "Animals That Might Be Disposed of in the Event of War," August 31, 1939, folder "LZS: Reports etc. regarding War Emergencies and Bomb Damage," ZSL.

32. Seth-Smith, "Report of the Curator of Mammals and Birds to the War Emergency Committee."

306 Notes to Pages 88–98

33. W. S. P. Smith, "List of Animals on Hand at Whipsnade" (c. 1939), folder "LZS: Reports etc. regarding War Emergencies and Bomb Damage," ZSL.

34. "Animals at Zoo Shot," *Manchester Daily Herald*, September 9, 1939; clipping in ZSL.

35. Clare Campbell, *Bonzo's War: Animals Under Fire 1939–45* (London: Constable, & Robinson, 2013), 31, 50. Historian Hilda Kean provides a powerful account of British citizens' willingness to destroy their companion animals in *The Great Cat and Dog Massacre: The Real Story of World War Two's Unknown Tragedy* (Chicago: University of Chicago Press, 2017).

36. For lengthy discussions of the theological and philosophical roots of this worldview, see Keith Thomas, *Man and the Natural World: Changing Attitudes in England 1500–1800* (New York: Penguin Books, 1984); and Matthew Scully, *Dominion: The Power of Man, the Suffering of Animals, and the Call to Mercy* (New York: St. Martin's Griffin, 2002).

Chapter 7

1. "Cold in Netherlands Brings Arctic Birds," *New York Times*, February 15, 1940, 21.

2. Herbert L. Matthews, "29 Die in Train Wreck Near Naples as Six Inches of Snow Falls in Italy," *New York Times*, December 31, 1939, 12.

3. "Topics of the Times," *New York Times*, January 15, 1940, 11.

4. "My Childhood at Whipsnade Zoo," *WW2 People's War*, October 15, 2014, https://www.bbc.co.uk/history/ww2peopleswar/stories/65/a4004065.shtml.

5. Roland Baetens, *The Chant of Paradise: The Antwerp Zoo: 150 Years of History* (Tielt: Lannoo, 1993), 107.

6. Charles J. V. Murphy, "European Zoos," *Life Magazine*, December 6, 1948, 149.

7. Helmut Zedelmaier and Michael Kamp, *Hellabrunn: Gesschichte und Geschichten des Müncher Tierparks* (München: Bassermann Verlag, 2011), 76.

8. Evelyn Gottschlich, "Wiedereröffnung und Zerstörung (1928–1945)," in *Nilpferde an der Isar: Eine Geschichte des Tierparks Hellabrunn in München*, ed. Michael Kamp and Helmut Zedelmaier (München: Buchendorfer Verlag, 2000), 133.

9. P. L., "La plupart des animaux du Zoo ont fait le voyage de retours, mais . . . ," *L'Intransigeant*, final edition, February 9, 1940, 2.

10. Gottschlich, "Wiedereröffnung und Zerstörung (1928–1945)," 133.

11. John Keegan, *A History of Warfare* (New York: Vintage Books, 1993), 371.

12. J. P. Harris, "The Myth of Blitzkrieg," *War in History* 2, no. 3 (1995): 352.

13. The following account of the Ouwehand's Zoo's experience during the invasion of Holland is largely derived from "Ouwehands Zoo," *Andere Tijden* (Other Times), December 22, 2003, https://www.anderetijden.nl/aflevering/483/Ouwehands -Dierenpark. For a broader discussion of Dutch zoos during World War II, see Maarten Th. Frankenhuis, *Overleven in de dierentuin: De oorlagsjaren van Artis en andere parken* (Rotterdam: 20/10 Uitgevers, 2013).

14. "Dierentuinen in oorlogstijd," *NW&T*, October 15, 2019, https://www.biologie plusschool.nl/nieuws/de-klas-uit/dierentuinen-in-oorlogstijd-1.

15. BB-7526, "Walk in the Zoo" (1930–1934), Moving Images Collections, Rotterdam City Archive, https://stadsarchief.rotterdam.nl/zoeken/resultaten/?mivast

Notes to Pages 98–104   307

=184&mizig=317&miadt=184&miaet=14&micode=4016&minr=39665739&milang
=nl&misort=dat%7Casc&mizk_alle=diergaarde&mif1=34&miview=ff.

16. The following account is drawn from several sources: Frankenhuis, *Over-leven in de dierentuin*, 14; Maartje Kouwen, "Dierentuinen in oorlogstijd," *bioneuws*, May 5, 2016, https://www.natuurwetenschapentechniek.nl/nieuws/de-klas-uit/dierentuinen-in-oorlogstijd-1; Ingrid Smits, "Mei 1940: kogels, brand en bomen in de dierentuin," *Rijnmond*, May 12, 2015, https://www.rijnmond.nl/nieuws/129149/mei-1940-kogels-brand-en-bommen-in-de-dierentuin; Marcia Tap, "Diergaarde Blijdorp zou voorjaar 1940 openen: Dit is de bizarre geschiedenis van de dierentuin van Rotterdam," *Rijnmond*, December 7, 2020, https://www.rijnmond.nl/nieuws/201864/diergaarde-blijdorp-zou-voorjaar-1940-openen-dit-is-de-bizarre-geschiedenis-van-de-dierentuin-van-rotterdam;.

17. Even when ordered to kill their more "dangerous" animals, zoo staff frequently spared rare or expensive animals (e.g., polar bears) or those who were especially popular with patrons. Everything else—including such zoo mainstays as lions and tigers—was ultimately viewed as expendable.

18. Frankenhuis, *Overleven in de dierentuin*, 32.

19. Henry Quinque, "Jean Delacour, My Friend," trans. Howard Swann, *Avicultural Magazine* 94, no. 1–2 (1988): 10; Ruth Ezra, "Jean Theodore Delacour, 1890–1985," *Avicultural Magazine* 94, no. 1–2 (1988): 1.

20. David Askew, "The Gentleman Naturalist," *Dublin Review of Books*, available at http://www.drb.ie/essays/the-gentleman-naturalist.

21. Tom Lovel, "Jean Delacour," *Avicultural Magazine* 94, no. 1–2 (1988): 3.

22. Ernst Mayer, "In Memoriam: Jean (Theodore) Delacour," *The Auk* 103 (July 1986): 604.

23. In 1988, *Avicultural Magazine*, the journal of the world's leading avicultural (bird-rearing) society, devoted a two-issue memorial to Delacour's life and legacy.

24. Lovel, "Jean Delacour," 3.

25. Jean Delacour, *The Living Air: The Memoirs of an Ornithologist* (London: Country Life Limited, 1966), 35, 40. In addition to losing his family home, Delacour also lost his brother, who was killed while serving in the French military.

26. Lovel, "Jean Delacour," 4.

27. Delacour, *The Living Air*, 44, 46.

28. Jean Delacour, "The End of Clères," *Avicultural Magazine* 6, no. 3 (May–June 1941): 82.

29. Delacour, "The End of Clères," 81, 83.

30. Delacour, "The End of Clères," 83.

31. Delacour, *The Living Air*, 52, 158.

Chapter 8

1. This vignette is based on Lewis Gannett, "World's Greatest Ant Collection Stolen by Nazis from Holland," *New York Herald Tribune*, November 3, 1944, and "The Rape of the Ants," *Time*, November 20, 1944, both clippings at the London Zoo Archive.

2. Adolf Hitler, *Mein Kampf*, trans. James Murphy, Project Gutenberg of Australia, eBook No. 0200601.txt.

308   Notes to Pages 104–109

3. Norman Rich, *Hitler's War Aims: The Establishment of the New Order* (New York: W. W. Norton, 1974).

4. Dick Van Galen Last and Rolf Wolfswinkel, *Anne Frank and After: Dutch Holocaust Literature in Historical Perspective* (Amsterdam: Amsterdam University Press, 1996), 35.

5. Quoted in Ihor Kamenetsky, *Hitler's Occupation of the Ukraine (1941–1944): A Study of Totalitarian Imperialism* (Milwaukee: Marquette University Press, 1956), 35.

6. Vernon N. Kisling Jr., "Ancient Collections and Menageries," in *Zoo and Aquarium History: Ancient Animal Collections to Zoological Gardens*, ed. Vernon N. Kisling Jr. (Boca Raton, FL: CRC Press, 2001), 19.

7. Louise E. Robbins, *Elephant Slaves and Pampered Parrots: Exotic Animals in Eighteenth-Century Paris* (Baltimore: Johns Hopkins University Press, 2002), 225.

8. Nigel Rothfels, *Savages and Beasts: The Birth of the Modern Zoo* (Baltimore: Johns Hopkins University Press, 2002), 81–142.

9. John Berger, "Why Look at Animals?," in *About Looking* (New York: Pantheon, 1980), 19.

10. "Attractions at the Zoo," *Daily Telegraph*, April 22, 1916. Quoted in John M. Kinder, "Zoo Animals and Modern War: Captive Casualties, Patriotic Citizens, and Good Soldiers," *Animals and War: Studies of Europe and North America*, ed. Ryan Hediger (Leiden: Brill, 2013), 52.

11. Kai Artinger, "Lutz Heck: 'Der Vater der Rominter Ure': Einige Bemerkungen zum wissenschaftlichen Leiter des Berliner Zoos im Nationalsocialismus," *Der Bär von Berlin. Jahrbuch* (1994), note 62.

12. Leszek Solski, "Zoological Gardens of Central-Eastern Europe and Russia," in *Zoo and Aquarium History: Ancient Animal Collections to Zoological Gardens*, ed. Vernon N. Kisling Jr. (Boca Raton, FL: CRC Press, 2001), 122.

13. Diane Ackerman, *The Zookeeper's Wife: A War Story* (New York: W. W. Norton, 2007), 89, 94.

14. Solski, "Zoological Gardens of Central-Eastern Europe and Russia," 122.

15. "Warsaw Zoo Needs Help for Restoration," *Parks and Recreation*, 29 (July–August 1946): 254–55.

16. Ackerman, *The Zookeeper's Wife*, 95.

17. US Holocaust Memorial Museum, "Antisemitic Legislation 1933–1939," *Holocaust Encyclopedia*, https://encyclopedia.ushmm.org/content/en/article/antisemitic-legislation-1933-1939.

18. Peter Demetz, *Prague in Danger: The Years of German Occupation, 1939–45: Memories and History, Terror and Resistance, Theater and Jazz, Film and Poetry, Politics and War* (New York: Farrar, Straus & Giroux, 2008), 61–63; Solski, "Zoological Gardens of Central-Eastern Europe and Russia," 42.

19. Last and Wolfswinkel, *Anne Frank and After*, 36, 43, 47–48.

20. Maartin Th. Frankenhuis, *Overleven in de dierentuin: De oorlogsjaren van Artis en andere parken* (Rotterdam: Uitgevers, 2010), 46, 47.

21. Adolf C. van Bruggen, "Koninlijk Zoölogish-Botanisch Genootschap, the Zoological Gargen in The Hague, 1863–1943, a Retrospect after Seventy Years from the Point of View of a Zoologist," *Der Zoologische Garten*, N.F. 82 (2013): 201; Henrick C. Verton, *In the Fire of the Eastern Front: The Experiences of a Dutch Waffen-SS Volunteer, 1941–45*, trans. Hazel Toon-Thorn (Mechanicsburg, PA: Stackpole Books, 2010).

Notes to Pages 109–116   309

22. Not long after settling into his Vincennes apartment, Jünger spent several hours at the zoo before reacquainting himself with the rest of the city. Allan Mitchell, *The Devil's Captain: Ernst Jünger in Nazi Paris, 1941–1944* (New York: Berghahn Books, 2011), 20.

23. Gilles Perrault and Pierre Azema, *Paris Under the Occupation*, trans. Allison Carter and Maximilian Vos (New York: The Vendome Press, 1987), 17; quoted on 18, 11.

24. "Ein Besuch im Zoologischen Garten," *Der Deutsch Wegleiter für Paris*, no. 19, May 1, 1941, 20.

25. Frankenhuis, *Overleven in de dierentuin*, 84.

26. "Aus Łódź wird Litzmannstadt (Łódź Becomes Litzmannstadt)," US Holocaust Memorial Museum, https://collections.ushmm.org/search/catalog/irn1003805.

27. See David A. Harrisville, *The Virtuous Wehrmacht: Crafting the Myth of the German Soldier on the Eastern Front, 1941–1944* (Ithaca, NY: Cornell University Press, 2021).

28. On Pétain's "shield" theory of collaboration, see H. R. Kedward, *Occupied France: Collaboration and Resistance 1940–1944* (Oxford: Basil Blackwell, 1985), 32, 40.

29. H. R. Kedward, *Occupied France: Collaboration and Resistance 1940–1944* (Oxford: Basil Blackwell, 1985), 47.

30. Jan Vlasák, "'Snow-White' of the Prague Zoo: The Polar Bear Which Grew Up in a City Flat," *The Illustrated London News*, September 13, 1947, 302.

31. Frankenhuis, *Overleven in de dierentuin*, 113, 88, 175.

32. Frankenhuis, *Overleven in de dierentuin*, 125, 121, 56, 116.

33. George Packer, "We Are Living in a Failed State," *Atlantic*, June 2020, https://www.theatlantic.com/magazine/archive/2020/06/underlying-conditions/610261/.

34. Oscar Mohr, "Nazi Yoke Is Borne by Netherlanders," *New York Times*, August 11, 1940, 29.

Chapter 9

1. "Mayor Opens Zoo's New 'Veldt'; Doubts Aquarium Will Be Moved," *New York Times*, May 2, 1941, 23. A few years earlier, William Croft, a Toronto alderman, joked to a local reporter that the Reich's leader was the only creature fit for the Riverdale Zoo's decrepit beaver cage. When German officials demanded an apology, the politician told them to "go to Hell." Daniel Panneton, "Putting Hitler in the Zoo: How a Toronto Politician Offended the Nazis—and Refused to Back Down," *tvo today*, January 7, 2021, https://www.tvo.org/article/putting-hitler-in-the-zoo-how-a-toronto-politician-offended-the-nazis-and-refused-to-back-down.

2. George H. Gallup, *The Gallup Poll: Public Opinion, 1935–1948* (New York: Random House, 1972), 290.

3. No matter, it seems, was too small—not even a request, forwarded by the American vice consul of Japan in 1939, about the best method of feeding a Siberian bustard, a large terrestrial bird native to central Asia. The consul's office had received the inquiry from a zoo in Keigo, Japan, and had passed it along in hopes of fostering "international good-will" between the two nations. Though seemingly trivial, such gestures were part of a larger strategy to leverage American scientific know-how to project a benign influence in an increasingly dangerous world. (For what it's worth, Mann advised that a Siberian bustard should be "fed much the same

310   Notes to Pages 117–121

as ordinary poultry," suggesting a diet of cracked grains and vegetables with a supplement of ground-up oyster shells.) W. M. Mann to Nathanial P. Davis, January 25, 1940, folder 1, box 152, RU 74, SIA.

4. Lucile Quarry Mann Oral History Interview, June–August 1977 (henceforth Lucile Mann Oral History), RU 9513, SIA, 115, 116. A transcript can be found at the National Zoo Library. The collected oral history interview is also available at https:// siarchives.si.edu/collections/siris_arc_217681.

5. "Air Raid Precautions" (n.d.), 29, clipping provided by Temple University, which holds the records of the Zoological Society of Philadelphia.

6. William Bridges, *A Gathering of Animals: An Unconventional History of the New York Zoological Society* (New York: Harper & Row, 1974), 369; New York Zoological Society, 1917 Annual Report, 63–71.

7. "Bronx Zoo Ready for Air Raid in City," *New York Times*, December 18, 1941, 35.

8. Footage can be found at "William M. Man and Lucile Quarry Mann—1940 Smithsonian-Firestone Expedition to Liberia," Smithsonian Institution Archives, https://www.youtube.com/watch?v=y0p3NKz-uSk.

9. Lucile Mann Oral History, 132. Lucile Mann's casual racism was not limited to the occasional demeaning phrase. At one point in her diary, she derides the "hopeless attempt" to teach some Liberian children to count to twenty, noting that a "chimpanzee can count to eleven." William and Lucile Mann, Diary, Firestone Expedition to Liberia, 1940 (henceforth Lucile Mann Diary), 32, SIA, https://transcription .si.edu/project/7865.

10. Lucile Mann Diary, May 23, 1941, 55.

11. Lucile Mann Oral History, 135. "William M. Mann (1886–1960) and Lucile Quarry Mann (1897–1986) (1940)," Accession number: SIA2009-0984, Smithsonian Institution Archives, http://photography.si.edu/SearchImage.aspx?id=5798.

12. Lucile Mann Diary, June 14, 1941, 63.

13. "S.D. Zoo Ready for Emergency," *San Diego Union*, December 14, 1942, B 2:2.

14. "Air Raid Precautions," 29.

15. W. M. Mann, "Air Raid Instructions to Employees," March 8, 1943, folder 2, box 191, RU 74, SIA.

16. W. M. Mann, "Air Raid Instructions to Employees."

17. Robert Earnest Miller, "The War That Never Came: Civilian Defense in Cincinnati, Ohio during World War II," *Queen City Heritage* (Winter 1991): 8.

18. "Bronx Zoo Ready for Air Raid in City," *New York Times*, December 18, 1941.

19. "Zoo Ready for War," *Washington Daily News*, June 8, 1942, 16.

20. "Capitol Motoring No. 64," February 26, 1942 (script copy), in folder 1, box 213, RU 74, SIA.

21. For a nuanced discussion of the biopolitical implications of zoo escapes, see Kári Driscoll, "World, War, Zoo: Zoo-Break Narratives in a Biopolitical Frame," *Textual Practice* 37, no. 10 (2023): 1586–604, doi:10.1080/0950236X.2023.2264682.

22. Mary A. Bessemer to Dr. [William] Mann, c. Jan. 1942, folder 2, box 191, RU 74, SIA.

23. Gus Knudson, *Air Raid Defense at the Woodland Park Zoological Gardens*, folder 7, box 2, RG 8601, Woodland Park Zoological Gardens, Seattle, WA (hereafter Seattle Zoo Archives).

24. Lucile Mann Oral History, 166.

Notes to Pages 121–124 311

25. William Mann to Roger Conant, March 10, 1942, folder 2, box 191, RU 74, SIA.

26. J. A. Campbell to Ed Bean, February 6, 1942, Brookfield Zoo Archives.

27. "Air Raid Precautions," *Animal Kingdom* 45, no. 1 (January 1942): 31.

28. "Bronx Zoo Ready," *New York Times*, December 18, 1941.

29. Robert Bean to Conant (December 19, 1941), Brookfield Zoo Archives.

30. "Wartime Zoos," *Indianapolis Star*, February 15, 1942, 14.

31. Miller, "The War That Never Came," 8.

32. Mayumi Itoh, *Japanese Wartime Zoo Policy: The Silent Victims of World War* (New York: Palgrave, 2010), 153; Mark Rosenthal, Carol Tauber, and Edward Uhler, *The Ark in the Park: The Story of the Lincoln Park Zoo* (Urbana: University of Illinois Press, 2003), 73.

33. John M. Kinder, "'Our Faunal Defense in Africa': Imperial Survivalism, Anglo-American Conservation, and African Liberation in the Twentieth Century," *Journal of Colonialism and Colonial History* 23, no. 3 (Winter 2022). doi:10.1353/cch.2022.0026.

34. Henry Fairfield Osborn, preface to the 2nd ed., *The Passing of the Great Race or The Racial Basis of European History*, by Madison Grant, 4th rev. ed. (New York: Charles Scribner's Sons, 1923), xi. See also Garland E. Allen, "'Culling the Herd': Eugenics and the Conservation Movement in the United States, 1900–1940," *Journal of the History of Biology* 46, no. 1 (Spring 2013): 31–72.

35. Robert R. Weyeneth, "The Architecture of Racial Segregation: The Challenges of Preserving the Problematical Past," *The Public Historian* 27, no. 4 (Fall 2005): 12.

36. Susan Ciani Salvatore, *Civil Rights in America: Racial Desegregation of Public Accommodations* (Washington, DC: National Historic Landmarks Program, 2004/2009), 16.

37. Weyeneth, "Architecture of Racial Segregation," 18.

38. "Negroes' Day Is Set at Zoo," *The Oklahoman*, June 21, 1939.

39. Jesse C. Donahue and Erik K. Trump, *American Zoos During the Depression: A New Deal for Animals* (Jefferson, NC: McFarland, 2010), 92.

40. Christine Knauer, "Race and/in War," in *At War: The Military and American Culture in the Twentieth Century and Beyond*, ed. David Kieran and Edwin A. Martini (New Brunswick, NJ: Rutgers University Press, 2018), 176.

41. Alfred Lawton to Dr. William M. Mann (June 9, 1941), folder 8, box 189, RU 74, SIA.

42. Bob Mullan and Garry Marvin, *Zoo Culture*, 2nd ed. (Urbana: University of Illinois Press, 1999), 135.

43. Paul Breese and Jean DeMercer-Breese, *The Honolulu Zoo: Waikiki's Wildlife Treasure, 1915–2015* (Honolulu: Honolulu Zoo Books, 2015), 40.

44. Gus Knudson, *Annual Report*, December 31, 1945, folder 8, box 7, RG 5801-01, Seattle Zoo Archives.

45. "Zoo Vandals Are Hunted after Death of Ostrich," *The Sacramento Bee*, February 20, 1943, 18; "Shotgun Ready in Albuquerque for Zoo Vandals," *Carlsbad Current-Argus* (Carlsbad, NM), June 19, 1944, 2.

46. Lucile Mann Oral History, 165.

47. Writing in the *Detroit Free Press*, one Michigander blamed zoo vandalism on the "spare the rod" mentality that infected wartime public schools. Mary Decker, "Zoo Vandals," *Detroit Free Press*, June 2, 1945, 4.

48. Quoted in James Gilbert, *A Cycle of Outrage: America's Reaction to the Juvenile Delinquent in the 1950s* (New York: Oxford University Press, 1986), 29.

49. Gilbert, *Cycle of Outrage*, 24–41; Milton Lessner, "Controlling War-Time Juvenile Delinquency," *Journal of Criminal Law and Criminology* 35, no. 4 (1944–1945): 242–48.

50. Charles E. Tracewell, "This and That," *The Evening Star* (Washington, DC), October 13, 1944, 8.

51. "Funeral Planned Saturday Here for E. Untermann, Sr.," *The Vernal Express* (UT), January 5, 1956, 1, 5.

52. Ernest Untermann, "Modern Zoo Problems," Papers, 1933–1956, Wisconsin Historical Society, Milwaukee, WI.

53. Lucile Mann's Diary, February 1940, 4.

54. "Wild Animals Roar and Moan as Fire Destroys Circus Home," *Steuben Republican* (Angola, IN), February 28, 1940.

55. "35 Circus Animals Burned Alive in Cages as Fire Sweeps Tent While Horrified Crowd Watches; Gargantua and Toto Saved," *Star*, August 4, 1942.

Chapter 10

1. Derek Wood with Robert Mannion, *A Tiger by the Tail: A History of Auckland Zoo 1922–1992* (Auckland: Auckland City, 1992), 61.

2. On the myth of the "good war" in the American imagination, see Michael C. C. Adams, *The Best War Ever: America and World War II* (Baltimore: Johns Hopkins University Press, 1994); and John Bodnar, *The "Good War" in American Memory* (Baltimore: Johns Hopkins University Press, 2010). On the myth of the "Great Patriotic War" in Soviet Memory, see Jonathan Brudstedt, *The Soviet Myth of World War II: Patriotic Memory and the Russian Question in the USSR* (Cambridge: Cambridge University Press, 2021).

3. Philip Snow, *The Fall of Hong Kong: Britain, China and the Japanese Occupation* (New Haven, CT: Yale University Press, 2003), xxiv.

4. John W. Dower, *War Without Mercy: Race & Power in the Pacific War* (New York: Pantheon, 1986), 263–64.

5. On the founding of Southeast Asia's first zoos, see Sally Walker, "Zoological Gardens of Asia," in *Zoo and Aquarium History: Ancient Animal Collections to Zoological Gardens*, ed. Vernon N. Kisling Jr. (Boca Raton, FL: CRC Press, 2001), 215–50.

6. Timothy P. Barnard, *Imperial Creatures: Humans and Other Animals in Colonial Singapore, 1819–1942* (New York: New York University Press, 2019), 96.

7. Randy Malamud, *Reading Zoos: Representations of Animals and Captivity* (New York: New York University Press, 1998), 59.

8. Kees Rookmaaker, "Two Former Zoological Gardens in Singapore," *International Zoo News* 59, no. 5 (2012): 369.

9. Sharon Teng, "Punggol Zoo," *Singapore Infopedia*, March 14, 2016, https://www.nlb.gov.sg/main/article-detail?cmsuuid=1473095b-ceb1-460e-9f12-d4b8357743be.

10. Quoted in Barnard, *Imperial Creatures*, 99.

11. Teng, "Punggol Zoo"; Rookmaaker, "Two Former Zoological Gardens in Singapore," 370.

12. "Polar Bears in Singapore," *Singapore Free Press and Mercantile Advertiser*, March 13, 1937, 3.

Notes to Pages 130–135   313

13. Nalina Gopal, "Finding Basapa: In Search of a Pioneer and His Story," *Roots.gov.sg*, 2013, https://www.roots.gov.sg/stories-landing/stories/finding-basapa-in-search-of-a-pioneer-and-his-story/story.

14. Ken Kawata, "Tales from Japan's Zoos: The Sustaining Saga of Sakoku," *International Zoo News* 62, no. 6 (2015): 415, 416, 420.

15. Ian Jared Miller, *The Nature of the Beasts: Empire and Exhibition at the Tokyo Imperial Zoo* (Berkeley: University of California Press, 2013), 62, 84.

16. Sheng-kai Hsu, *Brief History of the Taipei Zoo: 1914–2014* (Taipei: Taipei Zoo, 2014), 14, 16, 29.

17. Mayumi Itoh, *Japanese Wartime Zoo Policy* (New York: Palgrave Macmillan, 2010), 195–96.

18. Leslie Glass, *The Changing of Kings: Memories of Burma 1934–1949* (London: Peter Owen, 1985), 138.

19. "Japs 'Dine' on Giraffes at the Zoo," *The Morning Herald* (Uniontown, PA), July 16, 1946, 2.

20. Gopal, "Finding Basapa."

21. Not all Asian zoos were destroyed in advance of the Japanese invasion. After Japanese forces occupied the Chinese city of Beiping (later Beijing) in 1937, for example, the city zoo managed to carry on for several years. As Japan's military situation worsened, however, the zoo spiraled into decline. In 1943, Japanese Army troops poisoned the zoo's large carnivores, and many zoo denizens died of starvation. By the war's end, China's oldest zoo contained only a few dozen animals.

22. Quoted in David Horner, "Australia in 1942: A Pivotal Year," in *Australia 1942: In the Shadow of War*, ed. Peter J. Dean (New York: Cambridge University Press, 2013), 11.

23. Meta Maclean, *The Singing Ship: An Odyssey of Evacuee Children* (Sydney: Angus and Robertson Ltd., 1941).

24. Jessica Mann, *Out of Harm's Way: The Wartime Evacuation of Children from Britain* (London: Headline, 2005), ebook.

25. "Child Evacuees in Australia (First Pictures)," *British Pathé*, https://www.youtube.com/watch?v=enrOBduJ9JU.

26. Kate Darien-Smith, "The Home Front and the American Presence in 1942," in *Australia 1942: In the Shadow of War*, ed. Peter J. Dean (New York: Cambridge University Press, 2013), 72.

27. Kim Beazley, foreword, *Australia 1942: In the Shadow of War*, ed. Peter J. Dean (New York: Cambridge University Press, 2013), xi.

28. Derek Wood with Robert Mannion, *A Tiger by the Tail: A History of Auckland Zoo 1922–1992* (Auckland: Auckland City, 1992), 60.

29. Ian Bevan, "War Strikes at Taronga," *Sydney Morning Herald*, September 30, 1942, 8.

30. Wood with Mannion, *A Tiger by the Tail*, 60.

31. "Mrs. Roosevelt Pays Call on Koalas," *Sydney Morning Herald*, September 9, 1943, 4.

32. US Army SWPA and Commonwealth Department of Information, Australia, *Australia Is Like This* (c. 1944), https://www.awm.gov.au/collection/C188878.

33. Catherine de Courcy, *The Zoo Story* (Ringwood, Victoria [Australia]: Penguin Books, 1995), 47.

314   Notes to Pages 136–146

34. "ARP in Full Swing at the Zoo," *The Daily News* (Perth), December 27, 1941, 24.

35. "Zoo Is a Menace in Wartime," *Sunday Times* (Perth), February 1, 1942, 5.

36. "Dogs' Home Ready for Air Raids: Koalas Would Leave for the Hills," *News* (Adelaide), June 5, 1942, 3; see also "Zoo Animals Will Be Shot if Bombed," *The Mail* (Adelaide), March 22, 1941, 9.

Chapter 11

1. Ian Bevan, "War Strikes at Taronga," *Sydney Morning Herald*, September 30, 1942, 7.

2. Derek Wood with Robert Mannion, *A Tiger by the Tail: A History of Auckland Zoo 1922–1992* (Auckland: Auckland City, 1992), 60.

3. Lizzie Cunningham, *The Taste of War: World War II and the Battle for Food* (New York: Penguin Press, 2012), 2, 4.

4. Cunningham, *The Taste of War*, 1.

5. Wayne Whittaker, "Soup's On at the Zoo," *Popular Mechanics* (April 1943): 82.

6. Belle J. Benchley, *My Life in a Man-Made Jungle* (Boston: Little, Brown, 1943), 30, 25, 26, 24, 25, 27, 25.

7. "Hard Times at the Zoo," *Star*, September 4, 1915.

8. *Rationing in World War II* (Washington, DC: GPO, 1946), 25.

9. Carl G. Hartman to E. S. Ward, June 20, 1944, folder 8, box 154, RU 74, SIA.

10. New York Zoological Society, *22nd Annual Report of the New York Zoological Society* (New York: 1918), 71.

11. *Reports of the Council and Auditors of the Zoological Society of London for the Year 1918* (Bungay, Suffolk: Richard Clay and Company, Ltd., 1919), 6, 5.

12. Outline of Radio Talk (1944), folder 7, box 12, RU 7293 (William M. Mann and Lucile Quarry Mann Papers, c. 1885–1981), SIA.

13. "Zoo News," *Fauna*, date unclear, 31; courtesy of the Philadelphia Zoo.

14. Stanley Field, "Report of the Chairman of the Building Committee," January 5, 1946, 1; copy available from the library of the Chicago Zoological Society (hereafter CZS).

15. "Report of the Chairman of the Building Committee for the calendar year 1944," January 15, 1945, 1; copy available in CZS.

16. "Rationing the Zoo," *Detroit Free Press* (n.d.), folder Scrapbook, 1/1945–5/1947, box 45, RU 365, SIA.

17. Roland Baetens, *The Chant of Paradise: The Antwerp Zoo: 150 Years of History* (Tielt: Lannoo, 1993), 107.

18. Catherine de Courcy, *Dublin Zoo: An Illustrated History* (Doughcloyne, Wilton, Cork: Collins Press, 2009), 141.

19. Reports of the Council and Auditors of the Zoological Society of London for the Year 1939 (Bungay, Suffolk: Richard Clay and Company, Ltd., 1940), 7.

20. Outline of Radio Talk (1944), folder 7, box 12, RU 7293, SIA.

21. "Der Zolli im Zweiten Weltkieg," Zoo Basel, https://www.zoobasel.ch/de /aktuelles/blog/3/zoo-geschichte/8/der-zolli-im-zweiten-weltkrieg/.

22. Wood, *Tiger by the Tail*, 59.

23. Benchley, *My Life in a Man-Made Jungle*, 20.

24. Outline of Radio Talk (1944).

25. "My Childhood at Whipsnade Zoo"; Sylvia Lucas, "A Zoo Put to Work," *New York Times*, December 31, 1939, 73.

26. *Reports of the Council and Auditors of the Zoological Society of London for the Year 1940* (Bungay, Suffolk: Richard Clay and Company, Ltd., 1941), 11.

27. Philip T. Robinson, *Life at the Zoo: Behind the Scenes with the Animal Doctors* (New York: Columbia University Press, 2004), 172, 171.

28. "Use of Ersatz Meat Averts Curb of Zoo Exhibits Here," *Washington Times-Herald*, January 26, 1943.

29. "Fecundity in the Chicago Zoo," *Life* 17, no. 15 (October 9, 1944): 41; "Rationing the Zoo," SIA.

30. Helmut Zedelmaier and Michael Kamp, *Hellabrunn: Gesschichte und Geschichten des Müncher Tierparks* (München: Bassermann Verlag, 2011), 74; "Rationing the Zoo," SIA.

31. "Zoo's Penguins Have Catsmeat Menu Now," *Daily Express*, October 11, 1939, located in *Newscuttings*, vol. 36, July 1939–March 1940, London Zoological Society; Albert Bourez, *Mes amies de capitivité ou le zoo dans la tourmente* (Paris: La Pensée Universelle, 1973), 19.

32. Daily Logs, folder 4/4, box 4, RG December 11, 1946; folder 9, box 2, RG 8601, Seattle Zoo Archives.

33. "Meat Ration Means Little to the Zoo," *The Oklahoman*, September 18, 1942, 13.

34. "Zoo Inmates Do Their Bit," *The Bakersfield Californian*, April 20, 1939, 3.

35. Lucile Q. Mann, "Post War Developments in European Zoos," folder 7, box 12, RU 7293, SIA.

36. Letter from Zoological Garden, Franklin Park (Boston) to Ed Bean, February 23, 1943, folder 1:3, box 112, Chicago Zoological Society, Office of the Director of the Brookfield Zoo, Edward H. Bean, Correspondence (1942), CZS.

37. Lorenz Hagenbeck, *Animals Are My Life*, trans. Alec Brown (London: Bodley Head, 1956), 214.

38. "War Making It Tough on Animals in Fascist Zoos," *Corpus Christi Caller-Times*, July 1, 1941, 4.

39. Extensive evidence is housed in the archive of the Schönbrunn Tierpark in Vienna, Austria.

40. Daniel J. Harkins to William Mann, January 10, 1943, folder 6: Care and Feeding, 1942, box 154, RU 74, SIA.

41. Robert Bean to Belle Benchley, June 15, 1943, CZS.

42. Ernest P. Walker to Robert T. Oliver, May 10, 1943, folder 9, box 154, RU 74, SIA.

43. Quoted in Robert MacMillan, "War Left Zoos in Pretty Fair Shape—Spectators Happy," *Chicago Daily News*, Sunday News, March 10, 1946, 60–61.

44. "Uncle Leo Bakes for His Pets as Rationing Comes to Zoo," *The Oklahoman*, February 5, 1943, 4.

45. "War Making It Tough on Animals in Fascist Zoos," 4.

46. Margo DeMello, *Animals and Society: An Introduction to Human-Animal Studies* (New York: Columbia University Press, 2012), 50–54.

47. Bharati Naik and Marie-Louise Gumuchian, "Danish Zoo Kills Healthy Giraffe, Feeds Body to Lions," CNN.com, February 10, 2014, https://edition.cnn.com /2014/02/09/world/europe/denmark-zoo-giraffe/index.html (accessed October 30, 2018).

316   Notes to Pages 150–155

48. "Zoo Animals Are Helpless Victims of Meat Rations," *The Oklahoman*, October 7, 1942, 13.

49. Image: "Gay's Lion Farm, El Monte," Los Angeles Library Photo Collection, Los Angeles Public Library; image and description online at https://calisphere.org/item/1144d8c87d1e800e76ed551925887916/.

50. Ward R. Walker, "Hershey Zoo Closes," *Parks and Recreation* 26 (January–February 1943): 133, 134.

51. Zedelmaier and Kamp, *Hellabrunn*, 73.

52. Evelyn Gottschlich, "Wiedereröffnung und Zerstörung (1928–1945)," in *Nilpferde an der Isar: Eine Geschichte des Tierparks Hellabrunn in München*, ed. Michael Kamp and Helmut Zedelmaier (München: Buchendorfer Verlag, 2000), 132.

53. Anna-Katharine Wöbse and Mieke Roscher, "Zootiere während des Zweiten Weltkrieges: London und Berlin 1939–1945," *Werkstattgeschischte* 56 (2010): 54.

54. Belle Benchley to Robert Bean, July 15, 1942, folder San Diego, box 14, General Correspondence 1941–1942 (S-T), CZS.

55. Ian Bevan, "War Strikes at Taronga," *Sydney Morning Herald*, September 30, 1942, 7–8.

56. Uhrmacher and Kück, "80 Jahre Tiergrotten/Zoo am Meer," 5–7.

57. "Zoo What?" (1947), clipping in scrapbook, folder Scrapbook, 1/1945–5/1947, box 45, RU 365, SIA.

58. Rebecca L. Spang, "'And They Ate the Zoo': Relating Gastronomic Exoticism in the Siege of Paris," *MLN* 107, no. 4 (September 1992): 752–73.

59. Harold Helfer, *True*, December 1946, SIA; Lucile Mann Oral History, 177.

Chapter 12

1. "Ladies Only—Ladies of the Zoo," *British Pathé*, 1941, https://www.britishpathe.com/asset/81288/.

2. Ward R. Walker, "Hershey Zoo Closes," *Parks and Recreation* 26 (January–February 1943): 134.

3. Gerhard Heindl, "Otto Antonius—ein Wissenshaftler als Tiergärtner," in *Otto Antonius: Wegbereiter der Tiergartenbiologie*, ed. Dagmar Schratter and Gerhard Heindl (Wien: Braumüller Verlag, 2010), 69.

4. Evelyn Gottschlich, "Wiedereröffnung und Zerstörung (1928–1945)," in *Nilpferde an der Isar: Eine Geschichte des Tierparks Hellabrun in München*, ed. Michael Kamp and Helmut Zedelmaier (München: Buchendorfer Verlag, 2000), 132.

5. Heindl, "Otto Antonius," 72.

6. *Reports of the Council and Auditors of the Zoological Society of London for the Year 1939* (Bungay, Suffolk: Richard Clay and Company, Ltd., 1940), 7.

7. Letter from Belle J. Benchley to Freeman M. Shelly (Philadelphia Zoo), May 2, 1942, CZS.

8. New York Zoological Society, *49th Annual Report for the Year 1944* (New York: New York Zoological Society, 1945), 62.

9. Chicago Zoological Society, *Report of the Chairman of the Building Committee*, July 20, 1944, 1; copy in the CZS; Andrea Friederici Ross, *Let the Lions Roar! The Evolution of the Brookfield Zoo* (Brookfield, IL: Chicago Zoological Society, 1997), 77.

10. Chicago Zoological Society, *Report of the Chairman of the Building Committee*, January 13, 1944, 2; copy in the CZS.

11. Helmut Zedelmaier and Michael Kamp, *Hellabrunn: Gesschichte und Geschichten des Müncher Tierparks* (München: Bassermann Verlag, 2011), 74.

12. Henry Hooper Oral History, Catalog no. 27807, Imperial War Museum, https://www.iwm.org.uk/collections/item/object/80026655.

13. "War Strikes at Taronga," *Sydney Morning Herald*, September 30, 1944, 7.

14. Ulrich Herbert, *Hitler's Foreign Workers: Enforced Labor in Germany Under the Third Reich*, trans. William Templer (Cambridge: University of Cambridge Press, 1997), note 1, 389. In addition to enslaving millions of foreigners, the Nazis also constructed "hundreds of special forced labor camps for German, Austrian, and Polish Jews." See Wolf Gruner, *Jewish Forced Labor under the Nazis: Economic Needs and Racial Aims, 1938–1944*, trans. Kathleen M. Dell'Orto (New York: Cambridge University Press, 2006), xiv.

15. Herbert, *Hitler's Foreign Workers*, 1.

16. Lorenz Hagenbeck, *Animals Are My Life*, trans. Alec Brown (London: Bodley Head, 1956), 216.

17. Mustafa Haikal and Winfried Gensch, *Der Gesang Des Orang-utans: die Geschischte des Dresdner Zoos* (Dresden: Sächsische Zeitung, 2011), 88.

18. Gary Bruce, *Through the Lion Gate: A History of the Berlin Zoo* (New York: Oxford University Press, 2017), 164.

19. Katharina Heinroth, *Mit Faltern begann's: Mein Leben mit Tieren in Breslau, München und Berlin* (München: Kindler, 1979), 132.

20. Hagenbeck, *Animals Are My Life*, 216.

21. Zedelmaier and Kamp, *Hellabrunn*, 81.

22. "European Zoos—How They Have Fared," *Fauna* 7, no. 3 (1945): 82–84.

23. Herbert, *Hitler's Foreign Workers*, 391.

24. Albert Bourez, *Mes amies de capitivité ou le zoo dans la tourmente* (Paris: La Pensée Universelle, 1973).

25. This account of Koenraad Kuiper's tenure at the zoo is based upon extensive correspondence with his son, the linguist Koenraad Kuiper, professor emeritus at the University of Canterbury in New Zealand.

26. David Grazian, *American Zoo: A Sociological Safari* (Princeton, NJ: Princeton University Press, 2015), 87.

27. J. Barrington-Johnson, *The Zoo: The Story of the London Zoo* (London: Robert Hale, 2005), 82.

28. Scrapbook (European Trip 1938), box 22, RU 7293, SIA. Although prewar zoos did not typically hire women as zookeepers, some did employ women in other roles. During the 1910s, for example, the Buenos Aires Zoo staff included several women, who worked in the zoo kitchen and cared for the baby animals. See "Jardin Zoológico: El día de un director," *Caras y Caretas* 55, no. 70 (May 14, 1912), https://babel.hathitrust.org/cgi/pt?id=uva.x030598347&seq=655. Thanks to Ashley Kerr for drawing this to my attention.

29. "A 'Bring 'Em Back Alive' Lady," *Toronto Star*, November 12, 1949. Clipping found in folder Scrapbook 1949, box 45, RU 365, SIA.

30. June Mottershead, with Penelope Dening, *Our Zoo* (London: Headline, 2014), 177.

318 Notes to Pages 160–163

31. "Delia in the Lion's Den," *Sunday Times* (Perth), May 5, 1940, 17.

32. "Girls, You Can Be a Life Guard or Zoo Keeper!," *Chicago Tribune*, November 9, 1942, 9.

33. Ian Bevan, "War Strikes at Taronga," *Sydney Morning Herald*, September 30, 1944, 7.

34. Catherine de Courcy, *Dublin Zoo: An Illustrated History* (Doughcloyne, Wilton, Cork: Collins Press, 2009), 136.

35. "Delia in the Lion's Den," 17.

36. Claire McNeilly, "Story of How Belfast's Zoo's Baby Elephant Was Kept in Backyard of Home during the Second World War Blitz to Be Made into a Film," *Belfast Telegraph* (online), November 4, 2013, https://www.belfasttelegraph.co.uk /entertainment/film-tv/news/story-of-how-belfast-zoos-baby-elephant-was-kept-in -backyard-of-home-during-second-world-war-blitz-to-be-made-into-film/29723722 .html.

37. Harry Milton Wegeforth and Neil Morgan, *It Began with a Roar: The Story of San Diego's World-Famed Zoo* (San Diego, CA: Pioneer Printers, 1953), 167.

38. "Women Drive Taxis and Work at Zoo," *The Advertiser* (Adelaide, SA), February 14, 1942, 10.

39. Catherine R. Hambley, "Problems of Zoos Are Outlined at Zonta Luncheon," *The Evening Star*, September 7, 1944, clipping in folder Scrapbook, 1941–1944, box 49, RU 365, SIA.

40. This isn't to say that women were completely invisible at zoos in Germany and Japan. At Tokyo's Ueno Zoo, for example, women served as tour guides, and Lutz Heck praised women's efforts in the aftermath of air raids. "Whether in chain passing buckets along or on burning roof or in the saving of animals," he wrote in his autobiography, "women 'played the man'—and some of them did more." See "Female Guide at Ueno Zoo," Getty Images (May 1940), https://www.gettyimages.com /detail/news-photo/fumie-imaizumi-a-guide-of-ueno-zoo-holds-a-boy-circa-may -news-photo/463591786; Lutz Heck, *Animals, My Adventure*, trans. E. W. Dickes (London: Methuen & Co., 1954), 110.

41. Mottershead, *Our Zoo*, 198.

42. Chicago Zoological Society, *Report of the Chairman of the Building Committee*, 1.

43. "She Fell in Love at Pets' Corner," *Daily Express*, December 13, 1939.

44. Elaine Tyler May, "Rosie the Riveter Gets Married," in *The War in American Culture: Society and Consciousness during World War II*, ed. Lewis A. Erenberg and Susan E. Hirsch (Chicago: University of Chicago Press, 1996), 131.

45. Daniel E. Bender, *The Animal Game: Searching for Wildness at the American Zoo* (Cambridge, MA: Harvard University Press, 2016), 240, 254.

46. The following sketch is largely drawn from three sources: Belle J. Benchley, *My Life in a Man-Made Jungle* (Boston: Little, Brown, 1943); Harry Milton Wegeforth and Neil Morgan, *It Began with a Roar: The Story of San Diego's World-Famed Zoo* (San Diego, CA: Pioneer Printers, 1953); and Margaret Poynter, *The Zoo Lady: Belle Benchley and the San Diego Zoo* (Minneapolis: Dillon Press, 1980).

47. Wegeforth and Morgan, *It Began with a Roar*, 130.

48. Benchley, *My Life in a Man-Made Jungle*, 184.

49. Benchley, *My Life in a Man-Made Jungle*, 276.

50. Benchley, *My Life in a Man-Made Jungle*, 34.

Notes to Pages 164–171   319

51. Benchley, *My Life in a Man-Made Jungle*, 18.

52. Benchley, *My Life in a Man-Made Jungle*, 5.

53. The following sketch is drawn from Katharina Heinroth's autobiography *Mit Faltern begann's: Mein Leben mit Tieren in Breslau, München und Berlin* (München: Kindler, 1979).

54. Heinroth, *Mit Faltern begann's*, 146.

55. Laura Penn, Markus Gusset, and Gerald Dick, *77 Years: The History and the Evolution of the World Association of Zoos and Aquariums* (Gland, Switzerland: WAZA, 2012), 38.

56. Kara Dixon Vuic, "Gender, the Military, and War," in *At War: The Military and American Culture in the Twentieth Century and Beyond*, ed. David Kieran and Edwin A. Martini (New Brunswick, NJ: Rutgers University Press, 2018), 204.

Chapter 13

1. Marlin Perkins to William Mann (May 17, 1943), folder 12, box 170, RU 74, SIA. The following letters derive from this same collection.

2. William Mann to Marlin Perkins (May 21, 1943).

3. Marlin Perkins to William Mann (June 30, 1943).

4. "Unemployed and Animals at Zoo," *Daily Examiner* (Grafton, NSW), March 26, 1940, 5.

5. "Brisbane Zoo Out of Question During War," *Courier-Mail* (Brisbane), October 3, 1941, 4.

6. Laura B. Rawstorn to James Carvetto (August 4, 1942).

7. This missive can be found in a collection of "freak" letters sent to the war between 1932 and 1959; see folder 7, box 249, RU 74, SIA.

8. Gary Bruce, *Through the Lion Gate: A History of the Berlin Zoo* (New York: Oxford University Press, 2017), 192.

9. "A Challenge" (1940), *British Pathé*, https://www.britishpathe.com/asset/47742/.

10. "Zoo to Hold Sing, Military Display," *The Cincinnati Post*, August 30, 1944, 18; "Dionne Quintuplets Sing for Victory at Toronto War Rally," January 15, 1943.

11. Sylvia Lucas, "A Zoo Put to Work," *New York Times*, December 31, 1939, 73.

12. On the topic of animal agency and performance, see *Animals and Agency: An Interdisciplinary Exploration*, ed. Sarah E. McFarland and Ryan Hediger (Leiden: Brill, 2009); Susan Nance, *Entertaining Elephants: Animal Agency and the Business of the American Circus* (Baltimore: Johns Hopkins University Press, 2013); and Karen Raber and Monica Mattfeld, eds., *Performing Animals: History, Agency, Theater* (University Park: Pennsylvania State University Press, 2017).

13. "Zoo Birds Go Outside in Spring with Rifles" (May 14, 1942), Sherman Grinberg Film Library, https://www.gettyimages.com/detail/video/aviary-at-the-bronx -zoo-flamingos-in-a-pond-a-bird-being-news-footage/502852313.

14. Harry Milton Wegeforth and Neil Morgan, *It Began with a Roar: The Story of San Diego's World-Famed Zoo* (San Diego, CA: Pioneer Printers, 1953), 165.

15. "Zoo Vandals Steal Eggs, Give Up Stick to Coati Mundi," *The Evansville Courier* (Indiana), April 27, 1943, 1.

16. Anna-Katharine Wöbse and Mieke Roscher, "Zootiere während des Zweiten Weltkrieges: London und Berlin 1939–1945," *Werkstattgeschischte* 56 (2010): 48.

320 Notes to Pages 171–179

17. "Ming the Giant Panda" (1940), *British Pathé*, https://www.youtube.com/watch?v=8np4_dTXiEw; "Ming's Return" (1942), *British Pathé*, https://www.youtube.com/watch?v=e7Jt2ff4QpI.

18. L. R. Brightwell, "London Zoo Sees It Through," *Animal Kingdom* 47, no. 1 (January–February 1944): 20.

19. Well into the 1900s, animal welfare societies like Our Dumb Friends League (Britain) and the Dumb Friends League (United States) regularly used the term "dumb" (lacking speech) to refer to animals, emphasizing the need for charitable humans to speak on their behalf.

20. Editorial from *The Oregonian*, Thursday, January 7, 1943, folder 4, box 152, RU 74, SIA.

21. Arthur M. Greenhall to William M. Mann (January 7, 1943), folder 4, box 152, RU 74, SIA.

22. On concerns about the moral hazards facing home-front troops, see Aaron Hiltner, *Taking Liberties, Taking Leave: American Troops on the World War II Home Front* (Chicago: University of Chicago Press, 2020).

23. Mayumi Itoh, *Japanese Wartime Zoo Policy: The Silent Victims of World War* (New York: Palgrave Macmillan, 2010), 27.

24. "The Zoo and the Forces," *The Times* (London), January 20, 1940, 4.

25. Belle Benchley, "The Zoo and Its Defense Activities," *Zoonooz* 14, no. 14 (February 1942): 7.

26. "Carrying on at the Zoo," *The Times* (London), October 22, 1940, 6.

27. Alex Downs Jr., "Zoos in War Time," *Fauna*, 52.

28. Bruce, *Through the Lion Gate*, 189.

29. Belle Benchley, "The Zoo and Its Defense Activities," *Zoonooz* 14, no. 14 (February 1942): 7. Interestingly, zoo leaders in the United States would return to this argument in the aftermath of the terrorist attack of September 11, 2001. In an article written for supporters, Mike Waller of the Milwaukee Zoo attested to the "the key role that the zoo, and other parks and open spaces play in times of stress. Since mid-September, many of you have told us how the zoo has become a refuge, a peaceful, safe sanctuary, not just for animals, but for all of us during an increasingly uncertain time." Mike Waller, "Dear Members," *@thezoo* (Winter 2001): 4, copy in the Milwaukee Zoo Archives.

30. R. J. Dunham, "Our Jobs," *8th Annual Report* (1942), Chicago Parks District.

31. L. R. Brightwell, "The Zoo Carries On," *The Field*, November 18, 1939.

32. Bruce, *Through the Lion Gate*, 231.

33. "Backyard Livestock," *The Times* (London), 31 January 1940, 11; Reports of the Council and Auditors of the Zoological Society of London for the Year 1939 (Bungay, Suffolk: Richard Clay and Company, Ltd., 1940); *National War-Time Utility Exhibition* (London Zoo, 1940).

34. Garret G. Epply, "Service Men in the Out of Doors," USO Outdoor Programs.

35. New York Zoological Society, *48th Annual Report for the Year 1943* (New York: 1944), 3, 5, 19; New York Zoological Society, *49th Annual Report for the Year 1944* (New York: 1945), 23.

36. New York Zoological Society, *48th Annual Report for the Year 1943*, 3; William Beebe, "Bathysphere Goes to War," *Animal Kingdom* 46, no. 3 (1943), 71; "Bathysphere

Used in War Research; Beebe Device Was of Service in Depth-Charge Experiments, Zoo Report Reveals," *New York Times*, January 12, 1944, 25.

37. William Bridges, "The Electric Eel Went to War," *Animal Kingdom* (March–April 1946): 73–75, 88.

38. Daniel E. Bender, *The Animal Game: Searching for Wildness at the American Zoo* (Cambridge, MA: Harvard University Press, 2016), 216.

39. "What's New at the Zoo," *Washington Post*, September 22, 1945.

40. R. A. Glennie, "Diggers Find Peace in Cairo Zoo," *New Castle Morning Herald and Miners' Advocate*, October 8, 1940.

41. PFC John L. Awkward to Superintendent Zoological Park, May 20, 1945, folder 11, box 154, RU 74, SIA; W. M. Mann to Private John Awkward, USMCR, May 30, 1945, folder 11, box 154, RU 74, SIA.

42. James Fisher, "The Zoo's Peace Aims," *Fauna* 5, no. 9 (February 1941): 13.

43. New York Zoological Society, *Forty-Seventh Annual Report* (New York: New York Zoological Society, 1942), 18.

Chapter 14

1. Our Special Correspondent, "13 Air-Minded Monkeys," *The Times* (London), October 15, 1942, 4.

2. Adolf Hitler, "Speech to the Reichstag, 1 September 1939," Yad Vashem Shoah Resource Center, https://www.yadvashem.org/odot_pdf/Microsoft%20Word%20-%203328.pdf.

3. John Falter, "'Give 'em the stuff to fight with.' Sacrifice for freedom" (1942), Hoover Institution Library & Archives, poster collection, https://digitalcollections.hoover.org/objects/40665/give-em-the-stuff-to-fight-with-sacrifice-for-freedom.

4. J. Stalin, "Order of the Day of the Supreme Commander in Chief, No. 95" (February 23, 1943), in J. V. Stalin, *On the Great Patriotic War of the Soviet Union* (Moscow: Foreign Languages Publishing House, 1946), 97, available at http://marx2mao.com/Stalin/GPW46.html.

5. Winston Churchill, "Speech to the Allied Delegates" (June 12, 1941), Jewish Virtual Library, https://www.jewishvirtuallibrary.org/churchill-speech-to-the-allied-delegates-june-1941.

6. Leszek Solski, "Zoological Gardens of Central-Eastern Europe and Russia," in *Zoo and Aquarium History: Ancient Animal Collections to Zoological Gardens*, ed. Vernon N. Kisling Jr. (Boca Raton, FL: CRC Press, 2001), 134–35.

7. Dimiter Kenarov, "Askania-Nova: The Ukrainian Serengeti," *Pulitzer Center*, April 7, 2015, https://pulitzercenter.org/stories/askania-nova-ukrainian-serengeti.

8. Solski, "Zoological Gardens of Central-Eastern Europe and Russia," 136.

9. Iryna S. Borodai, "Professor O. O. Brauners (1857–1941)—Founder of the Theoretical Foundations of Animal Science, Organizer of Experimental Work in Livestock of Ukraine," *History of Science and Biographical Studies* 2, no. 5 (2020), doi.org/10.31073/istnauka202002-05.

10. Solski, "Zoological Gardens of Central-Eastern Europe and Russia," 139.

11. Solski, "Zoological Gardens of Central-Eastern Europe and Russia," 137.

12. Tracy McDonald, "The Moscow Zoo in the Second World War and Its Aftermath, 1941–1950," unpublished paper, 13, 15.

13. Solski, "Zoological Gardens of Central-Eastern Europe and Russia," 165.

14. McDonald, "The Moscow Zoo," 5, 3.

15. Solski, "Zoological Gardens of Central-Eastern Europe and Russia," 138.

16. McDonald, "The Moscow Zoo," 11, 7.

17. Todd Tucker, *The Great Starvation Experiment: Ancel Keys and the Men Who Starved for Science* (Minneapolis: University of Minnesota Press, 2007), 8.

18. Darra Goldstein, "Women under Siege: Leningrad 1941–1942," in *From Betty Crocker to Feminist Food Studies: Critical Perspectives on Women and Food*, ed. Arlene Volski Avakian and Barbara Haber (Amherst: University of Massachusetts Press, 2005), 150–53.

19. Tucker, *The Great Starvation Experiment*, 8.

20. "The Leningrad Zoo," trans. Linsey Greytak, found at "The Leningrad Zoo: Under the Tsars, during World War II, and Today," Museum Studies Abroad (April 11, 2021), https://museumstudiesabroad.org/leningrad-zoo-blockade/; McDonald, "The Moscow Zoo," 5.

21. Natalia Mihailova, "If Animals Could Speak . . . ," *GB Times*, February 4, 2014.

22. Tim Brinkhof, "The Creatures That Devoured Leningrad," *History Today*, May 28, 2020, https://www.historytoday.com/miscellanies/creatures-devoured -leningrad.

23. Mihailova, "If Animals Could Speak . . ."; "The Leningrad Zoo."

24. "The Leningrad Zoo."

25. Goldstein, "Women under Siege," 3.

26. Homer Smith, *Black Man in Red Russia* (Chicago: Johnson Publishing Company, 1964), 113.

27. Goldstein, "Women under Siege," 143, 155.

28. My analysis of what is sometimes called the Great Zoo Massacre at Tokyo's Ueno Zoo draws from several sources, chief among them Frederick S. Litten, "Starving the Elephants: The Slaughter of Animals in Wartime Tokyo's Ueno Zoo," *The Asia-Pacific Journal* 38-3-09 (September 21, 2009); Mayumi Itoh, *Japanese Wartime Zoo Policy: The Silent Victims of World War* (New York: Palgrave Macmillan, 2010); and Ian Jared Miller, *The Nature of the Beasts: Empire and Exhibition at the Tokyo Zoo* (Berkeley: University of California Press, 2021).

29. Litten, "Starving the Elephants," 2, 4, 5.

30. Quoted in Litten, "Starving the Elephants," 6.

31. Litten, "Starving the Elephants," 7.

32. Litten, "Starving the Elephants," 7–8; Itoh, *Japanese Wartime Zoo Policy*, 43–47.

33. Litten, "Starving the Elephants," 8, quoted on 9.

34. Litten, "Starving the Elephants," 11, 10–13; Itoh, *Japanese Wartime Zoo Policy*, 50; for a broader discussion of the elephants' deaths in context, see Miller, *The Nature of the Beasts*, 120–62.

35. Brinkhof, "The Creatures That Devoured Leningrad."

36. Litten, "Starving the Elephants," 9; see also Miller, *The Nature of the Beasts*, 100, 131.

37. Itoh, *Japanese Wartime Zoo Policy*, 188.

38. Quoted in Emily Van Buskirk, "Recovering the Past for the Future: Guilt,

Memory, and Lidiia Ginzburg's *Notes of a Blockade Person*," *Slavic Review* 69, no. 2 (Summer 2010): 281.

39. Yukio Tsuchiya, *Faithful Elephants: A True Story of Animals, People, and War*, trans. Tomoko Tsuchiya Dykes (Boston: Houghton Mifflin Company, 1988), n.p.

Chapter 15

1. This account is drawn from several sources: Eric Rentschler, *The Ministry of Illusion: Nazi Cinema and Its Afterlife* (Cambridge, MA: Harvard University Press, 1996), 283; Evelyn Gottschlich, "Wiedereröffnung und Zerstörung (1928–1945)," in *Nilpferde an der Isar: Eine Geschichte des Tierparks Hellabrunn in München*, ed. Michael Kamp and Helmut Zedelmaier (München: Buchendorfer Verlag, 2000), 134; and an especially detailed Wikipedia article: "Gesprengte Gitter," https://de.wikipedia.org/wiki/Gesprengte_Gitter.

2. For one of the earliest and most eloquent articulations of such sentiments, see Vera Brittain's short essay "Massacre by Bombing," reprinted in *Fellowship* 61, no. 5–6 (May/June 1995): 5–6.

3. Even today, despite millions of dollars spent fine-tuning US targeting systems, the practice of killing from above frequently resembles little more than state-sponsored murder (or, to be generous, manslaughter). On August 29, 2021, a missile launched from an American drone struck a white car in the Afghan capital of Kabul, killing ten, including seven children. The Department of Defense initially defended the attack as a "righteous strike" against an ISIS-K operative moving containers filled with explosives. Within days, however, the DOD was forced to admit the truth: the driver, "Zamarai Ahmandi, was a longtime aid worker for a U.S.-based group and was hauling water cans for his family." Alex Horton, Joyce Sohyn Lee, Elyse Samuels, and Karoun Demirjian, "U.S. Military Admits 'Horrible Mistake' in Kabul Drone Strike That Killed 10 Afghans," *Washington Post*, September 17, 2021, https://www.washingtonpost.com/national-security/2021/09/17/drone-strike-kabul-afghanistan/.

4. Jörg Friedrich, *The Fire: The Bombing of Germany, 1940–1945*, trans. Allison Brown (New York: Columbia University Press, 2006), 18.

5. I discuss the *Blitzkrieg*'s effects on European zoos at length in chapter seven.

6. Diane Ackerman, *The Zookeeper's Wife: A War Story* (New York: W. W. Norton & Co., 2007), 61.

7. Scholars have spent decades analyzing the history and ethics of strategic bombing. While some insist upon subtle differences between various types of air warfare (area bombing, morale bombing, tactical bombing, precision bombing, terror bombing, etc.), others use "strategic bombing" as an umbrella term to describe a growing willingness, on the part of military leaders, to view civilians as legitimate targets of aerial attack. I've chosen the latter route, not only out of convenience but also because I believe it best explains how urban zoos wound up in the line of fire. Nuanced analyses of the theory and practice of strategic bombing include Michael S. Sherry, *The Rise of American Air Power: The Creation of Armageddon* (New Haven, CT: Yale University Press, 1987); Friedrich, *The Fire*; A. C. Grayling, *Among the Dead Cities: Is the Targeting of Civilians in War Ever Justified?* (London: Bloomsbury, 2006); and Kenneth P. Werrell, *Death from the Heavens: A History of Strategic Bombing* (Annapolis, MD: Naval Institute Press, 2009).

324 Notes to Pages 202–208

8. Brian Burridge, "The Trenchant Memorial Lecture," *Air Power Review* 8, no. 1 (Spring 2005): 9; Trenchard, quoted in Friedrich, *The Fire*, 55.

9. The term "morale bombing" is not uniquely euphemistic in this regard. See John M. Kinder, "The Embodiment of War: Bodies for, in, and after War," in *At War: The Military and American Culture in the Twentieth Century and Beyond*, ed. David Kieran and Edwin A. Martini (New Brunswick, NJ: Rutgers University Press, 2018), 217–39.

10. Carol Harris, *Blitz Diary: Life under Fire in World War II* (Cheltenham, UK: The History Press, 2010), 59–187.

11. Anna-Katharine Wöbse and Mieke Roscher, "Zootiere während des Zweiten Weltkrieges: London und Berlin 1939–1945," *Werkstattgeschischte* 56 (2010): 53.

12. Peter Pollard, "Chessington Memory" (unpublished), October 2, 2015, World War Zoo Gardeners Project, https://worldwarzoogardener1939.wordpress.com/2015/10/02/chessington-zoo-blitzed-2-october-1940-eyewitness-accounts/.

13. "Animals in Air Raids," *New York Times*, November 10, 1940, 86.

14. See Angus Calder, *The Myth of the Blitz* (London: Jonathon Cape, 1991); and Darren Kelsey, "The Myth of the 'Blitz Spirit' in British Newspaper Responses to the July 7th Bombings," *Social Semiotics* 23, no. 1 (2013): 83–99.

15. "There's No Danger of Bombs Opening the Cages," *The War Illustrated*, November 15, 1940, 527.

16. W. G. Sebald, *On the Natural History of Destruction*, trans. Anthea Bell (New York: Modern Library, 2004), 3.

17. Quoted in Sebald, *On the Natural History of Destruction*, 19.

18. Sir Arthur T. Harris, *Despatch on War Operations: 23rd February 1942 to 8th May 1945* (London: Frank Cass), 7.

19. This incident took place on December 27, 1939. Ironically, about half of Bremerhaven's animal deaths in the war resulted not from bombs but from a lack of fresh fish. Helmut P. Uhrmacher and Heike Kück, "80 Jahre Tiergrotten/Zoo am Meer," *Begegnungen der besonderen Art . . . der Zoo am Meer feiert seinen 80. Geburtstag*, https://zoo-am-meer-bremerhaven.de/files/seiten/unser-zoo/historie/80jahre_zoo_am_meer_lowres.pdf.

20. Lutz Heck, *Animals—My Adventure*, trans. E. W. Dickes (London: Methuen and Co., 1954), 93.

21. Gottschlich, "Wiedereröffnung und Zerstörung (1928–1945)," 134.

22. Heck, *Animals—My Adventure*, 93.

23. Sebald, *On the Natural History of Destruction*, 26–28.

24. Friedrich, *The Fire*, 167.

25. Friedrich, *The Fire*, 96.

26. "Famous Hamburg Zoo Lost Heavily in Raids; Main Problem Now Is Restocking and Food," *New York Times*, June 17, 1946, 23.

27. Heck, *Animals—My Adventure*, 93–94.

28. Gerhard Heindl, "Otto Antonius—ein Wissenshaftler als Tiergärtner," ed. Dagmar Schratter and Gerhard Heindl, *Otto Antonius: Wegbereiter der Tiergartenbiologie* (Wien: Braumüller Verlag, 2010), 74.

29. Anna-Katharina Wöbse and Mieke Roscher, "Zootiere während des Zweiten Weltkrieges: London und Berlin 1939–1945," *Werkstattgeschischte* 56 (2010): 56.

30. Heindl, "Otto Antonius," 74.

Notes to Pages 208–213   325

31. Heck, *Animals—My Adventure*, 96, 97–98, 101.

32. Heck, *Animals—My Adventure*, 130; letter from Heck to Antonius, Schönbrunn Zoo Archive.

33. Heck, *Animals—My Adventure*, 130.

34. Heck, *Animals—My Adventure*, 106.

35. "Au zoo de Berlin le gorille se réchauffe dans un abri de fortune . . . ," *L'Ouest-Éclair* (Caen ed.), December 9, 1943, 1.

36. Heck, *Animals—My Adventure*, 107.

37. Quoted in George E. Hopkins, "Bombing and the American Conscience During World War II," *The Historian* 28, no. 3 (May 1966): 451.

38. Little more than a year after the US entrance into World War II, Franklin Roosevelt's early concerns about the morality of targeting of cities had all but disappeared. Citing the Luftwaffe's firebombing of Poland, the Netherlands, and elsewhere, he committed US air forces to a policy of violent retaliation: "Yes—the Nazis and the Fascists have asked for it—and they are going to get it." Quoted in Hopkins, "Bombing and the American Conscience," 451.

39. Throughout the war's later years, Hitler's V1 and V2 programs continued to harass British citizens, their terror amplified by the utter randomness of their sites of destruction. Though British zoos experienced less destruction than many other cultural institutions, they did not emerge fully unscathed. The ZSL's 1944 report noted that Regent's Park "suffered very severely during the summer and autumn, both directly and indirectly, from the effects of flying bombs." One fell in the zoo garden, while another crashed in the nearby vicinity, damaging an aviary, the hippo house, and other buildings. Frank Foster, a circus performer who worked at the Chessington Zoo during the war years, witnessed a similar episode that same year, when a Doodlebug (V1 flying bomb) detonated just above the zoo's polar bear cage. The explosion ripped the exhibit's door off its hinges, tore open the monkey cage, and blew off the leg of an ostrich. (It landed ten yards away.) "Confused by the din and shock, I was certain the polar bear would be dead," he recalled not long after the war's end. The bear spent the next five days "lying prostrate and dejected on his slab, obviously suffering from shell shock," though it eventually recovered. Frank Foster, *Pink Coat, Spangles and Sawdust* (London: Stanley Paul, 1949), 158, 159.

Chapter 16

1. "Anti-Nazi Zoo," reprinted in the *Fort Worth Star-Telegram*, July 14, 1944, 6.

2. Saskia Hansen and Julia Zarankin, "A Founding Myth for the Netherlands: The Second World War and the Victimization of Dutch Jews," in *Reflections on the Holocaust*, ed. Julia Zarankin (New York: Humanity in Action, 2011).

3. Stephan Wilkinson, "The French Resistance: How Resistant?," *H-NET*, March 2011, https://www.historynet.com/french-resistance-resistant.htm.

4. On the assassination of Heydrich and its aftermath, see Peter Demetz, *Prague in Danger: The Years of German Occupation, 1939–45: Memories and History, Terror and Resistance, Theater and Jazz, Film and Poetry, Politics and War* (New York: Farrar, Straus & Giroux, 2008).

5. Interview with Robert Rene Boiteux-Burdett, http://www.iwm.org.uk/collections /item/object/80009634.

6. Adéla Macková, "František Vladimír Foit a Jiří Baum," September 24, 2010, https://plus.rozhlas.cz/frantisek-vladimir-foit-a-jiri-baum-6647192.

7. Thierry Borrel, *Achille Urbain (1884–1957), de la gloire à l'oubli: un vétérinaire pasteurien au Muséum national d'Histoire naturelle*, Université Claude Bernard—Lyon I, 2014, 537–39.

8. Diane Ackerman, *The Zookeeper's Wife: A War Story* (New York: W. W. Norton & Co., 2007), 93, 128, 314, 115, 169, 314.

9. Maartin Th. Frankenhuis, *Overleven in de dierentuin: De oorlogsjaren van Artis en andere parken* (Rotterdam: Uitgevers, 2010), 57, 59–60, 44.

10. Frankenhuis, *Overleven in de dierentuin*, 59, 79, 52, 53.

11. Frankenhuis, *Overleven in de dierentuin*, 92, 49, 58.

12. Frankenhuis, *Overleven in de dierentuin*, 57, 47.

13. Frankenhuis, *Overleven in de dierentuin*, 89.

14. Frankenhuis, *Overleven in de dierentuin*, 94–97.

15. Frankenhuis, *Overleven in de dierentuin*, 91; "Duifje van den Brink," *JOODS-AMSTERDAM*, March 18, 2021, https://www.joodsamsterdam.nl/duif-van-der-brink/.

16. On surveillance at the zoo, see Irus Braverman, *Zooland: The Institution of Captivity* (Stanford, CA: Stanford Law Books, 2013).

17. Lotte Strauss, *Over the Green Hill: A German Jewish Memoir, 1913–1943* (New York: Fordham University Press, 1999), 76–77, 77.

18. Quoted in Ackerman, *The Zookeeper's Wife*, 241.

19. "Oral History Interview with Benjamin Reed," March 1, 1990, US Holocaust Memorial Museum Collection, https://collections.ushmm.org/search/catalog/irn 504646.

20. See, for example, Brett T. Litz, "Resilience in the Aftermath of War Trauma: A Critical Review and Commentary," *Interface Focus*, 4:20140008, https://dx.doi.org /10.1098/rsfs20140008; Lisa A. Kirschenbaum, "The Meaning of Resilience: Soviet Children in World War II," *Journal of Interdisciplinary History* 47, no. 4 (Spring 2017): 521–35; Emily Underwood, "In War Zones and Refugee Camps, Researchers Are Putting Resilience Interventions to the Test," *Science*, February 28, 2018, https://www .science.org/content/article/war-zones-and-refugee-camps-researchers-are -putting-resilience-interventions-test.

21. Andrea Beetz et al., "Psychosocial and Psychophysiological Effects of Human-Animal Interactions: The Possible Role of Oxytocin," *Frontiers in Psychology* 3, no. 234 (July 2012): 11, doi:10.3389/fpsyg.2012.00234.

22. Hal Herzog, *Some We Love, Some We Hate, Some We Eat: Why It's So Hard to Think Straight about Animals* (New York: Harper, 2010), 82–85; Lian Hill, Helen Winefiel, and Pauleen Bennett, "Are Stronger Bonds Better? Examining the Relationship between the Human–Animal Bond and Human Social Support, and Its Impact on Resilience," *Australian Psychologist* 55, no. 6 (2020): 729–38, doi:10.1111/ ap.12466.

23. Joann M. Lindenmayer, "Animals as Key Promoters of Human Resilience," *African Health Sciences* 8, no. S (2008): 46; Jennifer W. Applebaum, Evan L. MacLean, and Shelby E. McDonald, "Love, Fear, and the Human-Animal Bond: On Adversity and Multispecies Relationships," *Comprehensive Psychoneuroendicrinology* 7, no. 100071 (August 2021), doi:10.1016/j.cpnec.2021.100071.

Notes to Pages 220–224   327

24. Of the many books on the history of the incarceration of Japanese Americans during World War II, useful starting points include Lawson Fusao Inada, ed., *Only What We Could Carry: The Japanese American Internment Experience* (Berkeley, CA: Heyday Books, 2000); and Roger Daniels, *Prisoners Without Trial* (New York: Hill & Wang, 2004).

25. "Salt Lake City Governors' Meeting," *Densho Encyclopedia*, October 8, 2020, https://encyclopedia.densho.org/Salt_Lake_City_governors%27_meeting/.

26. Natasha Varner, "Sold, Damaged, Stolen, Gone: Japanese American Property Loss During World War II," *Densho*, April 4, 2017, https://densho.org/catalyst/sold-damaged-stolen-gone-japanese-american-property-loss-wwii/.

27. "At 92, a Japanese-American Reflects on the Lessons of Internment Camps," *Up First*, December 8, 2016, https://www.npr.org/2016/12/07/504602293/at-92-a-japanese-american-reflects-on-the-hardships-of-internment-camps.

28. Etelka Lehochzky, "George Takai Recalls Time in an American Internment Camp in 'They Called Us Enemy,'" NPR, July 17, 2019, https://www.npr.org/2019/07/17/742558996/george-takei-recalls-time-in-an-american-internment-camp-in-they-called-us-enemy#:~:text=%22I%20was%20old%20enough%20by,sent%20there%2C%22%20he%20remembers.

29. Email forwarded from Sam Mihara to author, April 24, 2018.

30. "Shig Yabu Interview," February 23, 2010, *Densho Digital Archive*, Densho ID: denshovh-yshig-01.

31. "Shig Yabu Interview," 18.

32. Email forwarded from Sam Mihara.

33. US War Relocation Authority, General information bulletin (Cody, WY), series 12, September 17, 1942, California State University Japanese American Digitalization Project, https://cdm16855.contentdm.oclc.org/digital/collection/p16855coll4/id/9468.

34. Transcript, episode 3, *Look Toward the Mountain* podcast, https://www.heartmountain.org/wp-content/uploads/2021/02/LOOK-TOWARD-THE-MOUNTAIN-Episode-3-A-New-Normal-Transcript.pdf.

35. Manzanar National Historic Site, Museum Management Plan, Department of the Interior, National Park Service, Pacific West Region, 2011, 20; see also Albert Marrin, *Uprooted: The Japanese American Experience During World War II* (New York: Knopf, 2016), 118, and "Zoo May Be Started," *Manzanar Free Press* 1, no. 22, June 11, 1942, 3.

36. Marrin, *Uprooted*, 118.

37. "Letter, 1944 December 6, New York to Miss Estelle Ishigo, Heart Mt., Wyoming," Charles E. Young Research Library, Library Special Collections, UCLA, https://oac.cdlib.org/ark:/13030/hb7q2nb7wc/?brand=oac4; "Letter, 1944 November 9, Cheyenne, Wyo. to Estelle Ishigo, Heart Mountain, Wyo," Charles E. Young Research Library, Library Special Collections, UCLA, https://oac.cdlib.org/ark:/13030/hb496nb5gn/?brand=oac4.

38. Email from Hiroshi Hoshizaki to author.

39. Email from Takashi Hoshizaki to author. For more on his imprisonment and life after the war, see "Takashi Hoshizaki Interview," July 28, 2010, *Densho Digital Archive*, Densho ID: denshovh-htakashi_2-01.

40. "Shig Yabu Interview."

328 Notes to Pages 225–233

41. "Shig Yabu Interview." In 2007, Shig Yabu and illustrator Willie Ito published *Hello Maggie* (Camarillo, CA: Yabitoon Books, 2007), a children's book about the bird's life at Heart Mountain.

Chapter 17

1. Chester Marshall with Ray "Hap" Halloran, *Hap's War* (Collierville, TN: Global Press, 1998), 37.

2. I've derived additional details of Hap's confinement from his ex-POW biography and an oral history he gave to the Admiral Nimitz Museum and the University of North Texas Oral History Collection in 1998.

3. Marshall with Halloran, *Hap's War*, 47.

4. Marshall with Halloran, *Hap's War*, 47, 51.

5. San Antonio Zoological Society Inc., circular: "For sale or exchange and wish to acquire," March 1, 1944.

6. Leszek Solski and Harro Strehlow, *150 Jahre OO Breslau/150 lat Zoo Wrocław* (Wrocław: Zoo Wrocław, 2015), 126–27.

7. Harry Milton Wegeforth and Neil Morgan, *It Began with a Roar: The Story of San Diego's World-Famed Zoo* (San Diego, CA: Pioneer Printers, 1953), 174.

8. Mary Louise Roberts, *What Soldiers Do: Sex and the American GI in World War II France* (Chicago: University of Chicago Press, 2013), 27.

9. "Belgian Collaborators and German Troops Are Rounded Up in Antwerp" (September 1944), Imperial War Museum, https://collections.ushmm.org/search /catalog/irn1004406.

10. Roland Baetens, *The Chant of Paradise: The Antwerp Zoo: 150 Years of History* (Tielt: Lannoo, 1993), 107.

11. Anne Applebaum, "The Agony of Liberation," *National Post* (Toronto), November 18, 2013, https://nationalpost.com/opinion/anne-applebaum-the-agony-of -liberation.

12. "The War Years in the Zoo," personal memo, author's collection.

13. Memorialized in Cornelius Ryan's 1974 account *A Bridge Too Far* (and its film adaption a few years later), the operation ended when British paratroopers failed to secure the Arnhem Road Bridge across the Lower Rhine, thwarting their entry into the city. The northern end of the bridge was, and still is, less than three miles from the entrance of Burgers' Zoo.

14. WeBuzz by AnimalConcepts, episode 44 ("Jan van Hooff on Growing Up in a Zoo, Burgers' Zoo in World War II, and How Connecting with a Drill Shaped His Career"), May 22, 2021, https://www.animalconcepts.eu/blog/ibuzzjanvanhooff.

15. "Reinier van Hooff, dir. Burgers' Zoo, Arnhem WWII (1935–1964)," short biographical account courtesy of Burgers' Zoo, Arnhem; Johanna van Nieustadt van Hooff, *Burgers' Zoo 1913–2013: een familiebedrijf met passie voor dieren* (Burgers' Zoo: Arnhem, NL, 2013).

16. "Reinier van Hooff, dir. Burgers' Zoo, Arnhem WWII (1935–1964)."

17. Mayumi Itoh, *Japanese Wartime Zoo Policy: The Silent Victims of World War II* (New York: Palgrave Macmillan, 2011), 133.

18. Helmut Zedelmaier and Michael Kamp, *Hellabrunn: Gesschichte und Geschichten des Müncher Tierparks* (München: Bassermann Verlag, 2011), 81.

Notes to Pages 233–241   329

19. Gerhard Heindl, "Otto Antonius—ein Wissenshaftler als Tiergärtner," in *Otto Antonius: Wegbereiter der Tiergartenbiologie*, ed. Dagmar Schratter and Gerhard Heindl (Wien: Braumüller Verlag, 2010), 76.

20. See, for example, Gary Bruce, *Through the Lion Gate: A History of the Berlin Zoo* (New York: Oxford University Press, 2017), 199.

21. Itoh, *Japanese Wartime Zoo Policy*, 137.

22. Someone at the scene shot the gibbon—whether it was Sailer-Jackson, another zoo employee, or a soldier remains unclear. Sailer-Jackson's experience on the night of the Dresden firebombing is described in greater detail in Mustafa Haikal and Winfried Gensch, *Der Gesang Des Orang-utans: die Geschischte des Dresdner Zoos* (Dresden: Sächsische Zeitung, 2011).

23. Mickey Z., "Anti War, Animal Rights, Collective Liberation," *Counterpunch*, July 21, 2014, https://www.counterpunch.org/2014/07/21/anti-war-animal-rights -collective-liberation/; Thomas Goodrich, "Dresden, 1945," *Counter-Currents*, February 12, 2014, https://counter-currents.com/2014/02/dresden-1945/.

24. Solski and Strehlow, *150 Jahre OO Breslau*, 128–32.

25. On the Berlin Zoo in the Battle of Berlin, see Cornelius Ryan, *The Last Battle* (New York: Touchstone, 1966/95), 170, 408, 484.

26. Kevin Prenger, "Een dierentuin tussen de puinhopen van nazi-Duitsland," an excerpt of *Oorlogszone Zoo* (War Zone Zoo), November 9, 2021, *Historiek.net*, https:// historiek.net/een-dierentuin-tussen-de-puinhopen-van-nazi-duitsland/55688/.

27. "A Report on the Berlin Zoo," 1945/46, 11; author's collection.

28. On the firebombing of Tokyo, see Michael S. Sherry, *The Rise of American Air Power: The Creation of Armageddon* (New Haven, CT: Yale University Press, 1987), 273–88. Kato quote in Sherry, *Rise of American Air Power*, 276.

29. Richard Rhodes, *The Making of the Atomic Bomb* (New York: Simon & Schuster, 1986), 599.

30. Itoh, *Japanese Wartime Zoo Policy*, 54.

31. Itoh, *Japanese Wartime Zoo Policy*, 55.

32. HistoryNet Staff, "Michie Hattori: Eyewitness to the Nagasaki Atomic Bomb Blast," June 12, 2006, https://www.historynet.com/michie-hattori-eyewitness-to-the -nagasaki-atomic-bomb-blast/.

Chapter 18

1. Derrick Sington, *Belsen Uncovered* (London: Duckworth, 1946), 15–16.

2. On the many institutions and systems that made the Holocaust "thinkable," see Zygmunt Bauman, *Modernity and the Holocaust* (Ithaca, NY: Cornell University Press, 1989/2001), 13–14.

3. Arnold Arluke and Boria Sax, "Understanding Nazi Animal Protection and the Holocaust," *Anthrozoös* 5, no. 1 (1992): 10, 14.

4. Arluke and Sax, "Understanding Nazi Animal Protection and the Holocaust," 26.

5. John C. McManus, *Hell before Their Very Eyes: American Soldiers Liberate Concentration Camps in Germany, April 1945* (Baltimore: Johns Hopkins University Press, 2015), 72, 127.

6. Charles Patterson, *Eternal Treblinka: Our Treatment of Animals and the Holocaust* (New York: Lantern Books, 2002), 44.

330   Notes to Pages 241–246

7. Arluke and Sax, "Understanding Nazi Animal Protection and the Holocaust," 25.

8. Gedenkstätte Buchenwald, ed., *Buchenwald Concentration Camp 1937–1945: A Guide to the Permanent Historical Exhibition*, compiled by Harry Stein, trans. Judith Rosenthal (Wallstein Verlag: 2004), 89–90.

9. Patterson, *Eternal Treblinka*, 47.

10. Quoted in Dirk Rupnow, "Annihilating—Preserving—Remembering: The 'Aryanization' of Jewish History and Memory During the Holocaust," in *Cultural Memories: The Geographical Point of View*, ed. Peter Meusburger, Michael Heffernan, and Edgar Wunder (Dordrecht: Springer, 2011), 192.

11. Gary Bruce, *Through the Lion Gate: A History of the Berlin Zoo* (New York: Oxford University Press, 2017), 173–74.

12. Bruce, *Through the Lion Gate*, 165.

13. Michael Wang, "Heavy Breeding," *Cabinet* 45 (Spring 2012), https://www.cabinetmagazine.org/issues/45/wang.php.

14. Kai Artinger, "Lutz Heck: Der 'Vater der Rominter Ure,'" *Die Geschte Berlins: Verein für de Geschite Berlins e.V., gegr. 1865*, available at www.diegeschichteberlins.de.

15. Not all German concentration camps were aimed solely at the extermination of Europe's Jewish population. Early camps functioned largely as makeshift prisons to deal with those who, by dint of their actions or identities, resisted the Nazi regime. Over time, facilities like those at Dachau and Buchenwald evolved into "vast slave labor markets," in Gitta Sereny's words (99). Survival at such places was slim. Millions died from overwork, starvation, disease, and murder. Beginning in December 1941, however, Hitler's regime established a different kind of camp, one whose "sole purpose" was to kill people as quickly and efficiently as possible. All six of the extermination camps—Chelmno, Belsec, Sobibor, Treblinka, Majdanek, and Auschwitz-Birkenau—were located in occupied Poland, where they carried out their murderous work largely out of public view. By the war's end, staff at the extermination camps had slaughtered an estimated 2.7 million people, the vast majority of them Polish Jews. Gitta Sereny, *Into That Darkness: From Mercy Killing to Mass Murder* (New York: McGraw-Hill, 1974), 99. For more on the Nazi extermination camps (or death camps), see Yitzhak Arad, *Belzec, Sobibor, Treblinka: The Operation Reinhard Death Camps* (Bloomington: Indiana University Press, 1999); and Laurence Rees, *Auschwitz: A New History* (New York: PublicAffairs, 2006).

16. Vassily Grossman, *The Years of War (1941–1945)* (Moscow: Foreign Languages Publishing House, 1946), 386.

17. Richard Glazar—Treblinka, Film, Accession Number: 1996.166, RG Number: RG-60, US Holocaust Memorial Museum.

18. Chris Webb and Michael Chocholatý, *The Treblinka Death Camp: History, Biographies, Remembrance* (Stuttgart: Ibidem-Verlag, 2014), 77.

19. Sereny, *Into That Darkness*, 166.

20. Sereny, *Into That Darkness*, 148.

21. Transcript of the *Shoah* interview with Franz Suchomel (German translation by Uta Wallers, Summer 2012), 50.

22. Sereny, *Into That Darkness*, 200.

23. Quoted in Mark Celinscak, *Distance from the Belsen Heap: Allied Forces and the Liberation of a Nazi Concentration Camp* (Toronto: University of Toronto Press, 2015), 62.

Notes to Pages 246–250   331

24. Celinscak, *Distance from the Belsen Heap*, 62, 64.

25. Quoted in Ben Shepherd, *After Daybreak: The Liberation of Bergen-Belsen, 1945* (New York: Schocken Books, 2005), 112.

26. Claude Lanzmann Shoah Collection, interview with Paula Biren (1985), US Holocaust Memorial Museum, https://collections.ushmm.org/search/catalog /irn1003910.

27. Oral history interview with Amalie Petranker Salsitz (1990), Accession Number: 1990.389.1, RG Number: RG-50.030.0198, Jeff and Toby Herr Oral History Archive, US Holocaust Memorial Museum.

28. Oral history interview with Tamar Lazerson (1997), RG Number: RG-50.471*0016, Accession Number: 1998.A.0119.16, Oral History Interviews of the Hidden History of the Kovno Ghetto collection, https://collections.ushmm.org/oh _findingaids/RG-50.471.0016_trs_en.pdf.

29. Oral history interview with Carol Stern Steinhardt (1996), Accession Number: 1996.A.0195, RG Number: RG-50.030.0368, US Holocaust Memorial Museum.

30. Interview with Rose Warner, July 15, 1999, RG-50.549.02*0058, US Holocaust Memorial Museum, https://collections.ushmm.org/oh_findingaids/RG-50.549.02 .0058_trs_en.pdf.

31. Oral history interview with Ruth Reiser, Accession Number: 2014.191.10, RG Number: RG-50.751.0010, Jeff and Toby Herr Oral History Archive, https://collections .ushmm.org/search/catalog/irn85495.

32. Oral history interview with Charlene Perlmutter Schiff (2003), Accession Number: 2003.47, RG Number: RG-50.549.02.0068, Jeff and Toby Herr Oral History Archive, https://collections.ushmm.org/search/catalog/irn512894.

33. Tom Regan, *The Struggle for Animal Rights* (Los Angeles: University of California Press, 1987), 76–77. Quoted in David Sztybel, "Can the Treatment of Animals Be Compared to the Holocaust?," *Ethics & the Environment* 11, no. 1 (2006): 102.

34. Karen Davis, *The Holocaust and the Henmaid's Tale: A Case for Comparing Atrocities* (New York: Lantern Books, 2005), 2. On comparing atrocities against humans and animals, see Marjorie Spiegel, *The Dreaded Comparison: Human and Animal Slavery* (New York: Mirror Books, 1996); Roberta Kalechofsky, *Animal Suffering and the Holocaust: The Problem with Comparisons* (Marblehead, MA: Micah Publications, 2003); and Sztybel, "Can the Treatment of Animals Be Compared to the Holocaust?"

35. Quoted in Davis, *Holocaust and Henmaid's Tale*, 55.

36. Edgar Kupfer-Koberwitz, *Die Tierbrüder: Eine Betrachtung zum ethische Leben* (1947) (Mannheim, Germany: Höcker Verlag, 1994), http://www.hoecker-verlag.de /ebooks/Tierbrueder-eBook.pdf. Quotes are taken from an English translation reprinted at https://compassionatespirit.com/wpblog/books/animal-brothers/.

37. Quoted in Josephin Dolsten, "Holocaust Survivor Likens Treatment of Livestock to Shoah," *The Times of Israel*, October 7, 2016, https://www.timesofisrael.com /holocaust-survivor-likens-treatment-of-livestock-to-shoah/.

38. Quoted in Rachel Kurland, "Survivor's Life Experiences Prompted Animal Rights Advocacy," *Philadelphia Jewish Export*, May 3, 2017, https://www.jewish exponent.com/2017/05/03/survivors-life-experiences-prompted-animal-rights -advocacy/. Even Treblinka commandant Franz Stangl seemed to recognize a connection between the camps and the misery inflicted on animals. During his postwar

escape to Brazil, he was traveling on a train that stopped near some cattle pens: "The cattle in the pens, hearing the noise of the train, trotted up to the fence and stared at the train. They were very close to my window, one crowding the other, looking at me through that fence. I thought then, 'Look at this; this reminds me of Poland; that's just how the people looked, trustingly, just before they went into the tins.'" After this moment, he told his interviewer in a self-congratulatory manner, he could not eat meat again. Quoted in Sereny, *Into That Darkness*, 201.

39. Quoted in Patterson, *Eternal Treblinka*, 183.

40. To cite two recent examples, in 2011, the British animal welfare group Naturewatch condemned the Kiev Zoo as a "concentration camp for those with fur and feathers." Associated Press, "Kiev Zoo a 'Concentration Camp for Animals,'" CBC News, March 23, 2011, https://www.cbc.ca/news/world/kiev-zoo-a-concentration -camp-for-animals-1.1106751. Nearly a decade later, a High Court in Islamabad denounced zoos as "concentration camps for living beings" and ordered the removal of two dancing bears to an animal sanctuary in Jordan. Tom Embury-Dennis, "'Concentration Camps for Living Beings': Pakistan High Court Condemns Continued Existence of Zoos," *Independent*, December 15, 2020, https://www.independent .co.uk/news/world/asia/zoos-pakistan-islamabad-high-court-bears-suzie-bubloo -kaavan-elephant-b1774382.html.

41. Scholarly and popular critics of zoos frequently cite the need for readers to imagine themselves in the place of zoo animals. See, for example, Peter H. Kahn, "Please Don't Visit Zoos! Zoos Reify the Human Drive to Dominate the Other," *Psychology Today*, October 2, 2009, https://www.psychologytoday.com/us/blog/human -nature/200910/please-dont-visit-zoos.

Chapter 19

1. Keith Lowe, *Savage Continent: Europe in the Aftermath of World War II* (New York: Picador, 2012), 7; Ian Buruma, *Year Zero: A History of 1945* (New York: Penguin Press, 2013), 57; "Grim Europe Faces Winter of Misery," *Life* 20, no. 1 (January 7, 1946): 21.

2. Lowe, *Savage Continent*, xv.

3. "Grim Europe," 21.

4. Lowe, *Savage Continent*, 39.

5. Buruma, *Year Zero*, 59, 65.

6. Lowe, *Savage Continent*, xiv.

7. Quoted in Buruma, *Year Zero*, 60.

8. John Dos Passos, "Americans Are Losing the Victory in Europe," *Life Magazine*, January 7, 1946, 24.

9. "The Fate of Fauna" (n.d.), 12, 14, clipping at Philadelphia Zoo Archives.

10. Sgt. Robert S. Robinson, "Somewhere in Germany," *Fauna* 7, no. 2 (June 1945): 54.

11. "European Zoos—How They Have Fared," 1945, 84; clipping at Philadelphia Zoo Archives.

12. Leszek Solski, "Zoological Gardens of Central-Eastern Europe and Russia," in *Zoo and Aquarium History: Ancient Animal Collections to Zoological Gardens*, ed. Vernon N. Kisling Jr. (Boca Raton, FL: CRC Press, 2001), 123.

Notes to Pages 258–265   333

13. "Farm Fair Staged at Budapest Zoo," *Asbury Park Press*, September 15, 1946, 9.

14. Dorothy Seidel, "Wiederaufbau und 'drittes Hellabrunn' 1945–2000," in *Nilpferde an der Isar: Eine Geschichte des Tierparks Hellabrunn in München*, ed. Michael Kamp and Helmut Zedelmaier (München: Buchendorfer Verlag, 2000), 139.

15. Gary Bruce, *Through the Lion Gate: A History of the Berlin Zoo* (New York: Oxford University Press, 2017), 202.

16. Kevin Prenger, "Een dierentuin tussen de puinhopen van nazi-Duitsland," an excerpt of *Oorlogszone Zoo* (War Zone Zoo), November 9, 2021, *Historiek.net*, https://historiek.net/een-dierentuin-tussen-de-puinhopen-van-nazi-duitsland/55688/.

17. Quoted in Lowe, *Savage Continent*, 7–8.

18. "The 'Zoo Camp' for Displaced Persons—Hamburg 1945," *Imperial War Museum*, https://www.iwm.org.uk/history/the-zoo-camp-for-displaced-persons-hamburg-1945.

19. "Animal Collaborators Clear Ruins," British Movietone, December 6, 1945, https://newsroom.ap.org/editorial-photos-videos/detail?itemid=57b7b7a3d28e4029a31af7bb20a17025&mediatype=video&source=youtube.

20. Lorenz Hagenbeck, *Animals Are My Life*, trans. Alec Brown (London: Bodley Head, 1956), 225, 228.

21. "Animals in Trust," *The Times* (London), April 3, 1947, 5.

22. "Animals for the Zoo from Germany," *The Times*, April 2, 1947, 7.

23. "World's News Review," *The World News* (Sydney), August 13, 1949, 19, 20.

24. Evelyn Gottschlich, "Wiedereröffnung und Zerstörung (1928–1945)," in *Nilpferde an der Isar: Eine Geschichte des Tierparks Hellabrunn in München*, ed. Michael Kamp and Helmut Zedelmaier (München: Buchendorfer Verlag, 2000), 137.

25. Leszek Solski and Harro Strehlow, *150 Jahre OO Breslau/150 lat Zoo Wrocław* (Wrocław: Zoo Wrocław, 2015), 135. On the forced de-Germanization of Poland after World War II, see Gregory Thum, *Uprooted: How Breslau Became Wroclaw during the Century of Expulsions*, trans. Tom Lampert and Allison Brown (Princeton, NJ: Princeton University Press, 2011); R. M. Douglas, *Orderly and Human: The Expulsion of the Germans after Second World War* (New Haven, CT: Yale University Press, 2012).

26. Mayumi Itoh, *Japanese Wartime Zoo Policy: The Silent Victims of World War* (New York: Palgrave Macmillan, 2010), 161.

27. "Army Garbage Provides Food for Tokyo Zoo," *Brooklyn Daily Eagle*, July 17, 1946, 6.

28. "Army Garbage Provides Food for Tokyo Zoo."

29. Peggy Warner, "The Animals Are Sad in This Japanese Zoo," *Chronicle* (Adelaide, SA), October 9, 1947, 32.

30. "Mr. Nishida to Lt. Doe" (May 18, 1946), Zoos, Aquariums, and Botanical Gardens in the Kyoto-Nara-Osaka Area, folder 4, box 5865, RG 331, National Archives, Washington, DC.

31. Itoh, *Japanese Wartime Zoo Policy*, 177.

32. "Chi's Brookfield Zoo Plans Post-War Transformation," *The Billboard*, August 18, 1945, 49.

33. Stanley Field, "Report of the Chairman of the Building Committee," January 15, 1946, 4, copy in Brookfield Zoo Archives.

34. Gus Knudson to Belle Benchley, May 27, 1946, folder 9, box 2, RG 8601, Seattle Zoo Archives.

334   Notes to Pages 265–271

35. Clipping, "U.S. Zoos Best in World; Packed with New Animals," November 20, 1947, folder 1948, box 155, Brookland Zoo Archives.

36. Henry Trefflich (as told to Baynard Kendrick), *They Never Talk Back* (New York: Appleton-Century-Crofts, 1954), 174.

37. President, Washington Park Zoological Society to Fred Pabst (August 24, 1945), folder 1 (1944–1946), Milwaukee Zoo Archives.

38. Charles J. V. Murphy, "European Zoos," *Life Magazine*, December 6, 1948, 143.

39. *Reports of the Council and Auditors of the Zoological Society of London for the Year 1947* (Bungay, Suffolk: Richard Clay and Company, Ltd., 1948), 10–11.

40. Murphy, "European Zoos," 146.

41. "Zoo Baby from Africa's Only Elephant School," *The Australian Women's Weekly*, February 8, 1947, 21.

42. "Africa Resumes Trade in Wild Animals," *Cairns Post* (Qld.), April 1, 1947, 7.

43. "Zoo Baby from Africa's Only Elephant School."

44. Seidel, "Wiederaufbau und 'drittes Hellabrunn' 1945–2000," 140–41.

45. Robert MacMillan, "War Left Zoos in Pretty Fair Shape—Spectators Happy," *Chicago Daily News*, Sunday News, March 10, 1946, 60.

46. "Fecundity in the Chicago Zoo," *Life Magazine*, October 9, 1944, 41.

47. Murphy, "European Zoos," 153.

48. "Taronga Park Bargaining for Baby Gorillas," *Sydney Morning Herald*, December 3, 1949.

49. "37 Depart by Plane for Czechoslovakia; Alligators in Cargo," *Chicago Tribune*, May 10, 1948, 9.

50. Itoh, *Japanese Wartime Zoo Policy*, 164.

51. "Science: This Little Pig Came Home," *Time*, April 11, 1949.

52. "Myth of Pig 311 Finally Cleared," *Lewiston Daily Sun*, July 22, 1946, 2.

53. For more on the sage of Pig 311, see "Animals Used in Bikini A-Bomb Test Reported to Be 'Dying Like Flies,'" *Los Angeles Times*, July 15, 1946; and Alice Bingham Gorman, "Nagasaki, the Atomic Bomb and the Irradiated Pig That Haunts Me," *Salon*, May 25, 2016, https://www.salon.com/2016/05/25/nagasaki_the_atomic_bomb_and_the_radiated_pig_that_haunts_me/.

54. "Russian Ship in Port," *Cairns Post* (Qld.), October 31, 1951, 5.

55. "Russian Ship Has Baby Kangaroo," *Sydney Morning Herald* (NSW), November 30, 1950, 5.

56. "No Iron Curtain on Russian Ship," *The Daily News* (Perth, WA), December 2, 1950, 5.

57. Henry Fairfield Osborn Jr., "The Shadow of the Curtain," *Animal Kingdom* (November–December 1951): 161.

58. See J. W. Mohnhaupt, *The Zookeeper's War: An Incredible True Story from the Cold War*, trans. Shelley Frisch (New York: Simon & Schuster, 2019).

59. John M. Kinder, "Militarizing the Menagerie: American Zoos from World War II to the Early Cold War," in *The Martial Imagination: Cultural Aspects of American Warfare*, ed. Jimmy L. Bryan Jr. (College Station: Texas A&M University Press, 2013), 30.

60. Kinder, "Militarizing the Menagerie," 26.

61. Armand Sunier, "What Does Our Union Stand For?," reprinted in Laura Penn, Markus Gussett, and Gerald Dick, *77 Years: The History and Evolution of the World Association of Zoos and Aquariums* (Gland, Switzerland: WAZA, 2012), 182.

Notes to Pages 272–278   335

62. On zoo leaders' and conservationists' fears about wildlife in post-independence sub-Saharan Africa, see John M. Kinder, "'Our Faunal Defense in Africa': Imperial Survivalism, Anglo-American Conservation, and African Liberation in the Twentieth Century," *Journal of Colonialism and Colonial History* 23, no. 3 (Winter 2022).

63. Bernard Livingston, *Zoo Animals, People, Places* (New York: Arbor House, 1974), 160.

64. R. S. Deese, *We Are Amphibians: Julian and Aldous Huxley on the Future of Our Species* (Berkeley: University of California Press, 2014), 118.

65. Robert S. Norris and Hans M. Kristensen, "Global Nuclear Inventories, 1945–2010," *Bulletin of Atomic Scientists* 66, no. 4 (July 2010): 77–83.

66. On the threat of nuclear war to the health of the planet, see Jonathan Schell, *The Fate of the Earth* (New York: Knopf, 1982); and Alexandra Witze, "How a Small Nuclear War Would Transform the Planet," *Nature* 579 (March 26, 2020): 485–87.

67. "Official Statement of COSWA VII," *Bulletin of Atomic Scientists*, January 1962, 28.

68. Max Roser, Hannah Ritchie, Esteban Ortiz-Ospina, and Lucas Rodés-Guirao, "World Population Growth," *OurWorldInData.org*, 2013, retrieved from https://our worldindata.org/world-population-growth.

69. Colin Bertram, "Man Pressure," *Oryx* 7 (1963/1964): 98.

70. "Animals in Trust," 5.

71. C. G. C. Rawlins, "Zoos: A Brief History," *The Rotarian* 130, no. 1 (January 1977): 15.

72. Quoted in "Symposium: What's New at the Zoo?," *The Rotarian* 130, no. 1 (January 1977): 54.

73. Penn et al., *77 Years*, 62–118.

74. John J. Daley, "Zoological Gardens in America," *National Republic* (August 1950): 22.

75. Murphy, "European Zoos," 146.

76. Estelle Gaines, "European Zoos Making a Comeback, Mann Finds," clipping.

77. Lucile Q. Mann, "Post War Developments in European Zoos" (c. 1945), p. 2, folder 5, box 10, RU 7293, SIA.

78. Murphy, "European Zoos," 154.

79. Murphy, "European Zoos," 157.

Epilogue

1. Leningrad Zoo, "Exposition 'Zoo in the Years of Blockade,'" http://spbzoo.ru /en/about-us/zoo-history/.

2. There are exceptions, of course. In 2009, zoo employee Mark Norris launched the award-winning World War Zoo Garden Project at Cornwall's Newquay Zoo to give young visitors an intimate look at the problems faced by World War II–era zookeepers. Norris and volunteers cultivated a model "Dig for Victory" garden on the zoo grounds; he also created a blog to disseminate an invaluable cache of photographs, memorabilia, diary entries, and other historical artifacts of zoo life under fire. Served up with a heaping helping of "keep calm and carry on"–flavored nostalgia, World War Zoo nonetheless highlights the importance of sustainability and recycling in an era of rapid climate change. See "About World War Zoo Gardens," https:// worldwarzoogardener1939.wordpress.com/about/.

3. One of the Berlin Zoo's most vocal critics in past decades has been Werner Cohn, a retired American sociologist, who contacted the zoo in 2000 to request details about his father's share in the institution. Shareholders and their families are allowed free admission for life, and shares are frequently passed down through the generations. Cohn found it suspicious that, according to the zoo, his Jewish father had "sold" his share in 1938—right around the time the zoo was ramping up its restrictions against Jewish visitors. At first, the zoo's representatives proclaimed innocence. In one of several letters to Cohn, the zoo's legal counsel insisted that "no special treatment of any sort was ever applied to Jewish stockholders, not even during the Nazi period." Eventually, however, the zoo was forced to own up to its history of discriminating against Jewish shareholders and Jews in general. Until his death in 2018, Cohn posted his lengthy correspondence with Berlin Zoo officials on his website, https://wernercohn.com.

4. Quoted in Gary Bruce, *Through the Lion Gate: A History of the Berlin Zoo* (New York: Oxford University Press, 2015), 174.

5. For her in-depth study of the zoo's persecution of Jewish shareholders, see Monika Schmidt, *Die jüdischen Aktionäre des Zoologischen Gartens zu Berlin: Namen und Schicksale* (Berlin: Metropol, 2014).

6. For more on German zoos' efforts to whitewash their Nazi past, see Alexander Nabert, "Von Tieren und Nazis," *Jungle World* 51 (December 17, 2015); and Bruce, *Through the Lion Gate*, 171–78.

7. Quoted in Steffi Kammerer, "In the Cage of Forgetting," a translation of "Im Gehege des Vergessens," *Süddeutsche Zeitung*, October 12, 2000, by Werner Cohn, on https://wernercohn.com.

8. Jens Raschke, *Was Das Nashorn Sah, Als es auf die andere Seite des Zauns Schaute* (München: Theaterstückverlag, 2013).

9. John F. Burns, "Sarajevo Journal: In the Zoo's House of Horrors, One Pitiful Bear," *New York Times*, October 16, 1992.

10. D'Vera Cohn, "U.S. Zoos Aid War-Ravaged Counterpart in Kabul," *Washington Post*, November 30, 2001, A16; "Global Coalition Unites to Aid Animals of Afghani Zoo," *Journal of the American Veterinary Medical Association* 220, no. 4 (February 15, 2002): 434–35.

11. Sue Surkes, "Ministries, Non-Profits Partner to Rescue Captive Animals from Border Towns," *The Times of Israel*, November 9, 2023, https://www.timesofisrael.com/ministries-non-profits-partner-to-rescue-exotic-captive-animals-from-border-towns/.

12. You can read such messages at the Sulala Animal Rescue Society's X (formerly Twitter) account: https://twitter.com/SulalaSociety.

13. "Starvation and Airstrikes Killed Majority of Animals in Gaza Zoo," Al Jazeera English, November 28, 2023, https://www.youtube.com/watch?v=k70zujaqfnI.

14. For more on the fate of Gaza's zoo animals during the Israeli invasion, see Mohammed Salem and Bassam Masoud, "Hunger Hits Displaced Palestinians and Animals at Gaza Zoo," Reuters, January 1, 2024, https://www.reuters.com/world/middle-east/hunger-hits-animals-people-alike-gaza-zoo-2024-01-01/; Mohamad El Bardicy, "Another Side Effect from War in Gaza? Animals Starving in Its Besieged Zoos," NPR, February 1, 2024, https://www.npr.org/2024/02/01/1226006760/another-side-effect-from-war-in-gaza-animals-starving-in-its-besieged-zoos.

Notes to Pages 282–285   337

15. Sarah Kaplan, "Earth Is on Brink of Sixth Mass Extinction, Scientists Say, and It's Humans' Fault," *Washington Post*, June 22, 2015, http://www.washingtonpost.com/news/morning-mix/wp/2015/06/22/the-earth-is-on-the-brink-of-a-sixth-mass-extinction-scientists-say-and-its-humans-fault/.

16. Elizabeth Kolbert, *The Sixth Extinction: An Unnatural History* (New York: Picador, 2014), 269.

17. David Wallace-Wells, *The Uninhabitable Earth: Life after Warming* (New York: Tim Duggan Books, 2019), 6, 7, 71. Fire has been especially punishing in rural Australia, site of what Dermot O'Gorman, chief executive of WWF-Australia, called "one of the worst wildlife disasters in modern history." A series of bushfires in late 2019 and early 2020 threatened to incinerate more than a billion wild animals, including as many as a million wombats and five million kangaroos. Although it's impossible to determine how many animals managed to escape the blaze, news reports published images of flame-blackened koalas falling from the trees, their cute faces burned and scarred. Unless something was done, a parliamentary inquiry from New South Wales predicted that koalas would be extinct in the wild by 2050—victims of humans' willingness to unmake the natural world. Graham Readfearn, "'Devastating' More Than 61,000 Koalas among 3 Billion Animals Affected by Bushfire Crisis," *The Guardian*, December 2, 2020, https://www.theguardian.com/australia-news/2020/dec/07/devastating-more-than-61000-koalas-among-3-billion-animals-affected-by-bushfire-crisis.

18. Lee Foster, "A Special Kind of Zoo in the Catskills," *New York Times*, August 15, 1971.

19. Ben A. Minteer, Jane Maienschein, and James B. Collins, "Introduction: Zoos and Aquarium Conservation: Past, Present, Future," in *The Ark and Beyond: The Evolution of Zoo and Aquarium Conservation*, ed. Ben A. Minteer, Jane Maienschein, and James B. Collins (Chicago: University of Chicago Press, 2018), 3.

20. Minteer et al., "Introduction," 5.

21. Minteer et al., "Introduction," 3.

22. "Milestone: The Scimitar-Horned Oryx Downlisted from Extinct in the Wild to Endangered by IUCN," Sahara Conservation, December 11, 2023, https://saharaconservation.org/milestone-the-scimitar-horned-oryx-downlisted-from-extinct-in-the-wild-to-endangered-by-iucn/.

23. Helen Pilcher, "There Are Two Northern White Rhinos Left, Both Females. Here's How Science Hopes to Save Them from Extinction," BBC Science Focus, March 19, 2023, https://www.sciencefocus.com/news/white-rhino-extinction/.

24. Minteer et al., "Introduction," 2.

25. John M. Kinder, "'Try Telling That to the Polar Bears': Rationing and Resistance at the Wartime Zoo," in *Zoo Studies: A New Humanities*, ed. Tracy McDonald and Dan Vandersommers (Montreal: McGill-Queen's University Press, 2019), 161.

26. "Owner of Gaza Zoo Puts Last of Starving Animals Up for Sale," *Guardian*, March 7, 2016; "Gaza: The Abandoned Animals of Khan Yunis Zoo, Dying of Starvation Due to Years of Conflict," *The France 24 Observer*, March 25, 2016, https://www.youtube.com/watch?v=kRaMmG1uReM.

27. Aviva Cantor, "The Club, The Yoke, and the Leash: What We Can Learn from the Way a Culture Treats Animals," *Ms.*, August 1983, 30.

28. Gary Bruce, *Through the Lion Gate: A History of the Berlin Zoo* (New York: Oxford University Press, 2017), 170.

29. See Wallace-Wells, *The Uninhabitable Earth*, 24; John Freeman, ed., *Tales of Two Planets: Stories of Climate Change and Inequality in a Divided World* (New York: Penguin, 2020); Nicolas Taconet, Aurélie Méjean, and Céline Guivarch, "Influence of Climate Change Impacts and Mitigation Costs on Inequality between Countries," *Climatic Change* 160 (2020): 15–34, https://doi.org/10.1007/s10584-019-02637-w; and David Eckstein, Vera Künzel, and Laura Schäfer, *Global Climate Risk Index 2020: Who Suffers Most from Extreme Weather Events? Weather-Related Loss Events in 2019 and 2000–2019* (Bonn: Germanwatch e.V.: 2021), https://www.germanwatch.org/sites/default/files/Global%20Climate%20Risk%20Index%202021_2.pdf.

30. Margo DeMello, *Animals and Society: An Introduction to Human-Animal Studies* (New York: Columbia University, 2012), 222.

31. According to Marco Silva, the BBC's climate disinformation specialist, "Climate doomerism is the idea that we are past the point of being able to do anything at all about global warming—and that mankind is highly likely to become extinct." Marco Silva, "Why Is Climate 'Doomism' Going Viral—and Who's Fighting It?," BBC, May 23, 2022, https://www.bbc.com/news/blogs-trending-61495035.

32. Lawrence Anthony with Graham Spence, *Babylon's Ark: The Incredible Wartime Rescue of the Baghdad Zoo* (New York: St. Martin's Griffin, 2008), 14, 50, 237.

Index

Page numbers in italics refer to figures.

Ackerman, Diane, 78–79, 106, 201, 214
Adelaide Advertiser (newspaper), 161
Adorno, Theodor, 36–37, 246
Afghanistan, 280–81
Air Raid Precautions (ARP), 80–83, 89
air raids: American zoos and, 119–22; bomb shelters and, 8, 119, 177, 278 (*see also* bombing); labor and, 157; liberation and, 236; occupation and, 109; in Pacific War, 132, 135–36; preparing for, 77–81, 85, 87; press coverage of, 69; sacrifice and, 194, 197; sirens, 81, 109, 201, 207, 208, 236; in Spanish Civil War, 72; wardens, 8, 80–81; women's efforts during, 318n40; in World War I, 68
Albuquerque Zoo, 124
Al Jazeera, 281–82
Allied Bomber Offensive, 205
alligators: execution of, 87; liberation and, 235–38; Nagasaki remains mistaken for, 237–38; postwar restocking of, 269
Altoona Tribune, 74
American Association of Zoological Parks and Aquariums, 163
American Kennel Club, 223
American zoos: aerial bombardment, preparing for, 119–22; antelopes and, 121; anti-animal violence at, 124–25; bears and, 121; buffaloes and, 124; cages and, 120, 123–26; deer and, 124; economic issues of, 115; elephants and, 120, 122; fascism and, 115, 124; Hitler and, 115–17, 123; Jews and, 123–24; lions and, 121, 123; London Zoo and, 117, 121, 124; William Mann and, 8, 116–23; military service and, 155–56; monkeys and, 124–25; Nazis and, 115–17; neutrality and, 115–19; ostriches and, 124; after Pearl Harbor, 119, 122; postwar issues and, 264–66; racism and, 122–25; restocking and, 265–66; snakes and, 119–21; tigers and, 119–21; World War II and, 119–26; zebras and, 121; zookeepers in, 116–17, 120–23, 264–66
animal agency, 319n12
Anschluss, 36
antelopes: American zoos and, 121; Asian, 72; bombing and, 202, 205; in circus fire, 126; conservation efforts and, 284; Dutch zoos and, 98; Liberian expedition and, 118n; London Zoo and, 87; postwar issues and, 85, 267–68; saiga, 187; Spanish Civil War and, 72
Anthony, Lawrence, 287–88
Anti-Defamation League (ADL), 6

antisemitism: Churchill and, 127; Haeckel and, 37; Nazis and, 3, 36, 127; occupation and, 106–7; stereotypes, *242*; vivisection and, 32–33, 36

Antonius, Otto, 39–40, 155, 207, 233, 262

ants, 103–5

Antwerp Zoo: elephants and, 17; execution of animals at, 85; food and, 17, 85, 92, 145, 148; liberation and, *231*; postwar restocking and, 266, 269; van den bergh on, 6–7; weather and, 92

apes: bombing and, 157; evacuation of, 77; food and, 147; liberation and, 234; Nazi racism and, 37; postwar construction and, 265; at Sachsenhausen, 54; sexual behavior of, 19; Spanish Civil War and, 72–73; trained, 54, 295n21; weather and, 91–92

Arluke, Arnold, 149

Artis Zoo, *7*; in Plantation District, 217; refugees and, 8, 215–17; Sunier and, 61, *62*, 99, 107–8, 113, 215–17, 220, 271, 274

Aryanism: Jewish denigration and, 107–8, 112, 214, 330n15; Nazis and, 37, 94, 107–8, 112, 214, 219, 244, 251; racial purity and, 37

Askaniya Nova (New Ascania), 187–89

Associated Press, 126, 132, 150, 270

atomic bomb, 89, 181, 236–38, 269–70

attendance: economic issues of, 16–17, 150; in Great Depression, 24–26, 28–29; segregation at American zoos and, 123; wartime, 8, 111, 135

Auckland Zoo, 16, 127, 135, 146, 151

auctions, 18, 58, 66

Audubon Zoo, 28, 123

aurochs, 41–42, 207, 299n36

Auschwitz, 89, 216–17, 246–47, 330n15

ausländische Arbeitskräfte (foreign workers), 156

Austin, Denise Weston, 161

Australia: bushfires, 337n17; climate change and, 282; Great Depression and, 16–17, 18; international

cooperation and, 59; labor and, 161; Melbourne Zoo, 16, 129, 134–35, 161; Pacific War and, 129–30, 133–37; Perth Zoo, 16, 135–36; postwar issues and, 257, 267, 269–70; press coverage of animal suicide and, 16; Taronga Park Zoo, 135, 141, 156, 160, 267, 269; war effort and, 169, 179

Australia Is Like This (film), 135

Austria: *Anschluss* of, 36, 62; Antonius and, 39–40; international cooperation and, 59

B-29 bombers, 226–27, 236

baboons, 279–80

back-breeding, 41, 61, 243, 285, 299n36

Baghdad Zoo, 287

Báguena, Manuel, 72

Baratay, Eric, 24, 297n55

Barcelona Zoo: bombing and, 66–74, 79; Commissariat of Natural Sciences and, 70; de Sagarra and, 66, 69; elephants and, 72–73; food and, 66–71; poor condition of, 65–66; Spanish Civil War and, 64–72, *73*

barless design, 24, 28, 65, 276

Basapa, William Lawrence Soma, 129–30, 132

Batory (ship), 133–34

bats, 87, 223

Battle of the Bulge, 257

Bauhaus architecture, 22, 46

Baum, Jiří, 213

BBC, 21, 89, 338n31

Beal, W. P. B., 88

Bean, Ed, 145

Bean, Robert, 122, 149

Bear Hunt at KZ Buchenwald, A (Dittmar), 50–51, *52–53*

bears: Asiatic, 10; *Bärenzwinger* (bear enclosure), 46; Betti, 50–51, *52–53*; black, 280; bombing and, 78, 205; breeding programs and, 188, 268; brown, 113, 195, 235; Buchenwald and, 46, 49, 50–51, *52–53*, 54, 223; dancing, 332n40; Deutsche Zoo and, 43; Dutch zoos and, 96, 98; escape

of, 121, 163; evacuation or execution
of, 78, 85, 88, 89, 108, 190, 191, 193–
95, 232, 235; food and, 146–53; Great
Depression and, 18, 28; Himalayan,
228; Kodiak, 163, 180; KZ system
and, *240*; Malay, 266; occupation
and, 111–13; Pacific War and, 130;
postwar issues and, 262, 266; as
"prisoners of state," 25; remembrance and, 279–80; resistance and,
213, 216; restocking, 228, 266; Siberian, 279; Spanish Civil War and, 65,
67, 71–73; Three Bears General Store
and, 10; throwing prisoners to, 54;
weather and, 92. *See also* pandas;
polar bears
beavers, 53, 309n1
Beebe, William, 179
Beevor, Antony, 68
Belarus, 243
Belfast Blitz, 161
Belgium: Antwerp, 58; Clères, 99; international cooperation and, 58; labor
and, 156, 158; occupation and, 104;
resistance and, 211; weather and,
92. *See also* Antwerp Zoo
Belsec, 330n15
Benchley, Belle: press coverage of, 163–
64; San Diego Zoo and, 122, 151, 163–
64, 176–77, 265; as Zoo Lady, 163–64
Bender, Daniel E., 162
Bengal, 237
Bergen-Belsen, 239, 246
Berger, John, 105
Bergmann, Hans, 50
Berlin University, 103
Berlin Zoo: bombing of, 1–2, 205,
208–10, 235, *259*; Cohn on, 336n3;
evacuation of animals from, 207,
208; Goebbels and, 42–43; Lutz
Heck and, 8, 40–41, 61, 106, 157,
165, 176, 189, 205, 208, 210, 218, 243,
262, 278; Heinroth and, 164–65, *166*,
209–10, 235, 258; *Kraft durch Freude*
(Strength through Joy) and, 39; KZ
system and, 243; labor and, 157, 165;
liberation and, 232, 235; Nazis and,

39–42; occupation and, 106, 189;
postwar issues and, 258–59, 262,
271; propaganda and, 39; remembrance and, 278–79; reopening of,
259; size of, 9
Bertram, Colin, 273–74
Bible, 11–12, 78, 277, 282–84
Billboard (magazine), 264–65
Billig, Hugo, 27–28
Billig, Irving, 27–28
biology, 21–22, 25, 37, 61, 100, 187n
bioparks, 10, 284
Bischoff, Hans, 103–4, 105
bison: American, 61, 87, 195; evacuation
or execution of, 87–88, 195, 207;
Göring and, 38; Lutz Heck and, 61;
"meat value" of, 150; occupation
and, 106, 108; wisents, 38, 61, 187,
207
Black Death, 6, 255
Blamey, Thomas, 133
Blitz, 133, 201–4, 257
Blitzkrieg (lightning war), 78, 94, 101,
128, 201, 323n5
Blondi (German shepherd), 35
Blondin, Leo, 149
Blonk, Henk, 216
boars, wild, 47, 66, 77
Bochum Zoo, 38
bombing, x; American zoos and, 119–22;
animal victims of, 106, 189, 201–4,
205, 208–9, 233–34, 269–70, 325n39;
atomic, 89, 181, 236–38, 269–70,
273, 276; Barcelona Zoo and, 64,
68–73, 79; Belfast Blitz, 161; of
Berlin Zoo, 1–2, 208–10; Blitz, 133,
201–4, 257; bloodlust and, 204–5;
British Bombing Unit Survey, 19;
bunkers and, 203, 232, *278*; cages
and, 201, 203, 208, 325n39; carpet,
98, 102; cleanup after, 209, 258, *261*;
Clères and, 99, 101–2; as cowardice, 200; Doodlebugs and, 325n39;
Dresden Zoo and, 233–34; drones,
200, 323n3; Dutch zoos and, 96, 98;
evacuation or execution of animals
in preparation for, 78–89, 96, 141,

bombing (*cont.*)
190, 191, 197, 207; fascism and, 325n38; firebombing, 236, 325n38, 329n22; firestorms from, 98, 207, 233; France and, 96, 201; Göring and, 204; Hague Convention and, 68; Lutz Heck and, 189, 205–10, 318n40; Hellabrunn Zoo and, 205, 233; Hiroshima, 236–37, 273; Hitler and, 201, 204, 325n39; impact of, 1–3, 6–10; International Peace Conference and, 68; labor and, 155, 157–59; liberation and, 226, 230–37; London Zoo and, 3, 19, 68, 79, 85, 89, 121, 129, 201–3, 257; Luftwaffe and, 69, 325n38; Madrid Zoo and, 64, 68–71, 79; morale, 202, 323n7, 324n9; moral issues and, 205, 209–10; munition factories and, 204; Nagasaki, 235–38, 273; Netherlands and, 201, 325n38; nuclear, 273, 280, 335n66; Operation Gomorrah, 207; Operation Market Garden, 231–32; Pacific War and, 134–36; *Panik* and, 199–200; Poland and, 78, 157, 230, 325n38; postwar issues and, 255–58, 269–70, 273, 276; POWs and, 209; propaganda and, 204; remembrance and, 278; resistance and, 202; revenge and, 209; shelters and, 8, 119, 177, 278; shrapnel, 68, 72, 77, 199, 232; in Spanish Civil War, 64, 68–73, 79; strategic, 3, 201–2, 210, 323n7; suffering from, 2, 91, 197, 234, 325n39; total war and, 74, 99, 177, 201, 204–8; types of, 323n7; V1 and V2 programs of, 325n39; Warsaw Zoo and, 78, 201, 214; in World War I, 68, 200; in World War II, 199–210; zeppelins and, 68
Bostock, Frank, 89
Bourez, Albert, 158
Brains Trust, The (BBC), 21
Braitman, Laurel, 15
breeding: Antonius and, 39; Askaniya Nova and, 188; back-, 41, 61, 243, 285, 299n36; captive, 3, 268, 270,

283–84, 286; eugenics and, 56–57; Lutz Heck and, 41, 243; Huxley and, 22; KZ system and, 44; medical research and, 168; rats, 143
Bremerhaven Zoo, 151, 205, 324n19
Breslau, 32, 165; Breslau Zoo, 228–29, 234–35, 262–63
British Bombing Unit Survey, 19
British Pathé, 134, 154
Bronx Zoo: Crandall and, 102, 275; gardens of, 144; Grant and, 123; Hornaday and, 60; Luces and, viii; pandas and, viii–xiv; Pandora, viii; platypus acquisition, 266; security measures of, 120; Singer on, 250; war effort and, 117, 155, 178–79; as world's second-largest zoo, 29; World War I and, 144
Brookfield Zoo, 122, 145, 149, 155, 162, 264–65, 268, 269
Brown, Bruce, 267
Bruce, Gary, 258
Buchenwald: *A Bear Hunt at KZ Buchenwald*, 50–51, *52–53*; bears and, 46, 49, 50, 223; cages and, 50, 54; chickens and, 46; as concentration camp, 43, 44–55, *240*, 279, 330n15; crematorium at, 44, 55; deer and, 46–51; dehumanizing of prisoners in, 44–45, 48–51; disease and, 45; dogs and, 49–50; ducks and, 46; eagles and, 49, 51, 55; as Ettersberg Concentration Camp, 43; falcon house of, 46–47; food and, 49–51, 55; France and, 47; Göring and, 46; horses and, 46; human experiments in, 45; human leather and, 45; *Jedem das Seine* (To Each His Own), 46; Jews and, 45, 48, 50, *52–53*; Koch and, 45–49, *53*, 54, 300n15; KZ system and, 44–55; monkeys and, 46, 48, 49–50; rabbits and, 46; Singing Forest and, 45; SS and, 44–55; starvation and, 44–45, 48–50; torture at, 44–45, 48, 54; triangle identification system of, 45; voluntary levies of, 48–49; wolves and, 48, 51

Buck, Vera, 162
buffaloes: American zoos and, 124, 153; execution of, 85, 87; as victims of war, 276, 294n9
Buffalo Zoo, 168
Bulgaria, 59, 74, 230
bunkers, 92, 96, 203, 232, *278*
Burdelev, Trofim, 190
Burgers' Zoo, *206*, 230–33
Burma, 128, 132
Burns, John F., 280
butchering: cattle, 232; elephants, 71; to feed armies, 5; giraffes, 132; kosher, 36; rhinoceroses, 132; van Hooff and, 232; war and, 2; zoo animals for meat, 7, 85, 148, 151, 192, 197
buzzards, 51

Cadwalader, William, 296n23
cages: as "artificial environments," 5; barless design of, 24, 28, 65, 276; Buchenwald and, 48, 54; captured soldiers and, 226–27, 230, *231*; free enclosures and, 26, 28, 57; Halloran and, 226–27; Huxley on, 21; KZ system and, 242–43, 248, 250–51; "radiant prison of light," 276; resistance and, 213–17; weather and, 92
Calcutta Zoo, 122
camels: Bactrian, 168; Burgers' Zoo and, 233; dromedary, 71–72; Dublin Zoo and, 160; London Exeter Exchange and, 20; Mongolian, 263; occupation and, 106; Ueno Zoo and, 263; war effort and, 168, 170
Cameroon, 26
Canada, 30, 127, 171, 229
Cansdale, George, 276
Cantor, Aviva, 285
Capra, Frank, 127
Caricuao Zoo, 284
Casa de Fieras. See Madrid Zoo
Caspian sheep, 233
Catholics, 64–65, 103
cats: big, 108, 120, 141 (*see also specific big cats*); eating of, 67, 152; euthanized, 36, 89; food and, 144; Heart

Mountain Relocation Center and, 221, 223; Reich Animal Protection Act and, 33; September Holocaust and, 89; stray, 67; wildcats, 43
Catskill Game Park, 283
cattle, 331n38; Artis Zoo and, 215; Askaniya Nova and, 188; aurochs, 41–42, 207, 299n36; back-breeding, 41, 285, 299n36; Buchenwald and, 46; Chillingham, 88; as utility animals, 144; van Hooff and, 232–33; war impact on, 5, 257
Celinscak, Mark, 246
Central Park Zoo, 18–19, 27–29
Chad, 26, 284
Chamberlain, Neville, 79, 87
Changgyeong Palace, 131
charity, 17, 39, 113
cheetahs, 87, 267
Chelmno, 330n15
Chengdu, viii–ix
Chessington Zoo, 203, 325n39
Chester Zoo, 15, 19n, 85, 160–61
Chiang Kai-shek, viii
Chicago Tribune, 160
chickens, 142, 146, 257, 267; Buchenwald and, 46; and wartime food production, 67, 144, *173*, 178n
children: Antwerp Zoo and, 7; Artis Zoo and, *7*, 217; concentration camps and, 213, 216, 221, 223–24, 244; drone strikes and, 323n3; elephants and, 195–96, 198; evacuation of, 82–84, 133–34; fascism and, 37; Jewish, 7, 216–17, 218, 244; labor and, 59, 156; liberation and, 229, 234, 260; Lucile Mann's racism and, 310n9; Nazis and, 37, 39, 116; petting zoos and, 9, 22, 160, 223; propaganda and, 39, 109; remembrance and, 279; resistance and, 213, 216–18; Royal Children's Zoo, 23; Spanish Civil War and, 67, 70, 72, 74; Ueno Zoo and, 195–96; zoos and, 7, 174, 177, 285
Children's Overseas Reception Board (CORB), 133–34

Chillingham cattle, 88

chimpanzees: Babu, 83; bombings and, 98, 203; Boo-Boo II, 83; colonialism and, 60; evacuation of, 83; George, 80; Georgie, 171; Gert, 83; Hank, 171; labor and, 154, 160; petting zoos and, 22; postwar issues and, 263, 267, *272*; Punggol Zoo and, 130; racism and, 310n9; resistance and, 211, 216; restocking, 267; Rotterdam Zoo and, 98; Tiny Tim, 83; war effort and, 80, 170–71; war impact on, 294n9

China: Japan and, 128, 313n21; Mao, 271; National Revolutionary Army, 128; pandas and, viii–xiv

Christians, 109, 217–19

Churchill, Winston, 6, 85, 99, 127, 171, 186

Cincinnati Zoo, 120, 170

circuses: Cole Brothers', 125–26; labor from, 156; postwar issues and, 261, 269; Ringling Brothers', 126; zoos and, 17, 20

civets, 118, 202

Clères, 99–102, 275

climate change: disinformation, 338n31; World War Zoo Garden Project and, 335n2; zoos and, 11, 282–88

Coates, Christopher W., 179

Cocteau, Jean, 130

Cohn, Werner, 336n3

Cold War, 8, 9, 230, 265, 270–73, 276, 280

Cole Brothers' circus, 125–26

collaboration: German zoos and, 39; international cooperation and, 63; liberation and, 230, 260; occupation and, 104, 109–13, 278; resistance and, 8, 212–14; "shield" theory of, 309n28

collateral damage, 2, 99, 201

Cologne Zoo, 61

colonialism, 24–25, 57, 60, 129–31, 267, 271–72

Colonial Zoo, 24–25

communism, 280; Dos Passos and, 256; Dutch, 107; fascism and, 64, 115; *La Humanitat* and, 72–73; Osborn Jr. on, 271; Sachsenhausen and, 53–54; Soviet zoos and, 188; Spanish Civil War and, 64, 72–73; Stalin and, 16n, 30, 94, 127, 168, 186–87, 190, 196–97, 227, 270; Wahl and, 230

Como Park Zoo, 28

complicity, 2, 212, 278–79

concentration camps, 255; Auschwitz, 89, 216, 217, 246–47, 330n15; Belsec, 330n15; Bergen-Belsen, 239, 246; Buchenwald, 43–55, *240*, 279, 330n15; Chelmno, 330n15; children and, 213, 216, 221, 223–24, 244; crematoriums and, 44, 55; Dachau, 223, 241, 249, 330n15; disease and, 45; escapees from, 218; evolution of, 300n3; exterminations in, 241, 330n15; Final Solution and, 241–43, 246–47, 249–51, 330n15; Göring and, 33, 46; Hollandsche Schouwburg and, 216; human experiments in, 45, 92–93, 240–41; Japanese Americans in US, 220–25, 327n24; Kiev Zoo and, 332n40; KZ system and, 44, 239–51; liberation and, 223, 239, 246–47, 259–60; Majdanek, 330n15; Malchow, 248; PETA and, 6; "preventive custody" and, 44; Ravensbrück, 248; remembrance and, 279; resistance and, 330n15; Sachsenburg, 45; Sachsenhausen, 45, 53–54, 301n25; Singing Forest and, 45; slave labor and, 44, 46, 48, 50, 53, 127, 156–57, 162, 251, 259, 317n14, 330n15; Sobibor, 330n15; survivors of, 159, 246–48; Treblinka, 219, 244–46, 250, 330n15, 331n38; triangle identification system of, 45; women and, 216

Coney Island, 179

Conference on Science and World Affairs, 273

Cook, J. C., 130

cormorants, 63

COVID-19 pandemic, 114

Cowles, Virginia, 68

Cox, Geoffrey, 69
Crandall, Lee, 102, 275
cranes, 77, 268, 275
crocodiles, 95n, 294n9; bombing and, 79, 209; confinement of, 21; Dutch zoos and, 95–96; Rome Zoo and, 26; suicide, 16; weather and, 92
Cunningham, Lizzie, 142
cyanide, 194
Czechoslovakia: Hitler and, 62; labor from, 157; Langers and, 30; liberation and, 230; occupation and, 30, 104, 107; postwar restocking and, 269; resistance and, 212, 213, 230; Vltava River, 93; Zenkel and, 50
Czupalla, Hans-Peter, 279

Dachau, 223, 241, 249, 330n15
Daily Express (newspaper), 162
Daily Mail (newspaper), 68, 171
Daily Standard (newspaper), 105
Daily Worker (newspaper), 68
Daniel, Paul M., 257
Dark, Philip, 259
Darwin, Charles, 21, 100, 187
Dashina, Yevdokia, 191–92
Davis, Karen, 249
D-Day, 229
DDT, *260*
death squads, 78
deer: American zoos and, 124; bombing and, 73, 208; Buchenwald and, 46–51; Clères and, 101; execution or release of, 87, 132; as food, 88, 132, 280; food crisis and, 148; "meat value" of, 150; Nazis and, 35, 42; weather and, 92; wild, 257
Deese, R. S., 273
Delacour, Jean Théodore: American zoos and, 102, 121; Clères collection of, 99–102, 275; France and, 307n25; on wartime animal loss, 256
Department of Science, Popular Education and Cultural Affairs, 103
Der Deutsche Wegleiter für Paris (guide), 109
"Der Führer's Face" (Blanc), 171

Der Sturmer, 243
Detroit Zoo, 122
De Vico, Raffaele, 26–27
disease: animals and, 11, 70, 72, 189–90, 265, 281, 294n9; Black Death, 6, 255; Buchenwald and, 45; COVID-19, 114; human experiments in, 45; KZ system and, 241, 330n15; Spanish Civil War and, 67, 74; typhoid, 247; typhus, 45; war and, 142, 175, 255; war effort and, 178–79
Dittmar, Kurt, 50–51, *52–53*
Dittoe, Mrs. George, 161
Dmitry Donskoy (ship), 270–71
dogs: Barcelona Zoo and, 66; Blondi, 35; Buchenwald and, 49–50; eating of, 67, 152; euthanized, 36, 89; food and, 144; German shepherds, 35, 221; Göring and, *34*; Great Danes, 37, 66; Heart Mountain Relocation Center and, 221, 223; Hitler and, 35; Jews and, 36; KZ system and, 241, 247; petting zoos and, 160; Reich Animal Protection Act and, 33; September Holocaust and, 89; stray, 67, 285
Dogs' Rescue Home, 136–37
dolphins, 295n21
Doolittle Raid, 193
Dos Passos, John, 256
Douhet, Giulio, 68–69
Dower, John, 128–29
Downs, Alex, Jr., 176
Dresden Zoo, 39, 157, 233–34
Dublin Zoo, 145–46, 160
ducks, 38, 46, 93
Duisburg Zoo, 38
Dumb Friends League, 320n19
Dunham, R. J., 177
Dunn, William J., x
Düsseldorf Zoo, 228–29
Dutch East Indies, 129, 131
Dutch Nazi Party, 103
Dutch zoos: antelopes and, 98; Artis Zoo, 7, 8, 61, *62*, 99, 107–8, 113, 215–17; *Blitzkrieg* on, 94–99; bombing of, 96, 98; execution of animals in, 96,

Dutch zoos (*cont.*)
98; *Fall Gelb* and, 96; Great Depression and, 96, 98; Luftwaffe and, 96; Ouwehand's Zoo, 95–96, 306n13

eagles, 18, 294n9; Buchenwald and, 49, 51, 55; execution of, 89; war effort and, 174
East Berlin Zoo, 271
economic issues: American zoos and, 3, 115, 148; capital investment, 141; Great Depression, 2, 9, 15–20, 23, 28, 98, 159; international cooperation and, 56; Nazis and, 104, 106, 251; Pacific War and, 129; postwar, 33, 284; restocking zoos, 265–69; tourism, 20, 39, 55, 102, 109, 114, 130, 284; zoo attendance, 8, 16–17, 24–25, 29, 111, 123, 135, 150. *See also* labor
Edinburgh Zoo, 81
education: biology, 22; Department of Public Education and the Arts, 113; Huxley on, 21–22; occupation and, 103, 113; war effort and, 8, 174, 178–81; zoos as, 18, 20, 22
eels, 87, 179
Ehrlich, Anne, 273
Ehrlich, Franz, 46
Ehrlich, Paul, 273
elephants, 1–2, 5; American zoos and, 120, 122, *164*; Antwerp Zoo and, 17; Ba-Bar, 83; Barcelona Zoo and, 72–73; Betty, 191; bombing and, 78–79, 191, 204, 208; breeding of, 268; Caesar, 228–29; chained, 295n21; children and, 134, 195–96, 198; in circus fire, 126; cost of, 265; debris clearing by, 258, 260–61; Dutch zoos and, 95; evacuation or execution of, 77–78, 83, 161, 190, 191, 194–97, 228–29; food and, 10, 146, 148, 152–53; Hanako, 195–96, 198, 278; Indian, 83, 122, 152, 260, 262; Jon, 195–96, 198, 277; Júlia, 72–73; Kasia, 79; Kiri, 260, *261*; liberation and, 232–36; Madrid Zoo and, 71; Many, 260, *261*; Mo Po Ko, 83; Nelli, 233; Nona, 190;

occupation and, 105–6; orchestra of, 17; Pancho, 71, 73; *Panik*, 199, *200*; postwar issues and, 262–68; Ranee, 83; restocking, 266–67; Tonki, 195–96, 198, 278; war effort and, 71, 170; weather and, 91–92
elk, 150, 153
emus, *161*, 168, 203, 281
endangered species: Barbary lions, 73; breeding programs and, 268; Caspian sheep, 233; government petitions for, 275; northern white rhinoceros, 284; Przewalski's horses, 189; Rawlins on, 274; Schroeder on, 274; scimitar-horned oryx, 283–84
Enemies, a Love Story (Singer), 250–51
Entnazifizierung (denazification), 262
Erikson, Ruth, vii
Err, Saeed Al-, 281
Ethiopia, 27, 29, 60
eugenics, 21, 40, 56–57, 123
euthanasia, 36, 89, 150, 190
evacuation and war preparation: air raids and, 77–90; at American Zoos, 119–22; at Antwerp Zoo, 85; of children, 82–84; food and, 82–83, 88–89; in France, 77, 90; Hitler and, 78–81, 85, 89–90; at London Zoo, 79–84, 85–88, 90; Luftwaffe and, 78, 80; in Netherlands, 90; Operation Pied Piper and, 83; pets and, 89; in Poland, 78, 85, 90; refugees and, 83; sacrifice and, 84–90; stress of, 207–8; at Vincennes Zoo, 77–78; at Warsaw Zoo, 78–79; of women, 82–84; of zoo animals, 77–90
executions. *See* sacrifice
Executive Order 9066, 220
Exposition Colonial International de Paris, 24–25
extinction: aurochs, 41–42, 207, 299n36; back-breeding and, 41, 61, 243, 285, 299n36; current threat of, 282; global warming and, 282, 338n31; great auk, 2; hunting and, 256; IUDZG and, 274–75; koalas and, 337n17; Kolbert on, 282; mass, 273,

282; Nazi ideology and, 240; passenger pigeon, 2; Rawlins on, 274; Schroeder on, 274; scimitar-horned oryx and, 283–84; tarpans, 40; zoos' role against, 5, 11, 274–75

factory farming, 6
falcons, 46–47, 49, 55
Fall Gelb (Case Yellow), 96
Falz-Fein, Friedrich, 187
Farm Animal Rights Movement (FARM), 250
fascism: America and, xi, 115, 124, 325n38; animals and, 37; children and, 37; communism and, 53, 64, 115; Ethiopia and, 29; Italian, 26–27; modernism and, 26–27; Mussolini and, 16n, 26–27, 29, 64; Nazis and, 16n, 37, 106, 115, 128, 212–13; occupation and, 106; resistance to, 211–13, 217; Spanish Civil War and, 64
Fauna (magazine), 176
Feldman Ecopark, 4
Final Solution, 36, 212, 241, 246, 249
Finlayson, Janet, 81
firebombing, 236, 325n38, 329n22
Firestone, Harvey, 117
Firma Ruhe, 228
Fisher, James, 181
flamingos, 54, 154
Flewin, L. M., 262
Flood, Cedric, 160
Foch, Ferdinand, 100
Foit, František, 213
Fontenoy, Jean, 53–54, 301n25
food, 10; animal treats and, 145; Antwerp Zoo and, 17, 85, 92, 148; Barcelona Zoo and, 64, 66–67, 71–72, 74; Buchenwald and, 49–51; as central to WWII, 142; Depression Diets, 17; expense of, 17–18; famine and, 72, 192, 217, 237, 256, 263, 273, 281; Göring's love of, 31; hand-feeding, 22, 295n21; KZ system and, 55, 250; labor and, 158; Leningrad Zoo and, 191–93; liberation and, 228–31; Madrid Zoo and, 64, 66–67, 71, 74;

malnutrition and, 67, 72, 142, 151, 236, 257, 263, 275; William Mann on, 8, 145, 147, 149; mice as, 142–43, 149; milk, 17, 49, 67, 142, 178–79; occupation and, 111–13; patriotism and, 147–49, 150, 192, 193–96; postwar issues and, 255–56, 261–63, 267, 275; potatoes, 49–51, 67, 142, 144–49, 248, 258, 263; rationing, 30, 49, 67, 143, 148, 150, *172*, *173*, 179, 191, 192, 217, 228, 255, 267, 275; rats as, 142–43, 256; resistance and, 214–15; road-kill, 17; sacrifice and, 150–53, 190–96; San Diego Zoo and, 142–43, 146, 151; scavenging for, 50, 67, 157, 191; shortages of, 3, 5, 17–18, 49, 64, 67, 74, 88, 111, 144, 149–51; smuggling of, 214; Soviet Union and, 190–91; Spanish Civil War and, 64–67, 70–71, 74; superfluous eaters and, 149–51; vegetarians, 30, 33, 36, 197, 298n10; victory gardens, 144–46; war effort and, 170, *173*, 178–79; weather and, 92; zoo animals as, 88, 150, 152–53. *See also* butchering; hunger; starvation
Foster, Frank, 325n30
Fotonieuws (magazine), 113
foxes, 33, 43, 47, 51, 77, 88, 148, 245
France: Blum and, 47; bombing and, 96, 201; Buchenwald and, 47; capitulation of, 102, 119; Clères, 99–102, 275; Cocteau and, 130; colonialism and, 24–25, 119; Delacour and, 121, 275, 307n35; Deladier and, 47; evacuation and, 77–78, 90; *Exposition Colonial International de Paris*, 24–25; *Fall Gelb* and, 96; food shortages, 151–52; imperialism and, 26; Indochina and, 25, 100, 128–29; *Jeder einmal in Paris*, 109–10; labor from, 156–58; liberation and, 229; Normandy, 99, 155n, 229; occupation and, 104, 109, 111; postwar issues and, 258, 266, 275; resistance and, 94, 111, 211–14; Spanish Civil War and, 65, 69–70; Vichy, 102, 109,

France (cont.)
111, 212, 214; Vincennes Zoo, 24–26, 58, 77–78, 94, 102, 109, 214, 266, 269; West Africa and, 119; zoos, funding of, 6
Franco, Francisco, 64, 68–74
francolin, 118
Frankenhuis, Maarten, 113
Franklin Park Zoo, 148
free enclosures (*Freianlagen*), 26, 28, 57
Free Zone, 214
Friedrich, Jörg, 207
Fudge, Erica, 70
Fukuda, Saburō, 193–97

Gannett, Lewis, 104
gas, 77, 80–81, 83, 86, *180*, 244–45
Gaulle, Charles de, 212
Gaza, 281–82, 284–85, 336n14
gazelles, 133
Geary, James, 246
Gellhorn, Martha, 70
genetics: aurochs and, 41–42; back-breeding and, 41, 61, 243, 285, 299n36; eugenics and, 21, 40, 56–57, 123; extinction and, 41; innovation in, 283
Gensch, Winfried, 234
German shepherds, 35, 221
Gestapo, 211, 216, 218
ghettos, 213–14, 218–19, 247, 250
gibbons, 101, 234, 329n22
Gila monsters, 86
Ginzburg, Lidiya, 197
giraffes: bombing and, 79, 96, 201, 202; Boxer, 202; D-Day, 229; Dutch zoos and, 95–96; evacuation of, 77, 208; food crisis and, 147, 151; Hitler and, 38; Marius, 150; Pacific War and, 132; postwar issues and, 263, 268; Spanish Civil War and, 67; weather and, 92
Glass, Leslie, 132
Glazar, Richard, 244
global warming, 338n31
Glorious Revolution, 65
Goat 311, 270

goats: bombing and, *82*, 269–70; as food, 151; milking, 178; mountain, 35; Murcia-Granada, 66; National Zoo and, 28; petting zoos and, 160; as utility animals, 144
Goebbels, Joseph: Berlin Zoo and, 42–43; "eternal laws" of, 37–38; master race and, 35; monkeys and, 38; Olympics and, 42–43; *Panik* and, 199–200; on Paris, 109; propaganda and, 36, 43
goldfish, 67, 221, 294n9
Good Neighbor Policy, 147
gophers, 223
gorillas: caged, 21; in circus fire, 126; evacuation of, 82; international cooperation and, 60–61, *62*; Japie, 216; liberation and, 235; Meng, 82; Moko, 82; Pongo, 235; restocking, 266, 269
Göring, Hermann: as animal lover, 6, 32, 35; appearance of, 31; bombings and, 189, 204; Buchenwald and, 46; concentration camps and, 33, 46; extravagances of, 31–32; as Fat Hermann, 31–32; Lutz Heck and, 8, 41–42, 189, 207, 243, 262; Hellabrunn Zoo and, 38; hunting and, 35, 207; labor and, 155; lions and, 31–32, 41; Luftwaffe and, 31, 78, 101; morphine addiction of, 31; nature preserve of, 42, 189; propaganda and, 32; titles of, 31, 35; vivisection and, 33, *34*; zoo donation of, 38
Grant, Madison, 123
Grant Park Zoo, 123
great auk, 2
Great Danes, 37, 66
Great Depression, 2, 9, 15–29, 98, 159
Great Patriotic War, 196–97
great spotted kiwis, 4
Great Zoo Massacre, 194, 322n28
Grebbe Line (fortified trenches), 96
Greenhall, Arthur M., 174
Grossman, Vasily, 244–45
Grüne Polizei (green police), 212–13, 216
Grzimek, Bernhard, 39

Guam, 127
Guazzaloca, Giulia, 26
guinea pigs, 46, 190, 191

habu (*Protobothrops flavoviridis*), 179
Haeckel, Ernst, 37
Hagenbeck, Carl: free enclosures of, 24, 26, 28, 57–58, 65; Rome Zoo and, 26, 57, 297n55
Hagenbeck, Heinrich, 58
Hagenbeck, John, 58
Hagenbeck, Lorenz, 58, 157
Hagenbeck Zoo, 148, 157; bombing of, 205, 207, 210; after liberation, 259–62; as model for other zoos, 24, 26, 28, 57–58
Hague, The, 68, 108
Haikal, Mustafa, 234
Halloran, Raymond, 226–27, 328n2
Hamas, 281
Hamm Zoo, 38
hamsters, 168
Hanover Zoo, 147, 158, 159
Hansen, Saskia, 212
Hardouin-Fugier, Elisabeth, 24, 297n55
Harkins, Dan, 148, 149
Harris, Arthur, 204–5
Harris, J. P., 94
Hartman, Carl, 143–44
Hattori, Michie, 237
Hauchecorne, Friedrich, 60–61
hawks, 55, 89
Heart Mountain Relocation Center, 221–25
Heck, Heinz: acclimation experiments of, 92–93; back-breeding and, 41–42, 61; geo-zoo of, 57; Hellabrunn Zoo and, 40, 92, 113, 258, 262, 276; internationalism and, 57, 61; labor and, 156–58; postwar issues and, 258, 262, 276; Przewalski's horses and, 106
Heck, Heinz, Jr., 283
Heck, Ludwig, 40
Heck, Lutz: appearance of, 40; back-breeding and, 41–42, 243, 285; background of, 40–41; Berlin Zoo and,

8, 40–41, 106, 157, 165, 189, 205, 208, 209, 262, 278; bombing and, 205, 208–9, 318n40; Deutsche Zoo of, 43; fleeing of, 262; Göring and, 8, 41–42, 189, 207, 243, 262; Hauchecorne and, 61; international cooperation and, 61; KZ system and, 243–44; labor and, 157, 209; *Lebensraum* of, 243–44; Nazis and, 40–41, 43, 209; occupation and, 106, 189; Przewalski's horses and, 106, 189; war effort and, 176; women and, 318n40
Heidelberg Zoo, 38
Heinroth, Katharina: background of, 164–65; Berlin Zoo and, 165, *166*, 209–10, 235, 258; on bombings, 209, 235
Heinroth, Oskar, 165
Hellabrunn Zoo: bombing of, 205; food crisis and, 150; Heinz Heck and, 40, 92, 258, 262, 276; labor and, 155; liberation and, 233, 258; Nazi donations to, 38; restocking, 267–68; weather and, 92–93
Hershaft, Alex, 250
Hershey Zoo, 150, 154–55
Herzog, Gustav, 48
Heydrich, Reinhard, 212
Himmler, Heinrich, 35
hippopotamuses: Beauty, 191–92; bombing and, 208, 325n39; breeding of, 268; in circus fire, 126; Dutch zoos and, 95; evacuation of, 77; food and, *145*, 151, 192; Kyōko, 236; Leningrad Zoo and, 191–93; liberation and, 228, 234–36, 262; Maru, 236; occupation and, 106, 109; Pepe, 67; Pipo, 73–74; sacrifice and, 191–93, 197; Sheba, 151; Spanish Civil War and, 66–67, 71–73; as victims of war, 4, 197, 294n9; weather and, 92
Hirohito, 263
Hiroshima, 236–37, 273
Hitler, Adolf: American opinion of, 115; American zoos and, 115, 117, 123; as animal lover, 33, 35–36, 298n10; animal protection and, 33;

Hitler, Adolf (*cont.*)

antisemitism and, 3; Aryanism and, 37, 94, 107–8, 112, 214, 219, 244, 251; Austria and, 31, 36, 40, 62; bombing and, 201, 204, 325n39; Buchenwald and, 44; concentration camps and, 33, 43, 241–43, 246–47, 249–51, 330n15; Czechoslovakia and, 62; as enigma, 30; *Fall Gelb* and, 96; fascism and, 37, 64; France and, 99, 102; as *Führer*, 32, 35–36, 38, 43, *108*, 171, 298n10; international cooperation and, 57, 60; Jews and, 36, 78, 104, 107, 115, 123, 216, 218, 247, 278; KZ system and, 241–43, 246–47, 249–51, 330n15; labor and, 156–57; *Lebensraum* and, 78; liberation and, 227, 230, 233–34; Luftwaffe and, 78, 90; *Mein Kampf*, 104; nationalism of, 56, 64; Nazi ideology and, 32–43; New Order of, 104; occupation and, 104–9, 113; Operation Barbarossa and, 188–89; pets and, 35, 36; Poland and, 40, 78, 85, 90, 93, 104, 128, 189, 234, 247; postwar issues and, 256–62, 268, 276; racism and, 35, 37, 89, 104, 123; remembrance and, 278; resistance and, 211, 212–13, 216, 218; rise of, 56; sacrifice and, 185; Spanish Civil War and, 64; suicide propaganda and, 16n; thousand-year Reich of, 78; V1 and V2 programs of, 325n39; vegetarianism and, 30, 33, 36, 298n10; zoo donations by, 38

Hitler Youth, 127, 233, 247

Hollandsche Schouwburg, 216

Holocaust, *7*, 181; KZ system and, 239–42, 246–51; remembrance and, 279; resistance and, 214, 218

"Holocaust on your Plate" (PETA), 6

homosexuals, 45, 239

Hong Kong, xii, 131, 137

Honolulu Zoo, 124

Hooper, Henry, 156

Horkheimer, Max, 36–37

Hornaday, William T., 60

horses: Buchenwald and, 46; evacuation and, 83; as meat, 17, 111, 142, 146, 148, 149, 151, 191, 257; Nazis and, 33, 35; postwar issues and, 258; Przewalski's, 106, 187, 189, 207; Spanish Civil War and, 66, 67; tarpans, 40; World War II and, 5

Hoshizaki, Hiroshi, 224

Hoshizaki, Takashi, 224

Hudson, Robert G., 157

Hungary, 59, 91, 230, 255

hunger: Great Depression and, 18; Hunger Winter, 217; international cooperation and, 56; occupation and, 78, 111, 113, 189–93; postwar issues and, 255, 257; rations and, 142, 153; Spanish Civil War and, 67; war effort and, 178; of zoo animals, 10, 18, 196, 236, 280. *See also* starvation

hunting: bird, 79; Buchenwald and, 50–51, *53*; bug, 116; extinction and, 256; Göring and, 35, 41, 207; Hitler on, 33, 35; Mussolini and, 26; poaching, 35

Huxley, Julian Sorell: background of, 20–21; on cages, 21; petting zoos of, 22–23; war preparation and, 85, 117, 120; Zoological Society of London (ZSL) and, 21–22, 58; on zoos as educational, 22

Huxley, Thomas H., 20–21

hyenas, 20, 232, 235

Hygiene Institute, 240

hypothermia, 45, 197, 241

iguanas, 87, 153, 281

Il dominio dell'aria (The Command of the Air) (Douhet), 68–69

imperialism: French, 26; internationalism and, 57; Japanese, 6, 127–34, 137, 178, 193; Nazi, 133; Pacific War and, 129–31, 137; Roman, 26, 105; Vincennes Zoo and, 26; zoos and, 285–86

India: animal merchants of, 265; Great Britain and, 128, 129–30, 133

Indochina, 25, 100, 128, 129

International Brigades, 67, 72
international cooperation: Belgium and, 58; economic crisis and, 56; eugenics and, 56–57; golden age of, 56; Heinz Heck and, 57, 61; Lutz Heck and, 61; Hitler and, 56–57; imperialism and, 57; IUDZG and, 58–63, 188, 274–75; Japan and, 301n7; nationalism and, 56–60; resistance and, 63; science and, 57, 59; sterilization and, 57; united directors and, 58–60; Vincennes Zoo and, 58; in vogue, 56–57; zookeeping and, 59
Internationalen Verbandes der Direktoren Zoologischer Gärten (International Union of Directors of Zoological Gardens, IUDZG): history of, 58–59; postwar, 188, 274–75; prewar, 59–63, 188; Sunier and, 274
International Peace Conference, 68
International Union for Conservation of Nature, 275, 283–84
Iraq War, 287
Iron Curtain, 270–71
Ishigo, Arthur, 221, *222*
Ishigo, Estelle Peck, 223
Ismail, Tunku, 132
Israel, 281, 285
Italy: Douhet and, 68; Ethiopia and, 27; fascism and, 26–27; labor of, 156; Mussolini and, 16n, 26–29, 64, 91; Polish storks in, 79; prewar, 6; Rome Zoo, 26–27, 58, 60, 148, 257, 297n55; *Savoia* bombers of, 72; Spanish Civil War and, 68, 69, 72

jackals, 77, 136
jaguars, 88, 98
Japan: atrocities of, 128; China and, 128, 313n21; food and, 142–43, 147, 256; Greater East Asia Co-Prosperity Sphere and, 128, 227; Hirohito, 263; Hiroshima, 236–37, 273; Imperial, 6, 127–34, 137, 178, 193; international cooperation and, 301n7, 309n3; Kempeitai and, 226; liberation and, 226–27, 235–36; Manchuria

and, 6, 128; Meiji Restoration and, 130; Nagasaki, 236–38, 273; napalm dropped on, 236; night raiders, 120; Pacific War and, 127–38; Pearl Harbor and, vii–viii, 119, 135; Penang and, 122; plethora of zoos in, 130–31; poison and, 194, 313n21; postwar issues and, 256, 263–64, 269–70; propaganda in, 178, 186, 193–96; Russo-Japanese War, 131; sacrifice and, 186, 193, 196–98; *sakoku* of, 130; submarine torpedoes of, 127, 141; Ueno Zoo, 195 (*see also* Ueno Zoo); women and, 318n40; Yamato and, 129
Japanese Americans, internment of, 220–25, 327n24
Japanese Home Islands, 227
Jardin d'Acclimatation, 151
Jardin des Plantes, 25, 78, 102, 105, 151
Jedem das Seine (To Each His Own), 46
Jeder einmal in Paris (Everyone once in Paris), 109–10
Jennings, Allyn, viii
Jews: American zoos and, 123–24; animal protection laws and, 36–37; Aryanism and, 37, 94, 107–8, 112, 214, 219, 244, 251; Berlin Zoo and, 278–79, 336n3; *Blitzkrieg* and, 78; Buchenwald and, 45, 48, 50, *53*; children and, 7, 216–18, 244, 285; Czupalla and, 279; death squads and, 78; dogs and, 36; Dutch, 107–8; Final Solution and, 36, 212, 241, 246, 249; German, 36, 107; Hitler and, 36, 78, 104, 107, 115, 123, 216, 218, 247, 278; kosher butchering and, 36; KZ system and, 239–44, 247–50, 330n15; Nazification and, 106–9; under occupation, 104–8, 112–13; pets of, 36; as refugees, 8, 78, 214, 218; remembrance and, 278–79, 285, 336n3; resistance and, 212–19; science and, 36; *Singende Pferde* (singing horses) and, 241; viewed as animals, 241–43
Johor Zoo, 132

Jünger, Ernst, 109, 309n22
Junior Zoological Society, 257

Kabul Zoo, 280–81
kangaroos: bombing and, 204; bushfires
and, 337n17; eating of, 152; evacua-
tion of, 77; international cooperation
and, 58; restocking of, 228; Soviet
zoos and, 187; Spanish Civil War and,
72–73; Ukraine invasion and, 4; as
victims of war, 263, 270, 294n9; war
effort and, *173*; weather and, 92
Kato, Masuo, 236
Kawata, Ken, 130–31
Kean, Hilda, 306n35
Kempeitai, 226
Kennedy, Kathleen, 23
Kennedy, Robert, 23
Kennedy, Teddy, 23
Khan Younis Zoo, 284–85
Kharkiv, 4, *110*
Kiev Zoo, 105, 189, 332n40
Kisling, Vernon N., Jr., 105
Knauer, Christine, 123
Knudson, Gus, 121–24, 265
koalas, *136*, 137, 337n17
Koch, Artwin, 47
Koch, Erich, 104
Koch, Ilse, 45
Koch, Karl-Otto, 45–49, *53*, 54, 300n15
Koga, Tadamichi, 194, 263, 274
Kogon, Eugen, 54
Kolbert, Elizabeth, 282
Korea, 6, 131, 271
Kraft durch Freude (Strength through
Joy), 39
Krakow Zoo, 106
Krefeld Zoo, 38
Kuiper, Koenraad, 98–99, 108n, 158–59,
317n25
Kuiper, Sara, 158–59
Kung, H. H., x
Kupfer-Koberwitz, Edgar, 249–50
Kursaal Zoo, 89
Kyoto Zoo, 264
KZ system: Bergen-Belsen, 239; Berlin
Zoo and, 243; Buchenwald, 44–55,

240; cages and, 242–43, 248, 250–51;
children and, 244; concentration camps, 44–45, 53–55, 239–51,
330n15; crematoriums and, 44, 55;
disease and, 45, 241, 330n15; Lutz
Heck and, 243–44; Hitler and, 241–
43, 246–47, 249–51, 330n15; Holocaust and, 239–42, 246–51; human
experiments in, 45, 92–93, 240–41;
Jews and, 45, 48, 216, 239–44, 247–
50, 330n15; metaphor and, 246–48,
249, 250; moral issues and, 249–51;
Poland and, 243, 247–48, 330n15,
331n38; POWs and, 248; preventive
custody and, 44; reeducation and,
44; Singing Forest and, 45; slavery
in, 44, 48, 50, 68, 127, 156–57, 162,
251, 259, 330n15; SS and, 45, 240–41,
244–47; starvation and, 241; suffering and, 239, 249; triangle identification system of, 45; use of animal
terms in, 240–43; women and, 244

labor, 154, 162; air raids and, 157; *ausländische Arbeitskräfte*, 156; Australia
and, 161; Belgium and, 156, 158;
Berlin Zoo and, 157, 165, *166*; bombing and, 155, 157–59; cages and, 156,
158; captive workers and, 156–59;
children and, 156; circus, 156; concentration camps and, 44, 46, 48, 53,
159, 259, 317n14, 330n15; Czechoslovakia and, 157; France and, 156–58;
Göring and, 155; Great Depression
and, 16, 159; Heinz Heck and, 156,
157; Lutz Heck and, 157; Hellabrunn
Zoo and, 155; Hitler and, 156–57;
hunger and, 158; Italy and, 156,
160; London Zoo and, 155–56, 159,
162; military service and, 154–56;
National Zoo and, 119, 158, 162;
Nazis and, 156, 158; Netherlands
and, 157–58; patriotism and, 155;
Philadelphia Zoo and, 155n, 157; Poland and, 157; POWs and, 156–58; as
repetitious, 228; resistance and, 158;
San Diego Zoo and, 155, 161, 163–64;

shortage of, 154–56; *Singende Pferde* (singing horses) and, 241; slave, 44, 48, 50, 68, 127, 156–57, 162, 251, 259, 330n15; Soviet Union and, 156–59, 165; Ueno Zoo and, 318n40; Ukraine and, 157; unemployment and, 16, 19–20, 23, 27, 169; women and, 122, 151, 154, 156, 159–67, 176–77, 265, 317n28, 318n40; zookeepers, 159–62 (*see also* zookeepers); *Zwangsarbeiter* (forced laborer), 46, 48, 157–59, 215–16, 259, 278, 317n14

"Ladies Only" (newsreel), 154

La Humanitat (newspaper), 72–73

lambs, 67, 160

Langer, Adele, 30

Langer, Jan Misha, 30

Langer, Tommy, 30

La Vanguardia (newspaper), 74

Lawton, Alfred, 123–24

Lazerson, Tamar, 249

Lebensraum (living space), 51, 78, 243

Leigh, Elisabeth, 5–6

Le Journal, 26

lemurs, 281

Leningrad Zoo: Beauty, 191–92; food and, 191–92; preparation by, 191–92; remembrance and, 277; Soviet Union and, 142, 188–93, 196–97, 270, 277

leopards, 294n9; in circus fire, 126; evacuation or execution of, 18, 88, 136, 195, 235; London Exeter Exchange and, 20; Prospect Park Zoo and, 29; restocking of, 228; rising cost of, 265; Sarajevo Zoo and, 280; Spanish Civil War and, 66, 73

Levi-Strauss, Claude, 8

liberation: Antwerp Zoo and, *231*; Berlin Zoo and, 232, 235; bombing and, 226, 230–37; cages and, 230, *231*; children and, 229, 234; Cold War and, 230; collaboration and, 230; concentration camps and, 223, 239–40, 246; D-Day, 229; food and, 228–31; France and, 229; Hellabrunn Zoo and, 233; Hitler and, 227,

230, 233–34; hunger and, 233, 236; Japan and, 226–27, 235–36; Pearl Harbor and, 226; Poland and, 230, 234; POWs and, 328n2; refugees and, 232; resistance and, 230, 235; revenge on occupiers during, 229–33; Russia and, 230; shock and, 229; Soviet Union and, 230, 234–35; SS and, 235; starvation and, 232, 235–36; suffering and, 234; Ueno Zoo and, 226–27, 236; Ukraine and, 237; Wehrmacht and, 227, 235; women and, 229; zookeepers and, 233–34

Liberia, 117–19, 267, 310n9

Life Magazine, 268, 276

Lincoln Park Zoo, 122, 177

lions, 105, 294n9; American zoos and, 115, 121, 123; Barbary, 73; Bluton, 66; bombing and, 208; breeding of, 268; caged, 21; in circus fire, 126; evacuation or execution of, 78, 85, 88–89, 98, 136, 141, 191, 307n17; food and, 18, 30, 148, 150; Göring and, 31–32, 41; labor and, 160; liberation and, 232, 235; London Exeter Exchange and, 20; Madrid Zoo and, 65; Marjan, 280; Micci, 66; misery of, 19; Mussolini and, 26–27; Nazis and, 31–32, 37–38; petting zoos and, 160; as "prisoners of state," 25; Prospect Park Zoo and, 29; restocking, 267–68; Sarajevo Zoo and, 280; Spanish Civil War and, 65–66, 71, 73; war effort and, *176*; weather and, 91–93

Litten, Freddy, 194, 196

Liverpool Zoo, 79

Livingston, Bernard, 272–73

lobsters, 33

Łódź Becomes Litzmannstadt (film), 110

Loisel, Gustave Antoine Armand, 65

London, Joan, 125

London Exeter Exchange, 20

London Zoo: American zoos and, 117, 121, 124; bombing and, 68, 79–88, 121, 202–3, 204, 257; butchering and, 151; charity ball of, 17; comeback of, 275–76; evacuation and

London Zoo (*cont.*)
preparation of, 79–88, *86*, 90; food crisis and, 146–47, 151; Huxley and, 85, 117; labor and, 155–56, 159, 162; postwar issues and, 274, 275–76; reopening of, 90; vandalism and, 124; war effort at, 80, 170–73, 175–76, 178; Zuckerman and, 3, 19–20

looting: of art, 32, 106; of Ethiopia, 27; of graves, 213; of occupied zoos, 2, 9, 63, 101, 103–6, 189, 215

Lorenz, Konrad, 39

Lowe, Keith, 255

Lubetkin, Berthold, 57

Lucas, Sylvia, 170

Luce, Henry, viii

Luftwaffe, 31, 69, 78, 80, 96, 101, 325n38

Lyautey, Maréchal, 24

lynxes, 106

Lyons, James J., 115

macaws, 77

MacBride, E. W., 15

MacDonald, Roderick, 59

MacMillan, Robert, 268

Madame Chiang, viii–xi

Madrid Zoo: bombing of, 66–71, 79; eating animals of, 67; elephants and, 71; food and, 66–71; Franco and, 73–74; reopening of, 71; Spanish Civil War and, 64–74, 79

magpies, 87, 221, 224–25

Maidstone Zoo, 170, 203–4

Majdanek, 330n15

Malaysia, 130, 132

manatees, 87, 235

Manchester Daily Herald, 85

Manchuria, 6, 128

Manini (ship), 127

Mann, Lucile Quarry: on Antwerp Zoo, 148; profile on, 159–60; racism of, 310n9; travels of, 116–19, 125, 275; at USDA, 116; on vandalism, 124; Zonta Club and, 161–62

Mann, William: Basapa and, 130; on diet, 8, 145, 147, 149, 179; female workers and, 159, 162; Greenhall

and, 174; National Zoo and, 116, 119–22; Perkins and, 168; postwar issues and, 270, 275; travels of, 116–19, 275–76; war effort and, 168, 174, 179–80

Manzanar War Relocation Center, 221, 223

Mao, 271

Marai, Sandor, 255

marmosets, 54

Marrin, Albert, 223

marten, 47

Marvin, Garry, 124

Matsumura, Clarence, 223, 224

May, Earl Chapin, 28

McCarthy, Joseph, 270

McDonald, Tracy, 190

meerkats, 281

Meiji Restoration, 130

Mein Kampf (Hitler), 104

Melbourne Zoo, 16, 129, 134–35, 161

Mengele, Josef, 92–93

mice: as food, 142–43, 149; Heart Mountain and, 223; medical experiments on, 46, 178n, 190, 241

Miedzyrzecki, Benjamin, 218–20

milk, 17, 49, 67, 142, 178–79

Miller, Bert, 220

Miller, Ian Jared, 131, 301n7

Milwaukee Zoo, 125, 266, 320n29

Mimile (marmoset), 54

Mitchell, Peter Chalmers, 21

Mitteleuropäische Zoodirecktorenkonferenz (Central European Conference of Zoo Directors), 58–59

Mohr, Oscar, 114

monkeys: anti-animal violence and, 124–25; bombing and, 79, 201, 208, 325n39; Buchenwald and, 46, 48, 49–51; in circus fire, 126; Dutch zoos and, 98; food and, 143, 145, 149; Goebbels and, 37–38; KZ system and, 239, 243, 248; liberation and, 226, 232, 235; occupation and, 109, 132; Pacific War and, 132, 134; from Physiological Institute, 185; postwar issues and, 263; preparation and,

86; restocking, 266; sacrifice and, 185; Spanish Civil War and, 72–73; suicide, 15–16; as victims of war, 4–5, 294n9

morale: bombing and, 202, 323n7, 324n9; public, 176; zoos' efforts to boost, 171, 176–78

moral issues, 8, 9; bombing, 205, 209–10; hedonism, 109; hunger and, 67, 113, 256; KZ system, 249–50; Nazis, 33, 37; Reich Animal Protection Act, 33; remembrance, 279, 287; resistance, 212, 215; sacrifice, 196; unemployment and, 20; war effort, 171, 175–77, 320n22

Morton, Patricia A., 24

Moscow Zoo, 17, 30, 178n, 185–90

Mottershead, George, 85, 160–61

mouflon, 47

Mullan, Bob, 124

Munich Conference, 79

Munich Pact, 85

Murphy, Charles, 276

Mussolini, Benito, 6; hunting and, 26; as Il Duce, 26, 27; lions and, 26–27; patriotism and, 26; Spanish Civil War and, 64; suicide propaganda and, 16n

"muzzle and claw" epidemic, 62

My Friends in Captivity or The Zoo in Turmoil (Bourez), 158

Nagasaki, 236–38, 273

napalm, 236

Napoleon, 65, 99, 105, 109

nationalism: Lutz Heck and, 40; international cooperation and, 56–60; jingoism of, 12; Olympics and, 42–43; Spanish Civil War and, 64, 66, 68, 72, 74; war effort and, 181

Nationalist Party (Spain), 64, 66, 68, 72, 74

National Zoo: American empire and, 131; elephants and, 122; food crisis and, 144–47, 149; game dinners of, 152–53; during Great Depression, 28; labor and, 119, 162; Lucile Mann

and, 116; William Mann and, 116–23; postwar issues and, 270; safety of, 120; snakes and, 121, 179; victory gardens and, 144; war effort and, 179

natural world: atomic bomb and, 237; extinction and, 337n17 (*see also* extinction); Heinroth and, 165; Nazis and, 6, 32, 38, 43, 48, 240, 245; scientific biology and, 187n; zoos and, 3, 22, 38, 245, 273–76, 286–87

Naturewatch, 332n40

Nazis: animal protection laws and, 33–37; antisemitism and, 3, 36, 127; Aryans and, 37, 94, 107–8, 112, 214, 219, 244, 251; *ausländische Arbeitskräfte* and, 156; Berlin Zoo and, 39–42; *Blitzkrieg* of, 78, 94, 101, 128, 201, 323n5; Buchenwald and, 44–55; cages and, 38, 243; captive labor and, 156–59; closet, 89; complicity and, 2, 212, 278–79; Delacour and, 102; denazification, 262; economic issues and, 33; extinction and, 240; *Fall Gelb* and, 96; fascism and, 37, 106, 115, 212–13; Final Solution and, 36, 212, 241, 246, 249; Gestapo, 211, 216, 218; Heinz Heck and, 40–41, 258; Lutz Heck and, 40–41, 43, 209; hierarchical view of nature, 240; hunting and, 33, 35, 41, 50–51, 53; ideology of, 3, 6; imperialism and, 133; KZ system, 239–51; labor and, 156, 158; *Lebensraum* and, 51, 78, 243; lions and, 31–32, 37–38; moral issues and, 33, 37; natural world and, 6, 32, 38, 43, 48, 240, 245; Netherlands and, 103; New Order of, 104; occupation and, 103–9, 111–14; Olympics and, 42–43, 56, 60; Operation Barbarossa and, 188–89; pets and, 31, 33, 35–36, 213; postwar issues and, 257–58, 262, 268; prison-state of, 301n25; racism and, 37, 57; rats and, 37, 241; Reich film policy, 199–200; remembrance and, 278–79, 285, 336n3; resistance and, 211–19, 330n15; slavery and, 44, 48, 50, 68,

Nazis (*cont.*)

127, 156–57, 162, 251, 259, 330n15; sterilization and, 57; survival of the fittest, 37, 240; swastikas, 38, 43, 60; total war and, 74, 99, 177, 201, 204–8; *Untermenschen* (subhumans) and, 37; vivisection and, 32–36; *Volk* concept and, 35; as zoo-lovers, 38; zoos and, 3, 6, 8–9. *See also* concentration camps; Hitler, Adolf; *Schutzstaffel* (SS); Wehrmacht

Netherlands, ix; Artis Zoo and, *7*, 8, *62*, 99, 107, 113–14, 215–17; bombing of, 96, 98–99, 325n38; Dutch zoos and, 94–99, 306n13; evacuation and preparation in, 90; as Germanic Brother Nation, 104; international cooperation and, 59, 61; labor and, 157–58; Nazis and, 103; occupation and, 104, 107–8, 113–14; Occupied Dutch Territories and, 107; resistance and, 211–12, 215–17; weather and, 91

neutrality, 29; abandoning pretense of by Nazis, 36; American zoos and, 115–19; postwar IUDZG membership and, 274; Switzerland, 215

New Caledonia, 179

New Deal, 28

New Guinea, 135, 137

New York Times, 28, 32, 114, 170, 185, 203, 256, 280, 283

New York World's Fair, ix

New York Zoological Society: Jennings and, viii; Osborn Jr. and, 2, 57, 123, 271; Shoemaker and, 74

New Zealand: animal suicide and, 16, 19; Auckland Zoo, 16, 141; Pacific War and, 127, 135; Tee-Van and, ix; Wellington Zoo and, 16

Nibelungenlied, 41

Nicholas II, 187

Nixon, Richard M., 271

Noah, 11–12, 277, 283–84

Norris, Mark, 335n2

Nunn, Robert, 258–59

Nuremburg Zoo, 116, 157

occupation: air raids and, 109; antisemitism and, 106–7; of Belgium, 104; Berlin Zoo under, 106; bombing and, 106; children and, 109; collaboration and, 104, 109–13, 278; communism and, 107; of Czechoslovakia, 30, 104, 107; economic issues and, 104, 106; fascism and, 106; food and, 111–13; of France, 104, 109, 111; Hague Zoo under, 108–9; Heinz Heck and, 106; Lutz Heck and, 106, 189; Hitler and, 104–9, 113; hunger and, 111, 113; imperialism and, 105; *Jeder einmal in Paris* and, 109; Jews and, 104–8, 112–13; looting under, 2, 9, 27, 32, 63, 101, 103–6, 189, 213, 215; moral issues and, 113; Nazification and, 106–9; of Netherlands, 104, 107–8, 113–14; Pacific War and, 132; Packer on, 114; of Poland, 104, 106; propaganda and, 109–11; resistance and, 111, 211–25; revenge and, 229–33; Russia and, 104–6; SS and, 103, 106, *108*, 111; starvation and, 104; of Ukraine, 104, 106; Vincennes Zoo under, 109; Wehrmacht and, 8, 94, 102, 109–10, 119; zookeepers and, 105, 114

Ōdachi, Shigeo, 194

okapi, 82, 92

Olympics, 42–43, 56, 60

Onslow, Richard, 175

Operation Barbarossa, 188–89

Operation Gomorrah, 207

Operation Market Garden, *206*, 231–32

Operation Pied Piper, 83

orangutans, 79, 83, 98, *166*, 266

Orwell, George, 67–68

Osborn, Henry Fairfield, Jr., 2, 57, 123; *Animal Kingdom* editorials of, 271

Osborn, Henry Fairfield, Sr., 123

ostriches: anti-animal violence and, 124; Askaniya Nova and, 187; bombing and, 98, 325n39; breeding of, 17; restocking of, 269

Ouadi Rimé-Ouadi Achim Faunal Reserve, 284

Our Dumb Friends League, 320n19
Ouwehand, Cornelis, 95–96
Ouwehand's Zoo, 95–96, *97*, 306n13
Overton Park Zoo, 123
owls, 224

Pacific War: air raids and, 132, 135–36, 193; Australia and, 129–30, 133–37, 141; bombing and, 135–36, 235–38; cages and, 226–27; children and, 133–35; Doolittle Raid and, 193; evacuation or execution of zoo animals in, 132, 135–37, 193–98, 236; as "good war," 127, 312n2; Hitler and, 127–28; imperialism and, 128–31, 133–34, 137; India and, 128; Japan and, 127–38, 193–98, 226–27, 235–38; William Mann and, 130; Midway and, 138; National Zoo and, 131; New Zealand and, 127, 135; occupation and, 128, 132; opening stages of, 131–32; patriotism and, 133, 136; Pearl Harbor and, vii–viii, 119, 122, 127, 131–32, 135, 293n1; racism and, 128; submarines and, 127, 135, 141, 143; Ueno Zoo and, 130–31, 193–98, 226–27, 236; white man's burden and, 129; zookeepers and, 129–30
Packer, George, 114
Palestinians, 281–82, 285
pandas: Bronx Zoo and, ix, xiii–xiv; Chengdu and, viii–ix; China and, vii–xiv; evacuation of, 77, 82; food crisis and, 147; Ming, 82, 171, *172*; Pan-Dah, xiv, 271; Pan-Dee, xiv, 271; Pandora, viii; Pearl Harbor and, vii–viii, xiii, 293n1; restocking, 266, 271; Tang, 82; war effort and, 171
Panik (film), 199–200
Pankiewicz, Czeslaw, 219
panthers, 20, 71, 73, 98, 132, 191
Panzers, 99
passenger pigeon, 2
patriotism: food and, 143, 147–49, 150, 192, 193–96; Great Patriotic War, 196–97; labor and, 155; Mussolini and, 26; Pacific War and, 133, 136;

resistance and, 216; sacrifice and, 192–97; singing ship and, 133; Spanish Civil War and, 67; war effort and, 8, 170–77
Patten, Robert Anthony, 135, 141, 160
Patterson, Charles, 241
Pavlov, Ivan, 185
Payne, Robert, 36
peacocks, 47
Pearl Harbor, vii; American zoos and, 119, 122; Executive Order 9066 and, 220; Pacific War and, vii–viii, 119, 122, 127, 131–32, 135, 293n1; pandas and, vii–viii, xiii, 271, 293n1; war effort and, 177
pelicans, 67
Penang, 122
Pender, Lucy, 146
penguins: Artis Zoo and, *7*; bombing and, 203; food and, 142, 147, 154; liberation and, 231; petting zoos and, 22; rockhopper, 4; Tecton Group and, 57
People for the Ethical Treatment of Animals (PETA), 6
Perkins, Marlin, 168
Perth Zoo, 16–17, 135
Pétain, Philippe, 109, 111
pets, 4–5; benefits of, 220; bombing and, 207; eating of, 5, 191; feeding of, 144; Göring and, 31–32, 41; Heart Mountain Relocation Center and, 221; Hitler and, 35–36; Huxley on, 22; of Jews, 36; London Zoo adoption scheme and, 146; Mussolini and, *27*; Nazis and, 31, 33, 35–36, 213; Reich Animal Protection Act and, 33; Ruhe and, 158; September Holocaust, 89
Pets Corner, 22, 162
petting zoos, 9, 22–23, 160, 223
pheasants, 124, 153, 233
Philadelphia Zoo: attendance at, 16; Cadwalader and, 296n23; food and, 144; international cooperation and, 59; labor and, 155n, 157; postwar issues and, 257, 275; preparation at,

Philadelphia Zoo (*cont.*)
119; Shelly and, 275; war effort and, 176, 179
Philippines, xii, 128, 137
phosphorous, 190, 207–8
Physiological Institute, 185
Piel, Harry, 199–200
Pig 311, 269–70, 334n53
pigs: bombing and, 269; Buchenwald and, 46, 49–50; equating Jews as, 241; labor and, 156, 160; petting zoos and, 160; rationing and, *173*; Whipsnade Zoo and, 146; World War II deaths of, 5
Pitiful Elephants, The (Tsuchiya), 198
poison: cyanide, 194; gas, 77, 80–81, 83, 86, 244–45; Heinroth and, 165; Japan and, 193–95, 313n21; postwar issues and, 237, 256; radiation and, 237; rat, 27–28; reptiles, 78, 305n26; snakes, 58, 99, 121, 132; strychnine, 30, 194–95; of zoo animals, 10, 194–95
Polak, Rudolf, 215
Poland: bombing and, 78–79, 157, 189, 230, 325n38; execution of animals in, 78; Hitler and, 40, 78, 85, 90, 93, 104, 128, 189, 234, 247; international cooperation and, 59; KZ system and, 243, 247–48, 330n15; labor and, 157; liberation and, 230, 234; Luftwaffe and, 78, 325n38; occupation of, 104, 106; postwar issues and, 263, 333n25; refugees of, 78–79; science and, 106; Soviet Union and, 90, 104, 230, 234, 248; Warsaw Zoo, 78–79, 106, 201, 214, 219
polar bears: bombing and, 78, 205, 325n39; breeding of, 188; Dutch zoos and, 96; evacuation or execution of, 190–91, 195, 307n17; food crises and, 147, 149, 151; liberation and, 232; Madrid Zoo and, 65; Maxie, 96, *97*; occupation and, 111–13; postwar issues and, 262; Punggol Zoo and, 130; Snow White, 111–13, *112*; Spanish Civil War and, 65, 71–72
Popular Front, 115, 125

Popular Mechanics, 142
Population Bomb, The (Ehrlich and Ehrlich), 273
porcupines, 72, 127, 168
Portielje, A. F. J., *62*
Portland Zoo, 144, 174
postwar issues: American zoos and, 264–66; at Antwerp Zoo, 266, 269; in Australia, 257, 263, 267–70; at Berlin Zoo, 258–59, 262, 271; bombing, 255–58, 261, 268–70, 273, 276; children and, 260; clearing debris, 258–59; Cold War, 265, 270–73, 276, 280; collaboration, 260, 275; communism, 271; concentration camps, 255, 259–60; denazification, 262; disease, 255–56, 265; empty cages, 257–60, 263, 266; food, 255–56, 261–63, 267, 275; in France, 258, 266, 275; at Hagenbeck Zoo, 260–62; Heinz Heck and, 258, 262, 276; at Hellabrunn Zoo, 258, 267–68; Hitler and, 256–62, 268, 276; hunger, 255–56, 257, 263, 273; in Japan, 256, 263–64, 269–70; at London Zoo, 257, 266, 274–76; malnutrition, 257, 263, 275; William Mann and, 270, 275; measuring cost of war, 255–57; morality, 256; at National Zoo, 270; natural world and, 273–76; neutrality, 274; nuclear war, 280, 335n66; at Philadelphia Zoo, 257, 275; poison, 256; in Poland, 263, 333n25; population growth, 273; refugees, 259; restocking zoos, 265–69; restoration, 255–76; revenge, 255; at San Diego Zoo, 274; in Soviet Union, 258–62, 265, 270–73; suffering, 275; trials, 262; at Ueno Zoo, 263, *264*; at Vincennes Zoo, 266, 269; Wehrmacht and, 258, 275; zoo births, 268
potatoes: food issues and, 49–51, 67, 142, 144–49, 248, 258, 263; patriotic diet and, 147–49; sweet, 67, 144, 147; victory gardens and, 144–46
POUM militia, 68
POWs, 45, 156–58, 209, 248, 328n2

Poznan Zoo, 230
Prague Uprising, 230
Prague Zoo, *93*, 111–13, 269, 278
Prelude to War (Capra), 127
President Coolidge (ship), vii–viii, xii–xiii, 293n1
Priemel, Kurt, 59, 62
propaganda: Berlin Zoo and, 39; British, 133, 204; Department of Public Education and the Arts, 113; film and, 110, 127, 130, 134, 135, 181, 199–200; food and, 153; Goebbels and, 36–37, 43, 109; Göring and, 32; *Jeder einmal in Paris* and, 109–10; occupation and, 109–11; Olympics and, 43; sacrifice and, 185–86, 192–98; *The Subhuman*, 241; war effort and, 170–71, *172*, *173*, 178–81
Prospect Park Zoo, 19, 29
Prussia, 42–43, 106, 152
Przewalski's horses, 106, 187, 189, 207
pumas, 92, 280
Punggol Zoo, 130, 132
Putin, Vladmir, 4

rabbits: Angora, 46, 190; Buchenwald and, 46; food crises and, 67, 143, *173*, 191; Heart Mountain Relocation Center and, 221, 224; September Holocaust and, 89; Taronga Park Zoo and, 160; vaccine testing on, 190; vivisection and, *34*; war effort and, 178
racial hygiene institute, 57
racism: at American zoos, 122–25; Aryans and, 37, 94, 107–8, 112, 214, 219, 244, 251; embracing, 114; eugenics, 56–57, 123; genetic destiny and, 56–57; Hitler and, 35, 37, 40, 89, 104, 123; Hornaday and, 60; Hygiene Institute and, 240; Lucile Mann and, 310n9; master race and, 35; Nazification and, 106–9; Pacific War and, 128; slavery and, 44, 48, 50, 68, 127, 156–57, 162, 251, 259, 330n15; stereotypes and, 117, 229, *242*; sterilization and, 57; *The Subhuman*, 241;

Untermenschen (subhumans), 37; white supremacy and, 123
Raffles Natural History Museum, 130
Randow, Heinz, 158
Rangoon (Burma) Zoo, 132
Raschke, Jens, 279–80
rationing, 143, 150, *172*, *173*, 178, 192
rats: antisemitism and, 241; as food, 142–43, 149, 256; lab, 241; Nazis and, 37, 241; poisoning of, at Central Park Zoo, 27–28; San Diego Zoo and, 142–43
Rawlins, C. G. C., 274
Rawstorn, Laura, 169–70
Red Army, 186, 188, 230, 234, 258
Red Menace, 270
Reed, Theodore, 270
refugees: Artis Zoo and, 8, 215–17; Britons, 83; climate change, 282; Delacour and, 102; evacuations and, 78, 83; Jewish, 8, 78, 214, 218; liberation and, 232; Luftwaffe and, 78; Polish, 78–79; postwar "displaced persons," 259; resistance and, 214, 218
Reich Animal Protection Act, 33
Reid, Anna, 196
Reiser, Ruth, 248
remembrance: at Berlin Zoo, 1–2, 278–79, 336n3; bombing and, 278; children and, 278–79, 285; concentration camps and, 279; Holocaust and, 279; Jews and, 278–79, 336n3; at Leningrad Zoo and, 277; Nazis and, 278–79, 336n3; at Prague Zoo, 278; Ueno Zoo and, 277–78; World War Zoo Garden Project, 335n2
Republicans (Spain), 64, 66–71, 79
resilience, 133, 220
resistance: Artis Zoo and, 8, 215–17; Belgium and, 211; bombing and, 202; cages and, 213–17, 221–25; collaboration and, 212–14; concentration camps and, 330n15; Czechoslovakia and, 212–13; exaggeration of, postwar, 212; fascism and, 211–13, 217; France and, 94, 111, 211–14; Hitler and, 211–12, 216, 218; Holocaust and,

360 Index

resistance (cont.)
214, 218; honor of, 211–12; Japan and, 220–23; Jews and, 212–19; labor and, 158; liberation and, 230, 235; Lidice and, 212–13; moral issues and, 211, 215; Nazis and, 211–14, 217–18, 330n15; Netherlands and, 211–12, 217; occupation and, 111, 211–25; patriotism and, 216; in plain sight, 218–19; refugees and, 214, 218; vs. resilience and, 219–20; revenge and, 216; "Righteous Among the Nations" and, 214; smuggling and, 214, 217, 219; Sunier and, 215–17, 220; Switzerland and, 215, 218; torture and, 215; Urbain and, 214; Vincennes Zoo and, 214; Warsaw Zoo and, 214, 219; zookeepers and, 63, 213–17
revenge, 205, 209, 216, 230, 255, 262
rhinoceroses: bombing and, 208, 233; butchering of, 132; as endangered species, 60, 284; evacuation of, 77, 191; Mari, 190; Raschke on, 279–80; restocking, 267; Toni, 233; weather and, 92
"Righteous Among the Nations," 214
Ringling Brothers' circus, 126
Ritvo, Harriet, 295n20
Robbins, Louise E., 105
Roberts, Mary Louise, 229
Robinson, Robert, 257
Rödl, Arthur, 50
Roger Williams Park Zoo, 17
Rolfe, Edwin, 72
Roma, 239
Romania, 4, 230
Rome Zoo, 26–27, 58, 60, 148, 257, 297n55
Rommel, Erwin, 99
Roosevelt, Eleanor, 135, *136*
Roosevelt, Franklin D., 28, 119, 209–10, 220, 325n38
Roscher, Mieke, 207–8
Rosenstock, Odette, 246
Rothfels, Nigel, 57
Rotterdamsche Diergaard, 96–99, 158
Rousset, David, 55

Royal Air Force, 204, 208, 233
Royal Australian Air Force, 160
Royal Canadian Air Force, 171
Royal Children's Zoo, 23
Ruhe, Hermann, 158–59
Russell, Herband Arthur, 100
Russia: labor and, 156–57; liberation and, 230; Moscow Zoo and, 17, 30, 178n, 185, 187–90; Nicholas II and, 187; occupation and, 104–6; postwar issues and, 260, 265, 270–71; sacrifice and, 128, 187–93, 197; *The Subhuman* and, 241; Ukraine and, 4; war effort and, 168. *See also* Soviet Union
Russo-Japanese War, 131
Ryan, Cornelius, 328n13

Sabine, Jacqueline, 162
sabotage, 103, 121
Sachsenburg, 45
Sachsenhausen, 45, 53–54, 301n25
sacrifice: air raids and, 194, 197; Allied powers and, 185–86; American zoos and, 120–22; Antwerp Zoo and, 85; Axis powers and, 185–86; Berlin Zoo and, 189, 205–10; bombing and, 189–91, 197; butchering and, 192, 197; cages and, 193, 196; Churchill on, 85; communism and, 188; deciding factors in, 10–11; disease and, 189–90; Dutch zoos and, 96–98; food and, 150–53, 190–96; Great Zoo Massacre and, 194, 322n28; Lutz Heck and, 189; Hitler and, 185, 188–91; hunger and, 189–96; idealism of, 186; Japan and, 186, 193, 196–98; Leningrad Zoo and, 188–93; London Zoo and, 187, 193; moral issues and, 196; Operation Barbarossa and, 188–89; patriotism and, 192–97; Perth Zoo and, 135–36; pets and, 191; poison and, 194–95; Poland and, 189; politics of, 196–98; preparations for, 84–90; propaganda and, 185–86, 192–97; San Diego Zoo and, 122; science and, 185, 187; September

Holocaust and, 89; shooting and, 10, 85, 96, 106, 113, 191; Soviet Union and, 128, 185–93, 196–98; starvation and, 186, 190–97; strangulation and, 10, 78, 195; suffering and, 186, 189, 194–97; Ueno Zoo and, 193–96; Ukraine and, 188–89; Vincennes Zoo and, 77–78; Warsaw Zoo and, 78–79; Wehrmacht and, 185, 189; women and, 190; zookeepers and, 197

Sagarra, Ignasi de, 66, 69

Sahara Conservation, 284

Sailer-Jackson, Otto, 233–34, 329n22

Salsitz, Amalie Petranker, 247

San Antonio Zoological Society, 228

Sanders, Clinton, 149

San Diego Zoo: aerial bombardment, preparing for, 119, 122; Benchley and, 122, 151, 163–64, 176–77; D-Day, 229; food for, 142–43, 146, 151; labor and, 155, 161, 163–64; rats and, 143; Schroeder and, 274; war effort at, 171, 175–76

Sarajevo Zoo, 280

Schalkwijk, Van, 217

Schiff, Charlene, 248

Schönbrunn (Vienna Zoo), 39, 155, 207–8, 233, 262, 315n39

Schroeder, Charles R., 274

Schulz, Christoph, 113

Schutzstaffel (SS): Buchenwald and, 44–55; donation campaign of, 39; KZ system and, 240–41, 244–47; liberation and, 235; occupation and, 103, 106, *108*, 111; Piel films and, 199; *The Subhuman*, 241

science: Commissariat of Natural Science, 70; Conference on Science and World Affairs, 273; conservation, 283; dehumanizing, 181; Department of Science, Popular Education and Cultural Affairs, 103; human experiments, 45, 92–93; Huxley and, 21–22; international cooperation and, 57, 59; Jewish, 36; KZ system and, 251; patriotic diets, 147; Polish, 106; politics and, 12, 20–22,

103, 251; postwar issues and, 273; promoting interest in, 23; race, 89; Soviet Union and, 185, 187; vivisection, 32–34, 36; war effort and, 181

scimitar-horned oryx, 283–84

sea lions, 16, 26, 88, 96, 124, 151, 295n21

seals, 130, 142, 151, 207, 231, *264*

Seattle Zoo (Woodland Park Zoo): aerial bombardment, preparing for, 119–20, 121, 122; food and, 148; Knudson and, 121, 124, 265; poor conditions of, 169–70; women and, 162, 165, 167

Sebald, W. G., 207

September 11, 2001, zoos and, 320n29

September Holocaust, 89

Serengeti Shall Not Die (Grzimek), 39

Sereny, Gitta, 245, 330n15

Seth-Smith, David, 82, 87

Seyss-Inquart, Arthur, 107–8

Shannon, Peggy, 160

Shelly, Freeman, 275

Shetland ponies, 83, 170

Shoemaker, Henry W., 74

shooting: Buchenwald and, 51; caged animals, 106; finding pleasure in, 35, 257; hunting and, 35, 51; Jewish dogs, 36; New Year's Eve party of, 106; occupation and, 106, 113; Pacific War and, 132, 136; sacrifice and, 10, 85, 96, 106, 113, 191; toy guns, 171

shrapnel, 68, 72, 77, 199, 232

Siberian bustard, 309n3

Siegmann, Georg, 243

Silva, Marco, 338n31

Simon, Walter, 243

Singapore, ix, 128, 129–30, 132, 266

Singer, Isaac Bashevis, 250–51

Singing Forest, 45

singing ship, 133

Sington, Derrick, 239, 247

Sinti, 239

Sixth Extinction, The (Kolbert), 282

sloths, 20, 266

Smith, Alfred, 29

Smith, Ellison D., 123–24

smuggling, 214, 217, 219

snakes, 17; American zoos and, 119–21; boa constrictors, 180; bombing and, 79; defanged, 121; Dutch zoos and, 99; evacuation or execution of, 85–86, 132, 190, 195; food and, 143; international cooperation and, 58, 62; National Zoo and, 121; Pacific War and, 132, 141; pythons, 21, 130, 195, 266; rattlesnakes, 4, 86, 178, 195, 221, 224, 294n9; war effort and, 178–80

Snow White (polar bear), 111–13

Sobibor, 216, 330n15

social media, 4, 281, 285

sociozoologic scale, 149

Solidaridad Nacional (newspaper), 74

Solomon Islands, xiii, 137, 179

Solski, Leszek, 106, 188

Soong Mei-ling, viii–xi

Soviet Union: Bolshevik Revolution and, 187–88; division of Germany, 258; food shortages and, 142, 190–91; Iron Curtain and, 270–71; Kabul Zoo and, 280; KZ system and, 244; labor and, 156, 159, 165; Leningrad Zoo and, 188, 190–93, 196–97, 270, 277; liberation and, 230, 234–35; making zoos in, 187–88; occupation and, 104, *108*; Operation Barbarossa and, 188–89; People's Commissariat for Internal Affairs and, 188; Poland and, 90, 94, 230, 248; postwar issues and, 258, 262, 265, 270–73; purge of intellectuals in, 30; Red Army, 186, 188, 230, 234, 258; revenge and, 230, 235; sacrifice and, 128, 186–93, 196–98; Stalin and, 16n, 30, 94, 127, 168, 186, 187, 196–97, 227; war effort and, 168; weather and, 91, 190–91

Spanish Civil War: Barcelona Zoo and, 64–72, *73*; bombing and, 64, 66, 68–72; *Casa de Fieras* and, 65; children and, 67, 70, 72, 74; Commissariat of Natural Science, 70; communism and, 64, 72–73; disease and, 67, 70–74; as dress rehearsal, 64; fascism and, 64; food shortages during, 64, 66–67, 69–72, 73–74; France and, 65,

69–70; Franco and, 64, 68–74; Hitler and, 64; Italy and, 68–69, 72; *La Humanitat* and, 72–73; Leigh and, 5–6; Luftwaffe and, 69; Madrid Zoo and, 64–74, 79; moral issues and, 67; Mussolini and, 64; Nationalist Party and, 64, 66, 68, 72, 74; patriotism and, 67; Republicans and, 64, 66–71, 79; science and, 66, 70; World War II and, 74

Speer, Albert, 36

Stalin, Joseph, 16n, 94, 127–28, 168, 186, 190, 196–97, 227, 270; purge of intellectuals by, 30; Soviet zoos and, 30, 186–88

Stangl, Franz, 245–46, 331n38

starvation: bombing and, 210; Buchenwald and, 44–45, 48–50; Clères and, 101; enforced fasting and, 73; famine and, 72, 192, 217, 237, 256, 263, 273, 281; in Great Depression, 18; KZ system and, 241; liberation and, 232, 235–36; malnutrition and, 67, 72, 142, 151, 236, 257, 263, 275; under occupation, 104; postwar, 255, 263; sacrifice and, 186, 190–97; Spanish Civil War and, 69–74; of targeted groups, 142; of zoo animals, 4, 9, 11, 150, 210, 281–82, 284, 287, 294n9, 313n21

Steinhardt, Carola Stern, 247

stereotypes, 117, 196, 229, *242*

stereotypy, 289

sterilization, 57

St. Louis Zoo, ix n, 28, 121

storks, 42n, 79

strangulation, 10, 78, 195

Straubing Zoo, 38

Strauss, Lotte, 218

strychnine nitrate, 30, 194

Subhuman, The (SS booklet), 241

submarines, 127, 135, 141, 143

suffering, 2, 8–11; animal, as weaponized, 234; bombing and, 2, 69–70, 91, 99, 121, 170, 189, 197, 203, 234, 325n39; Buchenwald and, 54; food and, 151–53; future, 282, 286–88; KZ system and, 239, 249; misery, 19, 54,

71, 195, 229, 234, 256, 331n38; Nazis and, 33, 54; postwar, 275; resistance and, 219; sacrifice and, 186, 189, 194–97; Spanish Civil War and, 69–73; suicide, 15–16, 19; war effort and, 170, 176–77; weather and, 91–93

suicide: animal, press coverage of, 15–16; of Antonious, 262; human relationship with natural world and, 287

Sulala Animal Rescue, 281

Sunday Observer, 255

Sunier, Armand Louis Jean: Artis Zoo and, 61, *62*, 99, 107–8, 113, 215–17, 220, 271; IUDZG and, 61, 274; occupation and, 107–8, 113; resistance and, 215–17, 220; theft and, 113

Suo, Ken, 221

Supreme Commander for the Allied Powers (SCAP), 263

survival of the fittest, 240

swans, 263

swastikas, 38, 43, 60

Sweden, 59, 248

Switzerland: Bern Zoo, 163n; IUDZG and, 59; neutrality of, 215; resistance and, 215, 218

Taiwan, 131

Takei, George, 221

Taliban, 280–81

tapeworms, 221

tapirs, 20, 191, 266

Taralunga, Sebastian, 4

Taronga Park Zoo, 135, *136*, 141, 156, 160, 267, 269

tarpans, 40

Tarzan (Burroughs), 123

Tause, Vicente, 69

Tecton Group, 57

Teeuwisse, Arie, 216

Tee-Van, John, ix–xiii

terns, 63

theft, 2, 9, 27, 63, 101, 103–6, 189, 205, 213–15, 241, 243, 257, 266, 272, 276, 286; Sunier and, 113. *See also* looting

Theory and Practice of Hell, The (Kogon), 54

Thomas, Keith, 3

Thula Thula Game Reserve, 287

tigers, 5; American zoos and, 119–21; Apay, 130; bombing and, 208; caged, 21; in circus fire, 126; Dutch zoos and, 95, 98; evacuation or execution of, 78, 85, 87–89, 98, 191, 307n17; food and, 148, 197n; Goebbels and, 38; labor and, 154, 160; liberation and, 232, 235; London Exeter Exchange and, 20; occupation and, 105; Pacific War and, 130, 132, 136, 141; as "prisoners of state," 25; rising cost of, 265; Sarajevo Zoo and, 280; Siberian, 28, 58, 87–88; Spanish Civil War and, 65, 71, 73; suicide, 16; Sunier and, 61; weather and, 92

Times (London), 85, 261–62

Timor, 137

Toronto Zoo, 127, 170

tortoises, 21–22, 87, 124

torture: of animals, 33n, 48; at Buchenwald, 44–45, 48, 54; Kogon on, 54; resistance and, 215

totalitarianism, 16n

total war, 74, 99, 177, 201, 204–8

tourism, 1, 20, 39, 55, 102, 109, 114, 130, 284

Treblinka, 219, 244–46, 250, 330n15, 331n38

Trefflich, Henry, 265

Trenchard, Hugh, 202

Tsuchiya, Yukio, 198

Tucker, Todd, 191

typhus, 45

Uekoetter, Frank, 35

Ueno Zoo, 9; food and, 148, 263; founding of, 130–31; Fukuda and, 193–97; Great Zoo Massacre and, 194, 322n28; Halloran and, 226–27; labor and, 318n40; liberation and, 236; postwar issues and, 263, *264*; preparation by, 193–96; remembrance and, 277; sacrifice and, 193–98; war effort and, 175; women and, 318n40

Ukraine: Kiev Zoo, 105, 189, 332n40; KZ system and, 245; labor and, 157;

364 Index

Ukraine (*cont.*)
man-made famines of, 237; occupation and, 104, 106; Putin and, 4
unemployment, 16, 19–20, 23, 27, 169
United Nations, 282
United Press, 67, 263
Untermann, Ernest, 125
Urbain, Achille Joseph, 25–26, 58, 77, 214, 266–67
US Army Signal Corps, 135

vandalism, 124–25, 311n47
van den bergh, Walter, 6–7, 92, 266, 276
van den Brink, Duifje, 217
van Hooff, Jan, 232
van Hooff, Reinier, 231–33
vegetarianism, 30, 33, 36, 197n, 298n10
Venezuela, 100, 284
Vetulani, Tadeusz, 40
Vichy government, 102, 109, 111, 212, 214
victory gardens, 144–46
Vila, Antoni Gispert, 69, 72
Vincennes Zoo: evacuation and preparation of, 77–78; France and, 24–26, 214; imperialism and, 26; international cooperation and, 58; Jünger and, 109, 309n22; occupation and, 102, 109; opening of, 25–26; pensioners of quality of, 94; resistance and, 214; restocking, 266, 269
vivisection, 32–35, 36
Vlasák, Jan, 111–12
Vltava River, 93

Wagner, Richard, 36, 285
Wahl, Veleslav, 213, 230
Waikiki Bird Park, 124
Walker, Ward R., 150
wallabies, 4, 101, 270
Wallace-Wells, David, 282–83
Waller, Mike, 320n29
war crops, 144
Ward, Yvonne, 160
war effort: air raids and, 170–71; at Antwerp Zoo, 17; Australia and, 169, 179; bombing and, 169–70, 177, 181; at Bronx Zoo, 178–79; cages and,

170, 171, 174, 178; calming effects of zoos and, 175–77; children and, 174, 177; disease and, 175, 178–79; eagle and, 174; education and, 8, 174, 178–81; food and, 170, *173*, 178–79; Lutz Heck and, 176; Holocaust and, 181; hunger and, 178; Japan and, 170, 178, 181; at London Zoo, 170–78; William Mann and, 168, 174, 179, 180; military discounts, 175–76; Ming, 171, *172*; morale and, 171, 176–78; moral issues and, 171, 175–78, 320n22; nationalism and, 181; at National Zoo, 179; patriotism and, 8, 170–77; Pearl Harbor and, 177; Perkins and, 168; at Philadelphia Zoo, 176, 179; propaganda and, 170–74, 178–81; at San Diego Zoo, 171, 175–76; science and, 181; soldier's queries and, 179–81; Soviet Union and, 168, 181; suffering and, 170, 176–77; at Ueno Zoo, 175; women and, 171, 175, 177; zookeepers and, 178
War Emergency Committee, 79–80
Warner, Peggy, 263
Warner, Rose, 248
Warsaw Zoo: bombing of, 78–79, 201, 214; execution of animals at, 78; looting of, 106; reopening of, 257; resistance and, 214–15, 219
warthogs, 67
Wasmann, Erich, 103
weather, 218; climate change and, 11, 282–83, 285, 287, 335n2, 338n31; food crises and, 92, 190–91; Heinz Heck and, 92; snakes and, 121; winter of 1939–1940, 91–93
Wegeforth, Harry Milton, 163
Wehrmacht: *Lebensraum* and, 78; liberation and, 227, 235, 258; occupation and, 8, 78, 94, 102, 109–10, 119, 189, 275; resistance and, 218; sacrifice and, 185
Wehrmacht Days, 170
Wellington Zoo, 16
Wells, H. G., 21
West Africa, 119

Weyeneth, Robert R., 123

Weygand, Maxime, 100

What the Rhino Saw When It Looked on the Other Side of the Fence (Raschke), 279–80

Whipsnade Animal Park, 81–83, 87, 88, 92, 146, 171, *172*

white supremacy, 123

Whittaker, Wayne, 142

wildfires, 282–83, 337n17

William Land Park Zoo, 124

Winterhilfswerk des Deutschen Volkes (Winter Relief of the German People), 39

wisents, 38, 61, 187, 207

Wöbse, Anna-Katharina, 207–8

wolves: Buchenwald and, 48, 51; Deutsche Zoo and, 43; evacuation or execution of, 78, 87–89, 108, 191; food and, 30, 148; Nazis and, 43; petting zoos and, 22; Spanish Civil War and, 73

wombats, 337n17

women: air raids and, 318n40; *ausländische Arbeitskräfte* and, 156; Benchley, 122, 151, 163–65, 176–77, 265; Black, 123; Breslau and, 234; evacuation of, 82–84; Heart Mountain Relocation Center and, 221; Lutz Heck on, 318n40; Heinroth, 164–65, *166*, 209–10, 235, 258, 319n53; KZ system and, 216, 241, 244; "Ladies Only" newsreel and, 154; liberation and, 229; Lidice and, 213; macaws' screams and, 77; William Mann and, 159, 162; Rosie the Riveter, 162; Royal Canadian Air Force and, 171; shaved heads of, 230; Ueno Zoo and, 318n40; war effort and, 171, 175, 177; as zoo workers, 154, 159–67, 176–77, 190, 191–92, 265, 317n28, 318n40

Woodfine, Tim, 284

Works Progress Association (WPA), 28

World War I: air raids and, 68; Belgium and, 58; bombing and, 200; Bronx Zoo and, 144; Delacour and, 100; German Air Force and, 68; Lutz

Heck and, 40; Hindenburg and, 94; Koch and, 45; privation and, 79; trench warfare and, 94; Urbain and, 25

World War II: American zoos and, 119–26; animal deaths during, 5, 11, 294n9; anti-zoo commentary and, 169–70; bombing zoos in, 199–210 (*see also* bombing); Churchill and, 6, 85, 99, 127, 171, 186; contemporary zoos and, 277–88, 335n2; context of, 1–12; D-Day and, 229; Dutch zoos and, 95–99, 306n13; existential threat of, 2; food crises and, 141–53; as "Good War," 127–28; as Great Patriotic War, 197; impact of, 3, 6, 286–88; Japanese Americans and, 220–25, 327n24; KZ system and, 44–45, 239–51; labor and, 154, 159–63, *166*, 167; liberation and, 226–38, 239–40; measuring costs of, 255–57; occupation and, 114; Pacific War and, 127–38, 141; postwar issues, 255–76; resistance and, 8, 211–25; Roosevelt and, 28, 119, 209–10, 220, 325n38; sacrifice and, 185–98; Spanish Civil War and, 64, 74; starvation and, 4, 9, 11, 294n9, 313n21; as torrent of death, 78; victory gardens and, 144–46. *See also* Holocaust; Nazis

World War Zoo Garden Project, 335n2

Wrocław Zoo, 106

Yabu, Shigeru, 221, 224–25

Yad Vashem, 214

Yoshimura, Akira, 221

Yoshinaga, Aiko, 221

Young, Floyd S., 122

Yuanshan Zoo, 131

Yugoslavia, 280

Żabińska, Antonina, 159, 214–15, 219–20

Żabiński, Jan, 214–15

Zarankin, Julia, 212

zebras, 294n9; American zoos and, 121; bombing and, 79, 202–4; Dutch zoos and, 96; food crisis and, 147;

zebras (*cont.*)
Lutz Heck and, *41*; liberation and, 233; occupation and, 106; Spanish Civil War and, 69, 73
Zenkel, Peter, 50
Zionism, 218
Zonta Club, 161–62
Zoo Camp, 260
Zoodirektorenkonferenz (Conference of Zoo Directors), 58
zookeepers: American zoos and, 116–17, 120–23, 264–66; captive workers and, 156–59; colonialism and, 129–30; internationalism of, 58–60; military service and, 154–55; Nazification of, 37–40; Norris on, 335n2; occupation and, 105, 114; post–World War II, 251; resistance of, 213–17; sacrifice and, 197; socio-zoologic scale and, 149–50; Spanish Civil War and, 67; war effort and, 178; women as, 154, 159–62, 190, 192, 317n28
Zookeeper's Wife, The (Ackerman), 78–79
Zoological Society of London (ZSL), 21–22, 79, 81, 146, 175, 325n39
zoomorphic language, 246
"Zoo's Peace Aims, The" (Fisher), 181
Zuckerman, Solly, 3, 19–20, 296n34
Zwangsarbeiter (forced laborer), 46, 48, 157–59, 215–16, 259, 317n14